BRIDGES
of
MEMORY

BRIDGES
of
MEMORY

CHICAGO'S SECOND GENERATION
OF BLACK MIGRATION

TIMUEL D. BLACK JR.

WITH FOREWORDS
BY LERONE BENNETT JR.
AND VALERIE GERRARD BROWNE

NORTHWESTERN UNIVERSITY PRESS
EVANSTON, ILLINOIS

DUSABLE MUSEUM OF AFRICAN AMERICAN HISTORY
CHICAGO, ILLINOIS

Northwestern University Press
www.nupress.northwestern.edu

DuSable Museum of African American History
Chicago, Illinois 60637

First paperback printing 2008

Printed in the United States of America

10 9 8 7 6 5 4 3 2 1

ISBN-13: 978-0-8101-5194-9
ISBN-10: 0-8101-5194-4

Publisher's Note

Northwestern University Press has been honored to
work with Timuel D. Black Jr. on this groundbreaking
oral history of the first and second generation of
African-American migration from the American South
to Chicago. The book's title, *Bridges of Memory*,
describes well the art of oral history. Memory, like
all things human, is influenced by emotion and
perception, both of which can change over time.
Occasionally in the text, minor details and the spellings
of place-names, businesses, and people's names have
been corrected. But for the most part, the book's editors
have let Tim and the interviewees speak for themselves,
and the result is a living history rather than a static
record of events.

Bridges of Memory is not meant to be a scholarly
account of African-American migration to Chicago.
Rather, it is a lively first-person story of how a thriving
community arose in Chicago, a story told in the voices
of those who created the community. The hope is that
their memories, however accurate or however hazy, will
enable readers to appreciate the accomplishments of
the past and gain understanding that will help them to
face the challenges of the future.

The Library of Congress has cataloged the original,
hardcover edition as follows:

Black, Timuel D.
      Bridges of memory. Chicago's second generation of
   Black migration / Timuel D. Black, Jr. ; with forewords
   by Lerone Bennett, Jr. and Valerie Gerrard Browne.
         p. cm.
      Includes index.
      ISBN 0-8101-2295-2 (trade cloth : alk. paper)
      1. African Americans—Illinois—Chicago—
   Interviews. 2. African Americans—Illinois—
   Chicago—History—20th century. 3. African
   Americans—Migrations—History—20th century.
   4. Migration, Internal—United States—History—
   20th century. 5. Chicago (Ill.)—Biography.
   6. Chicago (Ill.)—Social conditions—20th century.
   7. Chicago (Ill.)—Race relations. I. Title.
   II. Title: Chicago's second generation of Black
   migration.
   F548.9.N4B555 2006
   977.30049607300922—DC22

                                        2006022273

♾The paper used in this publication meets the
minimum requirements of the American National
Standard for Information Sciences—Permanence of
Paper for Printed Library Materials, ANSI Z39.48-1992.

CONTENTS

Foreword vii
Lerone Bennett Jr.

Foreword ix
Valerie Gerrard Browne

Introduction xi

Jewel Stradford Lafontant 3
Eddie Casey 22
Muriel Chandler 31
Reverend A. P. Jackson 42
Lawrence Kennon 54
Bill Adkins 78
Alvena Henderson 88
Earl Neal 93
Reverend Dr. Louis Rawls 100
Sam Nolan 107
Ella Saunders 116
Fred Rice 128
LeRoy Winbush 143
Floyd Campbell 151
Clark Burrus 158
Burnett "Bo" Carter 167
Jerry "Iceman" Butler 173
Mattie Butler 187

Jesse Brown 203

Dr. Emil Hamberlin 209

Dillard Harris 226

Roger Salter 242

Professor William Daniels 259

Wilks Battles...277

Milton Davis 283

Doris Smith...293

Betty Stell 306

Standish Willis 312

Sylvia Walton 330

Charles Mingo 345

Hermene D. Hartman 360

Conclusion...381

Index 383

FOREWORD

————

LERONE BENNETT JR.

There are only two kinds of scholars: observer-participants who know that all scholars are condemned to observe the world from their space in the world and observer-participants who think they can observe the world, like God, from a space outside the world. Timuel D. Black, like Fanon, like DuBois, like Drake and Cayton, is a citizen, scholar, witness, and participant of the first world. In an exemplary career spanning over fifty years, he has taught, theorized, criticized, mobilized, testified, marched, preached, and raised hell—with accompanying footnotes—from his space in one of the worst and best spaces of the modern world, the South Side of Chicago. In the process, he has lifted up his space and has reminded us, at a time when many need reminding, of the power and potential of an engaged intellectual who knows that struggle is a form of analysis, perhaps even the highest form of analysis.

Somebody said that the South Side of Chicago is the most studied community in the world, which may be its greatest burden. For the South Side has been studied too often in the wrong ways by the wrong people who asked the wrong questions for the wrong reasons from the wrong perspectives.

Timuel Black, who is his own question, and answer, asks the right questions from the right perspective—from the South Side's own perspective—in this major oral history project that carries the dialogue to a new level. The first volume of his study dealt with middle- and upper-income African-Americans who grew up in Chicago in the 1920s, 1930s, and 1940s. Some people will question the lack of more working-class survivors, but it should be remembered that most of the upper-income people who were interviewed grew up in working-class families and that others were raised by working-class mothers. Priscilla Johnson, for example, arrived in Chicago in 1929 with a four- or five-month-old baby and two boys, two and four years old. Although she had never worked before, she got a job and survived with style, and her two-year-old, George Johnson, went on to create the multimillion-dollar Johnson Products hair care empire.

There are also victims here, of course, and gamblers and hustlers—who can write a history of black Chicago without talking about the victims of a system that creates victims the same way that Detroit assembly lines turn out cars? But there are also heroes and sheroes who challenge that system and the continuing attempts to deny to them the elementary rights which America guarantees to its other citizens, even those who have most recently arrived on our shores.

One of the great questions of the African-American experience is: Can I get a witness? Can I get someone to tell my story and confirm my reality? *Can I get a witness?* In *Bridges of Memory*, Timuel D. Black answers what he calls "the voices" with his own voice and makes us all witnesses and participants in a truth that is still testifying and taking names.

FOREWORD

VALERIE GERRARD BROWNE

Not so many decades ago, before the 1960s, the history collected and preserved by archivists and oral historians was largely limited to the accounts of politicians, businessmen, and celebrities. Nearly all of them were white and male. My late husband, Archie Motley (1934–2002), shared with Timuel Black a determination to widen this restricted vision. At the Chicago Historical Society Archie was among a small vanguard in the archival profession who led the way in collecting papers and writings to document urban history, especially the history of Chicago's African-American community. Just as he fought the battles of a racially infused society and documented the struggles of those at the grassroots, so Timuel Black has been a tireless and creative oral historian with the same goal in mind. I know this pathway well from my years as archivist for the Women and Leadership Archives at Loyola University Chicago, collecting the history of grassroots women of achievement.

In *Bridges of Memory*, Tim Black has given us a gift of extraordinary and lasting value. He has followed the advice I once heard Studs Terkel, another great oral historian and close friend of Tim, give: find oral history subjects who can speak articulately not only for themselves but as representatives of their community. Tim has done this so well because he has been rooted in black Chicago his whole life. His oral history interviews read more like conversations between old friends recounting shared experiences and battles than a series of cold questions and answers between two distant parties. They capture and preserve life stories in the words of those who lived them, preserving a rich legacy that might otherwise have been lost to us.

The interviews are poignant, moving, inspiring. They bring history alive, and in so doing, they document the lives of the underdocumented in our society. We learn about the rich culture of African-American Chicago—the music, art, and literature. We read about people who survived and even thrived despite the all-pervasive racism that was part of their everyday lives.

My late father-in-law, Archibald J. Motley Jr. (1891–1981), devoted his life to depicting the lives of his people through his art. Many of us are familiar with his vibrant paintings of Bronzeville in the 1930s and 1940s. We see people speaking on the streets, in the clubs, in the churches. In *Bridges of Memory* we actually hear the voices and, through them, learn more about the context of the world he painted.

Taken together, all these forms of documentation provide us with a much fuller historic record and a greater understanding of the rich legacy of black Chicago and the significant contributions of its people. Historians will be able to write more informed histories that reflect more clearly the contributions of African-Americans to the rich fabric of human existence. Yes, we stand on the strong shoulders of those who have gone before us, those who survived hardships and still managed to find joy and keep the dream of a better future alive. The more we understand them, the better we understand ourselves and future possibilities. Though our lives and the challenges we face may be different, the spirit that inspired and motivated the people who went before us is also alive within us. Tim Black has given us the gift of memory. It is up to us to preserve and build on it.

INTRODUCTION

———

LET'S BUILD A STAIRWAY TO THE STARS . . .

This second volume of *Bridges of Memory* continues and completes my edited conversations with interviewees of the first generation of the First Great Migration (1915–50) of African-Americans who grew up in Chicago. Though they grew up in a similar racially segregated physical environment, each of these sixteen individuals has a unique story to tell. For example, artist LeRoy Winbush explains how his interests and talents led him to become the first African-American window display artist for the major department stores in Chicago's downtown area. His story is quite different from that of corporate attorney Jewel Stradford Lafontant, who tells how her family fled to Chicago just prior to the terrorism and riots in Tulsa, Oklahoma, in 1921, and then goes on to reminisce about her childhood experiences in a privileged section of the black South Side. Eventually she was able to follow in her father's footsteps to Oberlin College and from there to become the first African-American woman to graduate from the University of Chicago Law School, which, in turn, led to her becoming deputy solicitor general for two Republican presidents of the United States. These are only two examples of the unique personalities in this volume who are part of the first generation of African-American experience as it has evolved here in the city of Chicago.

The second half of this volume of *Bridges of Memory* comprises conversations with fifteen members of the second generation of African-Americans to have lived in Chicago. In their number we find vivid personalities such as rhythm and blues pioneer (and now Cook County Commissioner) Jerry Butler telling of the experiences of his family leaving Mississippi when he was a toddler and settling in the small black community on the North Side of Chicago, where he had to learn to deal with racial prejudices in education, housing, and other aspects of the socio-economic environment that were prevalent at that time, and how those experiences led him and his friends to create new musical sounds without the benefit of instruments as a means to cope with those situations psychologically, eventually leading to his national fame and glory, as well as academic and political success. His sister Mattie Butler, who was also a part of his musical group, tells of her own childhood experiences of coping with the adversities of racism on the North Side and the West Side of Chicago and of her current struggle with racism and classism in regard to the gentrification of the Woodlawn neighborhood on the South Side.

In another chapter, Professor William Daniels recalls growing up in the home of loving foster parents in the community that lived in the Grand Boulevard neighborhood and shares his memories of Willard Elementary School and of DuSable High School, where I first made his acquaintance when he was one of my students. Particularly interesting is his reminiscence of how a white counselor, after looking at his rather low scores on the type of standardized test that was mandatory during that period, advised him to keep on working at Sears Roebuck in order to give his foster parents some relief from the economic "burden" that he was placing on them. Fortunately, an agent for the Pullman Foundation recognized his potential and helped him to obtain an academic scholarship to Upper Iowa University, where he became an honors student, and then went on to be awarded Woodrow Wilson Fellowships for his master's and doctorate degrees in political science. In subsequent years he has taught at several prestigious colleges and universities and has been a political adviser to several members of the U.S. Supreme Court, including the late Thurgood Marshall.

Hermene Hartman, who grew up in Chicago as a member of a very distinguished black business family and who is the niece of the renowned ballad singer, the late Johnny Hartman, tells of her experiences in the civil rights movement and how these experiences led her to become the founder and publisher of N'Digo, an influential and progressive weekly newspaper that is distributed throughout the Chicago area.

These are just a few examples of the struggles and achievements of the first two generations of African-Americans living their lives in Chicago. In future volumes, I would like to continue with more conversations with individuals of the second generation and conclude with the stories of members of the third generation who are now attempting to create a legacy of their own. All of these oral histories demonstrate that even here in the "promised land" of Chicago the universal human struggle for survival, success, and progress as well as the promise of liberty, justice, equality, and freedom for all have continued to be marred and tainted for African-Americans, no matter what their personal degree of social or intellectual attainment, by those impediments that are directly associated with pervasive racial discrimination.

In closing this introduction, I would like to express enormous appreciation to the main transcribers of *Bridges of Memory*, Gene and Estella Walsh. The quality of this work has been greatly enhanced by their editing and advice. Thanks so much, Gene and Tedda, for your hard work and continuing friendship. Thanks are also due to Elizabeth Hollander and the Monsignor John J. Egan Urban Center at DePaul University, Sunny Fischer and the Richard H. Driehaus Foundation, Warren Chapman and the Joyce Foundation, and Judith Hochberg and Judith Types for their contributions to this book. Thanks also to Sue Betz and Stephanie Frerich at Northwestern University Press, to Muriel Chandler, Sadie Hampton, Bridgette McCullough, and Sherry Fox. And last but not least, I would like to thank my wife, Zenobia Johnson Black.

BRIDGES
of
MEMORY

JEWEL STRADFORD LAFONTANT

AMBASSADOR-AT-LARGE

Because I knew both her and her brother, the late Cornelius Francis Stradford, since our teenage years, I will just refer to her as Jewel in this introduction — and she was, in fact, a precious jewel to all who had the privilege of knowing her.

Jewel was a member of one of Chicago's most historically important and prestigious African-American families. Her father and grandfather were both successful lawyers and businessmen in Tulsa, Oklahoma, in the period that existed prior to the tragic 1921 race riot that terrorized and destroyed the prosperous black community that had popularly been known as T-Town. When their family left Tulsa, they moved directly to Chicago's South Side, where Jewel was born. Jewel, her father, and her grandfather all graduated from Oberlin College in Ohio. After that, Jewel had the distinction of being the first woman of Afro-American descent to earn a law degree from the University of Chicago, and that is where she met and married her first husband, John "Jack" Rogers, who is now a retired judge. From that marriage, one child was born, a son: John W. Rogers Jr., who became the founder, chairman, and chief investment officer of Ariel Capital Management LLC, a firm that currently manages billions of dollars of corporate investments.

Jewel, her forebears, and her own nuclear family have always been and still remain Republicans. In addition to a lucrative law practice and the administration of several prestigious government posts, Jewel was an active member of many corporate and philanthropic boards throughout her long and highly successful life. I am so glad that I had the opportunity to have this conversation with her before she passed, for otherwise these words that she spoke would be forever lost.

TB: Jewel, were you born in Chicago?

JL: Yes, I was born and raised in Chicago. I went to grade school at Willard, and then from Willard I went on to Englewood High School. DuSable had just been opened up, but my father and mother did not want me to go there because they thought that DuSable had been built to take the black students out of Hyde Park High. My brother, Cornelius, had already gone to school at Hyde Park, and so I was also enrolled in Hyde Park, but I was only there for about a week when the principal called me and said, "You don't live in this district," and so they put me out. That's why I enrolled in Englewood.

TB: Were you living in Englewood's district?

JL: No, I wasn't living in Englewood's district either, but they permitted me to stay there. You see, my parents did not want me to go to an all-black school because they had always fought any form of segregation every step of the way, going back to when my grandfather was in Tulsa, Oklahoma.

TB: Was he born in Tulsa?

JL: No, my grandfather was originally from Burnside, Kentucky. Then, after he married, he and his wife moved to Ohio in order to attend Oberlin College.

TB: As I understand it, there is something of an "Oberlin tradition" in your family.

JL: That's right. My father and mother also went there. Many people don't know it, but Oberlin was the first school in this country to admit women along with men. Then it also became among the first to admit blacks. So they had an established history of being liberal, but, even so, there never were a lot of blacks at Oberlin. As I understand it, after my grandfather left Oberlin, he went west and sought his fortune in Tulsa, Oklahoma, because there was oil there.

TB: This would have been in the 1870s or eighties?

JL: No, somewhat later than that because my father moved to Tulsa to join him after he had finished Columbia Law School, which would have been about 1916.

TB: Your grandfather was also a lawyer, wasn't he?

JL: Yes, he obtained his degree at the University of Indiana Law School before moving to Tulsa.

TB: So, after completing their educations, your parents went west to join him.

JL: That's right, and my brother, Cornelius, was born in Tulsa in 1918. By that time my grandfather was well established there. He owned a hotel called the Stradford Hotel and had established a library, the Stradford Library, but just a little later during the Tulsa riots both of those buildings were burned down to the ground!

TB: Was your family still there during the Tulsa riots of 1921?

JL: No, my father must have decided to leave just before then because he told a story of going to court and trying to argue his cases by telling the judge what the law was by reading to him from the law books, and when he did that, the judge just looked down at him and said, "Well, the law here is as I see it." So that was when my father knew it was time to leave, and shortly after that is when the riots took place. Whenever you have riots like that, whites get killed as well as blacks, but those riots came out of the jealousy that some whites felt toward those blacks who were becoming successful. You see, back then you already had a lot of blacks in Tulsa who were very rich, and my grandfather was one of them, and so that's why they tried to indict him for murder!

TB: Your grandfather?

JL: Right, but he escaped, and then my daddy had to fight against the extradition proceedings from his office here in Chicago. So, when I was growing up, I was always hearing my grandfather saying, "There are not many fathers like me that can attribute their lives to their own sons," and that's why I thought that being a lawyer was just the greatest thing that you could possibly do. Being a lawyer, you could save lives!

TB: Did your grandfather come up to Chicago and live with your family?

JL: Yes, my grandfather moved in and practiced law with my father. Then he opened up a candy store, and later on he had a barbershop right there at Fifty-first Street and what is now King Drive.

TB: Which was then Grand Boulevard.

JL: That's right.

TB: John Hope Franklin's family was also from Tulsa. He was born there.

JL: Yes, but I only met John in later years. He would have been much younger than my father.

TB: Did your mother outlive your dad?

JL: Yes, my father had a series of strokes, and he died in '63. My mother didn't pass away until '72.

TB: During his lifetime, your father ran for several offices, didn't he?

JL: Yes, he had run for the state legislature against Noble Lee, and in the primary he claimed he had won, but it seems that the night before all the ballots had been "mysteriously" destroyed!

TB: That sort of thing had been going on for a long time.

JL: Yes, but this time my dad took his case to court, and eventually he was awarded the salary that he would have gotten, but by the time that happened his term in office had already expired! After that, my father ran for office several times and never won.

TB: Did he ever run for Congress against Dawson?

JL: No, he was a close friend of Dawson, and so when Dawson turned Democrat, he tried to get my father to come over with him.

TB: But he didn't.

JL: No, he didn't because he could never forgive the Democrats for what they had done in the South.

TB: Now, going back to your mother . . .

JL: Well, my mother was from Charleston, South Carolina, and she always said that when she was a little girl she remembers seeing Africans returning to Charleston. The story is that the original slave was brought there from Africa and sold to a family called Vaughn. He was taught ironwork, and he did that sort of work so well that he was able to earn some money, and he bought his freedom. We have copies of the original court records that show that Vaughn granted him his freedom, and in his will Vaughn said he was to be given his tools and this, that, and the other thing that was needed for him to maintain his independence. He mated with a Cherokee woman, and then on his deathbed his sons promised him that they would return to their native land. Only one of them made it back, but he was able to find his father's people in a town called Abeokuta about a half hour's drive from Lagos. He recognized these people because the tribal marks on their faces matched those that had been on his father's. So this son decided to stay there, and he established a Methodist church, and later on he became a doctor. I've heard this story all of my life. I finally went to Nigeria in '63 and went to the grave site where that son is buried.

TB: Did your mother ever get a chance to visit Nigeria before she passed?

JL: No, but my aunt from New York—Aunt Sara—spent a whole month there with our relatives. One of our cousins, Lady Kofo, was the first Nigerian woman to finish her education at Oxford. She married the chief justice of the Nigerian Republic, and my mother and I gave a reception for them when they came over here in '52.

TB: So your mother's heritage is a very rich intercontinental heritage and your father's heritage is deeply rooted in the American experience.

JL: I have a cousin on my father's side—his grandmother and my father were sister and brother—who's considered to be the historian of the family, and he told me the story of how our ancestor was an African slave whose owner's daughter took a liking to him and taught him how to read and write. During the evening he would hide out in the haystacks and practice his reading and writing. Eventually he got to be so good at it that he was able to write his own pass out of that particular area. That's how he made his escape and went to Canada. He had this pass that he had made, and so people assumed that he was not a slave. Well, when he went to Canada, he saw the sign of a city called Stratford, and he decided to assume that name for himself, but instead of spelling his name "Stratford," he spelled it "Stradford" with a D.

TB: It's very important for us to know stories like that because so much of the established history that we've been given to read emphasizes the so-called passivity of those held in slavery.

JL: They weren't passive. They were tough!

TB: They had to be or they would not have been able to survive the brutal conditions of their lives. They constantly had to struggle just to survive, and at the same time they were constantly seeking to find another way out. I saw some of that spiritual strength in my own granddaddy. He was ninety-nine when he died, and I was just four, but I can still remember the strength of his character and the kindness he showed me.

JL: Yes, and I was also brought up to be very proud of the fact that I had this kind of heritage.

TB: Going back just a little, there were a lot of interesting people as well as yourself who came through Willard during the period that you were there. Can you remember any of them?

JL: Yes, Dorothy Donegan, Dempsey Travis . . .

TB: The great bass player, John Levy, who's older than either of us, also went to Willard at about that same time. He was the bassist for Billie Holiday, and he still manages Nancy Wilson and Joe Williams.

JL: He was older, but I think he may have been a senior when I was a freshman.

TB: There was also a family whose mother taught at Willard, and her brother went to the University of Chicago when he was only about fifteen years old.

JL: Oh, yes, that would be J. Ernest Wilkins. He was the most outstanding student at Willard when I came there. He later became assistant secretary of labor in the Eisenhower administration.

TB: To have that many people in the same school who would later become known beyond the local level is really quite remarkable.

JL: Yes, and everyone knew everybody else. I still remember when I used to walk down the street with my second husband, who was from Haiti, I'd say to almost every person that passed us by, "Hello, how are you?"—and he would say, "Who are all these people?" So I'd say, "I went to grade school with them" or "We went to high school together." His reaction was, "Well, the whole world must have been in your school!"

[*Laughter.*]

But that was because everyone around here knew each other. In later years once I met a girl on the El—I don't remember her name anymore—but she told me that she had nine children. "And my last daughter," she said, "I named after you." Well, I hardly knew that girl, but that's the way we all were. We made friends with everybody, and they stayed our friends and didn't move out of the neighborhood.

TB: The community was stable.

JL: Yes, when I lived on Washington Park Court, those people that I knew there are still friends of mine. Those kids who weren't as fortunate as we were our friends, and we shared the same aspirations. They may have been near the bottom of the heap financially, but not spiritually, and they aspired to be a doctor or a lawyer just like I did. Now it's just about impossible for so many of our young people to have those kind of hopes because the people they look up to are just like they are, and so they have no vision of ever doing anything that might be better.

TB: That block you're talking about, Washington Park Court, is between Forty-ninth and Fiftieth Streets, just around the corner from where Provident Hospital was.

JL: Yes, and we had a real sense of community. The people all knew each other and watched each other's kids so that none of us ever got into any sort of trouble.

TB: That was also true around where my family was living. I was always getting into trouble, and when our neighbors saw what I was doing, they wouldn't wait even a minute to call my mama!

[*Laughter.*]

JL: My father usually treated me just as if he thought I was a boy. He taught me how to play pool, and I never wore a dress until after I got into high school. I wore knickers all the way through grade school. If I remember correctly, I had about five pairs of knickers—blue and green—and I wore a cap. I was really "Little Miss Tough," and I had fights!

TB: Really? It's hard for me to imagine that.

JL: The other day I was telling my present husband about how I used to fight, and he couldn't believe it!

TB: Well, I can't either!

[*Laughter.*]

JL: My fighting days ended when I finished Willard, but back then I was pretty tough. I also used to perform on street corners when I was at Willard. I was double-jointed, and I used to be an acrobat, but my parents never knew about that side of me either.

[*Laughter.*]

TB: Now, after you graduated from Willard and then Englewood High, you went on to Oberlin.

JL: Yes, I went to Oberlin in 1939. I could not go to a black college like Fisk or Howard because I think my parents thought somewhere in the backs of their minds that I would become too socially active in places like that, and I think that means that they knew me pretty well!

[*Laughter.*]

As a matter of fact, I was not allowed to date until I was twenty-one. That's why I couldn't go to my own senior prom.

TB: At Englewood?

JL: Yes, because I couldn't date.

TB: You could have taken Cornelius.

JL: Well, that came up too, but, no, you don't go to a prom with your brother or your daddy! So I didn't go, and I can still remember my father arguing with my mother about whether I should be allowed to go or not. She was always pressing him to be a little less rigid. As a matter of fact, my brother eventually left home because of that rigidity, but I also remember my father saying to me, "Forget about this prom. The day will come when you will be invited here, there, and everywhere because you're going to be a great woman one of these days"—and I said, "But, Daddy, there will never be another prom."

TB: Which is true.

JL: Anyway, so I went to Oberlin, and there the emphasis was certainly on academics. You were in an environment there where the school did not permit sororities or fraternities or having a car of your own. The emphasis was never on what you had financially or how well you dressed or what kind of parties you went to. So, in many ways, maybe that was the best place for me to be at that particular time of my life, and being at Oberlin was in most ways a pleasant experience for me. It was also a difficult experience, of course, because the average IQ in a place like that is 150 or higher.

TB: Yes, the competition must have been very keen.

JL: As a matter of fact, I thought I could play the piano until I went to Oberlin, but when I got there I realized I just couldn't compete with the others in terms of music. So I went off into sports to satisfy my self-esteem, and I became the captain of the volleyball team, and I also played a lot of tennis. I never became a Phi Beta Kappa like my father wanted me to be, but I did become an all-around athlete. In fact, I went back to Oberlin recently to speak to the honors group there, and when the president of Oberlin introduced me, he said, "You won't believe this but she was on our intercollegiate volleyball team." So I got up and said, "You didn't do your homework. I was the *captain* of that team for four years!"

[*Laughter.*]

Another thing about Oberlin that wasn't altogether pleasant was that when I first went there my father didn't want me to stay in the dormitory.

TB: Why was that?

JL: Well, as you know, when you grew up in our black community, if you went to college, you were going to college to learn, to achieve something, and not to be like those white girls who would go there just to get a husband. You were there to achieve and to help your people. Those were the guidelines. So my father put me in a house that was owned by a Ms. Thomas, thinking that she would watch over me. He said, "Just stay here the first year, and then the second you'll go into the dormitory." Well, that first year wasn't too bad because there were three other girls living there with me, and I could date and do pretty much what I wanted to do, but then at the end of that first year that Ms. Thomas filled my dad's head with all the "terrible" things that she said I was doing. She told him that I was dating a man "not worth my little finger" and that I'd go with him to see a show every single Tuesday night. Woo! My dad thought that was just awful, and so I had to stay at Ms. Thomas's house for another two years, but I didn't speak to her the whole time! What's more, the other young women in the house wouldn't speak to her either. So it was not such a pleasant three years that I spent there, but then the fourth year I went into a dormitory and that was a wonderful experience for me. I made the most out of that last year both socially and academically.

TB: Then it must have been in 1943 that you graduated from Oberlin.

JL: Yes, and then after that I went directly to the University of Chicago Law School.

TB: How many women were in your class?

JL: Only two.

TB: And you were the only woman of color.

JL: Yes, and I was the first and only woman up to that point to graduate from the University of Chicago Law School. This was in 1946.

TB: That's still very recent, especially given the fact that the University of Chicago has been in business since about 1896 or so.

JL: Well, it was a great school, but there was also a great deal of prejudice, and that kind of thing still continued as late as '58 when I had my baby at the University of Chicago's hospital.

TB: Billings?

JL: Yes, as I'm sure you know, when I was in law school, blacks could not serve as doctors at Billings. In fact, blacks could not even go there as patients, but in '58 when I was pregnant, I was accepted at Billings. Then, years later, a woman came to my office, sat down, and said, "You don't remember me, do you? I was your nurse at Billings when you were pregnant, and you were on a floor that was supposed to be for whites only, and they wanted to move you, but you said you wouldn't be moved!" She said, "So I went to shut the door, and you said, 'Why are you shutting that door?' 'Because I don't want them to see you,' and you said, 'Open that door! I *want* them to see me'"—and then she said, "You know, I was so frightened for you."

TB: And this was in 1958.

JL: Yes, 1958.

TB: During that same period, your dad's office was still up on Fifty-fifth Street, wasn't it?

JL: Right, and I had worked for my dad during the summers all through grade school, high school, and college.

TB: Were you working with your father when he handled the restrictive covenants cases for Carl Hansberry?

JL: Yes, I was involved with all of that because, like I said, I was working as his secretary.

TB: What about the later case that Earl B. Dickerson took to the Supreme Court?

JL: That was a continuation of the same case. You see it was necessary for my father to go to Supreme Liberty and Life in order to get some financial help with all the necessary mortgages, and that's how Earl B. Dickerson got involved in the case. My father had been involved in that case from the very beginning, and he wrote all the briefs, and so we all assumed that he would be the one who would argue that case before the Supreme Court, but Truman Gibson, who was president of Supreme Life at that time, and his son, T.K. Jr., decided that Dickerson should be the one to argue the case at the higher level. Of course it was still a joint effort, and they depended heavily on the briefs that my father had prepared and submitted, but the person who stands up and argues the case is the one who gets the glory. There's no doubt about that, and Dickerson—although my dad liked him very much—was a very selfish person. He liked the PR and was only too happy to take all of the credit. It was certainly a landmark case, and I was always proud of my father's involvement with it, and so, as I was saying, it was always understood that I was going to practice law with my father, but when I married Jack, my father didn't even speak to me for seven years! So that's when I had to go out and earn my keep.

TB: Really? He wouldn't speak to you just because you got married?

JL: Yes, he had said I wasn't supposed to even date until after I was twenty-one, and then, even after that, Daddy managed to find something wrong with every guy that came up to the house, and he would bar them from ever coming back. I remember one day he said to me, "I know you think that I've been hard and that I don't want you to have any boyfriends, but that's not really true"—and then he went through the whole history of what was wrong with every fellow toward whom I'd ever showed any sort of affection. So I went on to law school, and who would surface on opening day? Jack Rogers! He had been a Tuskegee Airman. He was a real hero. He had graduated from the University of Chicago. He even owned some property.

TB: It would seem he had all of the right qualifications! What's more, Jack was almost a neighborhood boy because he had graduated from Willard, too! [*Laughter.*]

JL: Yes, he certainly met all the requirements — so Jack and I started dating, and, after a while, I said to Daddy, "Jack and I, we want to get married." My father said, "Did you ask him or did he ask you?" I said, "Daddy, he asked me" — and he said, "Well, first you are going to finish school and take the bar." Then, after a few weeks, he got very ill, and we thought he might die, and that's when he flat-out said, *"There'll be no marriage!"* Just like that! So that's when I knew I had to leave home, and so I called Jack and said, "Looks like we're going to have to get married sooner than we planned" — but, until we could make all the necessary arrangements, my dear brother took me in to live with him because back then there was no such thing as getting your own apartment. In those days you were considered to be a "fallen woman" if you lived by yourself. So I went to live in Cornelius's apartment, and we arranged for the wedding to be there. Well, my mother came to our wedding but not my father. Then, a little while later, I graduated, and when I passed the bar, my mother went with me to be sworn in — but once again not my father! He didn't speak to me for the next seven years even though I made all kinds of efforts for reconciliation.

TB: So, after you passed the bar, you definitely weren't able to practice law with your father as you had originally planned.

JL: That's right, and after I passed the bar, Jack was still in law school, and so I had to find a job for myself.

TB: What kind of job did you find?

JL: My first job was with the Social Security Administration as a manager. I took the exam and did very well and worked in Springfield for about six months.

TB: Only six months?

JL: Yes, because back then Springfield was so prejudiced that there wasn't even any place where a person like myself was allowed to sit down and eat lunch or dinner!

TB: This was when?

JL: January 1947.

TB: Even in 1947!

JL: Yes, so I came back here to Chicago and volunteered my services to the Legal Aid Bureau. At first I think they only gave me twenty-five dollars a week to pay for my transportation. That was all, but they must have liked the way I handled court cases because pretty soon they hired me as a trial lawyer. This was a first because up to that point they had never had anyone of color working at the Legal Aid Bureau, and so I continued to work there for about five years. Meanwhile Jack had graduated from law school, and so he and I formed a firm: Rogers and Rogers. Later on Earl Strayhorn joined us as a partner, and then, after that, we brought in Raymond Hunt.

TB: When did you start getting into politics?

JL: I think I started in politics when I was about twelve years old because by then I was already taking petitions around and getting them signed for my father when he ran for the state legislature. Later on, back in the forties, I remember being a precinct captain in the Sixth Ward, but then Jack and I moved over to the Twenty-fourth Ward on the West Side.

TB: When was this?

JL: When Dewey and Truman were running.

TB: That was '48.

JL: Yes, and the Democrats in the Twenty-fourth Ward were so afraid that we as two *black* Republicans might have so much impact on the other blacks in that ward that the Democratic precinct captain threatened to attack Jack!

TB: Physically?

JL: Yes, they played rough in those days.

TB: The First, the Twentieth, and Twenty-fourth wards were the toughest West Side wards back then, but about the time when you and Jack moved into the Twenty-fourth Ward, the area around Douglas Park was just beginning to turn.

JL: That's right. So we bought a building on St. Louis in Douglas Park, but after the Republicans lost that election, we decided to move back to Hyde Park on the South Side.

TB: Where were you living?

JL: In a co-op at Fifty-first and Ellis.

TB: I think my wife and I lived in that same building a little later on. It was at 5059, wasn't it? Right on the corner?

JL: Yes, but we only lived there for a short time because we bought a three-flat building with the McGees and Allison Davis at 1131 East Fiftieth Street. We stayed there until I became an assistant U.S. attorney in 1955.

TB: That was during the Eisenhower administration.

JL: Yes, Eisenhower was responsible for me becoming a U.S. attorney, and I stayed in the U.S. attorney's office until Johnny was born in '58.

TB: Were you working out of the Chicago District office?

JL: Yes, and I was the *first* black female assistant U.S. attorney in the entire nation.

Senator Dirksen and state Representative Elwood Graham were my backers, and Dirksen is the one who submitted my name, but then the Communists tried to keep me from getting the job.

TB: Could you explain what you mean?

JL: Well, it was taking so long for me to be approved that *Jet* and some of the other periodicals had started writing articles about how I *wasn't* going to get the job. So I went to my immediate superior—the man who was the U.S. attorney in the Chicago district office—and asked him what was the reason for the delay. He told me that he liked me and wanted me to be on his staff, but then he said, "I'm going to tell you something that I'm not supposed to say, which is that the FBI has some damaging material about you being a 'pinko,' and the only way I'm going to be able to take you on is if we can refute those charges, but I'm sure we can because I know you're not." It turned out that there was a former Communist that I had known named Ira Latimer who had at one time been head of the Chicago Civil Liberties group. The Communists called it that in order to fool people into thinking that they were associated with the American Civil Liberties Union, which I was on the board of and which was most emphatically *not* a Communist front organization. So, when I was up for the job—this was during the McCarthy days when so many former Communists were baring their souls to Congress and saying, "I'm going to give them all the names of my fellow travelers"—Latimer gave them my name!

TB: That's right. He wrote a letter to the FBI naming all of his former associates.

JL: And my name was on his list! But you know something? I never really hated that man because in his letter he described me as "Party, but beautiful"!

[*Laughter.*]

So I set about proving to them that I wasn't Communist and that, as secretary of the NAACP, I had always taken an active public stand against the infiltration of communism into that organization or any other organization with which I was involved. So then they went on and accused my father of being a Communist because he had been the head of the National Negro Congress! So I went to my father and said, "Do you know what's holding up my being clear? It's you!" He said, "What do you mean?" I told him, "They say that you are a Communist because you headed up the National Negro Congress." Later on, the National Negro Congress *did* become Communist, but in the earlier days of the struggle for civil rights—when my father was involved—the policy was to accept the support of anybody that was going our way, and so Communists and all sorts of other radicals came to the meetings. Anyway, they all voted and made my dad president of the organization, but then a friend of his who was chair of the overall umbrella group in New York called him and said, "Stradford, I am going to confide in you: this is a Communist organization." So that's when my dad withdrew completely from the organization.

TB: They made him president because they wanted the respectability that he would provide.

JL: That's true, but, even back then, I realized the importance of not having any sort of blemish on your record. Not that I thought the job I was trying to get was so great, but I knew that if I were labeled as a Communist or "fellow traveler" or even "pink," then that label would be pinned to me for the rest of my life. So, anyway, we finally were able to clear up all those false accusations, and I became assistant U.S. attorney.

TB: Did you handle any criminal cases?

JL: No, when I was in the U.S. attorney's office, I did not handle any criminal cases at all because they had the attitude that women were always supposed to be gracious and soft-spoken and sheltered from any sort of potentially violent situation.

TB: That was the military view as well.

JL: But, after I resigned and Johnny was born in '58, I finally got back into the practice of law with my father, and that's when the friends that I had made in the U.S. attorney's office started sending a lot of criminal cases over to me.

TB: Did Jim Montgomery come into that office while you were still there?

JL: No, as a matter of fact, I recommended Jim as my replacement.

TB: So now you were finally able to practice law with your father.

JL: Yes, it was always understood that I was going to practice law with my father, and, besides that, I never had any desire to join a major law firm because at that time a person like me couldn't even rent office space down in the Loop, much less join an already established, primarily white law firm.

TB: Was your office with your dad still on Fifty-fifth Street?

JL: Yes, and, since we were living in Hyde Park, it was easy for me to take Johnny with me to work. So I had flexible time, and this was long before they had "flexible time" as any established kind of concept. I didn't make much money back then, but, even so, I was practicing law, and I was also able to spend a lot of time with Johnny, and I never regretted that a single bit.

TB: So, as you were saying, it was during this period of time that you started to handle some of the criminal cases that were passed down to you from the state attorney's office.

JL: Yes, that's when I started to develop a criminal practice. I even handled some police brutality cases where I sued the city, but most of the work that I was doing was handling the divorce cases that came through my father's office. During this same time, there were some marital problems of my own, and we divorced. Then, after that, in '61 I formed a partnership with my father and my new husband, and we moved my father from Fifty-fifth Street downtown to 69 West Washington.

TB: Which, of course, was a prime location.

JL: Yes, well, one of my husband's clients was S. B. Fuller, and the only way we could get into that building was to use Fuller's name as the tenant, but we didn't really lie about that because at that time he was, in fact, our main client. I'm afraid, however, that the realtor just might have been under the impression that the "Fuller Products" which we represented was Fuller Brush and not Fuller Beauty Care!

[*Laughter.*]

Anyway, we were good tenants and quickly developed a good practice. Eventually we had about a dozen other lawyers working with us, and we stayed in that same location for a period of twenty years.

TB: Were you still handling divorce cases?

JL: Yes, the last divorce case I handled was in '76 when my client was the wife of Muhammad Ali.

TB: When did you start to become involved in the corporate world?

JL: I started going on corporate boards in '68. The first one was Jewel Companies. Then in '70 or '71 representatives of Trans World Airlines flew in and asked me to get on their board of directors because they knew the people at Jewel and had heard about the work I'd been doing. After that, one board led to another. Some of those corporations were giving me legal business as well, but one day one of them said to me, "I have given you as much business as I can give to a small firm. You're just not equipped to handle anything any larger." So I decided then and there to get "equipped," and so I accepted an offer to join Vedder Price, which was a much larger firm. I did that because I realized that you have to be with a major firm in order to represent the really big corporations.

TB: What year would this be?

JL: As I remember, it was about 1980.

TB: In terms of those corporate boards, how do you account for the fact that you were not only the first *woman* but also the first *black* person to be included?

JL: Well, when I went on the Jewel Board of Directors, it's true that there weren't as yet any other women or any other blacks, and oftentimes my women friends who were professionals would say to me, "Why are you doing this?" But what they didn't seem to realize is that you not only get paid a healthy retainer but, in addition, you also begin to learn from the inside just how these large businesses are actually run, and business is what has made America great!

TB: Timing is also of the utmost importance, and, during this period, opportunities were beginning to open for black women because of what had been accomplished by the civil rights movement.

JL: Yes, and throughout America they were already starting to talk about affirmative action. Back then a person who was black and female was what they called a "two-for"—and so when I went on the Jewel Board, they said about me, "She's black. She's female—and her name is Jewel!" But by now that sort of attitude has really changed a lot due to the fact that more of us are being put in positions where we can actually show that we can think just as well or even better than the next person.

TB: But not everything has changed all that much for the better.

JL: Well, I must admit that what you say is true. What I particularly regret is that we don't have many blacks going into the scientific fields where there are so many great opportunities. You know, I'm on the board for GenCorp, which owns Aerojet, and we put the equipment on the space shuttle, but I suppose our past history has been that we've been kept out of certain areas such as this, and, therefore, we tend to stay with what is tried and true. Even so, there's really no excuse for young blacks not taking advantage of all these new opportunities that are starting to open up.

TB: Well, maybe with people like you on their boards, some of these corporations have become somewhat liberalized, but most often young blacks don't have any way of knowing that those sorts of opportunities actually exist.

JL: That's because there isn't the right kind of networking going on. In fact, it seems that the only kind of networking that most of them have is networking with people who don't have any more than they themselves have got. Now they've got to learn how to network with people who have the right kind of information and can point out the opportunities that are starting to open up.

TB: Yes, but for the majority of our young people that kind of networking just isn't available. What's more is that even though some of these companies are opening up in terms of whom they will hire, the ones that they hire have to be experts in their field, and unfortunately you cannot dispute the fact that last year in the entire country there were only *three* blacks who earned Ph.D.s in physics and another three in mathematics. So, although the numbers may be going up slightly, they're not going to be going up very fast anytime in the near future.

JL: Well, that's because our people are so burdened with the race issue that most of them don't get the opportunity to see the larger picture. They reach out only to people that they already know and trust because those people have exactly the same kind of problems that they have. That's why all forms of segregation have got to go out the window! Our young people have got to go out and get in the mix in order to be recognized for their talents and capabilities.

TB: In terms of "getting into the mix," let's talk for a few minutes about your continuing political activities.

JL: Well, I continued to be active in the Republican Party, and I attended the '56 Convention although I was not elected or delegated, but then, at the next convention in 1960, they made me a delegate-at-large, and the day before the nomination, much to my surprise, they asked me to give the seconding speech. So I went right over to the hairdresser and wrote my speech under the dryer!

[*Laughter.*]

No one corrected that speech or even read it before I presented it to the convention, which came as another surprise to me because I felt that they would have wanted to make sure that I didn't get up there in front of all those people and say something outrageous. But, anyway, I gave that speech just as it was written, and it was quite an exhilarating experience for me.

TB: Yes, and those of us who were watching on television were very proud. I said, "I know this lady!"

[*Laughter.*]

JL: It was easy for me to do because I really liked Richard Nixon. People say, "Everybody has to have an angel if they are going to succeed." Well, as far as opportunities to serve our government are concerned, Nixon was an angel for me. He appointed me to everything there was to be appointed to. My first appointment, I believe, was to the Minority Business Enterprise board, which was something that Nixon had initiated. After that, he appointed me as a delegate to the United Nations, and that was the first time an American black had ever been a full delegate and not just an alternate.

TB: That must have been a very interesting experience.

JL: What made it easy for me was that I was also still on the board of Trans World Airlines, and so I had a free pass and could shuttle back and forth all the time. I would go to Washington, say, on a Monday, come back to Chicago on Wednesday, and then go back to Washington on Friday.

TB: What period of time were you living in Washington?

JL: I started that kind of commuting in '72, but I always had my real home here in Chicago.

TB: Tell me something about your recent government appointment involving the problems of refugees.

JL: President Bush appointed me in April of '89 to be ambassador-at-large and U.S. coordinator for refugee affairs. This meant that I reported directly to the president of the United States and recommended policy on all refugee issues. I recommended to him yearly the number of refugees that should be blocked from the United States for resettlement as well as from what parts of the world others should be allowed to enter. In this role I worked with all the agencies of government that had anything to do with refugees, including the Immigration and Naturalization Service. Every Monday their representatives would meet in my office, and we'd discuss the problems that had arisen during the week.

TB: Through your efforts, were you able to modify or "liberalize" the U.S. position in regard to any of those refugee issues?

JL: I think so. Although our government wouldn't like to admit it, our whole immigration policy has been racist from the very beginning in the sense that we have always favored those coming here from Europe to the exclusion of everyone else. So, through our efforts, for example, we were able to bring in eleven thousand Haitians who had a credible claim for refugee status.

TB: This was under Bush?

JL: Yes, well, at first the State Department didn't want to do this. They said, "Aristide has just been elected president, and if we let in these refugees, it would be like slapping him in the face." So I told Secretary Eagleburger, "Well, let's wait a year and just see what happens." Then, sure enough, a few months later, they had another coup, and that's when we were able to bring those refugees into our country.

TB: Did you travel very much to see firsthand what was happening in the rest of the world?

JL: I've been all over Asia: Hong Kong, the Philippines, Thailand, Indonesia—wherever there are refugees.

TB: What about Africa?

JL: Well, prior to getting this job, I had traveled all over West Africa—Ghana, Nigeria, Ivory Coast, Senegal—but now I was able to go to South Africa, Swaziland, Zimbabwe, Kenya, and Ethiopia. I made a special point of visiting Malawi because that was the only country I had heard of that actually welcomed refugees. It has a population of only about eight million, and yet they took in over five million refugees! It's a poor, poor country which was run by a man who was president for life—Hastings Banda—and who had been educated in the United States at the University of Chicago back in the 1930s.

TB: After your experiences with contemporary refugees, looking back on your own family's history, would you say that they were also refugees from the racism that they had experienced in Oklahoma?

JL: Yes, definitely. My grandfather would have been killed if he had remained.

TB: Now, after you left government service, you came back to Chicago and resumed your law practice.

JL: Yes, in January of '93, but I became a full equity partner in a new law firm.

TB: "Full equity partner"? That means what?

JL: An "equity partner" means that you have an interest in the whole partnership. You share in all the successes as well as the failures. Whatever happens to the firm also affects you for better or for worse, which means profits as well as losses. Whatever happens you are definitely in the mix!

TB: Just how big is this firm?

JL: One hundred and thirty lawyers.

TB: How many of those are of color?

JL: There are four of us altogether: one man and three women.

TB: I understand that you recently have been given a new assignment at the Chicago Housing Authority.

JL: Yes, I've been appointed to reorganize the entire legal department and help them find a new general counsel.

TB: This comes as a result of the recent fiscal mismanagement scandal.

JL: Yes, but we don't have anything to do with changing the environment of the people who live in the projects. Our job is strictly a legal one: to set up a decent legal system and determine what core business ought to be handled in-house by the staff and what things should be sent outside.

TB: Now, at this point in your life, having seen what you have seen, in your reflection what has been your opinion of your life as you have lived it here in this city of Chicago?

JL: Well, first of all, I must say that I have been saddened over the degree of control that the former Mayor Daley had over the city, especially over our people. I resented all the blacks having to march to the beat of one drummer. I had always been brought up to be independent. To be different—well, maybe not so "different" that they'd put you out in the Elgin mental institution—but to always be your own person and do what you think is right, no matter what others might think. If you don't agree with them, don't just go along! I've never admired the people who get in lockstep just to secure some temporary advantage.

TB: Did you ever have any direct dealings with the late Mayor Daley?

JL: I was offered positions here in the city, but I always refused to be part of the machine. So Daley never bothered me personally because I was never in any sort of competition with him. I was a Republican, and most of my work was done on a national basis, but, even so, of all the places I've been in the world, to me, Chicago is the very best.

TB: It's home.

JL: But, more than that, it just has more to offer. First of all, I like cities. I don't want to live in a little community. That is because most of those little towns when I grew up were very narrow-minded, and I would hate to be dependent upon narrow-minded people like that for my survival. That's why I like to go to cities where I can be close to a wide variety of people. I can see the shops. I can see the industry. I can see what people are doing and be part of what is going to happen—and, out of all those cities that I've ever been to, it seems to me that Chicago is the very best, even with all its warts. Compared to New York, it's more livable. You can earn a living here. This part of the city is gorgeous. You are not confronted daily with the slums. Not that you can escape from them completely, but here at least you have a beautiful setting, and I don't know any other city where we have that. People here are also a little more open, and they respect you for what you are. Perhaps I have been successful because I have been much more fortunate than many others, but what I have been able to accomplish in my life is mainly because of the fact that I had two loving parents. My parents are the ones who made everything that has happened possible for me.

TB: Yes, but, even so, in spite of all that—

JL: Well, "you are still black, and don't you ever forget it!"

TB: Yes, that's the major point. No matter how much success you may have achieved, you always have to keep that fact in your consciousness and all the pain that goes along with it. You have to learn to carry that burden without letting it destroy you or stand in the way of what you want to accomplish.

JL: True, we have got too much to give to let anything like that stand in our way.

June 20, 1994

EDDIE CASEY

TALENTED ATHLETE AND SOCIAL ACTIVIST

The late Eddie Casey and I were friends for more than seventy years. Though in our youth we lived in different neighborhoods, those neighborhoods were adjacent to each other, and even though this meant that sometimes we were rivals, most often it meant that we were teammates on various basketball, softball, and football teams. We were also classmates at Wendell Phillips and DuSable high schools. Right from the beginning I recognized that Eddie was probably a pretty smart guy because he seemed to always have a pencil placed behind his ear whenever that pencil was not in his hand writing something down.

Eddie's brother, Stanford, also now deceased, was a star baseball player on the sandlots and the high school playing field. He was so good that I am sure that back then, if he had been born white, he would have gone on to play in the major leagues. During that period of time, the neighborhood in which all of us lived was considered to be rather rough, and so Stanford was always there to be his younger brother's protector. Everyone knew that "nobody better not mess with Eddie."

In later years Eddie became a self-taught intellectual who was interested and active in local, state, national, and international affairs. He read voraciously and personally participated in matters concerning economics, politics, and racial justice. Because of his wide range of knowledge and intellectual activity, he was able to introduce me to two of the persons whose conversations with me are to be included in these volumes: Fred Smith and Junius Gaten. Eddie Casey was one of those so-called ordinary people who help to accomplish extraordinary things that are of benefit to

everyone. I miss him but will always remember him with fondness and reverence.
Thanks again, Eddie . . .

TB: Eddie, where were you born and when did you first come to Chicago?

EC: I was born September 7, 1918, in Laurens, South Carolina. It's a little town near Greenville. My brother Stanford was also born there, a year earlier, on April 14, 1917. Then my father died in 1920, and my mother brought my brother and myself up here to Chicago in 1924.

TB: Did you already have any relatives that were living here?

EC: Yes, I had an uncle that came to Chicago much earlier, around 1910 or '12 or something like that. He went into World War I from here in Chicago, and he was involved in the whole shebang of us being over there.

TB: What was his background in terms of education?

EC: Surprisingly enough, he had attended Benedict College in South Carolina, but I don't know whether he got a degree or not because I only learned about his having been there after he died. The important thing is that he always comported himself with great dignity and gave serious thought to whatever he said or did.

TB: Was he the first member of your family to come to Chicago?

EC: Yes, and after he sent for us, just a little later, he also sent for my grandmother, my grandfather, and his youngest sister.

TB: What line of work was he doing?

EC: My uncle was in the moving business, and he also sold used furniture and other things. He was always very resourceful.

TB: So he became the leader of all three generations of your family.

EC: That was because we all respected his judgment.

TB: Did your father have any other sisters or brothers?

EC: Yes, my father had eight sisters and one brother that remained in South Carolina.

TB: Do you happen to remember when your grandfather was born?

EC: Well, he always said he was three years old when the slaves were freed, and my grandmother was about five years younger.

TB: So, when your grandparents and your mother and your brother and sister came to Chicago, you were all more or less under the supervision of your uncle.

EC: Right, and we all lived together on the second floor, above my uncle's store. Because she could read and write and my grandfather couldn't, my grandmother worked in the store while my mother did all the housework and cooking and stuff like that.

TB: Where was that store located?

EC: It was in a four-story red brick building at Forty-eighth and State. We lived there for a while, and then my mother got married again, and we moved away, but in 1930 my stepfather got killed in an automobile accident. So after that happened, we moved back here to Chicago.

TB: You knew that whenever there was a crisis like that, you could always come back here to Chicago.

EC: Yes, that was because my uncle was such an exceptional man, and we all looked up to him as a father. When my mother couldn't provide, he was the one who bought shoes and clothes for us. He did everything for us just as if we were his own children. After we came back—this is in '32 or '33—my uncle bought a two-flat frame building across the street at 4841 State, and we moved ourselves and his business over there. That's where we were living when I graduated from Coleman School.

TB: Did your uncle have any children of his own?

EC: No, and when he finally did get married, some of the members of our family became jealous of his wife.

TB: I can understand that. It was because a new person like her must have seemed like an intruder.

EC: That is exactly how some of us felt.

TB: What year did you graduate from Coleman?

EC: In June of '32. Stanford graduated just before me in February of that same year.

TB: Yes, that's right. We had half-year graduations at that time. I remember that because I graduated from Burke at exactly the same time: June 1932. So what did you guys do for fun until you got ready to go to high school?

EC: Mostly we played softball in the Coleman schoolyard. The girls played jacks, hopscotch, jump rope, and things of that sort. To earn money to go to the show, we would fill little baskets full of chopped-up wood scraps and sell them at three for a quarter to our neighbors. Some of the braver fellows would also sometimes go up to the coal yard on Federal and steal some coal and sell that in order to make some money.

TB: They could make money doing that because most of the apartments at that time were heated by either coal or wood.

EC: I remember when we had gas jets for light, we used to have to go to the drugstore and buy a fuse or something like that which you put in the jet. Then you'd turn the gas on and strike a match to get it going. Looking back, it's a wonder to me that we didn't ever blow up that old house we were living in!

TB: Well, actually, very few of those old dry wooden buildings over on Dearborn and Federal ever burned. Now, during that period, were most of your activities confined to the east side of the tracks?

EC: Well, you could go over there but just not very far.

TB: What would happen if you decided to go over on the west side of the railroad tracks?

EC: You would run into white folks over on Swann Street or Wentworth, and also there were some hostile groups of blacks over there that might have caused you some trouble.

TB: But by then was it mostly blacks that were living in that neighborhood on the east side of the tracks?

EC: Yes, but we had quite a few Italians that were also living east of the tracks. As a matter of fact, there was an Italian boy in my graduating class, and in Stanford's class I think they had a couple of Italian boys and a Jewish boy and girl.

TB: Was the Owl Theatre still there?

EC: Yes, that's where we saw Hoot Gibson and all the other cowboys, but I never did get a chance to see Tom Mix because they showed his movies on Sunday, and we couldn't go to the show on Sunday on account of my grandmother. She was strictly religious, and so you couldn't go to the movies or play cards—but you could play dominoes, and so that's what we did!

[*Laughter.*]

Another thing that I remember is that because my uncle had access to used furniture from his moving business we always had a piano in the front room, and a white lady used to come by and teach me to play for fifty cents a lesson. My mother and aunt would watch what she was doing, and after she'd gone, they would put their specs on and try to pick out the proper notes on the piano for themselves!

[*Laughter.*]

TB: So now you move away for a while, but fairly soon you move back in with your uncle. Where did you go to high school?

EC: In 1932 I went into Wendell Phillips High School at Thirty-ninth and Prairie, and I stayed there until January of '35, when part of it burned down. After that, my brother and I went into New Phillips.

TB: What are some of your recollections of your experiences at the old Phillips?

EC: I have many pleasant memories.

TB: Several of your classmates went on to become well-known musicians, didn't they?

EC: Well, there was Nat King Cole, of course, and then there was also Clyde

Winkfield, who played concert piano and later went on to be the accompanist for Etta Moten.

TB: Was Ray Nance still there?

EC: No, he had already graduated in June, just before I got there.

TB: Do you remember anything about Alonzo Parham? He was there just before you.

EC: Yes, he was the first black from Chicago that was appointed to West Point.

TB: That's right. He was appointed by Oscar DePriest.

EC: Well, I knew all about him. In fact, he was one of my idols, but I never met him until about two years ago when we were both at an art exhibit.

TB: How did you feel about the quality of education that you were getting at Phillips?

EC: Well, I thought the quality was very good, but I wasn't too much concerned with taking advantage of what was being offered. The classes that I enjoyed the most were ones in which I got the better marks. Others like math and so forth, I didn't do well in, and I didn't enjoy them at all, but I've always been interested in history. So, therefore, I scored pretty high in black history and world events.

TB: Who did you have for history?

EC: Mrs. DePriest. We had a lot of discussions in her class about modern history because at that time—this was '35—Mussolini was marching in on Ethiopia, and she was irate about what was happening. So I scored well in her class because I also had strong opinions about those events.

TB: Your history teacher was Lydia DePriest. She was Oscar DePriest's sister-in-law, and she was my teacher as well. Later on her daughter taught at the New Phillips, which, of course, became DuSable.

EC: But I didn't stay there long enough to graduate because in 1937 I decided to drop out and get a job.

TB: Back then a lot of other guys were also dropping out. What kind of job did you get?

EC: I worked for a while at a grocery store at Fiftieth and South Park, and then I got a job working on a Coca-Cola truck making deliveries in the neighborhood. I was making four dollars a day.

TB: Which was pretty good money for that time.

EC: Yes, but then in 1940 I got a better job at Swift & Company.

TB: And where was that located back then?

EC: At Forty-first and Ashland.

TB: What did you do there?

EC: Well, I ended up being what they called an order filler, but actually I was a shipping clerk. You see, that was a position which was held by whites until the country went to war, and when they had to hire blacks to fill those jobs, they didn't want to elevate blacks to that title. So that's the reason why they called us order fillers instead of shipping clerks.

TB: How long did you stay there?

EC: For eighteen years, until '58, when they decided to close down their major operation here in Chicago.

TB: During those eighteen years that you were working there, did they continue to hire many blacks?

EC: Most of the blacks that worked there were hired during the war years.

TB: Where did they come from?

EC: About 90 percent of them came from Mississippi.

TB: So, when you left there in '58, did you already have a family of your own?

EC: Yes, I was married in '42, and by then we had two children. So I was off of work for about a year, but during that time, I was able to get my insurance broker's license, and then in '59 I went to work at the Metropolitan Mutual as a debit agent.

TB: What kind of experiences did you have while working at the Met?

EC: Well, mostly it was not a good experience for me there because they had become rich by selling those little nickel-and-dime policies—such as burial insurance and so forth—and they did not seem to want to advance and be competitive in the developing market. So they fought against change, and I became disillusioned.

TB: And now outside competition from the white insurance companies is also beginning to move into the marketplace.

EC: Before then, those companies totally ignored the needs of blacks. Even a black doctor or lawyer couldn't get a policy that was worth more than a thousand dollars from any of those white folks.

TB: During that period, did you know Langford Spraggins?

EC: No, not personally, but Langford Spraggins and Cirilo McSween were the Jackie Robinsons of the insurance business for blacks in those days. They were our idols.

TB: Langford became the first black to become a member of the Million-Dollar Round Table because he was able to sell one million dollars of insurance in a single year, mostly to those same people that Chicago Met was still ignoring.

EC: Pretty soon a lot of other blacks left Chicago Met because they also became frustrated, and they went over to those white-owned companies and started setting sales records of their own. In fact, for a brief period I went over to Bankers Life and Casualty and led them in the selling of life insurance for one of the months out of the year that I was there, but I left them because I also became disillusioned with them. The reason for that was the fact that their policies were not the kind of policies that you could sell to your customers in good faith. MacArthur, who owned Bankers Life and Casualty, was the most sued man in America at that time. There were over ten thousand lawsuits in the courts against him!

TB: So, when you left Bankers Life and Casualty, where did you go?

EC: Well, my wife and I separated in 1960, and that's when I got another job working for a private company in Skokie—the Prestige Casualty Company—as an automobile claims adjuster.

TB: How long did that job last?

EC: For another eighteen years, and then I retired.

TB: Now, Eddie, going back to those early years, what kind of memories do you have of your life on the South Side?

EC: Well, the South Side was really beautiful back then because you didn't have to be afraid of anything.

TB: Whatever the physical condition of the neighborhood might have been, there was a quality of life in the community that made people feel comfortable.

EC: Yes, and safe. What's more is that there was a lot of camaraderie with all the fellows that I knew. In order to look good and make the proper kind of appearance at all the different dances and social events, we always used to share each other's shoes, shirts, pants, or whatever else we needed. When you look at all those old photos, we always look all dressed up in different clothes, but back then I don't think that any of us had more than one suit!

[*Laughter.*]

Whenever we would go out, we always wanted to look our best—especially when we went strolling down the avenue and had our girlfriends with us! Maybe all we had was two dollars in our pockets, but that was sufficient in those days. There were lots of places to go and inexpensive places where you could get something to eat. Do you remember those chicken shacks they used to have?

TB: What were the names of some of those places that you remember?

EC: Willie Gray's Chicken Shack, Ruby Henderson's Chicken Shack, Charlie and Ella Mae's Chicken Shack—places like that.

TB: Do you remember that place on Fifty-eighth Street where Nat Cole and his band used to play?

EC: Of course I do.

TB: Did you know back then that he could sing?

EC: No, after he went out to California, the first time I heard "Straighten Up and Fly Right" on the radio, I said, "Who's that?"

[*Laughter.*]

TB: You also were involved in sports, weren't you?

EC: I sure was, but I didn't play anything at all when I was in high school because I hadn't grown much yet. I was still short, but just a year or two later I was playing basketball with the Trojans Club and then with the Rockets over at the Wabash YMCA. Dan Gaines was one of our sponsors, and he bought all the uniforms for us. At that time he was the only black in the entire nation who had an authorized Ford dealership.

TB: So, as you describe it to me, during these times, you were poor but not poverty-stricken. There was a network of good relationships between people in the family and all the people out on the street. So there was a sense of community, and there was also a feeling of safety and hope for the future. Even though you might not get rich, there was always the hope that at least sometime soon you were going to be better off than you were at present.

EC: Right, and there was also a respect toward the elders. If ever an older person was around, you didn't use any swear words. You didn't let them hear that sort of thing, and if you ever happened to do anything that was wrong, the grapevine would always get a report about it back to your house before you could get there yourself!

TB: So these were a kind of glory days that you've been describing as your memories of growing up in Chicago.

EC: Yes, looking back, I've had a lot of experiences—some good and some bad—but all of them taken together are what has molded my character and made me what I am. Even those bad experiences, they taught you how to survive, how to know when you are in danger, how to be able to size people up in uncertain situations, how to cope with adversity and not get in trouble, how to make an honest living no matter what else was going on. You know, back in the thirties, the only fellas that I knew that had much money were the guys around Forty-fourth and State who used to steal off of trucks. They lived fast, but most of them died while they were still in their twenties. The rest of us learned what we could and did what we had to do. None of us were professionals, and yet we all lived a decent life. We worked jobs for twenty or thirty or forty years. We raised our families, and did you know that two of the guys that I knew while I was growing up now have children that are on the faculty at Harvard? That's a hell of a jump from Federal Street!

TB: How do you see things for the young people growing up today as compared with that time when we ourselves were young?

EC: Well, I think that we are advancing and backing up at the same time.

TB: Please explain exactly what you mean.

EC: Although you don't see much of it in the newspapers or on the television, there are a lot of success stories—increased opportunities and all of that—but the ones who are backing up are the ones who have no education and no hope for the future. They are the ones who are lowest on the totem pole, and so there is a growing separation between them and those who have become successful.

TB: When we were growing up, we had all kinds of examples of talent and success that were living right here in the neighborhood with us, but now our young people don't get to see those kinds of people in the flesh anymore. At best all they have is their images on television, and that is something that's very, very different.

EC: Yes, that's not the same thing at all. I wrote a letter last year to Michael Jordan asking him if he might be able to show up impromptu and speak to a group of our young people, but he never even responded.

TB: That may not be because he didn't want to. I think that people like him have become isolated by their own management. You have to go through a block of other people before you can make any sort of contact. Oprah is the same way. I mean, she is a good person, but you can't get through to her. She's given millions away, but you can't speak with her directly anymore. Bill Cosby's just the same.

EC: Like you say, you can't get close to them and get them involved.

TB: But somebody reads their mail, and someday your letter will be read, and perhaps one day they will respond. Meanwhile, they just stay where they are and do what they do and continue to be successful.

EC: And the problems for our young people who are not successful remain the same or even get worse.

TB: And the gap gets wider and more solidly constructed.

EC: That gap has got to be closed.

TB: That is exactly what we are trying to do. Thank you, Eddie.

August 31, 1992

MURIEL CHANDLER

SIGNIFICANT CONTRIBUTOR TO THIS WORK

I first met Muriel Chandler through my friend Jamie Kalven. At that time Muriel was transcribing some materials for one of the Hyde Park social agencies, and with Jamie's help I was able to obtain her services as one of the major transcribers of the audiotapes that form the basis for Bridges of Memory. *During that process I learned that she was reared on the South Side and that she had some vivid and richly important memories of those years that were central to her personal and social growth.*

Muriel possesses a charming, informed, engaged, entrepreneurial personality. I am certain that she can be a tough customer to deal with for anyone who might be so foolish as to attempt to mess with her mind or social values. However, she is always compassionate and very concerned about the affairs and conditions that exist in Chicago for all less-advantaged people, particularly blacks. It was my good fortune to meet, work with, and have this conversation with such a strong-willed and lovely person.

TB: Muriel, since you've been such a great help to me by transcribing so many of these conversations that I've had with my friends and acquaintances, I'm pretty sure you already know the first question that I'm going to ask you.

MC: Where was I born?

[*Laughter.*]

TB: That's right.

MC: I was born in Detroit, Michigan, on March 5, 1926. March 5 also just happens to be the same day of the year that my mother was born.

TB: Where were your mother and father born?

MC: They were both originally from Georgia, but they did not know each other when they were in Georgia. She was born in Carrollton, and he was born in Palmetto. They met in Detroit.

TB: Rather than migrating to Chicago, each of them migrated separately from Georgia directly to Detroit?

MC: Yes, the automobile industry was the main attraction. You see, she was the seventh of nine children, but her mother died when she was only about fourteen years old, and by the time she had finished school in Carrollton, one of her older sisters had already gotten married and migrated to Detroit. So then she and her sisters and her father all decided that they should also move up to Detroit.

TB: What about her brothers?

MC: Her two brothers stayed in the South.

TB: And about which year would this be?

MC: Let me think about that. My mother was born in 1906, and her mother died fourteen years after that—so my grandmother must have died in 1920, and, since my mother didn't finish school until she was about seventeen or eighteen, that means that my mother and her father and sisters must have come to Detroit sometime around 1923 or 1924.

TB: When they got to Detroit, did they stay with her sister?

MC: No, they got a place to live of their own. They all lived together, which made things very difficult for my mother and her sisters because my grandfather was such an autocratic man.

TB: What do you mean by saying that he was autocratic?

MC: Well, back in those days most of the people that we knew had nice, kind fathers, but my grandfather was always very severe with his children. He believed in whippings and beatings. That is the reason why all his sons left his house just as soon as they were old enough to run away. So it wasn't a very happy childhood for any of them, but my mother always said that at least he wasn't ever mean to her. Pretty soon, after they'd been in Detroit only a little while, I believe that the girls all got together and asked him to leave their home. They said, "Papa, we are grown now," and then they told him they had decided that it was no longer going to be the way it was in the past where he made all the decisions about everything and laid down all the rules.

TB: Did you ever have the chance to meet your grandfather?

MC: I was ten years old when he died. So I knew him up to that point. Of course by that time he had mellowed quite a bit. I would sit in his lap and rub his bald head, and I really loved him.

TB: How old was he when he died?

MC: Oh, he must have been only about sixty-three or somewhere around that age.

TB: What kind of work did he do? Did he work in the automobile industry?

MC: I think he did, but he was quite proud of the fact that he had also worked on building that bridge that connects Detroit with Canada.

TB: You mentioned that your father also came from Georgia.

MC: Yes, he left when he was still a very young man. I think he ran away. Those were times when young black men, if they spoke out and said the slightest sort of "wrong" thing, they could get hurt or even killed. So something must have happened, but he never did explain to me exactly what it was. He only said that he knew when it was time for him to leave the South, and so he hit the road and came to Detroit.

TB: Did he know anybody who was already there?

MC: No, he always said he came to Detroit knowing no one and making his own way. So he got a job in the automobile industry, and he worked for Ford all the rest of his life. That's the only job that he ever had!

TB: How did he meet your mother?

MC: Well, in those days the church was the center of all social activities, and they both had been raised in the AME Church. So one of the AME churches in Detroit is where they met.

TB: And you spent your first years in Detroit?

MC: Yes, but my parents divorced when I was about six years old, and my mother moved here to Chicago when I was seven. So almost all of my education was here.

TB: Did you have any brothers or sisters?

MC: No, I am an only child.

TB: What was the first school you went to?

MC: The first school was Forrestville, but I spent most of my time at Willard, and that was where I graduated from elementary school. I have the greatest memories of the time that I was at that school! Did you ever go there?

TB: Yes, I did. Do you remember any of your teachers there? Were any of them black?

MC: Well, in those days most of our teachers were white because there were so few blacks who could make it through all those hurdles that were in place back then, but I do remember Ora Marlow, who taught art, and another woman named Thomas or Thompson.

TB: Was Ruth Fosche also there?

MC: Yes, she was my music teacher.

TB: Of course at that time a lot of prominent people were living in the Willard area. Charles Murray, who was the founder of Murray's Superior Products Company, lived in the neighborhood.

MC: And then there was that man who was an attorney that went into the Eisenhower administration.

TB: Yes, Ernest Wilkins, who later on went on to become the undersecretary of labor.

MC: But he died soon after that. In fact, he died before he had finished his term of office.

TB: One of his sons—the math whiz—received his Ph.D. from the University of Chicago when he was only nineteen. He was the youngest person ever to get a Ph.D. from that university, and then he went on to work on the Manhattan Project, which is where they discovered how to make a nuclear bomb.

MC: That reminds me. I believe at one time his mother was a teacher at Willard.

TB: Yes, she was. You know, when I was there, the school was so crowded that we were on triple shift. You, of course, are younger than me, and I wonder if the school was still that crowded when you were there.

MC: When I was there, they had only two shifts. One group would come in at 8:30 A.M. and stay until noon, and another group would come in at 12:30 or 1:00 P.M. and stay until 3:00 P.M., but then when you got to the seventh and eighth grades, you stayed all day. That's when they were beginning to have teachers specializing in certain subjects, and so we had to move from room to room throughout the day. I would go to Ms. Fosche for music, Ms. Marlow for art, and someone else for science. They said they were moving us around like that to prepare us for the kinds of programs that we'd be having in high school.

TB: Do you remember any of the students that were there at that time?

MC: Well, Oscar Brown Jr. was one of my classmates. We graduated at the same time, but he was never in any of my classes. I just knew him and that he was already doing radio programs and that sort of thing. He was always such an innovative person!

TB: As you remember it, what was the neighborhood around Willard like?

MC: It was a nice, quiet neighborhood, not at all like it is today. We were living at Forty-fifth and Prairie, and that's a long way from Willard, but I'd walk there every school day. Eventually I got used to doing that. Listen, I was what they used to call a latchkey kid. I wore a key to the apartment on my neck from the time I was seven years old. When we first came to Chicago and I was going to Forrestville School, my mother was working. My little key was on my neck. That was so I wouldn't lose it, and nobody ever bothered me. Sometimes my mother would be working at night, especially when she would get an elevator job. She would go to work at eleven o'clock, and then she would get back home by eight o'clock in the morning to fix breakfast for me and get me ready for school.

TB: And you never had any problems with being a latchkey kid like that?

MC: No, I didn't.

TB: When did you graduate from grammar school?

MC: I graduated from grammar school in '39, and from there I went to DuSable.

TB: Did you graduate from DuSable?

MC: No, I only stayed there for a year, and then I transferred to Englewood.

TB: Why was that? Did you think you'd be getting a better education?

MC: No, it was nothing like that. I think we had very good teachers at DuSable, and I am not saying anything against those teachers. The problem was that the kids at DuSable liked to fight and do things that worried my mother. You see I was always very small, and I was her only child. She was afraid that I'd get beat up.

TB: Oh, I'm sure they wouldn't have done anything like that to you.

MC: Of course they wouldn't. I knew enough by then to just get out of their way when necessary!

[*Laughter.*]

But my mother didn't know that I knew how to do that.

TB: And so you transferred to Englewood in 1940.

MC: Yes, and I graduated from there in 1943.

TB: Were you still living at Forty-fifth and Prairie?

MC: No, by that time we were living at Fifty-second and South Park.

TB: So now you're living in Englewood. What was the neighborhood like back then?

MC: By the time I got there, Englewood was maybe 10 percent black. Englewood was always a kind of blue-collar neighborhood, and so most of the white kids, of course, came from that blue-collar white element, mostly Italians and Polish.

TB: And you all got along together pretty well?

MC: Yes, everything was just fine, but when prom time came around, that's when we split into separate groups. That's why Margaret Burroughs and some of her friends established the Purple and White Club as a sort of umbrella organization that would help us through all the problems we were having. So all we had to do was just to follow along with what they set up for us, and that made our prom a very nice one for all of us.

TB: Before that there had been an organization called the Circe Ceroines, which was formed by some of the students at Englewood for the very same reason.

MC: Well, I wouldn't know about that. That was before my time. I keep on telling you, Tim, I am just a little bit behind you, and I don't know about things like that!

[*Laughter.*]

TB: As far as school is concerned, we are only just about eight years apart.

MC: Well, back then it was a *big* difference.

TB: Aside from the academics, what sort of activities were you involved with at Englewood?

MC: Well, I was so small that I was always ashamed of my size, and so I was not at all athletic, but I was in the speech club and that sort of thing.

TB: Was Ms. Espenchez still in the music department?

MC: Yes, she was, but my favorite teacher was an Irish woman named Ms. O'Brien, who was my homeroom teacher.

TB: Was she your homeroom teacher all the time you were there?

MC: Yes, until I graduated in 1943. She was a real doll. I just liked her, and she liked me. So she was very kind to me, and I became a kind of secretary for her. That's the reason I got to know so many people.

TB: What about the social side of things during that period of your life?

MC: Well, there were always so many activities going on that we would have to plan our weekends ahead of time, and so we formed social clubs. We started a little club like that when I was still in high school. There were maybe five or six of us, and we would pay our little dues of about ten cents a week or something like that so that we could save up our money and rent a little hall where we could have a dance—and, of course, we also went to the dances that the other social clubs were having.

TB: Did you ever go to any of the nightclubs?

MC: Yes, when I was a little older, my dad came from Detroit to visit us one time, and he took my mother and me to the Club DeLisa. You know, when you first went in there was just a little bar in front, but in the back there was this whole big place with a stage and everything. That was my first time going there. I remember they would let you bring your own bottle for drinking, but they'd charge you something like five or six dollars for glasses and ice. They called that a setup.

TB: The wait staff made most of their money from tips, and the management made most of their money from the gambling that was going on down in the basement!

MC: I didn't know that.

TB: All that other stuff was just a front.

MC: Yes, but whenever you went there you always saw a good show.

TB: Always!

MC: After I graduated, the war was still going on, and I had to decide what I was going to do.

TB: What was your decision?

MC: Well, my mother did not have that good an education, but somehow she could always manage to get some kind of factory job. Sometimes she also worked as an elevator operator and things like that, but her earnings were always meager. So I knew that when I graduated I would have to get a job. College wasn't on my mind—well, actually it was, but I knew it just wasn't for me. If there were any kinds of scholarships around that I could have applied for, I just did not even know that they existed. I would ask around at Englewood about things like that, but they would not tell me any of the things that I needed to know.

TB: Was that because those receiving the available scholarships were all hand-picked?

MC: That's right. It was all a matter of politics. If only I had known then what I know now, I would have been scrambling around to get whatever I could, but I didn't know what to do beyond the fact that I needed to get a job, and the WACs had just started, and I was wondering if I had the stamina to do something like that, but by that time a lot of civil service jobs were also opening up for blacks, and they were not so discriminatory in their hiring policies as they had been previously.

TB: That's because so many men had gone into the service, and now they had a serious labor shortage on the home front.

MC: Exactly, and so jobs were opening up for women, but the white women would always gobble up the best jobs that were available, and so the black women had to take whatever was left. Well, anyway, I went in and took an exam and got a job in the federal government. I worked for the Signal Corps. Do you remember that Motorola and Zenith used to have factories here that built radios for the military? Well, my job was to learn how to inspect those radios before they shipped them out. So I went into training for that for about three months, and then they asked if I wanted to work in an office instead. I was qualified for that because when I was at Englewood I had taken shorthand and typing, but in the meantime, I got married, and so I decided to quit!

[*Laughter.*]

I got married in 1945, and my husband was still in the service. So I moved out to Oklahoma to join him.

TB: At Fort Sill?

MC: Yes, and we lived in a little cottage for the military staff that we shared with another couple. To go into town you would have to take a local bus, not a military bus. So it was a segregated bus, and we had to ride in the back. Well, one night we went to the movies, and coming back we were there in the back of the bus, and here is this white soldier also sitting back there, and he is as drunk as a skunk. He starts telling us about how angry he is that soldiers in uniform who've signed up to risk their lives for their country have to sit like this in the back of the bus. Well, this was my first time ever being in the South, and what he was saying really disturbed me. It made me want to not ever live in the South and just to get out of there as soon as possible.

TB: You had not had that kind of specific experience previously?

MC: No, I certainly had not. So I stayed there for a while, but the marriage was not going very well, and I decided to come back here to Chicago and go back to work for the federal government, but after doing that for a few years, I realized that this kind of work was not getting me anywhere. I would always be some kind of a clerk or stenographer. So I said to myself, "Hey, there has to be something better out there!"—and that's when I went back to school.

TB: What school did you go to?

MC: I went to DePaul at night, and at the same time I was still working for the government moving from job to job and getting promotions whenever and wherever I could, but I hung in there, and I got through and graduated at the same time I was still working at a full-time job.

TB: Now, while all of this is happening in your life, the mood of the city is changing, and the communities within it are also changing.

MC: Yes, when I was growing up, most of the neighborhoods where we were living on the South Side were all pretty much stable. Of course, back in those days, if the man of the family had a job in the post office or on the railroad, that was considered to be a good job. There were only just a few pockets of poor people that were living over around State Street and some of the other areas. Then, when the war ended, all of those people started coming up here from the South. I remember that very clearly because I was working downtown on LaSalle Street, and every morning a fellow that I knew would pick me up, and we'd drive down Michigan Avenue to get to our work. We'd be there about eight o'clock, just as the train coming in from the South was letting its passengers off, and we'd see all these black folks carrying their cardboard boxes that contained all of their belongings.

TB: Are you talking about the old Twelfth Street Station?

MC: Yes, that station on Michigan Avenue at Twelfth Street, that's where you'd see all these black folks coming in from the South. Farms were going out of fashion down there, and they couldn't make a decent living. So they were coming up here, and, like I said, all they had was just cardboard luggage tied up with a string to hold their stuff together. Some of them just had paper sacks to put their possessions in.

TB: This, of course, was part of the second migration to Chicago from the South.

MC: Yes, and now here are all these people starting to come in that don't know the first thing about how to live in the city, and so the neighborhood starts to change, and you say to yourself, "I got to get out of here!" So people moved. We moved to a place on Fifty-second Street.

TB: During that period just after the war, as I remember, housing was very hard to get.

MC: Yes, in order to get a decent place to live you had to pay a lot under the table. What they would do is say that in order to get this apartment you must also buy the furniture that's in it.

TB: And that furniture might be just a chair.

MC: That's right, and if you wanted that apartment, you'd have to pay them five hundred dollars or maybe a thousand for that chair or whatever else might be left in there. So, in order to avoid all of that, my mother and I ended up buying an old tumbled-down house at Sixty-first and Michigan.

TB: Now, at about this same period of time, new job opportunities are also beginning to become available.

MC: Yes, but the reason for that is that the white men who were coming back from the service were taking advantage of the GI Bill and going back to school to complete their educations, and after graduating, believe me, most of them weren't going back to their old prewar jobs. They left those for black guys to fill. That's why you were beginning to see black streetcar motormen and even black police officers.

TB: Lots of black women were also starting to get jobs in the post office.

MC: That's right. Everything was changing, and another thing to remember is that with gas rationing ending and their salaries increasing, more and more whites are moving out of the city and into the suburbs, and that leaves no one else but blacks to take over their old jobs.

TB: Now, by the time you graduated from DePaul, are you and your mother still living at Sixty-first and Michigan?

MC: No, I didn't graduate until 1963, and we sold the house and moved out to Lake Meadows in 1958. That is where we lived for ten years, until 1968.

TB: What was Lake Meadows like when you moved there?

MC: It was very nice and pleasant. At that time crime wasn't bad, and you could go out at night feeling carefree.

TB: And you were never fearful?

MC: Well, we had to be a little careful, but crime was not rampant anything like it is now.

TB: You said that you left Lake Meadows in 1968. Where did you go?

MC: I moved to Washington, D.C.

TB: What kind of work were you doing?

MC: I was working as an analyst for the Social Security Administration. It was an interesting job, and I liked Washington, but it is very expensive to live there. Even though I got a promotion and made a couple of thousand dollars extra, every bit of salary was being spent just to pay for rent and expenses. So I said to myself that this is not what I want, and I came back here to Chicago and got a job at the Social Security office here in the city. That was my last job! In 1978, I retired because my mother became ill. She had the final stage of kidney disease, and I had the chance to retire before retirement age. So I decided to quit my job in order to take care of her, but that was a hard decision for me to make, and those were hard, hard days.

TB: Did you move back to living in Lake Meadows when your mother became ill?

MC: No, when I came back from Washington, we moved to Hyde Park and lived at the University Park Apartments. My mother was ill for about eleven years before she passed away in 1989. Those were difficult years, but I managed, and everything worked out OK. So that brings my career up-to-date.

TB: Now, looking back on all the years that you have lived here in Chicago, how would you summarize your experiences?

MC: It is hard to answer something like that. I only know that I always think about being a black person and having to struggle for everything I've been able to achieve. In every job I've ever had, that thought has always been in my mind. Don't get me wrong. I get along all right with white people—most of them—but there is always that little seed back in your head where you know that you don't know whether the person you are talking to is sincere or not. You do not know if they might be going to throw a monkey wrench at you at anytime during your conversation!

[*Laughter.*]

So I don't know if it's just Chicago or if it's the times we grew up in, and I just happened to be in Chicago when certain things happened, but I still remember when I was working with the Signal Corps—this was the first job I ever had—and they sent me downtown to some office space they had rented in a big, beautiful building at 1 South LaSalle. At that time I didn't know anything about buying lunch out from home. Usually I'd just take a little sandwich with me and eat in, but then, as I started making a little bit more money, I started to venture out a little, and I saw that some white people were going into a coffee shop right there on Madison and getting themselves something to eat. So I went in there, and I just stood there and stood there with the waitress completely ignoring me. It took me a while to realize what was happening, but I finally caught on. Blacks weren't welcome there.

TB: And this is 1945, and there is a war going on, and you are working for the Signal Corps.

MC: Yes, and you know, when I was a kid, we would come downtown, and you could go on State Street to any place you wanted and get something to eat, but this job I had was on LaSalle Street, and this is the business area. This is the banking area, this is the money area, and a different set of rules had been estab-lished.

TB: That kind of treatment caught you by surprise.

MC: I wasn't expecting it. You know, when I started working in those government offices, I would always be one of the few blacks that were hired. There were maybe ten of us at the very most out of the whole group that was there, and I'll never forget one woman who was working in the files section. She was very fair. In fact, she looked like she was white. Her name was Lucille, and she lived over there on Forty-fifth near that Washington Park Court area. She was a very nice woman, and when these white people in the office would start talking about blacks, she would not hesitate to put them straight right away. "Listen, you are talking to a *black* person!" She got married during the Depression to a man with a much darker complexion, and her children, of course, were brown. Well, jobs were hard to get, and her husband couldn't get a job, but she discovered that she could by passing as white. So that's what she did for a time, but what stopped her from doing that was one day she was coming home on the bus with one of her kids, and she realized that her children had become accustomed not to speak to her in a public place because they knew she was passing.

TB: Do you think with your skills and personality that you would have done better in someplace other than Chicago?

MC: Maybe, but who knows? Listen, these are the cards I was dealt, and these are the cards that I've got to play. I really don't worry about what could have been. Well, I may think about it sometimes, but I don't let anything like that get in my way. I guess I could have been an activist, but I was never around enough people who were activists to get me involved with any of that. But if my path had crossed those types of people, I would have been right there with them because it was so disturbing for me to see the sorts of things that were happening and not be able to change those things and make them better.

August 25, 1995

REVEREND A. P. JACKSON

TOWER OF STRENGTH

The late Reverend Abraham Patterson Jackson and his sister Aileen were longtime friends and classmates of mine at the old Wendell Phillips and then the new DuSable high schools. I can still remember quite vividly the time in 1935 when their family had to move out of their nice apartment in the six-flat building at Forty-third and Michigan Avenue because the soon-to-be heavyweight boxing champion of the world, Joe Louis, and his wife, Marva, had bought the building and needed all the available space for their own entourage. It wasn't very long after that before Abe's dad was able to find another equally nice apartment nearby—so, of course, they were never out on the street or anything like that!

Later on, during the time that Abe was a student at Morehouse College in Atlanta, Georgia, one of his fellow students was Martin Luther King. Though King was a bit younger and, therefore, at a lower academic level, they became close friends, and their friendship continued uninterrupted until King's assassination in 1968. During the period of King's ascendancy to world fame as a civil rights leader and nonviolent strategist, contrary to many of the boasts that may have been heard in subsequent years, King was not welcome in and did not receive support from the majority of churches in Chicago or anywhere else. That was not the case at Liberty Baptist Church, however, where he was welcomed with open arms and spoke to crowds that filled the church and flowed out into the streets. Then, in the spring and summer of 1966, when Dr. King accepted the invitation of the Coordinating Council of Community Organizations to come to Chicago in order to protest housing segregation and to organize and lead

marches into certain tightly segregated neighborhoods, he was berated by the estab-
lishment (both economic and political) and denounced by some black political office-
holders as nothing but a troublemaker. As a result, at that time the majority of
churches and community organizations, both black and white, were reluctant or
afraid to welcome Dr. King or offer him any form of open support. Nevertheless, de-
spite political threats, Reverend A. P. Jackson opened the doors of his church to
Dr. King and his supporters for their rallies and organizational meetings—and in
those tumultuous days that show of support required great moral conviction and guts!
The community remembered this, and later on, in April of 1968, when Dr. King was
assassinated, there were no riots anywhere in or around Liberty Baptist Church—only
deep shock, sadness, peaceful mourning, and a series of eloquent and beautiful shared
memories and deeply felt tributes that were meant to express the heartfelt loss and
abiding love and respect that continued to be felt within the community for this very
great man.

That same combination of moral leadership and intestinal fortitude was also very
much in evidence again during the days of the struggle against South African
apartheid, when Bishop Desmond Tutu and other activists were invited to be guests
at Liberty Baptist Church—and, well, I could go on and on about the many contri-
butions that were made by my late friend, Reverend A. P. Jackson, but to close these
remarks and to give some idea of the admiration and respect that were felt for this re-
markable man, when he passed, so many people from all walks of life wanted to pay
homage and eulogize his impact on their lives that it took two days to complete his
funeral service, and even after the service was over, people were still waiting in line
outside so that they would also be able to pay their final respects. Amen, amen, and
amen . . .

APJ: My father was from Sardis, Mississippi. They had a little college down there—
　　Mississippi Industrial College—and that's where he got his college education.
TB: What about your mother?
APJ: My mother only finished as far as the eighth grade.
TB: Which, of course, is typical for that time. So when did they come to Chicago?
APJ: My father left Mississippi in 1923. He came up here about two years before us.
　　That was the way they did things like that back in those days. The man would
　　come up North, get a job, and save enough money to send back down home for
　　his wife and children to join him. So, when my father first came up here, like so
　　many others, at first he worked at a series of odd jobs.
TB: Such as?
APJ: Well, he worked for a time at South Water Market unloading freight cars when

the fruit would come in from Florida, but then he got a better job as a carpenter at West Pullman. He made railroad cars.

TB: Where did he learn that trade?

APJ: At Mississippi Industrial College they taught everyone a trade. So now that he had a better job, he was able to save some money, and all the rest of us came up here in 1925. My mother, my two sisters, my two brothers, and me.

TB: Where did you live when you first got here?

APJ: When we first moved here, we lived at Fifty-third and Dearborn, across the street and down the block from Service Link, which was a black-owned ice-cream parlor.

TB: Service Link later became the basis for Baldwin Ice Cream, didn't it?

APJ: That's right. The man who started Service Link was a man by the name of Kit Baldwin. His store was at Fifty-third and State. Most of the Negroes were living on State, Dearborn, and Federal streets in those days.

TB: Where did you go to school?

APJ: We went to Farren School for a year. Then my folks moved to Forty-fifth and Dearborn, and so I went to Coleman School. I stayed at Coleman until about the fourth grade. Then I went to Forrestville School and stayed there through the seventh grade.

TB: Didn't Forrestville go to the eighth grade?

APJ: No, it only went up to the seventh grade.

TB: Why was that? Was it because Forrestville was so crowded?

APJ: No, it was because they had a junior high school system in Chicago back then, and so I left Forrestville and went over to Phillips Junior High School.

TB: Were your classes in the same building as the senior high school students?

APJ: No, the senior high was in the permanent building. Junior high was out in the portables, which were cottages with coal-burning stoves.

TB: Was it crowded?

APJ: Of course it was crowded! Negroes could only go to one high school in those days, and that was Phillips. Negroes could not go to Tilden, Englewood, or Hyde Park—so all Negroes went to Phillips High School at Thirty-ninth and Prairie. Phillips was named after an abolitionist, and when they built the new school for Negroes, they named it New Phillips, until a little later on they changed that name to DuSable.

TB: How long were you a student at the old Phillips?

APJ: I never even got to finish my first year because the school burned down! So I never really finished grammar school. I only got one diploma, and that was from high school.

TB: What did they do with you and the other students after they had the fire?

APJ: When they had the fire, they moved us all out and over to New Phillips, which was still under construction. You see, our old school had gotten to be so over-crowded that they were already building this new school for us at Forty-ninth and Wabash.

TB: So you never really attended the old Phillips High School.

APJ: That's right.

TB: Where were you living at this time?

APJ: We had moved from Forty-fifth and Dearborn to Sixty-sixth and Rhodes. You see, in those days Negroes went house hunting every spring.

TB: Every spring was moving time!

APJ: Moving time, that's right!

TB: I do not care how good your present apartment was — in the spring you always went looking for another one!

APJ: That is right. Every spring we did just that!

[*Laughter.*]

TB: So now you're living at Sixty-sixth and Rhodes, which is a community that comes to be known as Woodlawn. What was it like back then?

APJ: It was a very nice neighborhood. There were Negroes, Japanese, Chinese, and Italians all living there at that time.

TB: When did your father take up his first ministry in Chicago?

APJ: While we were living at Forty-fifth and Dearborn, some other folks came up from the same part of Mississippi where he came from. They were all from Batesville or Sardis, and they knew he was here. So they persuaded him to organize a church for them.

TB: What was the church called? Where was it located?

APJ: The church was called Christian Home, and they met in an undertaker's parlor at Twenty-fifth and State Street. Now, at just about that same time, the Liberty Baptist Church, which was already very well established — the church had about five hundred members by then — that church split apart.

TB: Do you know why that happened?

APJ: The church had to split apart because one of their preachers was a crook!

TB: He was a crook?

APJ: Yes, of course he was. He stole something.

TB: What?

APJ: The congregation!

[*Laughter.*]

Because when he left he took just about everybody with him!

TB: Where did he take them?

APJ: He took them to the Methodist church on Thirtieth and Dearborn.

TB: The Allen Temple?

APJ: That's right. He took away the entire congregation except for seventeen members and several deacons. Well, those deacons went directly over to Olivet Baptist Church, where Dr. L. K. Williams was the pastor, to get some advice.

TB: Dr. Williams was also president of the National Baptist Convention at that time, wasn't he?

APJ: That's right, and he told them about this young preacher from Mississippi that was organizing a new Baptist church over on State Street. So they came over to my father's church in the funeral home, and they persuaded him to become their preacher. Well, at that time he already had a congregation of about fifty folks, and so he led his fifty folks and those deacons out of the funeral home, and they marched together around the corner, from Twenty-fifth and State to Twenty-seventh and Dearborn. When they reached the Liberty Baptist Church, there were those seventeen folks who did not go away with that other preacher standing on the steps just waiting for them to arrive! So my father conducted a joint service for them in that old church, and after that sermon he delivered, they asked him to be their preacher from then on.

TB: That sermon convinced them immediately?

APJ: Yes, because he was such a good preacher. A great preacher, and so he was able to combine those two churches right then and there. That's how Liberty got a new start with sixty-seven members in the congregation—and that is also how my father really got started. He was pastor of that church for twenty-five years, from 1925 until 1950.

TB: Now, that church was originally at Twenty-seventh and Dearborn. When did you move the church to Forty-sixth Street?

APJ: The church stayed there for another five years or so, but then most of the Negroes in the congregation started moving farther south. You know, it's a strange thing, Tim, but a lot of black folks do not know that just before this period that we're talking about Negroes were still living around Eighth and Ninth Streets in the downtown area.

TB: That's right.

APJ: As a matter of fact, a Negro by the name of Jones sold the land that he owned at Ninth and State to the Board of Education, and that is where they built the Jones Commercial High School.

TB: He sold them the land. They even named the school after him, but blacks were not allowed to attend that school.

APJ: So by this time, the late twenties, Negroes were moving much farther south. By then my family was living at Forty-third and Langley.

TB: The Regal Theater and the South Center Building were also built around this same period.

APJ: Yes, the Regal Theater opened to the public in February 1928. I remember that quite clearly because I used to pass out handbills so I could get in there on Saturday afternoons.

TB: In those days, if you wanted to see anyone at all in Chicago, all you had to do was just stand there on the corner of Forty-seventh and South Park, and they would all pass by sometime sooner or later!

[*Laughter.*]

Now, when I first knew you, you all were living in a building on the forty-third block of Michigan Avenue.

APJ: That's right. We were living right across the hall from Joe Louis.

TB: Were you there first or was he there first?

APJ: We were there first.

TB: That's what I thought.

APJ: But he bought the building!

[*Laughter.*]

TB: So Joe Louis and his wife, Marva, lived right across from you when you were growing up.

APJ: Yes, and he was the first to sign my autograph book when I graduated from DuSable. You see, Marva was a Trotter, and that whole family belonged to my father's church. My father even preached her mother's and father's funerals. That's how close they were.

TB: If my memory serves me right, after Joe Louis won the championship, they lived in the Rosenwald Building for a short while.

APJ: That's right. You know, the history of that building is very interesting. Old man Rosenwald was a great philanthropist, and so he built the Rosenwald Building as an experiment for low-income families in the year 1929. The only problem was that the Great Crash came the same year as its completion, and when that happened, there weren't very many low-income Negroes who could still afford to be living there!

[*Laughter.*]

As a matter of fact, at that time the only Negroes who could afford to live there were doctors, lawyers, preachers, postal workers, and railroad men. So that's how the Rosenwald Building became the most elite dwelling spot on the entire South Side. People like Archibald Carey and Jewel Lafontant all lived there. That was the place to be!

TB: But you all had larger living quarters back where you were living, didn't you?

APJ: Sure, we did. The apartments in the Rosenwald Building only had four rooms, and what's more, you had to walk up to the fifth floor, but it was brand new, and it had a garden on the roof! They had guards in that garden. I remember that because many a day I was removed from the Rosenwald roof just because I did not happen to live in that building!

[*Laughter.*]

TB: So now the new location of the Liberty Baptist Church was on Forty-sixth Street, right across from the Rosenwald Building.

APJ: That's right.

TB: What happened in terms of your education after you graduated from DuSable?

APJ: I went to Wilson Junior College for one year, and then I went down to Morehouse and enrolled as a sophomore. I was in my senior year there when the war broke out. So I left Morehouse and I came back to Chicago. When I got back here, I went right over to the draft board, which was located in the ward office on Forty-seventh Street, and I told the secretary of the ward that I wanted to enlist as a chaplain because I knew that if you were a chaplain you would automatically get the rank of second lieutenant when you went in. So the first thing she asks me is how old I am, and I say, "I'm twenty-one years old." Then she asks me if I have a seminary degree, and my answer, of course, is no. Well, she was an old lady, and she says to me, "Boy, this a man's army! You better go back home and get an education."

[*Laughter.*]

So I couldn't go into the army because I didn't yet have a seminary degree, and I got a full deferment as a student so that I could complete my education.

TB: Did you return to Morehouse?

APJ: No, during all the other war years, I was too busy assisting my father. So I didn't complete my education until after the war was over, and then I went to Garrett up at Northwestern.

TB: This would be in 1945?

APJ: Yes, that's right.

TB: Now, by this time your congregation has grown quite a bit, I would imagine.

APJ: Yes, what happened was that right from the beginning, just as soon as we moved to Forty-sixth Street, all the neighborhood people started coming over to Liberty on a regular basis.

TB: This was still during the Depression?

APJ: People didn't have either cars or carfare, and so those people that lived along Forty-seventh Street—from Michigan Avenue, Wabash, State, and Calumet— all of them came over to our church right away. Pretty soon we had a congregation of around seven hundred, and so the new building was already getting to be too small. The church got so crowded that folks used to actually run to church to be able to get a seat!

[*Laughter.*]

TB: Where were most of your members from?

APJ: The neighborhood.

TB: No, what I mean is, what were their backgrounds? Where did they come from originally?

APJ: Mostly Mississippi and Alabama, and every Sunday all those people used to crowd in, and some of them were even standing around against the walls just to hear my father's preaching. That's when we began to talk about moving again. So we started looking to find a larger church we could move into. Now a lot of people don't remember this, but in those days Negroes didn't build churches here in Chicago. What they did was to buy up white people's churches and synagogues.

TB: That's right. Most of the large black churches on the South Side were originally Jewish synagogues.

APJ: It's the same thing on the West Side as well.

TB: So your father was looking around on the South Side in hopes of finding a larger church or synagogue that he could purchase.

APJ: That's right, but he couldn't find any that were suitable, and so my father said, "Well, all right, then we are going to have to build a church for ourselves!" I told him I thought he was crazy, but he said, "We are going to have a five-year plan just like Stalin does in Russia, and that way I'm going to raise enough money to build my own church!" So we started a five-year building fund, and we put a big chart on the wall with a picture of a thermometer on it that indicated just how much money had been contributed. One thousand, ten thousand, twenty thousand, thirty thousand . . .

TB: So the fund was growing rapidly.

APJ: Yes, it was, but we still hadn't found a suitable piece of land on which we could build.

TB: By that time there was already very little vacant land on the South Side.

APJ: My father told me, "We have looked all around, but we can't find anything that's suitable." So I asked him, "Is it all right for me to take a look around and see what I can find?" He said, "Go ahead," and on the next day—Monday morning—I went over to Coleman Real Estate at Forty-seventh and State. They were the ones who had sold us the old church we were in on Forty-sixth, and so he knew right away who I was. "You're the preacher's son!" Well, when I went home that night, my dad asked me if I'd had any luck, and I told him they suggested the vacant lot that was on the corner of Forty-ninth and South Park. He said that the deacons of our church had already inquired about that property but had been told it was not available because an outdoor advertising company had a ninety-nine-year mortgage on it. So he advised me to forget about it and keep on looking, but then the very next morning Mr. Coleman called me and said that he could definitely get that lot for us if we could bring twenty-five hundred dollars to his office on the following day. After he said that, I was so excited that I ran all the way to my father's house. Now he was living at Sixty-second and Langley, and I was living at Sixty-second and Rhodes, and I ran all the way to his house— and when I got there, he was sitting on the porch dipping snuff!

[*Laughter.*]

I said, "Papa, we can get that lot on Forty-ninth and South Park!" I explained to him what was required, and so that night my dad called the deacons together, and a check was written for the exact amount that was required, and the next morning my father and I carried that check over to the Coleman Real Estate Company and gave it to them as was promised. This was on Wednesday, and on that very next Sunday—which also happened to be Father's Day that year—we had the title on that property.

TB: How did the congregation react to the good news?

APJ: They were shouting to God because now at last we had found the land on which to build our church!

TB: And you were the one who had found that lot for them.

APJ: Yes, but what we discovered was that in that neighborhood where we were moving most of the Negroes living around there were middle-class and had become accustomed to attending the Corpus Christi Catholic Church.

TB: They all were Catholics?

APJ: Well, they certainly weren't Baptists, and when they heard that a bunch of foot-stomping, hand-clapping Baptists were coming over, they said, "Oh my God, now the neighborhood will go to the dogs, and we can't let this happen!" So, when we started building the church, they used to break our windows, and twice they even tried to set the church on fire!

TB: Are you sure it was the Catholics that were doing this?

APJ: Yes, because on several occasions we caught the kids who were doing these things, and when we asked them why they were knocking the windows out of our church, they said, "That ain't no church. Not a real one."

TB: These were black kids?

APJ: Yes, students from the Corpus Christi School. They were knocking out our windows on the way coming and going from there. I asked them who had told them that our church wasn't a real church, and they said, "Our priest told us. That's a real church over there!"—and they pointed to Corpus Christi.

TB: Well, back at that time, as I remember it, the Catholic Church was making great efforts throughout the city to recruit black membership.

APJ: You know why? It was because the Catholic Church up to that time had been giving their full attention to the white immigrants coming here from Europe, but now that all of those immigrants and all of their children were already established in the Catholic Church, they were starting to look for a new area into which they could expand and that was when they discovered the Negro community!

TB: What you're saying is that the Catholic Church didn't bother much about Negroes until all the white immigrants got settled, and then they started recruiting in the black community.

APJ: And they didn't want any competition.

TB: Well, during that same period of time, when I was a young man working part-time in the post office, I remember that they used to be sending out a lot of literature, one of which was a little pamphlet called "Our Negro Harvest."

APJ: That's just what I'm talking about, and I must admit that in many instances their attempts at recruitment were successful, especially among the upper middle class. Robert Taylor was a Catholic. Ralph Metcalfe was a Catholic.

TB: Well, in a place like Chicago, if you were black, you couldn't break the political barrier unless you were Catholic.

APJ: That's right. Some Negroes became Catholic for political reasons. So anyway, as you can well imagine, there was a very long period of time before a good relationship was established between Corpus Christi and Liberty.

TB: But you didn't let anything like that interfere with the construction of the new church.

APJ: No, we certainly didn't. We came over here, and we dedicated this ground on July 9, 1950, but later in that same month Daddy went to the hospital in Rochester, and they discovered that he had cancer of the stomach. So he came back here and stayed with us, but he died in November, and he never saw a stone turned nor the ground broken in any way. He never even saw a picture of what the building would eventually look like.

TB: Did you hire an architect?

APJ: No, not at first. Before he died, my father had put me in as chairman of the building committee, and so I worked with the building committee, and together we designed this church.

TB: Were there any problems?

APJ: No, the older deacons respected me because I had been to college, and so I had no problems, and they decided to make me the acting pastor of the church. While I was acting as interim pastor, they went out and got the dean of the

Chicago Baptist Institute, and he preached the Sunday sermon the entire month of December, but, after that, they said to me, "Son, our mourning period of sixty days is now over, and we want you to be our pastor." So that was it! There was no one running against me. The church was not divided in any manner whatsoever.

TB: And so was construction of the new church building still going on during this time?

APJ: Well, there were a few delays involving legal problems, but during that time we were making plans, and we decided that we were going to build our church in three phases. At first we would build the basic structure, but it would be just a shell and nothing more. After we had built the shell, then we were going to put the balcony in. After we got the balcony in, then we were going to put in the downstairs and finish the job.

TB: Did your plans go the way you expected?

APJ: Things went very well. We didn't even have any doors in place, but we decided to expand by buying the property that was next door to the church.

TB: That was at one time a Sons of Wisdom shop, wasn't it?

APJ: That's right. After we bought that property and the church was nearing completion, new members started joining and giving us money and all sorts of support. We had just gotten new life!

TB: So at last the new church has been built, and this is the first brand-new church that was built from the ground up in the city of Chicago by a black congregation.

APJ: Yes, and so we came in over here on Thanksgiving Day of 1956.

TB: What was the reaction of the people in the community?

APJ: Well, at first some folks made fun of it because they had never before seen a building with so much glass. They called it the glass house. One day a lady came up to me and said, "Oh, aren't you the one that comes from that church that looks like a boat that's upside down?"

[*Laughter.*]

But I didn't mind her saying something like that. As a matter of fact, it pumped up my ego and made me feel good because she was a Methodist minister's wife!

[*Laughter.*]

APJ: Let me tell you one other thing. I must say this, and then I am through! When we started building this church, we did not have enough money to finish it, but we stuck with our three-phase plan, and this church has never had a mortgage on it of any kind!

TB: Remarkable. Absolutely remarkable!

APJ: But there's something else that you should know. You see, the construction on this church is still not entirely completed. There is supposed to be a bell tower in the courtyard outside the chapel. That bell tower will rise up for one hundred and twenty feet and have twelve bells within it, and when those bells ring, people from as far as five miles away will know that they are hearing the sound of Liberty!

August 15, 1992

LAWRENCE KENNON

———

ATTORNEY STRUGGLING FOR JUSTICE

I first met Larry Kennon in 1958, soon after his graduation from law school. At that time he was a very busy young man giving advice and counsel to the besieged and beleaguered Chicago branch of the NAACP. Back then this organization had three very active units: one on the South Side, one on the West Side, and one on the Near North Side. Larry was particularly active on the West Side, where members were working on such major issues as integration of public schools, open housing, and fairness in employment opportunities. Because the NAACP's president during that period, Willoughby Abner, who was also a labor leader, was aggressively pursuing these issues, the Chicago Democratic machine under the leadership of then Mayor Richard J. Daley used some of the community's black ministers that were obligated to him (as well as certain members of their various congregations) to infiltrate and neutralize the efforts of the NAACP in regard to the election of 1957. For reasons not publicly discussed, the national office of the NAACP decided to support that takeover and justified their decision by hinting that the more aggressive members of the defeated activist group were either Communists or supporters of the Communist Party and its ideals and tactics. Despite the fact that these accusations might have placed Larry's professional career in jeopardy, he never wavered in his principled position that freedom, justice, and equality were realizable goals for all Americans. He was always outspoken in his belief that he and we should always fight for these goals without any form of delay or compromise.

TB: I'm talking with Lawrence Kennon, whom I've known for about forty years.

LK: That's right, Tim.

TB: Tell me, Larry, where were you born?

LK: I was born right here in Chicago on the second of June in 1929.

TB: That means you'll be celebrating another birthday next week.

LK: Yes, next Monday I'll be sixty-eight years old.

TB: Tell me about your parents. Where were they born?

LK: They were both born in Mississippi. That's where my father met my mother.

TB: Did they get married before they left Mississippi?

LK: No, neither of them left Mississippi until they were fully grown, but my dad was the first to leave. He left Mississippi, I think, in about 1919, right after the war. As a matter of fact, he was run out of Mississippi like so many other black people were back then.

TB: Did he tell you what happened?

LK: He was working in a sawmill, but he was working in the front office because he was a mathematician, and he was doing the figures for them. Well, one day some white man made an error in addition or something like that, and so my father said to him, "I'm sorry, but that's wrong. Here's the answer." He said that because in mathematics you've either got it wrong or you've got it right. It isn't a matter of guesswork, but the white man said, "Nigger, are you calling me a liar?" So the boss was there, and he said, "Oh, no, I'm sure he didn't mean anything like that." He said that to protect my dad, but that other guy got really angry and stormed out of the sawmill. So the boss says to my dad, "Listen, that man is a very influential person around here, and he's very upset with you. Take my advice and get out of town before he comes back here." So that's when my dad left Mississippi.

TB: That kind of thing was not so very unusual back then.

LK: No, it certainly was not. My dad was what you would call the strong silent type. He never attacked anybody, but he never backed down from anybody either. When I was growing up, he'd always say, "You should always wear a silken glove but have an iron fist inside it!" So we learned that early on, and as you may know from my own approach to life, that's also what I always try to do.

TB: And where did he live in Chicago?

LK: Before he married my mother, my father lived around Twenty-ninth and Cottage Grove. Then, after their marriage, they moved to another place somewhere around Forty-second Street.

TB: They were still living on the South Side.

LK: Yes, and then they moved to 4401 South Vincennes, right across the street from Ebenezer Baptist Church, and that's where they were living when I was born. We stayed there until around 1933, and then we moved to the West Side, over near Polk and Damen.

B: Do you remember anything about those early years?

LK: Well, that was just after the Depression, and times were bad. We were living in a nine-flat tenement, and we stayed there until 1948. That was the year that my dad bought a house over in Lawndale, where we were living, at 3202 West Douglas Boulevard.

TB: Now, what kind of work did your dad do?

LK: My dad was in steel. In fact, he ended up being the superintendent of a steel warehouse.

TB: Is that right?

LK: Yes, he was the first black superintendent of a place like that in the entire country.

TB: What kind of education did he have?

LK: He had been a student down in Mississippi at Alcorn State University.

TB: Alcorn is way out in the country. It's a nice little country school now, but originally it was a school for the children of the relationships between a black woman and a white guy, I think.

LK: Is that right? My dad never mentioned that to me.

TB: Where did your mother get her education?

LK: She graduated from high school in Mississippi, and then she came up North and went to Indiana, but it wasn't very long before my father brought her from Indiana to Chicago, and they got married.

TB: When was that?

LK: That was, I believe, in 1924.

TB: So, after a while your family moves to the West Side, and that's where you spend most of your early years.

LK: That's right. As you may remember, the black South Siders and the black West Siders didn't get along too well in those days. In fact, there was a great deal of fighting between the two groups, and so blacks on the West Side would never go to the South Side.

TB: Or South Siders go over to the West Side.

LK: Well, for high school I went to Crane Tech, and I used to go over to the YMCA over on Wabash Avenue.

TB: Why there?

LK: The Y on Wabash was the only one that I could go to. Back then, all of the YMCAs were connected with the various high schools. So there was a Phillips Y and a DuSable Y and a Dunbar Y, but the Wabash Y was different in that they had kids there from all the different schools mixed in together. That meant that when I went there I began meeting young people from all the different schools on the South Side as well as the West, and pretty soon I began to run with the DuSable-ites and the Phillips-ites and all the rest of them. The result was that it wasn't long before all of the South Siders began to think that I was a South Sider, but, of course, back home on the West Side they always knew that I was still one of them! [*Laughter.*]

So that way I developed a broad scope of acquaintances. Much more than any of the other young people that I knew on either side of town, and that was probably the best thing that ever could have happened to me at that time because it really gave me the opportunity to know so many different kinds of people. Also at that Y in those days very often when some of the big stars in entertainment and athletics would come to town, since they couldn't rent rooms in the downtown hotels, they would have to stay there at the Y, and so that's when you'd get a chance to meet them.

TB: It was a meeting place.

LK: It was *the* meeting place! All those guys who were out on the road and just passing through, they'd stay there.

TB: That means a lot of the Pullman porters must have stayed there when they were in town.

LK: That's right, and you could sit around and hear all the great stories that they would tell.

TB: So you learned a lot from your experiences at that Wabash Y, and as a result, you sort of transcended the neighborhood in which you were living.

LK: Yes, like I said, I was living at Damen and Polk, which was right on the border of a white community. The south side of the street was black and the north side was white, but when we first moved there in 1934 or 1935, it was still white on our side of the street as well. So we lived in an integrated building.

TB: In those days the lines of demarcation were not as yet quite so tightly drawn.

LK: That's right. We lived in the same building with Italian families, and some days we kids would have our fights, but the next day we'd all be playing baseball together! [*Laughter.*]

Say what you will, but the thing about Italians, as I'm sure you know, is that when the blacks started to move in they didn't run away in the way that most of the other nationalities tended to do.

TB: So you were able to grow up in a somewhat integrated social setting.

LK: Yes, but primarily I ran with the young black guys from the Taylor Street crowd.

One of the main reasons for that was because there was a sort of antagonism that had developed between us and the blacks that lived across Roosevelt Road. So sometimes all the black guys from Taylor Street would go over to Union Park to have our little battles with them.

TB: What about the Italians? Were they any part of this?

LK: No, because they had gangs of their own, and the Italian Mafia was also very active in that neighborhood. I don't know if you remember or not, but there was a guy called the Mad Dog Killer whose real name was Morelli.

TB: Yes, I remember that name.

LK: Well, the different generations of the Morelli family lived above and below us in our building. We went to school together with their kids. One of them—a guy named Fred Morelli—was in my class. But the one who was convicted as the Mad Dog Killer was his older brother. I guess he must have still been a teenager, but it was rare back then for a teenager to have a gun. This was near the end of the Prohibition era, and the Italians were considered to be the really bad guys on the national scene at that time. So it was, of course, a matter of pride for us that we knew somebody who was a real gangster—and his family as well!

[*Laughter.*]

In addition to that, while I was growing up, in those days all the young guys used to hang out every night on the corner under a streetlight. Each corner had a group of guys who would hang out together and tell their stories as well as share the latest rumors and gossip. The corner of Damen and Polk Street was where the Polk Street crowd hung out, and there was another light over on Taylor Street, which was where the Taylor Street guys hung out. Well, when I was just getting into high school, I would be hanging out every night with those Polk Street guys, but pretty soon that got kind of boring for me. So I would leave and go down and hang out on the corner of Taylor Street with those other guys.

TB: They accepted you into their group?

LK: Well, these weren't gangs in anything like the sense of what we have today. These were just crowds of guys hanging out together on the street corner. Of course some of those guys didn't exactly appreciate you coming from another community into theirs, but somehow I was able to hang out with them because I would give them the gossip from Polk Street, and those Taylor Street guys really liked to hear that sort of thing. Then I would take the gossip that those guys told me, and I'd bring it back to Polk Street, along with all the dirty jokes and stuff that I had learned by being on Taylor Street. So I was kind of a liaison between those two groups. Later on, when I got to be a little bit older and went over to the South Side to meet some of my new friends that I'd met at the Y, the same sort of thing happened once again.

TB: Well, I would imagine that by becoming a sort of liaison between all these separate groups you most likely also became somewhat marginalized from each of them. Each of those groups could claim your loyalty, but they could not own it exclusively.

LK: That's exactly right, and, as a matter of fact, I have continued to do that same sort of thing throughout the rest of my life.

TB: So somehow quite early on you learned how to negotiate these differences and become trusted and accepted by all those separate groups.

LK: Listen, when I first went down to the South Side, I was just a very poor guy out of the West Side, and I thought all my new friends were other kids just like me, but then I went to some of their homes, and I saw that some of them lived in mansions, the kind of places that I'd only seen in the movies. This was 1946 or '47, and I remember sometimes we would go over to the South Side Community Arts Center and just take a peek in there because that was a kind of a never-never land, and those were the kind of people that you just shouldn't go in and bother. Back then I was only about seventeen years old, and so I felt that I wasn't supposed to go in there, but now, of course, as you know, I'm the vice president of the South Side Community Arts Center.

TB: When I was a kid growing up, the South Side Community Arts Center was a place of great intellectual stimulation. I could go there, and at any point of time I might see a Richard Wright or other people of that caliber and hear a radical and informative conversation. It was a place of haven, and younger people like me would just go there and listen to what was being said. You know, I knew *something* was wrong with the world, but I couldn't quite articulate what it was. So the people there and what they were saying helped me to understand what was wrong with society—why people didn't get along, why black folks were being kept down at the bottom.

LK: That was also true of those conversations that I listened to at the Wabash, and that reminds me of something else that was very important for me. One summer I had a job at a place called the Blackstone Manufacturing Company, which was at about 4800 West on Harrison Street. That was as far west as we ever went, and I had to take a streetcar to go out there. Anyway, there was a man out there in this Blackstone Manufacturing Company named Al who was a union organizer. Al was heavyset—potbellied actually—and he had this big, booming voice. He was a great orator, and when we would go down to change into our work clothes, he would talk to us about the same kinds of things you were just talking about—the injustices of society and all of that—and I was just overwhelmed. Now, my father is my greatest hero in the world, but Al was the person who initiated in me my desire to battle and fight the injustices of this society that we live in. So I told

Al many years later—in the presence of people we both knew—that he was the person who had gotten me started in the civil rights movement. He was the one who had inspired me into taking a stand and speaking out.

TB: In terms of your own experience, when did you first become aware of the fact that racial discrimination lies at the root of many of this society's most serious problems?

LK: Well, when I was thirteen years old, I was a patrol boy at Gladstone. Now, this was an integrated school. We only had probably 20 percent or less of blacks in that school, but my best friend was the captain of the patrol boys and I was the lieutenant. Every year there was an annual baseball outing for all the patrol boys from the entire city. Well, this is in 1943, which is my last year in grammar school, and there must have been maybe about twenty patrol boys in our group. So we went to the game, and after it was over, Mr. Fine, who was the gym teacher and was also in charge of the patrol boys, had a station wagon, and he could only take back home one-half of the group at a time. So he took my best friend and some of the other guys in the first group, and he told the rest of us he was going to come back and get us in the Armour Square Park in about forty minutes or so. We were told to go down through the park to Thirty-second Street and meet him at the foot of the park.

TB: That park was in Bridgeport, wasn't it?

LK: It certainly was. It was right behind the old White Sox Park, where we had been watching the game. There were about seven or eight white guys and myself and two or three black guys in our group, but I was the lieutenant, and so I was walking behind the rest of the group. Well, we passed by a group of seventeen or eighteen white teenagers that were playing baseball, and one of those guys called out at us, "Well, look at the niggers!" and they all started running after us. Because of my being behind the rest of them, they cut me off from the others, and they grabbed me, and at least half of the team started beating me.

TB: Did anybody come and try to help you?

LK: No, but there were so many of them beating and kicking me that I could scoot out under the legs of some of them, and I ran out and got away.

TB: How did the other guys in your group react when they learned what had happened to you?

LK: Well, we were a very closely knit group, that twelve of us, and the white boys in our group were just as upset about my being beaten as the black ones were, and so they decided that they were going to go back in the park and try to do something about it, but there was a policeman there who had been watching the whole thing. So they found some rocks and were beginning to walk back and find those guys when this policeman walks over to them and says, "What are you boys planning to do with those rocks?" So they tell him, "Well, those guys in there, they've just beat up our friend!" So the policeman says, "Don't any of you dare go in there because if you do, you're going to be arrested." "But those guys beat him up, and they can't get away with anything like that!" So he says, "Don't worry about them. They were just playing." That was the attitude of this big, white, Irish cop just standing there and watching me getting beaten and not doing anything about it.

TB: This is in 1943.

LK: Yes, 1943.

TB: Well, that tradition has remained intact!

LK: Yes, that tradition has remained. You know, I have been collecting news items documenting police brutality in Bridgeport over the years, and I think that it is fair to say that if you look at the overview of that community, it's definitely a terrorist community in terms of the consistent terrorism that is directed against black people trying to go through there. As a matter of fact, it's the same kind of situation that the United Nations attempts to prevent from occurring in other parts of the world.

TB: I'm an old man at this point, but only a few years ago I went over to Bridgeport to go to this shop and buy something. I've forgotten by now what it was, but I got in my car and went over there and got my stuff and came out of the store, and as I was getting ready to get in my car, two white guys come up to me and say, "Hey, nigger, what are you doing over here?" And this is, maybe, two years ago, and I'm an old man, you know, and I'm just going to the store. So that racist attitude is still embedded in that community, and until something happens to change the whole culture of that community that kind of attitude is going to continue to be there with them for a long, long time.

LK: There are a lot of problems that still have to be solved.

TB: So just how long have you been practicing law?

LK: Well, I graduated from law school in 1953.

TB: Which school did you graduate from?

LK: From DePaul. At that time I was twenty-three years old, and so, of course, the army was right there waiting for me just as soon as I graduated. I was blessed by the fact that I had been allowed to complete my education because at that time most blacks were drafted before they finished school so that the army could fill its quotas.

TB: Are you saying that the army would take the blacks before they finished school, but they would let the whites finish their education?

LK: Which is the reason why you see such a disproportionate number in that same age group of whites who graduated as opposed to blacks who did not.

TB: So where was your service?

LK: I stayed on stateside. From our part of Chicago, most of us went to Fort Leonard Wood for basic training, and from there I went to Fort Sill in Oklahoma, and a rather neat thing happened there. I had an opportunity to go to Officers Training School, but, as you know, if you were drafted it was for two years, but then if you went in for being trained as an officer it was for three years. So you see, it was a volunteer type of situation. You had to make a choice, and at that time I was trying to get out of the army just as quickly as possible! [*Laughter.*]

Listen, I'm not a military person. I'm not a violent person. I don't like to shoot rifles or guns or anything like that. But I was lucky because there were a number of other enlisted lawyers who were there at the same time who also felt exactly the same way. So what we did was to set up an organization of noncom legal officers.

TB: These other enlisted lawyers, were they also black?

LK: No, the other four were white. You see, there were five batteries, and each one of them had one of our lawyers in it. So we five guys would meet together, and we'd figure out ways to handle all of the legal problems for the officers in that entire battalion. We handled the court-martials. If there were AWOLs, we'd go out with the colonel's people and pick up the AWOLs, and we'd have a legal presence there. Then there were also all sorts of personal things that we would have to do for those officers.

TB: Such as?

LK: Well, such as if they wanted to buy a house or get a divorce. So they'd come to us for information concerning personal things like that, and that way we actually had kind of an unusual existence, considering the fact that we were still in the army.

TB: What you're saying is that you were also getting a lot of practical experience that would be useful later on in your career.

LK: Yes, but I had other sorts of experiences as well. You see, in my own company there was a racist captain named Captain Grimes from Macon, Georgia, and he was refusing to promote any blacks. What I'm saying is that I had been there nearly eighteen months, and during that entire time, no blacks had ever been promoted! Now, in our battalion we had not only a lawyer like myself but also graduates of college who were black, and what was happening was that graduates of high schools who were white were being given promotions, but the blacks were not.

TB: Did any of the whites that were promoted have any kind of college education?

LK: There were no white college graduates. They had one person who had graduated from a junior college and a few who had graduated from high school, but most of the others were high school dropouts—and these were the people that the captain was promoting over the well-qualified blacks. So I went to the inspector general's office and protested, saying that this was a form of racism. Well, under the military code of justice, if you bring an action against an officer and can't sustain it, it's the same as committing slander.

TB: And then you could be court-martialed for slandering an officer.

LK: That's right! So here I was an E-2 private, not even a private first class—I did reach private first class later on—but now I was bringing this action against the captain. Well, I was able to document exactly who had been promoted, what their backgrounds were, and everything that they had or had not done over the entire period of their enlistment. I was able to do this because, as a noncom legal officer, I was working in headquarters, and the white guys in the headquarters were friends of mine. More than half of them were from the North. So we documented all the promotions, and, of course, during that entire period, there were no blacks! There was one black sergeant, but he had come into the unit as a sergeant. So I brought this to the attention of the inspector general, and, as a result, they sent a black captain out of Ohio to Fort Sill to investigate to see if there was any racism in the system of promotions. Well, one fine day this black captain brought me in and talked to me about what a great guy I was. He had checked me out and said how I ought to be in Officers Training School, and so I said, "No, I don't want that. I just want to get out," and so forth. Then he says OK and he leaves. Well, the months go by, and I never hear anything about what kind of report that guy had written. So I went back to the inspector general and said, "I didn't get any report yet, and I was wondering about the present status of the investigation." His reply was, "Oh, it's already been investigated. It's all over." So I asked him, "What do you mean?"—and he said, "This captain,"—whatever the black captain's name was—"he talked to you, and he said you said that everything was fine." So I said, "That's not true, sir. If he said that, then he is lying!" "Are you saying that the captain is lying?" "Well, with all due respect, sir, yes, the captain's lying." So they sent someone else back out there again, and then after about another month or two—I only had sixty days to go by then—they came back and told me that according to the new report they had determined that all of my allegations were totally unfounded. So I said, "Well, tell me why." They said that the basis for their decision was that Captain Grimes and the black captain who had been sent there previously to investigate me both lived in the same area and that their children often played with each other. They considered that to be solid proof that Captain Grimes could not be a racist and that, therefore, all of my evidence to the contrary was inadmissible. So I said OK and they sent me back to my office, and pretty soon Captain Grimes himself walks in and says,

"All right, you sit right there where you are because I was found not guilty, and now we're going to court-martial you for slandering an officer. So I am ordering you to start writing up your own court-martial papers!" You see, he knew that my job had been to write up all the court-martials and see that they were run properly. So I said, "Well, all right, I'll follow orders, but you know just as well as I do that the facts I have gathered don't lie. The records show that you have never promoted anyone who is black, and so I am also going to write a letter to Adam Clayton Powell, and he will see to it that all the newspapers across the country get into this and help us to straighten these things out in a fair and proper manner." You see, my family had worked with the NAACP, and I knew about Adam Clayton Powell. So Captain Grimes says, "Stay right where you are and sit back down. That's an order!" And then, after about three hours of my sitting there at my desk, he comes back in and says, "OK, we're going to do something different from what I said before. We're going to transfer you out of this company." So I was able to avoid the court-martial by using the name of Adam Clayton Powell, and because of my being a lawyer, this captain thought that I actually *did* know Adam Clayton Powell.

[*Laughter.*]

What had been happening while this investigation was going on was that I had established a precedent, and so all the guys in the other units stationed there at Fort Sill would come over to me, and I would tell them how to bring up charges concerning the various forms of racial discrimination they were experiencing. For example, at that time, after someone graduated from the ROTC in college, all of them—black and white—had to go down to Fort Sill and get their training in artillery in order to get their field commission and become active second lieutenants. Well, the system down there was so racist that the black soldiers in this program were also having problems with getting their certification, and so they came to me and asked for my help. Now, of course, someone with my rank was not allowed to fraternize with lieutenants, and so I would have to go into town where we could meet secretly so that I could give them lessons on what to do, and, as a result, pretty soon they began bringing charges of their own!

[*Laughter.*]

So what happened was that we turned the whole post around, and on my last day at Fort Sill the inspector general called me into his office and said to me, "Kennon, you are a troublemaker. You are a rabble-rouser. Since you brought up your charges, we have had more complaints about racism than we have *ever* had before on this post, and we know exactly what you've been doing because we have been following you the entire time!" He goes on to tell me exactly where I'd been meeting in town with those lieutenants, and then he says, "You have been encouraging them to bring these actions against us, and you are the person that should be in jail because *you* are the person causing all this trouble — not these people. It's your kind that has set your race back twenty years!"

TB: When I was in the service, during basic training, all of my NCOs happened to be black, but that didn't seem to make much difference because they were intent on carrying out the orders of the white, racist officers who were their superiors. What's more, most of them were Southern rural guys, and so they had a personal thing against those of us who came from the North, because they thought that we thought that we were better than them. So I had to teach these black guys from rural Mississippi and Arkansas that I could take my sergeant's stripes off and whip their asses!

[*Laughter.*]

It finally got to the point that one of those guys challenged me, and so I had to say, "You don't know who you're fucking with," and I took my shirt off and licked his ass, but then, after it was over, I said, "Look, I ain't mad at you." So from that point on those guys accepted me and showed me respect, and later on whenever one of those guys would come to Chicago, they'd always look me up. So I handled that problem in the necessary manner, but it also meant that when I was overseas the word *troublemaker* was written on my record, and in every unit I'd go to the CO would always call me in and say, "Sergeant, we understand that you're a troublemaker, and we hope you won't make any trouble here." So I'd always say, "No, sir, I'm not going to make any trouble, sir," but then sometime about two weeks later or so, something would happen, and I'd be in trouble again!

[*Laughter.*]

Now, you come out of the army and immediately get involved in the civil rights movement.

LK: That's correct. When I went into the state's attorney's office in 1957, I joined the NAACP, and then I started to become actively involved with the Coordinating Council of Community Organizations.

TB: By that time there were already a number of litigations going on in the courts over discrimination in the schools. The NAACP was in the forefront of that struggle, but before very long, if I remember correctly, you were even more in the forefront in terms of aggressiveness than they were.

LK: There were three units of the NAACP at that time: the South Side, the West Side, and the North Side — and some were more aggressive than others.

TB: That's true. So sometimes we'd have to meet together in order to work out those problems and differences of opinion.

LK: Right.

TB: Now, do you remember the time when we were denounced?

LK: Yes, that was in 1958. How could I forget?

[*Laughter.*]

Were you also at that meeting in 1957 when Dawson brought out his warriors and came into the meeting to dethrone Willoughby Abner?

TB: Yes, Ted Jones had been given the assignment to overcome Willoughby Abner, and so Ted Jones gave a statement to the newspapers that one of the main reasons that he wanted to get to be elected the president of the local branch of the NAACP was that he wanted to oust the Communist-inspired people that were currently running it.

LK: Yes, and, of course, he was very, very careful not to really call us Communists. He only claimed that the West Side members were Communist-influenced and that the North Side members were also Communist-influenced.

TB: That was at a time when anyone who would stand up for black people would always be called a Communist or a Communist sympathizer.

LK: But to be called a Communist by someone like that! Let me tell you, I had never been so angry before in my entire life.

TB: And don't forget that the Hyde Park unit of the NAACP on the South Side was also supposed to be Communist-inspired. Please don't leave us out!

[*Laughter.*]

LK: That's right. I almost forgot!

[*Laughter.*]

TB: And that is the same sort of tactic that was used a little later on to break up the Negro American Labor Council. As you know, Mr. A. Philip Randolph was the national president, and in 1960, while I was the local president of that same organization, they tried to pin that same kind of label on us as well.

LK: Sometimes the labels change, but the tactics don't.

TB: So, now you've gotten actively involved in the civil rights movement, and although you are inside the mainstream of politics, in some ways you are also outside that mainstream and right on the cutting edge.

LK: Yes, by the beginning of 1958 I had become the head of the West Side NAACP Youth Council. So in addition to my legal actions, I was working with a man named William Henry—no relation to the politician—who was a *magnificent* human being, and I could never give him too many accolades. He gave his life for those young people who were in that group. He and I together had a series of training sessions for those young people. I should mention that my sister was also working with us, and we would give those young people a background in black history as well as a notion of what society was really all about. Now, at this same time the youth council that was associated with the South Side branch was more or less dormant. It had just about died out, and so we organized a series of nonviolent protests on the South Side with some of the young people from our West Side branch to demonstrate our sympathy with what was happening at the sit-ins in the South. You probably remember that at that time there was a five-and-dime store on Forty-third Street, and at that time it was the only local five-and-dime store in the entire black community—so we went out there and picketed that five-and-dime store on Forty-third and Prairie because of the racism that still existed in the operation of that chain of stores in their operations in the South.

TB: And this is also about the same time that you got involved in the demonstrations at Rainbow Beach.

LK: Well, as you know, prior to this period of time, Rainbow Beach was a beach in Chicago which was unknown to most of us black people because we were still having problems with being allowed to use the facilities at the Sixty-third Street Beach. Rainbow Beach is at Seventy-fifth Street, and so we didn't know much of anything about it until one day a woman came to the NAACP office and told the executive director that she had seen a black family being severely beaten by young white people just for being at the beach, and she thought we should do something about it. So we decided to take our West Side group over to Rainbow Beach and determine exactly what was going on. Now, at this time I was an assistant state's attorney under Benjamin Adamowski, who was the state's attorney. So before going down to Rainbow Beach, I went to Ben and told him what my position was with the NAACP and the youth council and about how I was going to take this group and attempt to deal with this problem of racism at Rainbow Beach. I said, "I'm not really asking your permission for my participating in a controversial situation where I may be arrested, but I know that I have a duty to let you know what I'm doing." Well, I thought I was going to have some opposition, but he says, "You know, Kennon, I'm a fighter, and you seem to be a fighter as well. I appreciate a fighter, and I just wish you all God's speed as long as you're fighting for your people. I believe in that, but just don't do anything to denigrate this office." So I always have respected Ben Adamowski because of that conversation, and so we went on out to Rainbow Beach. I think you were out there that Thursday, weren't you?

TB: Yes, I was.

LK: Then you remember that when we got there it was already crowded with white people, and we had to have a cordon of police to take us in. Then that crowd swelled up and attacked us.

TB: Larry, do you remember that it was at that very point, when they were most needed, that the police turned their backs on the mob and, therefore, let that angry mob have direct access to us?

LK: That's right. That's just what happened.

TB: As I remember it, all of those police were white.

LK: Yes, all of them were white. Before taking our group to Rainbow Beach, we had a meeting with the district captain and asked him if we could have an integrated police force on the scene, but the captain said, "Well, since this a racist sort of situation, we don't want to have any black policemen there because the crowd would isolate them and start small individual fights with them, and so we wouldn't be able to take care of the crowd in any coordinated kind of manner." So they had all whites, and when we got there, the crowd was hissing at us and calling us all sorts of ugly names. They had taken and turned over one of those very large metal garbage cans and were beating on it—boom, boom, boom, boom—and telling us to go back to Africa where we belonged! While all this was going on, one of the police officers walked up to me and said, "Aren't you Kennon from the state's attorney's office?" I said, "Yes, I am." Well, I was there in just a bathing suit, but I was glad this guy recognized me because he went back, and word got around among the other policemen that someone from the state's attorney's office was there watching them.

TB: They thought you were there officially.

LK: Yes, and it was a good thing that they did. Just after that it was necessary for me to escort some of the young black girls from our group up to the public washroom, and as I was standing outside waiting for them, some of the policemen came over and said that they had come there to protect us from the crowd.

TB: That's only because now they knew who you were.

LK: Exactly. But then one of them says to me, "Maybe you'd better leave right now because this situation is getting too tense for us to handle," and I replied, "No, I'm not leaving those girls here. It's your job to make sure all of us are safe!" So when those girls came out, we walked on back to join our group, and, believe me, *those* policemen did not turn their backs on us.

TB: But all the rest of them—when that crowd was calling us names and throwing rocks, and people were being injured—those cops didn't do a damn thing! So I called Police Superintendent O. W. Wilson and told him what had happened— about the physical attacks and all of that and how the police force there was not properly integrated—and so he promised, "The next time you go back there they will be."

LK: Yes, but also before I left the park, I spoke to the commander in charge as well and demanded that an integrated force be present when we returned, and so when we went back out there the next Sunday, there were black cops standing there wearing their uniforms and with guns in their holsters, and, as a result, it was quite a different kind of scene.

TB: It was quiet for one thing.

LK: Well, occasionally some white guy would say something confrontational, but when that sort of thing happened, one of those black cops would just walk over and stare at him, and that guy would shut up!

[*Laughter.*]

TB: It was like the difference between night and day to have those black cops out there.

LK: Yes, and the only violence was when we started to leave. That's when they all ran toward us and threw things at us. So, of course, we had to go back there again, and eventually it took us almost three years to overcome that situation.

TB: And so the police also had to be out there with you every single one of those Saturdays for those three years.

LK: Yes, and during those years I went to the beach more times than I had ever been before or have been since!

[*Laughter.*]

Then in 1963 I went to the March on Washington, and after that, I went down to Mississippi, where they had the Freedom Democratic Party and where SNCC was helping them to register black voters. I told those courageous people that I wanted to be able to help protect those who were being arrested, and the first thing they told me was, "Whatever you do, don't tell anything to the FBI. They are our enemies. Just stay away from them!" Well, although I knew that the FBI wasn't exactly what the newspapers said they were, I really had no idea that they could be as bad as they were.

TB: How long did you stay down there?

LK: I came back in 1965 because there was a riot over on the West Side that had been started when some white firemen had backed over a little black girl. So I told Fannie Lou Hamer and all those people that I was working with down there that something serious was happening back home and that there were some urgent things I had to do. So that's when I left Mississippi and came back to Chicago in order to defend the people on the West Side who were being arrested.

TB: That serves as an excellent indication of how closely matters in the South were connected to the things that were also going on in the North.

LK: Yes, people need to remember that our struggle was connected all across the country.

TB: Now, in terms of your legal career, let's talk about some of the important cases in which you have been professionally involved.

LK: Well, first of all, let me mention that my entire professional life has been dedicated to addressing directly the unresolved racial problems of this country. So in that regard, I suppose the biggest case that we handled—at least the one that got the most national attention—was the Attica trial, in which there were seventeen black convicts who were accused of killing three white guards during a riot that had occurred down there. The trial went on for close to two years, but eventually we won the case.

TB: Yes, I remember that trial very well because I attended some of those sessions. What do you believe was the major factor in your winning that case?

LK: Well, I think the prosecution would have won the case if they had charged only three people with the killings, but they wanted to clean up the gang structure that existed in that prison, and so they charged all those others as well. By over-charging—as they usually do with black people—they hurt the case they were trying to present, and so we began to show the inconsistencies of their case. You see, the people they were using as witnesses for the prosecution were also convicts, and so we were able to prove that they were giving these people all kinds of rewards for testifying against the others.

TB: So your strategy was to attack the integrity of the testimony of the witnesses.

LK: Yes, but we were also attacking the integrity of the prison system and by inference the entire criminal justice system as well. In addition to the lying and perjury, there was manufactured evidence. As a result, in many ways our strategy was quite similar to that which Johnnie Cochran used in the O. J. Simpson case. We showed that the authorities in their overzealousness to get a conviction had either exaggerated or manufactured evidence, which, of course, is still not an uncommon occurrence in our present system of justice.

TB: Especially when it is black people who are on trial.

LK: Yes, in my experience that is where that sort of thing most frequently occurs.

TB: And so, with these seventeen black men who were on trial, how many were acquitted?

LK: They were all acquitted!

TB: Were they set free?

LK: No, you see, all of these were people who were in that prison on other terms anyway. That's where they were when there was a riot and those guards were killed. So they still were spending the remaining portions of their sentences at Attica, but they had nothing to do with the murders of those guards, and that's what we were able to prove.

TB: During that time—and previously and subsequently as well—you worked on a whole lot of civil rights cases.

LK: There was a group of lawyers—myself, Anna Langford, Leo Holt, Jean Williams—who volunteered to be of full-time service to the civil rights movement. We were always involved in something almost every single day!

TB: Jean Williams? She's Claude Holman's niece, isn't she?

LK: Yes. Later on she became a judge in Phoenix, Arizona. As a matter of fact, as I'm sure you must remember, her Uncle Claude had been an Uncle Tom alderman for the Daley machine.

TB: Yes, he was one of what we used to call the Silent Six, but what most people didn't know was that actually he was quite a brilliant guy.

LK: Well, no one ever said that he was dumb. That wasn't the problem. To put it bluntly, it was not a matter of his intelligence but of the fact that he sucked up to Mayor Daley!

[*Laughter.*]

He was Mayor Daley's boy all right, but he had originally started out as a fighter for civil rights.

TB: He did?

LK: He actually did! He started out as a strong advocate for civil rights, but then he got elected, and the mayor, I guess, must have rubbed him on the head or something because after that he changed completely!

[*Laughter.*]

But his niece, Jean, made up for that. She was a very, very radical—at least that's what they called us in those days—fighter for the cause. I should mention that Connie Toole also worked with us, because she was a very hard, vibrant fighter whom I hold in the highest regard.

TB: Yes, well, during the civil rights period of the sixties, we all knew that if you got arrested in the daytime, you were going to get released by the time the night was over, and the reason that would happen is because that team of people you just mentioned would always be down at the court demanding some kind of immediate action on behalf of those who had been arrested.

LK: Let me go back and explicate the context in which these situations occurred. As you know, this was a nonviolent movement for social justice, and so there was no question that we were not going to be attacking the police, but, even so, the police were attacking us just as though we were violent people, and so there were mass arrests. In fact, this was the first time in the history of our nation in which there was a continuous series of mass arrests like these, and the system didn't seem to know how to handle the problem that it had created. So what we did was to go through the chief justice—a big, tall, white fellow with white hair—and we demanded that they open the courts in the evenings so that the people who had been arrested during the day would not have to stay in prison overnight. As a result, at seven or eight o'clock in the evening they would reopen the courts, and the people who had been arrested during the day would be able to be free by that same night. Sometimes we would have to represent up to two hundred or more people each evening in those special night courts!

TB: I remember that very well.

LK: And so those lawyers who were handling these situations, we would start out at seven or eight o'clock at night, and we'd be there in the court till one or two in the morning, and after that was all over, then we'd have to go back and work extra hard the next day with our paying clients!

[*Laughter.*]

So all of us were working both day and night during that entire period. Most people didn't realize it, but we had to have regular clients that were paying us as well as all those pro bono cases that we handled every night. We were young back then, and this was a cause that we all believed in, and, of course, the cause was of such supreme importance that you did things that you would never have done for anything else in your normal existence. Later on, when I've had some clients who've told me that they wanted me to come over late at night and do some work for them, I'll always say, "Listen, you can't pay me enough to make me come out that late!" Yet during that period we're talking about, for free I'd be out there late at night every night working to free people who were arrested during all those nonviolent demonstrations.

TB: Yes, yes, it certainly was a remarkable period. What was the impact of all these events on the people living on the West Side?

LK: Well, percentage-wise what was happening was that we had developed an even larger progressive group on the West Side than you had on the South Side.

TB: What do you think are the reasons for that?

LK: On the South Side, of course, you had some people who were progressive and deeply committed to the movement, but the Dawson and Holman factions were so strongly attached to the Daley machine that most people said, "Don't fight the system over here." On the West Side things were quite different, and people were not as strongly connected to Dawson and what he represented. Also, on the South Side they didn't have the same racial situation that the majority of West Siders were in. On the South Side they were surrounded by mostly black people, and there was a lot of internal fighting in terms of trying to get a piece of the patronage that Mayor Daley had to offer, but on the West Side we were out there where the white folks were, and, therefore, every day we could see the injustices for ourselves. In fact, one of the main reasons I wanted to become a lawyer in the first place was that I wanted to help black folks obtain equal protection under the law, and I wanted to do that because I could see for myself what was happening.

TB: And that has always been a constant effort throughout your life, but now—during this period we're talking about—the political scene is beginning to change a little bit because Mayor Richard J. Daley starts to recognize that he can no longer depend on the black vote as solidly as had once been the case. There's a growing flexibility in the black community that becomes obvious when Ralph Metcalfe breaks away from the machine and runs for Congress without Daley's support and wins the election!

LK: And don't forget that in 1963, when Daley speaks to the NAACP convention in Grant Park and says that there are no slums in Chicago, he gets booed off the stage!

TB: That's right. They booed him right off the platform because he was saying there was no racism in Chicago, and everybody knew that was a lie.

LK: And something like that had never happened before.

TB: No, it hadn't, and that response from the crowd wasn't itself racist in any sense because those were the very same people who had been cheering for Paul Douglas when he spoke to them.

LK: Most people today don't realize how important that was because up to that point Mayor Daley was King Daley to most of the black people in the city, and people such as Dawson were still saying, "What's good for the machine is good for black folks as well," and people continued to believe him.

TB: You know, I ran for alderman that same year against Holman. People thought I might lose my life!

LK: You might have.

TB: Well, I didn't, but I lost the election, and after that Holman sent me a telegram saying, "You got one-third of the vote, and I got two-thirds—so who's the best man?" After that, if he saw me coming down the street, he would always cross the street to avoid me.

LK: That's when the mayor began making openly racist public statements in order to strengthen his power base among the new white ethnic groups that were arriving in the city, and then, of course, there was that incident in which Hanrahan and his forces killed Fred Hampton in a shoot-out on Monroe Avenue on the West Side.

TB: That's when a lot of the blacks on the West Side and elsewhere went over and cast their votes on the Republican side of the ballot. So now we're beginning to show a little more political independence, but after Daley's death, we band together again to support Jane Byrne as an independent candidate for mayor.

LK: Yes, Jane Byrne would never have been elected mayor in 1979 without the black vote.

TB: Not that we loved Jane Byrne so much.

LK: But that we loved Bilandic even less!

[*Laughter.*]

TB: So she gets elected and assumes that she has the black community in her pocket, but then—almost immediately—she is co-opted by the remnants of the old Daley Democratic machine, and so she says and does things that are an insult to those blacks that had given her their support.

LK: All of which leads to the effort to get Harold Washington to run for mayor.

TB: Do you remember the factors that led up to his selection?

LK: Yes, I do. Even before the Byrne election, I seem to remember that among these people who were looking for someone to run against the Democratic machine there was a guy named Tim Black and another strong person named Wesley South. Of course on the West Side for a time we also had Gus Savage, and all these guys and several others got together for a meeting at Wesley's house. We all knew Harold and his capabilities, and so we decided to ask him if he would be willing to run for mayor of the city of Chicago.

TB: This was back in 1977, and he refused.

LK: That's right, and so we put our support behind Jane Byrne and got her elected, but then she turned against us, and so in 1980, when she had that music festival in Grant Park, we organized a boycott, and we were able to persuade Stevie Wonder to forgo a very large fee to appear there.

TB: All of the other black musicians and some of the white that had been scheduled to perform followed Stevie's lead and also agreed not to appear there.

LK: So our efforts were successful, and that's when we began to organize a new power base, and that same group of people got back together and asked Harold once again if he would be willing to run as a candidate in the next mayoral election. We were so enthusiastic about Harold because he was probably the most articulate politician that any of us had ever heard.

TB: He could move a crowd, both individually and collectively.

LK: Plus we knew his background. He had done everything in politics. He had the knowledge and the experience. He was just the ideal person to be mayor.

TB: Yes, but once again he said he didn't want to run for that position because by now he's in the Congress and has been very instrumental in getting an extension of the Voting Rights Act.

LK: That's correct, and so he said, "I've been elected to Congress. I've got a job to do. I don't need the headache of coming back to Chicago," and he was very serious about what he was saying.

TB: At point a lot of black people still thought that we weren't ready for a black mayor, and Harold himself needed to be convinced.

LK: That's why he made those famous demands of his. We kept on insisting that he run, and so finally he says, "Well, OK, but only if we get us fifty thousand new registrations," and also, of course, if we were able to raise sufficient funds to be able to mount the proper kind of campaign. Now, the reason that he said this was because he thought he was making demands that we couldn't possibly meet, but we did! We met at the Independence Bank under the sponsorship of Al Boutte, and we raised all the necessary funds! What's more is that in an unbelievably short period of time, we were able to register 263,000 new voters. Well, when Harold learned what we had accomplished, he still insisted, "I really don't need this," but he had given us his promise, and so he consented to run. Well, that's when the campaign started. At first we didn't have much of any money, and so people were making their own signs, their own flyers, and even their own buttons in order to support Harold's campaign.

TB: That's right. If you weren't wearing a Washington button you were considered to be half-dressed! Bus drivers would say, "Where's your button?" The enthusiasm was just phenomenal!

LK: This was truly a classic, textbook example of a people's grassroots progressive movement.

TB: Even the preachers and politicians who had supported the Daley machine were beginning to be pressured by their constituents, who finally went and told them what they were supposed to do.

LK: And the enthusiasm continued to build. In the beginning people were saying, "Harold can't make it." Then they were saying, "Harold *might* make it," but now they are saying, "Harold's going to make it. He'll be our next mayor!" Then, when Harold would stand up and speak, he would always vindicate everything that we had done on his behalf. We all just felt a thousand feet high whenever Harold would speak. So he really came through for us.

TB: But then in the general election, running against a Republican in a Democratic town, he won by only forty thousand votes.

LK: We had an 80 percent registration in the black community and a 93 percent turnout of black voters for him in the election, but what you say is true because so many of the white voters who usually voted Democratic crossed over and voted Republican. He was running against an opponent who wasn't even competent, but that's what they did!

TB: And in all of their castigations of Harold, no one could ever say that he was in any way incompetent.

LK: And for people like that *not* to say that a black person was incompetent was in itself remarkable!

[*Laughter.*]

At first the news media attempted to attack him, but he out-talked them every single time, just as Malcolm X had done previously. So the reason that Harold earned their respect was that they knew they couldn't challenge him without being beaten, but when we actually won the election, the media were not prepared because they just didn't think that something like this would ever happen. Some of them even had tears in their eyes because the Daley dynasty had ended. Even with all the obstacles that the regular Democratic machine kept putting in our way, we continued the struggle, and Harold was elected for a second term, but then he suddenly died, and that was the biggest shake-up for all of us. Not a single one of us was able to hold back our tears, and then right away that Evans-Sawyer mess came about. I have to admit that at first I was for Evans because Evans had been a part of the movement whereas Sawyer was old-school, but, contrary to what we feared, for the brief time he was in office Sawyer turned out to be a great mayor. He did not let the mainstream forces dictate to him what he should do, and he stood up on many occasions to defend the interests of the black community by following the path that Harold had already established. Then, as you know, there was a legal challenge to Sawyer that was sponsored by the old machine politicians, and they called for an early mayoral election.

TB: That was the worst thing that could have happened to us at that time because now we had *two* black candidates who were running against one of theirs who was white, and that caused a split among black voters which allowed the white candidate to win.

LK: And so that's when another Mayor Daley got in!

TB: Yes, the present mayor of Chicago: Richard M. Daley.

LK: Yes.

TB: Larry, at this point what do you see politically as the future of the black community in Chicago?

LK: Well, first of all, sad to say, the Chicago black community is hardly a community anymore. During the period that we've been talking about, because of the integration we had achieved, blacks started moving back into the downtown area, up to the North Side, and out into the suburbs, and so now many of our younger people—particularly those who are well-educated and successful—are no longer part of that solid South Side and West Side base that we used to have. What's more, many of these successful young blacks feel that now that they are part of the corporate world, they no longer owe any kind of allegiance to the black community. Many of them have become Republicans, and some of them are even anti–affirmative action. Sometimes you hear people that are like this say, "I didn't get to where I am from affirmative action. I didn't get here because of any of those struggles that people fought so many years ago." They truly believe that they have gotten into their present positions because of who they are and what they themselves have accomplished. They don't seem to realize that we have had to fight every single step along the way in order for them to be standing where they are now.

TB: These young people don't know their history.

LK: They believe that somehow they are *above* history. So, at least in terms of politics, I think we are in a bad, bad situation. What's worse is that in our predominantly black high schools we now have a 70 percent dropout rate. For every one who graduates there are more than two that don't! I went back to my old high school, Crane Tech, and the principal told me that they were also having a dropout rate of 70 percent. Can you believe it?

TB: The same thing is true at Phillips, at DuSable, at almost every black high school.

LK: So can you project what that will mean ten years from now? It means that we will have more than two-thirds of the coming generation in the black community who are practically illiterate, and that means that they don't know and won't have the opportunity to learn history.

TB: And those who don't know history—

LK: —let others write it for them. We need to write our own history.

TB: And that is just what we are now doing.

May 31, 1997, and July 31, 1997

BILL ADKINS

TENOR SAX PAR EXCELLENCE .

Bill Adkins is one of those persons who attended high school in the late thirties and early forties who got caught up in the constant Chicago Board of Education redistricting schemes that were ongoing attempts to confine all black students to Phillips and DuSable high schools. Even so, Bill says that going to DuSable when he graduated from Carter Elementary School was the best thing that could have happened to him.

Being musically inclined though not a musician myself, I first met Bill when at DuSable we both came under the rigorous tutelage and discipline of the already legendary Walter Henri Dyett.

During that same period, Bill also met Joe Williams, the future jazz-blues ballad singer, and Eddie Johnson, who was to become a master of the tenor saxophone, both of whom lived just a little farther south of the place where he was living. From that point onward, these three became friends for life.

Within a few years, Bill was playing tenor saxophone with many well-known big bands. Later on he had problems with alcoholism that he was able to overcome because of the inherent strength of his character. Today he is back in constant demand as a highly successful and respected jazz musician.

TB: Now, first of all, tell me where you were born.

BA: I was born in Chicago in my dad's house at 5712 South Wabash.

TB: And when was that?

BA: I was born in 1927.

TB: Any brothers or sisters?

BA: I was second to the youngest of ten kids.

TB: Oh, man! I hope your dad was making a lot of money!
   [*Laughter.*]

BA: Well, he was working in the post office, and everybody was always kidding him all the time—even the deacons in the church! "How many you got now?"

TB: What church was that?

BA: That was Berean Baptist Church at Fifty-second and Dearborn.

TB: That was Reverend Braddan's church.

BA: He was a former military man just like Walter Dyett.

TB: That's right. I have a copy of the book he wrote about his experiences in World War I.

BA: It was called *Under Fire.*

TB: He was a brave and very strong person.

BA: That cat was made out of pure iron. Between him and my dad, who had been a blacksmith, they kept me straight while I was growing up. Believe me, you don't ever want guys like that to be mad at you—and then I walked into DuSable and immediately came under the scrutiny of Walter Dyett!
   [*Laughter.*]
   So all those years I never got a chance to do nothing wrong!

TB: Where was your family living while you grew up?

BA: We lived at 5712 Wabash, right across the street from Carter School. Our whole family went to that school, even my mother.

TB: Is that right?

BA: Only Carter School back at that time when she was young was where Betsy Ross is now.

TB: Was that school—except for her—all white back at that time?

BA: Just about, but she might have been the only spot on the cloth, as they used to say.

TB: I remember James T. Farrell writing in his books about how Studs Lonigan and the other Irish kids of his generation used to go ice skating out there in the playground at Carter back then.

BA: Well, that must have been at approximately the same time my mother went to school there.

TB: Was your mother born here in Chicago?

BA: I believe she was, but I'm not entirely certain about that. You see, she died while I was still quite young. It was around 1931 or some time like that. I was only four when she passed.

TB: Did your dad marry again?

BA: Yes, but that didn't last very long. There must have been just too many kids for her to handle.

TB: So your dad practically raised you by himself?

BA: It was more my older brothers and sisters that raised me. They just took charge. So we managed to get through growing up without much trouble. Of course the old man was always there to lay down the law, and you had to be out of your skull to try to break that law he had laid down because if you did you'd have a broken skull!

TB: But he kept you straight.

BA: Yes, he sure did. None of us played around. At one point I got to drinking a little bit and got in some trouble and put into the lockup, but my grandfather was a lawyer, and he called down there and got me out.

TB: What was your grandfather's name?

BA: Arthur Simms. He was a lawyer down around Forty-eighth Street when they had the court down there.

TB: Yes, I remember that old police station at Forty-eighth because I had to go down there lots of times to help out somebody who was in one kind of trouble or another.

BA: I remember once one of my brothers got in some trouble out in Harvey. I don't know what the heck he was doing out there, but my grandfather got word that the police had locked him up. So my grandfather got on the phone and said, "You got a young Turk out there named Nelson Adkins? You do! Well, let me talk to the desk sergeant." So he says to the desk sergeant, "Keep him there until he learns his lesson, and heat the pot till it's boiling!" So that was the first and last time Nelson ever had a problem like that!

TB: Tell me more about your dad. Where was he born?

BA: The birthplace for my dad was a little town called Providence Forge, Virginia. It was a rural district with a highway running through it. A grocery store on this side of the road and a gas station on the other. That was just about all there was.

TB: Now, what was the neighborhood like around Carter School while you were growing up?

BA: Listen, and this is as close to the truth as I can get. That block—the 5700 block on Wabash—was just like one big family.

TB: Did Reverend Braddan live on that block?

BA: No, Braddan lived over in the 5800 block on Wabash.

TB: But that was close by.

BA: Yes, it certainly was. There was a gas station there on the southwest corner, and right next to that gas station was Braddan's house. I still remember that house because it had such a lot of ivy growing on the front.

TB: It was a nice neighborhood.

BA: It was a beautiful neighborhood. All the people knew each other, but what that meant for a kid, of course, was that you couldn't get away with anything whatsoever because whatever you did somebody would always see you do it!

[*Laughter.*]

Whatever you did or didn't do your old man would know all about by the time he got home. So we all pretty much walked the chalk line all the time.

TB: Was Sylvester Washington living on Fifty-eighth Street then?

BA: Yes, old Two-Gun Pete lived right across the street from Reverend Braddan. There was a story going around that some cat was horsing around with one of his daughters, and somehow Pete got in the way, and that young guy must have clobbered him a good one. Well, of course, it may have been some kind of an accident, but, believe me, that guy was never seen or heard of again!

[*Laughter.*]

TB: Two-Gun Pete actually had two daughters, and one of them was about my age, and I was starting to date her, but then one day she says to me, "You know, you ought to meet my father," and I replied, "Oh, yeah, who's he?" "Sylvester Washington!" And that was the last time I saw her!

[*Laughter.*]

BA: But you didn't disappear, did you?

TB: No, I'm still here!

[*Laughter.*]

As a matter of fact, a little later on I became acquainted with Two-Gun Pete myself, but I never had any kind of trouble with him because of the fact that I had saved this boy who was the son of one of his lady friends from getting himself into some serious trouble with one of those tough guys over at the pool room on Fifty-first Street. Well, Two-Gun Pete always remembered me doing that, and so, whenever he saw me someplace where I shouldn't be, he would always say, "Hey, Shorty, what are you doing hanging around with these hoodlums?" And I'd reply, "Not much, Mr. Washington. I was just about to leave."

[*Laughter.*]

What about your high school experience? Which school did you go to?

BA: Well, we lived closest to Englewood, but somehow the Board of Education came to the conclusion that Fifty-ninth Street would be the boundary between Englewood students and DuSable students. I would assume that the reason for that was that they were trying to keep Englewood just as white as they possibly could. So they came up with that dividing line, which meant that if you lived south of Fifty-ninth Street, you stayed in Englewood, and if you lived north of Fifty-ninth Street, you went to DuSable.

TB: Now, going to DuSable, what was it like coming there from snooty Fifty-eighth Street and mingling with all those kids from Forty-seventh Street?

BA: Actually that turned out to be a blessing for me because right away I ran into Walter Dyett, and I never looked back!

TB: He wouldn't let you!

[*Laughter.*]

BA: You're probably not going to believe this, but when I first got there, I played football for about ten minutes until I got smacked in the mouth by one of the other players. Well, when Captain Dyett took just one look at what had happened, he said to me, "Either play ball or play horn! If you play football, you're going to get hit in the mouth. It's bound to happen. It can't be avoided." Now, as you know, that guy couldn't say good morning without cursing, and so he says, "God damn it! You play football or you play horn. One way or the other! It's just that simple." The man was right, and so that settled the argument right then and there because if I were to get hit in the mouth again, I'd be out of the music business before I ever got in!

[*Laughter.*]

TB: Well, in support of what you're saying, do you remember Marl Young?

BA: Remember him? I still keep in touch. He's living out in California now.

TB: Well, I remember when we all were still kids Marl was already a fine piano player, and he had even directed one of the musical shows we put on in our school, but then one day we were playing softball, and he hurt his finger pretty badly. When that happened, he became so frightened that he might not be able to play again that I think maybe that's when he decided he'd better get a law degree to back up his playing.

BA: That could well have been the deciding factor.

TB: So, now you're enrolled at DuSable, and Dyett puts you right away into the concert band.

BA: Yes, you had to be in the concert band. That was the prerequisite.

TB: What about the marching band?

BA: The concert band and the marching band were one and the same except that for the marching band you had to practice and rehearse the routines for the half-time shows. So he would take the older students who were more advanced and have them teach us one on one. That's the way that he worked. A guy named Roy Grant was one of my tutors. Johnny Griffin and I were in there together.

TB: Walter Dyett trained so many wonderful musicians!

BA: Listen, that man could have taught chemistry, science, English, or absolutely anything. With the kind of communicative skills he had, he could have made a drum talk! A whole slew of guys about my own age—Gene Ammons, Benny Green, and all the rest of them—came out of DuSable at about the same time that I did.

TB: Now, about this same period of time you started playing professionally, didn't you?

BA: Well, I was lucky from the get-go because we had clubs like the DeLisa. The big star professional musicians would be there working six nights a week, but, because of the friendships and connections that Captain Dyett had established, we young guys would be the band that played there for dancers on the off-nights. We would always make it to all the regular show rehearsals so our band would be able to play the tunes just as well as the older guys. We knew that we had to get it exactly right because those kids out there dancing are depending on what we're doing. They may not be musically trained like we are, but they can *hear* what we are playing, and if we'd make any kind of mistake, believe me, they'd let us know all about it!

TB: But there was also a kind of give and take going on. Of course the innovation of the music helped in the creation of those dances, but sometimes you guys would be playing on the beat and we'd be doing an off-step in counterpoint to it.

BA: That's right.

TB: So the music and the dancing were really like a form of call-and-response, which is, of course, a continuing part of our cultural heritage.

BA: Yes, that is true.

TB: It's something that we learn very early in the game. One of the first things that I can remember is that when they were washing the dishes my mama and daddy always used to sing together. You know they didn't have a dish-washing machine back then, and there was a certain rhythm to the way they were doing the washing, and pretty soon they would start to harmonize. My dad sang a low bass, and mama sang alto or contralto. Later on, when I heard them doing that, I knew enough by then to know when I could be included, and so I'd come in at certain times with my bad excuse for a baritone, and they would look around and smile at me. Those are precious memories.

BA: They certainly are.

TB: So now you're still in high school, but you're already starting to work as a professional musician.

BA: That's right. I got in the union and played my first professional job in '43. I was about sixteen years old or something like that, and I was playing with Dave Young, Eddie Smith, Red Saunders, and all those cats. Everybody in those bands that I worked with was old enough to be my father, and I will never get through thanking the powers that be for putting me in the middle of all those wonderful, talented men. That made all the difference in the world for a young man like me.

TB: You're absolutely right about that.

BA: I mean, here I am in those nightclubs night after night, six nights a week, surrounded by all these naked women, and those cats to a man—every damn one of them—said, "Leave that boy alone!"

[*Laughter.*]

In those days we were just learning how to play, so whenever they'd bring a new show into the Rhumboogie or one of the other clubs, we would always try to get into all the rehearsals so that we could learn something new. We were just young guys, but all these big-name guys—Tiny Bradshaw and cats like that—because we were musicians, they always let us in. What's more—let me tell you this is the God's own truth—never ever, not even once, did any of those guys refuse to talk with you. They would welcome you and listen to what you had to say. I will never forget the time that Prez—

TB: Lester Young.

BA: Lester Young was saying to us, "Listen, let me tell you young guys one thing that is so important you must never forget it. If you want to learn how to play a ballad or any kind of love song, you must always learn not just the chords and changes but the words as well so that you'll know what the hell you're supposed to be saying through your horn."

TB: The old-time jazz musicians were all like that.

BA: Well, they ain't anymore.

TB: The old-timers still are.

BA: Yes, you're right about that. The old-timers still are.

TB: I remember when these white kids used to come to the clubs. They wanted to be musicians, and the musicians would pull them in too and answer all their questions. That's how those white kids—such as Benny Goodman and Bix Beiderbecke—all learned how to play. The musicians would let them play with them, and every time one of those white kids would hit the wrong note they'd get a laugh or someone would say something, and that way that kid would learn what he needed to learn. You can't beat that for a learning experience!

BA: You can't learn things like that from just practicing by yourself or reading a book of instruction.

TB: Athletes were like that too. When I was just a kid, the Harlem Globetrotters used to live in the neighborhood, and sometimes they would come out to the

Carter playground or wherever it was that we were playing, and they would get in the game and say to me, "Hey, Shorty, here's the way to do that!"

BA: I know precisely what you mean.

TB: But I never had much of any musical training. My mama wanted me to take piano lessons, and so I learned how to play "Little Boy in the Boat," which was a kind of warm-up piece, but, instead of going up on State Street, where I was supposed to go for my piano lesson, I'd take that money she gave me and go to the Regal to hear someone I just had to hear. That way almost anyone in our generation or older who was playing was someone that I got to hear, and that's how my friends and I, even though we weren't musicians ourselves, grew up loving the music and understanding almost as much as if we were playing it ourselves.

BA: I know just what you mean. There was one of my brothers wouldn't know one note from another—whether it sat on his shoulder or bit him on the ass! But whenever I'd play something, I could never hit any kind of a wrong note because he'd always know exactly when I was screwing up.

TB: That's because we lived with the music. It was just as much a part of our personal culture as it was for the performer.

BA: That reminds me of something else. Let me tell you a little story before I lose it. One time I was sitting at the counter in Chili Mac's, and this cat was playing something on the jukebox, which was up in the front of the place. Well, it comes to the place on the recording where the tenor takes his solo, and, believe me, that cat was playing the hell out of his horn, and in the back there's the cook who makes the tamales standing by the register, and, Tim, he is *singing* every damn note that this cat is playing! I couldn't believe what I was hearing. I tell you we have some amazing people in our race.

TB: And his tamales were pretty good too, as I fondly remember!
[*Laughter.*]

BA: They certainly were. Now, let me tell you something else. Later on in all my travels around the country, there were just *three* things that people seemed to know about Chicago. Number one: the Italian gangster thing—Al Capone and all of that. Number two: the Club DeLisa, and number three: Chili Mac's!

TB: Everybody went to Chili Mac's.

BA: Yes, after the gig, that's where we'd all go.

TB: But now that place is gone.

BA: Yes, and nothing tastes like that anymore.

TB: So, now you leave high school and are working full-time as a professional musician and starting to travel all around the country. Tell me about some of your experiences.

BA: Well, I first went out on the road with George Hudson. That's the band I traveled with. Do you remember a group of singers called the Ravens?

TB: Yes, I do.

BA: Well, we were traveling with them. You see, we had what was called a package that played the black theater circuit.

TB: The Regal was part of that.

BA: Of course it was, but you also had the Apollo in New York, the Howard Theater in Washington, the Royal Theater in Baltimore—altogether there were about twelve or thirteen theaters in that circuit back then. At any rate, after we'd traveled all the way through that theater circuit and when there was no other place for us to go, we'd play what we called the chitlins circuit.

TB: And that was in the South.

BA: Yes, that's where you play in villages, hamlets, alleys, cotton fields, tobacco warehouses—just about anyplace at all because the people down there were so starved for music and entertainment of any kind. I even worked on the riverboats out of St. Louis for a short while.

TB: You did? I didn't know that. Now, about this same time that you're starting to make your mark as a professional musician, things are expanding rapidly, and black musicians are beginning to be in great demand in places beyond just Harlem and the South Side of Chicago.

BA: Yes, that's when I started working with Henry "Red" Allen, J. C. Higginbotham, and cats like that, and that bunch, they all put their arms around me and tried to help me out in every way that they could because to them I was still a youngster, but it wasn't so many years after that I got to play Carnegie Hall with Basie. That was the first and only time I ever worked with Billie Holiday.

TB: So at this point of time you are playing concerts in places such as Carnegie Hall, and some of the guys are beginning to make some serious money with their music.

BA: Well, yes, but in terms of my own career and making money with my music, I'll be point blank and up front with you. I had one hell of a time with alcohol, and so I missed a lot of opportunities. I don't know how much money I blew because once word gets out that you're a bottle baby, no one will hire you. If someone was looking for a musician, they'd call the local and ask, "Who've you got that's playing saxophone?" "We got Bill Adkins." "Him? Well, he's a nice cat, and he's a good player, but he's bad news. You don't ever know who is going to come to work: Jekyll or Hyde!" So, in order to get off that stuff, I had to come back home here to Chicago and get cleaned up, and then I married a girl I was in kindergarten with. So don't think that I mean for this in any way to be a negative type of story that I'm telling you.

TB: It isn't.

BA: That's right. It's a *positive* story because now I was able to return to the music—and that music has been my life!

November 17, 1995

ALVENA HENDERSON

LONGTIME CHICAGO RESIDENT

The late Jonas and Alvena Henderson were a very interesting couple that I got to know only briefly before each of them passed. They were the parents of my neighbor, Patricia Henderson Skyles-Hammonds, who is the president and chairman of the fifty-three–unit cooperative building at 4900 South Drexel in the Hyde Park–Kenwood neighborhood of Chicago. The Hendersons came to live with their daughter in order to comfort her after her first husband's death as the result of a brief illness, and it was then that they became my neighbors as well. It was not long before I learned that they both were college graduates, that they had held teaching and administrative positions at various educational institutions in the South before deciding to come to Chicago, and that they had established several successful businesses on the South Side before their retirement.

I found them to be a charming couple, eager to reminisce with me about their life experiences in the South and the North. Jonas Henderson was an avid sports fan, and so, having that in common, he and I had many interesting and informative informal conversations on sports and other related topics. They were never recorded and so, unfortunately, cannot be included within the context of the conversation that follows, in which his wife discusses some of her interesting experiences managing a record store located near the famous DeLisa and Rhumboogie nightclubs.

TB: Mrs. Henderson, I understand that back in those days when the South Side was filled with so much musical excitement and creativity you were running a very popular record store.

AH: Yes, I did that with my mother. We had a little place on Fifty-fifth Street in the basement called the Boulevard Record Shop. Mama worked there in the day, and I worked there at night.

TB: How late did you stay open?

AH: We stayed open until at least two o'clock! Can you believe that? You see, the DeLisa and the Rhumboogie and most of the other smaller clubs, all of them had live music, and some of their singers and musicians were starting to make recordings. But the only way those recordings could be heard was on the radio, and a lot of those disc jockeys had to be paid something before they'd play anything on the air. So what these artists used to do to publicize their music was that when they'd get a new record, they'd bring it right over to a record store like ours that had speakers out in front.

TB: So, after the clubs closed, they'd come over with their new recordings and ask you to play them so that people on the street could hear their music?

AH: Yes, so they'd give you a little box with twenty-five copies of their new record, and we'd be glad to play it for them because it was a real drawing card for us to have those people there in our shop while we were playing their music. People off the street would come in and buy a copy and get it autographed for themselves! I remember that when Pearl Bailey had her first recording our shop was the first place that she came to.

TB: And by the time you closed it was usually two o'clock?

AH: Or sometimes later, and then Henderson would pick me up—you see he was working nights at the post office back then—and we'd go over to the lake and have our lunch!
[*Laughter.*]
It was really late at night, but there was nothing for us to worry about. Nobody would ever bother you.

TB: It was a different world back then.

AH: That's right. It was a different kind of world.

TB: And the streets were full of music! Do you remember any of the other entertainers that used to stop by your shop?

AH: Sarah Vaughan, Dinah Washington, and lots of other people like that.

TB: Being open that late, did you ever have any kind of problems?

AH: No, we didn't ever have to worry about anything at all. That guy—what's his name—kept that corner clean.

TB: Two-Gun Pete?

AH: Yes, Sylvester Washington. Every so often he'd just come by and put his head in the door—and if any of the wrong kind of people were in there, that's when they'd leave!

[*Laughter.*]

There was a friend of mine—a white fellow that I knew—that owned a record shop on the West Side. This was in about 1954, and he had been selling mostly Lithuanian and Jewish kinds of music, but by then the neighborhood was changing because so many blacks were coming up from the South and moving into the area where his store was located. Where I used to see that fellow was at the M.S. music distribution house that used to be on Michigan Avenue just below Twenty-second Street, and one time when we both were there, I told him that if he ever needed any help to change over the kind of music he was selling to fit the needs of his new customers, he should give me a call. So I gave him one of my business cards and forgot all about him for a while. Well, then, about a year later, he gave me a call and told me that he needed some full-time help during the daytime. Now that was fine with me because my daughter, Pat, was just finishing grammar school, and when she started high school, I wanted to be able to be at home with her in the evenings. So I went to my mother, and I told her, "Mama, I can't work at night anymore. I've got a teenage daughter, and I want to be at home with her during the evenings." Mama understood exactly what I was saying, and so I went over there to the West Side, and that man just turned his store over to me to run it for him.

TB: Where was that record store located?

AH: It was right on the corner of Homan and Roosevelt Road, at 3400 West Roosevelt.

TB: Now, by this time, a lot of popular recordings were coming out by a wide variety of black artists.

AH: Most of the most popular music was coming out on the four big record labels: Columbia, Decca, Capitol, and RCA Victor.

TB: And all of those were white owned and managed.

AH: And so were all the distribution companies, but they hired a lot of blacks to do all the work for them—

TB: —as well as create all the music that they were selling.

AH: Yes, whites owned everything. Back then they segregated even the music, and Columbia put out its black music on the Okeh label and RCA Victor on Bluebird.

TB: Nat King Cole practically single-handedly made a success out of Capitol Records.

AH: Yes, but they didn't put him out on a separate label. His records came out on their own main label. You see, they were promoting him as a *singer* and not as a *black* singer. Usually labels like that wouldn't give a black musician the same kind of opportunities that they'd give to a white person. In that regard, RCA Victor was the worst of the lot. They were prejudiced as hell. They had signed up exclusively a whole lot of really great black artists, but they wouldn't ever want to release any of their recordings. So we had a lot of black artists that were better than Presley ever was, but nobody ever got to hear them!

TB: Remember Dr. Jo Jo Adams?

AH: Yes, that's a good example. That guy was just *so* far ahead of Elvis in terms of that kind of entertaining.

TB: Now, at that time, were there any black-owned record labels?

AH: The only one that comes to mind is Vee-Jay. All of your gospel music was on Vee-Jay, and they were going like a house on fire!

TB: Wasn't Al Benson, the well-known disc jockey, involved with that label?

AH: Yes, he took it over from the original founders and owners.

TB: Before getting involved with the music business, he used to be known as the Reverend Leaner, didn't he?

AH: Yes, he had a little church down on State Street. That's where he got his start.

TB: Well, in certain ways Al Benson revolutionized the disc jockey business.

AH: He certainly did, but he also did a lot of underhanded stuff. He'd sign up all these up-and-coming doo-wop groups that were out there standing on the corners singing their own songs and play their records on his radio show.

TB: At first his was the only radio show that would play that kind of music.

AH: So at least Al Benson did encourage a lot of those young guys to record their music, but unfortunately none of them ever got any kind of royalties because Benson didn't ever pay them any!

TB: He started playing blues as well as gospel and doo-wop, didn't he?

AH: Yes, but he never played any live music at all. Everything he played was on a record, and most of those records that he played were on the Vee-Jay label.

TB: And he never played any jazz at all, either live or recorded.

AH: That's right.

TB: Do you remember when the musicians' union took him to court?

AH: Yes, I do. They did that because before he was doing what he was doing almost all the music that you heard on the radio was played by live musicians. Every little radio show had its own little band.

TB: Sometimes it was just an organist.

AH: Yes, but a real *live* organist!

[*Laughter.*]

But the union lost that court battle, and now those programs could all start using some type of prerecorded music.

TB: What he did by doing that was to break the back of the black musicians' local.

AH: Yes, what Al Benson did was to put a lot of musicians—both black and white—out of work, and it left him completely free to promote his records without having to pay any musicians or any royalties whatsoever because he owned the rights to almost all of the music that he played!

September 25, 1994

EARL NEAL

CHAMPION OF SOCIAL JUSTICE

The conversation that follows provides a brief but insightful sketch of the life and times of a very well-known professional family whose legal and judicial careers have made an impact on many areas of Chicago's political world. Earl was born in Chicago, where his father had first established himself as a prominent attorney and later became a judge in the circuit courts during an era when becoming a black judge was nothing short of phenomenal. Through these established successes and contacts, young Earl Neal became familiar with local government and politics. After obtaining a law degree from the University of Michigan Earl did his service in the U.S. military (which is an interesting story in and of itself—as in my own experience, blacks were not promoted in the army and often served under less-qualified whites who became officers with no trouble at all). After the Korean War, Attorney Neal went into private practice with great vigor and style, backed up by solid knowledge and experience. Just to see him walk into a courtroom with such style and self-confidence was always a thrilling experience for me, but then to hear him eloquently explicate his legal position was even more rewarding—and so, because of this combination of unique personal and professional qualities, I myself and many others were extremely glad that Earl Neal was the one who represented Harold Washington in a court suit that he won but that otherwise might have damaged his career.

Earl and his wife are a charming couple, and his law firm, which is now headed by his son, Langdon, continues to be a prosperous one. As a matter of fact, not only is Langdon Neal a lawyer like his father and grandfather, but also he has recently become the chairman of the Chicago Board of Election Commissioners. This is a very powerful position—and so it seems that the Neal legacy will continue its honorable progression onward and upward into the future.

TB: I am about to interview Earl Neal, a prominent Chicago attorney, whom I have known for a very long time. Earl, let's begin at the beginning. Where were you born?

EN: I was born right here in Chicago at the old Provident Hospital at Thirty-fifth and Dearborn. That was in 1928. My father at that time was not yet a lawyer, and my mother was a schoolteacher. She taught in the public school system after having attended Wilson Junior College.

TB: Where did she teach?

EN: At Forrestville School.

TB: Now, going back a bit in your own family history, your mother and father, where were they born?

EN: Well, both my mother and my dad were born here in Chicago, Illinois, near the turn of the century, which is a bit of a rarity for blacks of my generation.

TB: Do you remember the years when they were born?

EN: In 1904 and 1906. My father was an only child, but my mother had a sister and a brother. Her brother was a very gifted and talented young man who was my father's best friend. Both of them were interested in becoming chemists or engineers, and they both went to the University of Chicago for their undergrad studies. After they graduated, the professors there expected them to teach in the South because there were no job opportunities at that time for blacks with their education in the North—but, instead of doing that, my father moved to New York City and enjoyed life with new friends such as Paul Robeson during the Harlem Renaissance!

[*Laughter.*]

After that, my father came back to Chicago, married my mother, and worked as a redcap by day and went to law school at night. He went for one year to the University of Chicago's law school, but then, because his shift changed and he had to work at night, he went to Chicago-Kent Law School, and he became a lawyer in 1935. The major case he handled—this was sometime around the early 1940s—was settling the estate of Dr. Richie Williams. Dr. Williams had left an estate of at least a million dollars, which, of course, was almost unheard of for blacks in those days. Dad said they just kept opening vault after vault with nothing but dollars coming out of each of them!

TB: What about your grandparents?

EN: My father's father worked on the railroad, and my father's mother was a beautician who had her own business. My mother's father was one of the first blacks to have a license to sell insurance. This was in the twenties. He was with the old Globe Insurance Company, and he got that job because he had worked for the principal owner of that company as a chauffeur and handyman.

TB: Do you have any brothers and sisters?

EN: No, as I said, my father was an only child, and I was also an only child, and my son was an only child! But he just had twins—a boy and a girl—so he now has four children, and the spell has been broken!

TB: Now tell me, where did you go to elementary school?

EN: I went to Forrestville Elementary School with people such as Johnny Griffin, the saxophone player. We were very close, and I still see him whenever he comes to Chicago. Bill Cousins was also there with me.

TB: Did you and Bill go to high school together?

EN: No, Bill went to DuSable and I went to Englewood, but later on, Bill and I both went to the University of Illinois at the same time.

TB: Where were you living when you went to Forrestville?

EN: We were living at Forty-first and Michigan, but then we moved out south to Sixty-eighth and Champlain, where there were a lot of homeowners, and it was a very stable neighborhood.

TB: Did you change schools?

EN: No, although we'd moved out of the district, I continued at Forrestville because my mother taught there. So I graduated from Forrestville and I went to Englewood High School. Of course where we were living was really much closer to Parker. Parker was at about Sixty-ninth and Stewart, and Englewood was at about Sixty-seventh and Stewart, but they had gerrymandered all the schools around there so that even though my mother was a teacher and my father a truant officer, they said we were living in the district for Englewood. The real reason was that we were black.

TB: Maybe, without intending to, they did you a favor. After all, there were a lot of wonderful people at Englewood during that period of time. What was the racial mixture?

EN: About fifty-fifty, black and white.

TB: And I imagine that every black that was there with you went on beyond high school in terms of education.

EN: Absolutely, and I am certain the same thing was true at DuSable as well.

TB: Yes, and that was because the teachers at both of those schools focused on the needs of their students. What did their students need to learn? What would be the best way to reach them and teach them? Back then those teachers really believed that you could learn and that they could teach you. Also they had the full support and discipline of the families and the community to back them up. That was a very important continuum from which you could not escape, even if for some reason you wanted to!

EN: So I graduated from Englewood in February of 1945, and I was cited by the *Chicago Tribune* as an outstanding graduate, although I was not the president of my class. I was the vice president. The president was a young black woman named Juanita. Then I went to the University of Illinois in February of 1945, and during that time, I had my first overt experience of undisguised racism. I was only sixteen, and there was a fast-food restaurant down there called the Steak 'n Shake, and they would not serve blacks inside—so they put my hamburger in a bag and told me to eat it somewhere else!

TB: What about your living conditions?

EN: Blacks were not allowed to live in the dormitories of a state school like that. So when I went there, I always lived in the Kappa house, and, later on, in 1976, when I was elected president of the board at the University of Illinois, I took the time and trouble to remind them that back in 1945 they would not serve me food and I could not stay in their dorms!

TB: Back in '45, the university had about how many black students?

EN: Oh, well, during the war, the university was quite small, and so I would say there were only about ten or twelve thousand students, and of those about five hundred or so were black. For the men we had a Kappa house with thirty in it, and there were another thirty in the Alpha house, and then there were two sororities: the Delta house and the Alpha Kappa Alpha house for the young black women who were there at the time. The reason why they had even that large a number of blacks back then was that Missouri was close by, and if you were black and you wanted to advance your education, the State of Missouri would rather pay for your education outside of the state than let you into their own law school or med school. So what that meant was that a lot of black students from there and elsewhere were paying their tuition in Illinois because they were not allowed to go to schools in their own home states.

TB: And when did that change?

EN: Well, as a matter of fact, that ingrained attitude of racism at the University of Illinois began to change during the time when I was there, and that was because we did a whole lot of picketing during that entire time!
[*Laughter.*]

TB: So you were already really active by then.

EN: Yes, we were all active as students. So as a result, by the end of my time there, we all could eat in the restaurants, and we even had a few of our people living in the dorms.

TB: And so as a result of those efforts, a tradition was being laid down for those who would come later.

EN: An old tradition was ended, and a new one had begun.

TB: Now, after you did your undergraduate work at the University of Illinois, what did you decide to do?

EN: I applied for law school at the University of Michigan.

TB: By now, had your dad already become a judge?

EN: No, he's still practicing law, and my mother is still teaching. You know, my mother taught for forty-three years, until my father was finally a judge, and then she immediately quit!

[*Laughter.*]

And then I went to the University of Michigan because of the quality of its reputation and also because of a friend of mine named James Baker. His father—Oscar Baker—started his law practice in Bay City, Michigan, in 1903, and he became the most successful personal injury lawyer in that region. He was, I believe, one of the most successful trailblazers for black lawyers in this entire country. His first son was Oscar Jr., and he also became a successful lawyer. His second son was my friend Jim, who was a year ahead of me and who was able to make it possible for me to live in the Law Quad. No black had ever lived in the Law Quad before except for James Baker and Hobart Taylor. Taylor was the first black who had ever lived in the Law Quad, and he went on to become a very brilliant and successful lawyer in Washington. So that's why I went to Michigan, and I graduated and passed the bar in Michigan in 1952, but then I went into the army in January of 1953.

TB: What rank were you when you were discharged?

EN: I rose to the rank of corporal.

TB: Bill Cousins has a similar story. He also rose through the ranks. Did you see service overseas?

EN: Yes, the Korean War was on, but instead of that, I went to Europe. I lived just outside of Paris, as a matter of fact, for about a year, and then I came back, got discharged, and passed the bar here in Illinois.

TB: Where did you first start your law practice?

EN: I started my practice here in Chicago with my father in a suite that had been occupied at one time by Bill Dawson.

TB: Where was that located?

EN: We were located at 180 West Washington, in one of the only two buildings in the downtown area that would accept minorities as tenants. You could not get an office downtown anywhere else! Anyway, we rented almost an entire floor in that building. Eventually we had seven lawyers working out of that suite, and what is remarkable about that is that we had only one secretary—or maybe two on a part-time basis—to do all of that work for us. Something like that would be unheard of today! Just think how good she must have been to take on all of that work we were handing her, but that one secretary was all that we could afford.

TB: Was it about that time that George Leighton joined in with you?

EN: Yes, and you know, George is still working just as hard as ever now that he's eighty-five!

TB: Well, he's been an inspiration to me because whenever I look at him I always say to myself, "He's still here—so that's how it must be done," and I think that I've got to keep on keeping on just a little longer.

EN: When my own kids were working here, I was worried about what would happen if they came into the firm and if their names might not get confused with my own, but then I thought about it, and I told them that there wouldn't be any problems like that because I won't still be practicing law by the time they get here. That's when my son said, "Yes, but maybe you'll be like Leighton!" [*Laughter.*]

TB: Well, as Duke said when somebody asked him, "Duke, when are you going to retire?" he said, "Retire to what?" [*Laughter.*]

EN: That's right. Duke was a good friend of all of us. He was a close friend of my father's. I remember once when I handled a legal matter for Duke I was working night and day on ironing out all the details because there was just no way that I was not going to win for him!

TB: And so you did!

EN: Yes, so I did, but you know something? In those days, as I look back, you know somehow it seems as if there were more fine, respected black lawyers back then than maybe there are today.

TB: Well, I very clearly remember that period about which we've been talking, and it seems to me that back then it was such an honor to overcome the obstacles that were in place to prevent you from becoming a lawyer that once those barriers had been passed you most likely had attained a certain maturity and dignity that deserved the utmost respect.

EN: Yes, but today what troubles me most is that although young black lawyers now have so many opportunities to enter these large, predominantly white legal firms, they very quickly become frustrated—and they come back here and talk to me about things like this every single week—because they discover that no matter where they go, no matter how hard they work, no matter how talented and intelligent they might happen to be, they will always be an *assistant* to someone else. That is the only title that they will ever hope to get in the corporate world unless things change even more than they already have.

September 1994

REVEREND
DR. LOUIS RAWLS

MINISTER AND SOCIAL ACTIVIST

The late Reverend Dr. Louis Rawls was a well-known social-activist minister on the black South Side of Chicago during and after World War II. He was particularly active during the acceleration of the civil rights movement, starting in 1948, and continued his social concern and involvement until the time of his death in 2002. For all those many years his Tabernacle Missionary Baptist Church at 4130 South Indiana was both a place of worship and a haven for thousands of blacks coming to Chicago from the South. He had the ability to make everyone he met feel comfortable and welcome. Those of us who were already residents of Chicago frequently used the large sanctuary of his church for rallies and organizing meetings. For example, in 1960 this is where we held our organizing rallies for the huge march on the Republican National Convention in which we were protesting for more equitable civil rights and civil liberties for all Americans. Such luminaries as Paul Robeson, Dr. Martin Luther King, A. Philip Randolph, Fannie Lou Hamer, and many, many others who were leaders in the struggle for social justice also spoke there on certain memorable occasions.

Dr. Rawls was always involved in many other social concerns that were of great benefit to the community. At one time he created a much-needed hospital on Garfield Boulevard in the near southwest section of black Chicago to serve the needs of a mostly very poor clientele. He kept it open as long as he could, but unfortunately it closed down after only a few years because of lack of funding.

This brief conversation does not fully reveal all of the many contributions that Dr. Louis Rawls made to our community. Suffice it to say he was a very great man and one of our unsung heroes, who should be remembered by future generations.

———

TB: Tell me, where did you come from before you came to Chicago?

LR: I was born in Johns, Mississippi, on July 16, 1904.

TB: Which makes you now ninety-two years old. Congratulations!

LR: And in just a few months I'll be ninety-three! I'm really looking forward to that. I'm just so lucky to still have the retention and the continuing interest in what's going on.

TB: When did you first come to Chicago?

LR: I first came here from Mississippi in 1922.

TB: What was this neighborhood like when you first came here?

LR: Most of this neighborhood was homeowners, but from 1937 to 1945, this was a stress area. We were just coming out of the Depression, and it was nothing to see people eat out of garbage cans or go out behind any of the butcher shops in the neighborhood where they threw out the bones and then take those bones and go back home and make soup out of them.

TB: You could get about three pounds of neck bones for twenty-five cents or so, but some people just didn't have that twenty-five cents.

LR: Or if they did, those twenty-five cents were just too precious to part with! I can still remember how I used to walk through the stockyards and be able to get all the meat that anyone would want to eat for fifteen or twenty cents. Of course it would have to be tripe or hog oysters. Remember those?

TB: Mountain oysters but from pigs not cattle.

LR: That's right, and sometimes we could also get chicken feet, chicken necks, chicken livers and gizzards, but those were great days, you know, because we had fellowship. To ride the street cars cost just five cents, and you could get an extension—a coupon is what they called it—for seven cents, and you could ride all the way from here to Evanston or Morgan Park for those seven cents. At that time I was living at 4130 State Street, just three blocks from right here where we are right now.

TB: So you've been at home in this neighborhood for almost your entire adult life. When did you first go into the ministry?

LR: I first went into the ministry on Mother's Day, 1932. All during those Depression years, I was preaching at Canaan Missionary Baptist Church on State Street. I served there for ten years, and during that time, we were helping to feed the people as well as preaching to them.

TB: When did you move over to this church?

LR: We came over here in September of 1941 and bought this land from the Catholic Church.

TB: I've had the honor of being in your church many times. In fact, I've had relatives who were members of this church, but most of them are gone. Has anyone ever kept some kind of a history of Tabernacle? Is there a history that's been written down?

LR: Yes, there is. It's all been written down. The first building we owned, what we paid for it, where we got the money—all of that sort of thing.

TB: I'd like to borrow a copy of that sometime.

LR: Well, I wouldn't let you have it to take out with you, but you could read it here whenever you want. It has the whole history of our church. I've married over a thousand people here, and we've had funeral services for at least sixteen hundred—and it's all there: the dates of marriage, the dates of death.

TB: As I remember it, back during World War II, your church became a haven for black soldiers who would be either ignored or insulted in most of the other places in this part of town. They would come to your church, and very often your parishioners would take them to their homes for food and fellowship.

LR: Right, but we would also feed them down here as well. On any given Sunday, we would be feeding at least seventy-five to a hundred people.

TB: So your church has always been a service center in addition to being a spiritual center for the community.

LR: And this is also where Mahalia Jackson had her first major concert because at that time we were the only place that had enough room for all the people that wanted to hear her sing. We could seat about forty-one hundred people.

TB: Yes, and I've been here many times when this church was full to capacity. As a matter of fact, one time when I came here to hear Sam Cooke, I had to stand up all the way at the back!

LR: Yes, we had to turn 'em away from here like that on many occasions. I still remember that when Bishop Holly died we had to turn 'em away in droves because we'd completely run out of room.

TB: Bishop Holly was the founder of one of the Pentecostal churches.

LR: Yes, the Apostolic Church of God in Christ at 3749 Indiana. Bishop Brazier is over at Sixty-third and Kenwood, and then you have Reverend Finney at Sixty-third and Cottage Grove, right there on the corner.

TB: Now, coming back to Sam Cooke, he was your nephew, wasn't he?

LR: Yes, and Sam Cooke's daddy just died this year. He was Bishop Cook of the Church of God in Christ.

TB: And then, of course, there's Lou Rawls!

LR: Yes, he's just like my own son 'cause I took him in and adopted him.

TB: Two great singers coming from the same family!

LR: Did you know that Lou was in the hotel with Dr. King when he was assassinated?

TB: Yes, I remember.

LR: Marian Anderson also sang here—and so did Josephine Baker, Aretha Franklin, Shirley Caesar—almost all the great black singers!

TB: This church has a really fantastic history. Please tell me a little more about it.

LR: Well, this building you are sitting in now is one hundred and one years old. You can see the date engraved on the corner over there.

TB: And you said it was formerly a Catholic church.

LR: Yes, and we were the first Protestants in Chicago to buy a piece of property like this from the Catholic Church. Since that time, of course, many others have done much the same sort of thing.

TB: When did you buy this property?

LR: Well, we came here in '41, and then five years later we bought these other three buildings from them.

TB: You mentioned Mahalia Jackson, but I know that you have been the host to many other famous people here in this church.

LR: Let me see. In politics we've had Oscar DePriest, Mrs. Bethune, A. Philip Randolph, Marcus Garvey, the Honorable Elijah Muhammad, Adam Clayton Powell and his father, Martin Luther King—Senior and Junior!—and Dr. King's mother and his wife—all of them have spoken here! We never had Ida B. Wells-Barnett here because she died in 1931, but when I first came to Chicago, I was the chauffeur for that family, and I used to take Ida and her daughter Freda all around town.

TB: Freda was the first black woman who graduated from the University of Chicago, to the best of my memory.

LR: And she and her husband, Ben Duster, were here in this church just last week.

TB: And I also remember that when we organized the march with Willoughby Abner during the 1960 conventions, it was done right here in this church.

LR: That's right, and before then, back in 1949 or 1950, this is also where Paul Robeson gave one of his greatest concerts. He came here because all the other places were just too small, and, if you remember, even places like the Armory wouldn't be open to let blacks come in and use their facility.

TB: Not someone like Robeson anyhow!

[*Bitter laughter.*]

LR: Yes, and it didn't even matter what color he was. It was because he spoke out openly against the racism of America, and that made him so many enemies that he was barred from almost anyplace where he could perform.

TB: Well, that concert must have been a glorious experience.

LR: Yes, it was a great experience to have so many people coming here to hear this black Moses speak and sing.

TB: How was the concert publicized? How did people learn about Robeson coming here?

LR: On the Jack L. Cooper radio show.

TB: And, of course, there was no television back then.

LR: Yes, but we had the *Bee*, the *Whip*, and the *Chicago Defender*!

TB: Was it a mixed congregation that came to hear him?

LR: Oh, yes, many whites came here to see Paul Robeson. He had his own accompanist, but there was no choir. He just sang and then talked about the racism in this country and how things needed to be changed.

TB: Did you know that his father was a minister, and also his brother?

LR: They were Methodists, weren't they?

TB: They both were ministers in the African Methodist Episcopal Church.

LR: Back then, Robeson wasn't the only one who didn't have a place he could speak. There were quite a few other people—such as the Honorable Elijah Muhammad, Malcolm X, Farrakhan—that also had nowhere to speak, and so I let them come here.

TB: Also at one time even Jesse Jackson didn't have a place to speak.

LR: Yes, and I brought him here too. Operation Breadbasket started here, and then PUSH started here as well. Before that, during the war years, the Golden State Mutual Life Insurance Company, which is the second largest black insurance company, also got its start right here in this building.

TB: Most people may not realize or remember just how important your church has been to this community and all the services which you have rendered so unselfishly.

LR: I've just tried to keep the faith.

TB: At one time you established a hospital.

LR: A hospital, a car wash, two funeral homes. We even had the first licensed nursery for blacks in the city of Chicago. We kept it open and met every standard for thirty years, but then, when they changed the code and demanded we put in a sprinkling system, we had to close it down.

TB: During all these years, you must have seen a lot of changes in this neighborhood.

LR: Yes, they wanted me to sell this church and move out in the suburbs, but I wouldn't go! The Honorable Elijah Muhammad wanted to buy all this property, and his people, they offered me fifty million dollars for what we owned from this corner to the next, but I told them, "No, I'm going to stay right here because the city is going to move back." That's what I was preaching about twenty-three years ago. I told them that by the year 2000 you will have a series of new housing projects being built down State Street and throughout this neighborhood because the white people are going to move back into the city, and the blacks will be the ones who will be left out there in the suburbs.

TB: It seems that you were and are an accurate prophet.

LR: I said they are not going to let the blacks take the lake for themselves. Pretty soon they're gonna want to take it back!

TB: During all these many years, you have continued to be one of the few truly inspirational leaders of our community. Where did we lose the rest of that kind of leadership which once we had?

LR: In my opinion, although we didn't know it at the time, integration was the worst thing that ever happened to us.

TB: We thought we were doing the right thing.

LR: See, there's one God, and there's only one race: the human race! All of these churches, all of these denominations, all this racism in all of its forms, all of that is nothing but artificial dividers between people—but the minute we started to become more fully integrated that's when we started to lose our positions as schoolteachers, as lawyers, as doctors, even as family providers!

TB: Right now most of our families are in serious trouble.

LR: Especially our young boys. The first Cook County Jail at Twenty-sixth and California was built in 1928. Then they built a new one in 1984, and they built another new one in 1996.

TB: And they still don't have enough room for all the young black men that they have arrested!

LR: Seventy percent of all the prisoners at the county jail are black. They have no freedom. A lot of it is because of drugs, because drugs have such an enormous market, but it can't be the blacks that are using all those drugs because they are the ones that they are locking up!

TB: Yes, and that's exactly the kind of thing that Robeson was fighting against.

LR: Yes, he fought against it, and the Honorable Elijah Muhammad fought against it. S. B. Fuller fought against it. Oscar DePriest fought against it.

TB: But now, at this point in our history, we don't have that kind of leadership that should be bringing us together. What do you think is the reason for that?

LR: It's because of racism. See, racism has messed up our lives.

TB: It has messed up the lives of all Americans.

LR: That's right. It's not just the blacks anymore. It's the whole of America. The way it is now, the whites per capita are worse off than we are. You have somewhere about sixteen or eighteen or twenty families that are running America, and all the rest don't even seem to care. The way things are now it's too bad. It didn't have to be this way, but I suppose it's just a fact of life because it's the way that things have come to be.

TB: Where does most of your congregation come from now? From this neighborhood?

LR: From all over.

TB: But most of them used to live within walking distance.

LR: Yes, from across the street and all around here, but now only about 15 percent of the people who come here live in the neighborhood. A lot of the people come here from the suburbs for the Sunday morning service, but most of them don't want to come back here on Sunday night. I'd have to say that about 50 percent of my congregation doesn't ever come to the Sunday night service, and yet it used to be filled to capacity. Now there's nobody here, and it just breaks your heart, but that's just the way it is.

TB: It's a different world and a different time.

LR: Yes, but one thing has remained constant.

TB: And what is that?

LR: We are a refuge!

February 28, 1997

SAM NOLAN

LONGTIME POLICE OFFICER

This conversation with Sam Nolan came following his retirement from the Chicago Police Department after more than thirty-five years of service, part of which time he served as the head of the Youth Division and then later as the temporary superintendent of the entire department. Not long after our conversation, he moved to Hilton Head, South Carolina.

It was back during the time that he was head of the Youth Division that I first got to know Sam. At that time I was teaching at Hyde Park High School in Chicago, and the Blackstone Rangers had just begun to emerge and solidify as a powerful street gang. There had been a series of attacks and other acts of violence in and around the schools in the Woodlawn area, and Sam Nolan and his staff immediately began to move in on this escalating problem because he and his fellow officers were already familiar with the source and knew what might be the appropriate remedy. This was particularly true of the black officers, who already were thoroughly familiar with the neighborhood where these problems were concentrated. At that time it happens that the future leader of the Blackstone Rangers, Jeff Fort, was still a student in one of my classes, and I knew how to handle him, and I believe that he knew that I knew how to handle him. However, while I was away for a week attending a conference on race that was convened by President Lyndon Johnson, officials from the administration of Hyde Park High School expelled Jeff Fort and several of his associates. During the ensuing chaos, I have been told by friends of mine who were members of the police back then that all the black police officers were removed from duty in that area and were replaced by white officers. Sam Nolan was one of those who were replaced, and so, as the result of this policy, the gangs went on an unimpeded rampage, destroying parts of Woodlawn and then going on to other areas as well.

In this conversation we will hear Sam Nolan's perspective on his early experiences and how they helped to prepare him for a life of service to the people of his community.

––––––

TB: Your mother and dad, were they born here?

SN: My mother was born in Collinsville, Illinois, and my dad was born in College Grove, Tennessee, which is a place that's right outside of Nashville.

TB: Do you have any brothers or sisters?

SN: I had one sister. She was born and raised here in Chicago. She died at the age of forty-six, and she left three daughters—my nieces. Two of them are still living here, and one is in Nashville, Tennessee, at the present time.

TB: Where were your parents living when you were born?

SN: At Thirty-sixth and Vincennes—3632 Vincennes to be exact!

TB: Do you still remember any of your early experiences living there?

SN: Well, for one thing, I remember very well the time I fell out of my grandfather's vegetable wagon and into the sewer!

TB: Your grandfather sold vegetables?

SN: Yes, he sold vegetables in the city five days a week from a horse-drawn wagon.

TB: Did you go down the alleys?

SN: Yes, but sometimes we'd park on the corner. It was an after-school job for me just as soon as I was old enough to make change for a dollar. You know what I mean? Old enough to sell a ten-cent pail of sweet potatoes and not make any kind of mistake!
[*Laughter.*]
As soon as I was able to do that, I got a job on the truck.

TB: How old were you when you started working on your granddad's truck?

SN: About seven or eight years old.

TB: And so in your life you learned very early that there was something you had to do besides just play.

SN: In our house that was a must! My grandfather was stricter than my father, but the strictest one of the bunch was my mother. Anyway, it was no big thing for me to work like that. Dealing with people has always been a pleasure for me. Always a real pleasure!

TB: What all did you sell?

SN: Green beans, sweet potatoes, collard greens, corn—anything that was in season. People would call down to us from the third floor or wherever they were living, and they'd say, "Boy, bring me up a pail of potatoes!"

TB: Where did your granddad get his produce?

SN: From the market over at Twenty-second Street. He would go there at about four in the morning to get his vegetables, and then he'd bring 'em back, and the rest of us—me and my uncles—we would go and help him sell 'em after school was over.

TB: How many of you were there?

SN: Well, there were four of us. My three uncles were all young guys close to my own age. William Jr. was my grandfather's youngest son. Walter was the middle one, and Clifford was the one who was nearest my own age. As such, all of us come together. We all lived in an old two-story house: my mother and dad, my grandfather, my uncles, my sister, and me.

TB: So there were three generations living under one roof!

SN: Yes, but we liked it like that. We felt comfortable with that arrangement. We felt we were lucky. We felt we were rich.

TB: Your granddad was from where?

SN: My mother's father also came out of Collinsville, Illinois. That was his home.

TB: Was he born during the period of slavery?

SN: Yes, but he was born a free man.

TB: It's important for people to know about things like that because many people think that all black folks that live in America are descended from slaves, and that doesn't happen to be true.

SN: Well, in my case it wasn't.

TB: Now, by this time we're talking about, both you and your sister are going to school. What elementary school did you go to?

SN: My first one was Fuller School at Forty-second and St. Lawrence.

TB: I also went to kindergarten at Fuller.

SN: If you did, then you know all about it, and from there I went to Willard at Forty-ninth and St. Lawrence.

TB: When did you go to Willard?

SN: I left Fuller in the middle of the first grade and went directly to Willard and stayed there until the fourth grade. Then I went out to McCosh and stayed out there until I graduated in '33. So consequently, I must have started out at Willard School about 1928 or '29.

TB: What was the neighborhood like physically and socially during that period of time from when you started at Fuller until you went out to McCosh?

SN: I guess I was old enough to realize that blacks were moving farther south in the city, and what I remember so vividly is that we were in the first of that flow, and when I used to come home from school I always had to run all the way from Champlain to South Park or else take a licking from the white kids. One of the guys that I had the biggest problem with turned out to be a good friend of mine later on. His name was Douglas Block, and he was a nephew of a fellow named Sam—I forget his last name—who was the only guy giving credit to blacks when they wanted to buy watches. He'd come around every payday and collect fifty cents to a dollar from anyone who wanted a watch. That's how he sold all his watches!

TB: He probably made a mint!

SN: Probably, but even so, none of the others would sell to blacks. Not on credit! You'd have to walk into the store with all the money in your hand if you wanted to buy a watch or anything like that.

TB: What was the neighborhood like physically back then?

SN: When I was going to school at Willard, we were living at 5017 St. Lawrence, and most of the blacks in that neighborhood were living in apartments, and some owned their own homes. Jewel Lafontant and her relatives lived around there, didn't they?

TB: Yes, and also the first black pediatrician in Chicago, whose name I forget right now. He had an office on Thirty-fifth Street, in the old Supreme Life Building.

SN: You mean Anthony Beasley? He turned out to be the doctor for Joe Louis's children.

TB: That's right, and Joe Louis's trainer—Chappie Blackburn—also lived in that same block.

SN: It was a wonderful neighborhood with a lot of great people and beautiful homes.

TB: But then your family went on to Woodlawn.

SN: Yes, we went from there to 6424 Champlain, which was in the heart of Wood-lawn, and in that neighborhood the people were different, and they had their own circle, and it was tough for us to break into that social circle. For them, if you were light skin, you ran with a certain group. If you were dark skin, like myself, you may know them, you may speak to them, you may even play with them, but you are not included in their in crowd, if you know what I mean.

TB: I certainly do! There was a class within a class that had developed which was based entirely on degree of pigmentation.

SN: And that's what we discovered for ourselves when we moved to Woodlawn.

TB: At about that same time in the early thirties, when the great sociologist E. Franklin Frazier was getting his doctorate at the University of Chicago, he said that Woodlawn was the most solidly middle-class black community in the entire country—and he knew exactly what he was talking about because he had to live in Woodlawn himself. You see, back then he wasn't allowed to live on the U of C campus.

SN: Well, at least my mother didn't seem to be too much troubled by any of that nonsense. You see, she and my father had separated by then, and so I suppose she didn't have much time to worry about social life, or who knew who, because she was so busy doing day work. Back then all my mother had time to do was to go to work and come back and make sure that we kids had something to eat and proper clothes to wear. She would not want us to be seen anywhere unless what we were wearing was clean and pressed. She died in '46, and—God bless her!—we always tried to remember all those things she taught us.

TB: That sense of discipline and self-respect.

SN: Especially the discipline! Let me give you just one example of that discipline. One Sunday, when I was just a little guy about four or five years old, I had to go to church with my mother. It was the Baptist church at Thirty-seventh and Langley, and after the service we had to walk back to where we were living, at 3632 Vincennes. Well, my mother had me all dressed up in a white suit, and I thought I was really something! I wanted an ice-cream cone, and she said, "No!" So I said, "But I want an ice-cream cone!" and she said no again. So I started to throw a fit, and that woman—oh my, the strength she must've had—she took a picket off a fence—just tore it off—and whipped my fanny from Thirty-seventh and Vincennes all the way down to Thirty-sixth Place!
[*Laughter.*]
So I know all about discipline, and I know it well because I was taught by one of the champions.

TB: Yes, as I recall all too well, parents of that particular period recognized the importance of good behavior, and, therefore, they were always willing to enforce it on their children whenever and wherever they might have happened to be.

SN: Strong enforcement like that is something I guess we will always remember.

TB: When your family moved to Woodlawn, what grade were you in?

SN: Oh, I must have been in about the seventh grade.

TB: So this is about 1931.

SN: Nineteen thirty-one or '32.

TB: And that neighborhood was just beginning to change.

SN: Yes, like I said, we were one of the first black families to move into that community.

TB: Do you remember any of the other blacks that lived in that neighborhood?

SN: Yes, there was this large police officer that they used to call Big Six. He lived right next door to St. Anselm's Church, and I remember one morning he was coming home from work carrying a bottle of milk, and he fell and cut a tendon in his hand when he fell on the glass from that bottle. I don't think he could have had too much use out of that hand after that, but he still had all of our respect.

TB: That name had a lot of reputation.

SN: He was someone you'd always look up to. We never called him Big Six. What we'd say is, "Here comes *Mr.* Six!"

TB: The reason I'm familiar with that whole neighborhood is because in the thirties, after I graduated from high school, I got a job as a grocery boy at that grocery store that was at 5919 Michigan Avenue.

SN: That was right near the El, next to a cleaning shop, wasn't it?

TB: That's right.

SN: After a little while my family moved over to 6043 Calumet, but I still went to McCosh, and I stayed there until I graduated. You know, Tim, after I was in the department, they called me back to give a speech to the graduating class, and that year one of the people that received an award was Mrs. Campbell. She had been my music teacher, and it was such a treat for me to see that woman again! The assembly hall was smaller than I remembered, but the kids had it all painted up and placed a lot of interesting stuff on the walls. It was just a beautiful day!

TB: So when you graduated from McCosh, you then went to where?

SN: In 1933 I went to Englewood High School and stayed there until I graduated.

TB: What was your experience like at Englewood?

SN: It was very good because many of us had already had some experience in integrated schools. So I was just fine in terms of breaking in there. I was a member of the school patrol and all that stuff. I ran track out there, and we had a great track team. Buddy Young won the state championship while I was there.

TB: What was the percentage of black students at Englewood back then?

SN: Well, when I got ready to graduate, we were up to about a third. That's where I met my wife in '36. Two years later we were married.

TB: What about the faculty?

SN: The faculty was not very integrated. In fact, all I can recall are three black teachers, and one of them—our algebra teacher—was so light that most people didn't think much about what color she was!

TB: When you left Englewood, what did you do?

SN: Well, in 1937 I went down to Tennessee State University—at that time they called it Tennessee A & M—and I had a couple run-ins of a racial nature.

TB: Such as?

SN: Well, for example, in the town I ran into this guy who was walking around barefooted wearing these mean-looking bib overalls. He was just looking as crummy as could be, and he was telling me that I've got to call him sir.

TB: Until then you'd had no experience like that at all?

SN: No, and so I discussed the situation down there with one of my uncles, and he advised me to come back to Chicago and enter one of the junior colleges. Well, I decided to follow his advice, but when I got back here, I found out that this girl that I'd been dating was starting to date someone else, so I asked her to marry me, and she did! So now I'm a married man, and I have some financial responsibilities, and pretty soon I found out that money was not as easy to make as I had thought it might be, and so instead of going back to school, I had to take a job mopping floors at a drugstore at Thirty-ninth and what is now King Drive. It was owned by a bunch of brothers who had three or four drugstores on the South Side.

TB: The Mirsky brothers?

SN: Yes, that was them. I also worked for a while in their store on Roosevelt Road over at Western Avenue. Then I worked for them at Fifty-eighth and Calumet. Fifty-first and Michigan was the last store of theirs that I worked in, and one day a girl that I knew came in there while I was wiping off the stools at the lunch counter, and she said, "Sam, you come from Englewood. You ran track, and you always had good grades. What are you doing here? Why aren't you in school?" So I told her that I'm making money to feed my family because that was exactly what I was doing, and I wasn't bashful about it. Before that, I'd gone downtown and shined shoes, wiped floors, run errands, and things of that nature. Sometimes I made as much as seventy-five cents a day in tips, and back then that seemed like big money to me. At the end of the day I would go home and take the money and lay it out on the bed. Then my wife and I would count it, but first we'd close the bedroom door to make sure nobody was keeping tabs on us! [*Laughter.*]

TB: But you did go back to school, didn't you?

SN: Yes, but not till after I joined the police force.

TB: When did you join?

SN: It was in 1945. Congressman Dawson had been complaining about the lack of black police officers in Chicago, and the mayor—I forget just who the mayor was at that time, but it might have been Kelly—agreed with him to hire one hundred new black officers. I was lucky to be one of that one hundred! We came in as temporaries, like I said, because of Congressman Dawson, but then in 1947 they gave us an examination, and out of those one hundred guys, only thirteen made it. Now that's not a very good percentage, but some of those guys really didn't like police work anyway, and so it was only thirteen of us that stayed in there.

TB: How many blacks in total were on the force at that time?

SN: One hundred and twenty-six.

TB: Out of a force of how many?

SN: About six thousand.

TB: There were already a few high-ranked black officers back then. Was Sylvester Washington still on the force?

SN: Yes, he was on the force at that time, but the guy we really looked up to was Harry Deas, who was commander of the Fourth District. At that time we had no black lieutenants. We had one captain, six sergeants, and all the rest were patrolmen.

TB: So as part of your training, they sent you back to school.

SN: Yes, a lot of people think that it was O. W. Wilson that started the educational requirements for the police department, but it was Timothy J. O'Connor. He—along with the mayor—set up the junior college program for incoming officers and also the master's program at the Illinois Institute of Technology. That's why the training academy is named after him.

TB: What school did they send you to?

SN: I started off at Wright Junior College because the police department had a class there. Later on, I took a lot of classes at the University of Chicago, Roosevelt University, and DePaul University. I learned a lot, but I never got a degree.

TB: When you first started out on the force, where were you assigned?

SN: When you first start out, they always put you on the dogwatch, which is from twelve at night until nine o'clock in the morning.

TB: This is as a foot patrolman?

SN: Yes, and the area that I patrolled was all the way from the station down to Thirty-first Street and Cottage Grove. Now that's a lot of territory for one new patrolman on the midnight shift, and I was worried about it, but I was scared to mention anything for fear of being fired. As it turned out, the sergeant must have read my mind because he said, "Don't worry. There will always be a patrol car—Number 149—close by to watch out for you rookies if there is any trouble." So that eased my mind a little, but what he didn't tell me was that if there weren't enough white police officers on duty to put in that patrol car, then that car stayed in the garage during that midnight shift I'd been assigned to.

TB: On those occasions you were out on your own.

SN: Well, it worked out all right, and a little while later they transferred me over to the Woodlawn Station at Sixty-third and Harper.

TB: At that time what was the racial composition of the neighborhood?

SN: This was in 1947, and it was pretty well integrated at that time—about fifty-fifty—but there was still a great distinction between black and white police officers in that district. Back then there was a problem with blacks crossing over on Cottage Grove, and I'll never forget that one of the white guys I was working with told me to remember just one thing: "We both wear the same badge. Those white SOBs over there want to start some stuff, but we won't let them. We're going to keep the peace here by working together to keep Cottage Grove from being crossed by either whites or blacks!" So that's what we did.

TB: How long did you stay there at the Woodlawn Station?

SN: I was there less than two years because most of the black policemen were re-assigned to areas west of Cottage Grove. My territory was South Park and Sixty-first up to St. Lawrence and Sixty-third. The guy I was working with was Charlie Younger. I don't know if you knew Charlie.

TB: Yes, I had Charlie Younger's kids in my classes at Hyde Park.

SN: Well, a lot of people don't know this, but, putting aside all the goofy things he did, Charlie Younger could have been the first black superintendent of the Chicago Police Department if only he had put his mind to it.

TB: I can believe that because I got to know him quite well during the '68 riots. I went with him over to the West Side. What we were trying to do was to get those kids off the street. We both knew that some of those other cops would take advantage of the situation and blow those kids away.

SN: And they did exactly that to some of them.

TB: If you gave them any indication that you were out of order, they didn't give you a second chance. So Charlie asked me to go with him, and we went over there. I was scared to death, but Charlie went on in there, and I was amazed at how well he functioned.

SN: Here's the thing about Charlie. When it got down to real police work, nobody was any better than he was, and he was really proud of the fact that there was nobody any better than he was. There wasn't a dad-blasted one of them in the entire force that knew police work and could act out on the street as effectively as he could. He could always tell who should be treated with kid gloves and who he should stand up to and dare them to make a move or put their hands anywhere near their pockets. I learned so much from him, but I was never able to put any of it to much practical use.

TB: And why is that?

SN: Because after all that, I was reassigned once again, and there is a lot that you cannot do when your job is to sit behind a desk.

May 14, 1993, and May 21, 1993

ELLA SAUNDERS

JAZZ AFICIONADO

Ella Saunders is the widow of the late Ted "Red" Saunders, the legendary drummer and bandleader at the now demolished though still warmly remembered Club DeLisa. Visitors—black, white, brown, or any other possible mixture, famous or unknown, local, national, or international—always found time to visit the DeLisa when in town, and, of course, people who happened to live in Chicago went there on a regular basis. Guests would always plan to set aside at least one evening during their stay to go to the club to hear and see Red Saunders's great band and the artists and celebrities who gathered there to perform and also to be entertained.

I first met Ella Saunders when I visited their home on East Fifty-fifth Place, near Washington Park. It was always a thrilling experience for me to go there because I knew that I might get the opportunity to meet one of the jazz giants who happened to be in town, such as Johnny Hodges of the Duke Ellington Orchestra or some other famous or soon-to-be-famous person. I got this unique opportunity because of my neighbor and friend Bill Allen, who was a drummer in Captain Walter Dyett's band at DuSable High School. Red Saunders was eager to help Bill (and many others as well) learn to improve his musical techniques. Ella was very supportive of this and was, in fact, like a big sister to all these aspiring young musicians.

Ella was born of mixed parentage and raised in Chicago. She had been a trained dancer and appeared professionally on the stage, but after she and Red were married, she confined herself to rearing their children and being his most ardent booster.

After Red's death, in my conversations with Ella, I learned more about their personal and professional life together, and also much more about the social, economic, and political culture of the jazz music industry as it once existed here in Chicago.

TB: I'm here talking with Ella Saunders, who is a longtime friend and aficionado of music, about her life and her memories of the Jazz Age in Chicago.

ES: Well, to start with, as you know, I was born here in Chicago. My father was born here too, in 1890. He died in 1967. Mama was from Nashville, and she died when she was 48. My dad's mother was from Albany, New York, but her family was originally from Germany. I remember Grandma saying that her sister Elizabeth was born on the boat that brought them to America. Since she was older than Grandma, that would mean that my grandma was born in the United States. She and her family must have come to live here in Chicago sometime before the Great Fire of 1871 because she told me that their home was damaged by the fire and that they had to go to the lake to get away from the smoke.

TB: What about your father's father? What was his ancestry?

ES: Dad's dad was born in Detroit. His mother was Cherokee Indian, and his father was mulatto. They both looked white, but they were very strong race people. Daddy was too, and I'm sure you remember how fair Daddy was!

TB: What do you remember about your mother's parents?

ES: My mama's mother was also Cherokee Indian. She was born in Lookout Mountain in the Cherokee Territory, and she told us stories about how the soldiers ran them out. She lived to be over 103 years old, but she never lost her mental faculties. Grandy looked Indian, and yet she had those bright blue eyes because her daddy was a white man. When her mother died, her mother's sister raised her, and then when her aunt died, her father—this white man—raised her himself, and she was well educated.

TB: How many sisters and brothers did you have?

ES: I had five sisters and four brothers. There were ten of us.

TB: Where was your family living when you were born?

ES: They were living with my grandmother in her house on the South Side, either on Bryant Avenue or Browning Avenue. There is something about that that I still remember, and this is something that I think is very beautiful. We weren't raised within the race. We had an interracial house. We had all these Germans in the house, and race was never discussed. We just judged people by who they were and not by the color of their skin. You were either good people or you were bad people—so we had friends of all colors and all languages. My godmother was also German. When she died, she still had that very strong accent that she'd always had.

TB: Have you and your family lived on the South Side most of your life?

ES: Yes, I remember as a kid that we were living right down there at 3024 Prairie.

TB: That was a nice neighborhood.

ES: A very nice neighborhood. Back then I thought we were rich! Our next-door neighbor was Elijah Johnson, who was a real estate man. His wife was named Lolita, and their chauffeur used to take their children and all of us over to the park.

TB: Back in that period, that neighborhood was still part of the Gold Coast. Black people from the South were beginning to move into the area, but these were people who had pretty good middle-class standards—people like Ida Mae Cress and her brother Ernest Griffin—and so it continued to be a mixed neighborhood for quite a while.

ES: Yes, as a matter of fact, Ernest Griffin remembered knowing Daddy. We lived there when my brother Earl was born in 1921, and so we must have moved there just before then.

TB: That was just after the race riot.

ES: The race riot was in 1919, and I was still an infant—so I didn't know anything about the race riot.

TB: My own family came to Chicago at about the same time from Birmingham, and I didn't know anything about it either.

ES: We were just too young to know.

TB: Which schools did you go to?

ES: The first school I went to was Drake. Then, when the family began to get bigger, we moved to 441 East Forty-eighth Place, and I went to Willard School.

TB: I also went to Willard, but it was overcrowded, and so I went to Burke a little later.

ES: I wasn't there for more than a year myself because we moved to Morgan Park in 1928, and I went to Shoop School and graduated in June of '29.

TB: Did you go to Morgan Park High School?

ES: Yes. It was very highly rated at that time.

TB: And you met your future husband, Red, right after high school, didn't you?

ES: No, as a matter of fact, I first met Red while I was still in high school. I met him through the Denisons, who were friends of our family.

TB: Would that be the family of Colonel Denison, who was the head of the Eighth Regiment in the 1916 Mexican campaign and in France during World War I?

ES: Yes, but he was dead by then. We always called Edna, his wife, Mama Denison. I don't remember who was the oldest of her children, but there was

Dorothy, George, Frank, Denise, and the baby, Jacqueline. Well, anyway, Denise was about my age, and she was working after school at the Indiana Theater. I had already asked Daddy to let me work after school so I could have some fun on the weekend, and he'd said, "No, you can't do it." But then, when Denise asked Daddy if I could also work as an usherette at the Indiana Theater, Daddy thought that if Mrs. Denison thought it was all right for her daughter to work there, maybe it would be all right for me as well, so Daddy agreed and let me do it!

TB: The Indiana Theater was on Forty-third Street, between Indiana and Prairie.

ES: Yes, and the Denison home was at Forty-third and Vincennes—so we would stay at Mama Denison's house on weekends. You see, my sister Sue and I both got jobs as usherettes, and pretty soon whom do you think I met?

TB: Red?

ES: Red! You see, I had to go back home Sunday night, and Mama Denison didn't have a car at that time. So I had to take the trolley all the way out to Morgan Park, and that was quite a long ride! Well, Red had this little car—the kind they called a tin lizzie—and sometimes he would drive me home.

TB: How did your father feel about that?

ES: When my father found out that this musician was driving me home, he was ready to kill me! He told Mama that he didn't want a musician like that in the house or anywhere near his family. You see, in those days musicians were supposed to be trashy—and jazz musicians especially! But I had already met Red's family, and they seemed to be very nice people. They certainly weren't trashy people. Not at all!

TB: So at that time his family was living here in Chicago.

ES: Yes, but his mother had died when he was five years old, and his sister Lucille was the one who had raised him.

TB: His family originally came from New Orleans, didn't they?

ES: No, as a matter of fact, none of Red's family was from New Orleans. Red was born in Memphis, and he was twelve years old when his family moved up to Chicago. When they first came here, they lived with Louis and Lil Armstrong at Forty-sixth, right off of South Park. You see, Lil and Lucille, Red's older sister, had gone to school together in Memphis.

TB: Do you remember anything about Red's parents? Where they were from or anything like that?

ES: His father—J. H. Saunders—was originally from Alabama, and his mother was from Mayersville, Mississippi. As a matter of fact, his father owned the town! He was white, and Red's mother was black, and they never married.

TB: We had a lot of that sort of thing going on back then—and it didn't mean that they didn't like each other either. Sometimes couples like that were very much in love, but the law and customs of that time—

ES: They didn't allow them to marry.

TB: Even so, many of those fathers tried to provide a good education for their children. But getting back to Red and your dad, it seems that a sort of struggle was beginning to develop between them.

ES: That's right. Daddy forbade him to come into our house. One summer night when Red dropped me off at home, there was my father in the living room, pretending to read a newspaper, just waiting for me to arrive. You see, he knew Red would be bringing me home, and he had already told me I shouldn't see him. Anyway, Red said hello in the politest possible manner, but Daddy just grunted back at him. I mean, if he said hello, you certainly didn't hear him—and then he looked up from his newspaper, and that's when Daddy read him the riot act. He told him that he was not to see his daughter anymore and that in his opinion musicians like Red were just the lowest. You see, my father worked down in City Hall, but he also worked in the evenings as a waiter in some of the nightclubs, and so he thought he knew all about musicians and the kind of life they lead.

TB: Your dad was just making an assumption that was based on some of the people that he had seen. Which nightclubs did he work in?

ES: The Dreamland, the Sunset, and the Plantation.

TB: Those were the big clubs. The Dreamland was at 3518 South State, and the Sunset and the Plantation were facing each other on Thirty-fifth Street, near Calumet. I remember them so well because my dad used to go back to Thirty-fifth Street a lot because he continued to have a great many friends that lived around there. But I'm also quite sure that he went there because it was a very exciting place to be and to witness the emergence of our music. Was Red playing drums at the Indiana Theater?

ES: Yes, but Red hadn't been playing there for very long. He had only been playing professionally for maybe five or six years at that time.

TB: Was the Regal Theater open by then?

ES: No, they still had those big mansions there back then. The Regal and the Savoy weren't built until '27 or '28. Around that same time, while we were living down at Forty-eighth Place, one day Grandma decided that it was time for me to have dancing lessons. So she took me to the Net Studio, right there upstairs at Forty-seventh Street, and I had ballet lessons, and Hazel Thompson Davis was my teacher for tap. Well, Daddy didn't approve of that either. He said, "No dancing!" But Grandma—she was his mother, and in those days she was the matriarch; she ran the household—she told me, "You keep on taking those lessons. They'll give you poise and grace."

TB: This was in the late twenties?

ES: No, this was in the early thirties, and, believe me, that poise and grace came in handy because after I graduated from high school there were no jobs.

TB: The Depression had broken out by then.

ES: Yes, and that's why we moved to Morgan Park. Before that, we had a fifteen-room house at Forty-eighth Place, but Daddy decided to make an apartment out of the ballroom, which was on the top floor. I didn't understand why he wanted to rent out an apartment like that, but now I know that it was probably because the times were getting tough. I remember that we had a chandelier with cut-glass prisms above the dining-room table. Once a month I had to stand on the table and take all those prisms down. Sue had a dish in which to wash them and a dish in which to rinse. Mama would supervise what we were doing, and she'd hand them back to me, and I had to put them all back up. There had to be a million of those prisms—and I used to wish that damn thing would just fall down from the ceiling!

[*Laughter.*]

A little later, after we moved to Morgan Park, I said to Sue—I was a regular little devil, see?—"Let's go back and take a look at our old house." So we went and knocked on the door, and I told the lady that was living there that we had moved away and that I loved the house because I was raised there. "Could we look in?" Well, she was nice, and she let us in. There was the big reception hall, and then there were two parlors. From the second parlor you could look right into the dining room, but now there was a string light fixture hanging from the ceiling. Oh, my goodness, our beautiful chandelier was gone! I said thank you to the lady, but I was hurt because the chandelier was not there anymore. Many years later, when I had already started working down at City Hall, where Daddy had been working all the time we were growing up, I told him about the time we went back to our old house, and that was the first he ever knew about our ever going back because he would have killed us for doing a thing like that. I said, "Daddy, they had this string light coming out of the ceiling, and our beautiful chandelier was gone!" Daddy just laughed, and he said, "They never saw that beautiful chandelier," and that was because he himself had sold it! He said we needed the money—and that's why we eventually had to give up the entire house as well.

TB: Things were tough. Even my daddy lost his job—and back then weren't no welfare, weren't no Social Security, weren't none of that! But, of course, we didn't have much of anything, and so we didn't have much of anything to lose.

ES: Well, I think Grandma had some money put away, but then all of this cut glass and beautiful stuff that she had gradually started to disappear! I didn't think anything of it at the time. As a kid, it just meant something I wouldn't ever have to wash again, but I suppose if it hadn't been for her doing that, we would have really been in bad shape. So anyway, we moved out of a fifteen-room mansion and into an eight-room house in Morgan Park. At that time my father was working two jobs in order to take proper care of us, and so during all that time, we never knew a single hungry day.

TB: Were you still seeing Red?

ES: Well, as I said, Daddy told me that I was not supposed to see him anymore—so after that, I would always make Red leave me off a few blocks away, and I would walk the rest of the way home. Daddy would be out there on the porch waiting to see that I got home all right—so I defied him and kept on seeing Red anyway! [*Laughter.*]

Then one day Red tells me that the show *Harlem Scandals* is auditioning for chorus girls and musicians and that he had already been hired by Curtis Mosby, the bandleader, as a drummer, and so I decided that I would go to those auditions as well! The show was originally from California, and I guess they had lost part of their cast along the way—so they were regrouping here in Chicago because they were on the Balaban and Katz circuit, and then they were going to hit the road again. The auditions were being held at the Vincennes Hotel on Thirty-sixth Street, where they had this big ballroom that we rehearsed in.

TB: The clarinet player that used to play there was Jimmie Noone.

ES: Yes, I knew Jimmie Noone, but anyway, I went there and auditioned and was accepted and became one of the fifteen girls in their chorus line. I told Mama about this, but, of course, I didn't tell Daddy. Oh, seventy-five dollars a week— that was a lot of money in those days! Up till then I couldn't even get a job paying twenty-five dollars weekly. I could only find work on the weekend at the Indiana Theater, and some of those weekends I didn't even work because they only needed one usherette. So anyway, I told Mama, and I brought her to meet the people that I was working with in the show. There was Norman Thomas, who played the piano and who, as it happened, already knew my father. His own son was one of the dancers in the show. Earl Shanks sang, and Freddy Crump was a sensational drummer who was featured in the show. Well, after she met all of them, I decided to tell Daddy and bring him to see the show. Mama was with me, and she said, "They seem to be nice people, Matt," but Dad said, "They're damn show people. Musicians! I'll bet she's with that musician again!" Well, by this time Red is asking me to marry him, but I hadn't told Daddy about any of this. I knew if I did he was going to kill me for sure! "Marry that trash!" Anyway, Daddy says, "I don't want you going down there rehearsing anymore," but he knew me. He knew that I was stubborn. He knew that I was going to defy him, and so I told Mama, "I don't care what he says. I can't get any kind of a job around here, and I don't have money to go to college—so I'm going to take this job no matter what he says," but, even so, I didn't ever lie to him. I told him where the rehearsals were and everything. Well, anyway, so Mama goes with me, and guess who shows up at the rehearsal but Daddy himself, and he sees Norman Thomas, and Mr. Thomas introduces him to Curtis Mosby. Well, the two of them are the ones that own the show, and Mr. Thomas tells him, "Don't worry about her. I'll keep an eye on her. She'll be well taken care of. We don't bother with any kind of foolishness around here." Daddy still said, "I don't want her with that trashy drummer," but he finally broke down and bought me some luggage and even helped me to pack!

TB: Sounds like a daddy all right!

ES: But he still said he didn't want me to be with Red. What he didn't know was that Red had already given me this little chipped diamond ring. It was so small you couldn't even find the diamond!

[*Laughter.*]

The first stop we made after we left Chicago was in Milwaukee, at the Alhambra Theater. After we left Milwaukee, we played several smaller cities in Wisconsin, doing week-long shows, and then we started hitting those little hick towns out west, and we'd do some one-nighters. After that, we had to come back to Chicago to get new costumes and everything. Capezio made our shoes. They took the prints of your feet, and, after that, we could always order new dance shoes wherever it was that we happened to be. Anyway, when we came back to Chicago, I showed my father this little chipped diamond ring that Red had given me, and he just raised holy hell. He said, "You are not going back on that show!" But I did, and so Red and I got married in Indianapolis instead of back here. I really wanted for my family to be with me, and I've always said that if Daddy hadn't pushed so hard against my marrying Red, I probably wouldn't have married him right then but would have waited till a little later.

TB: Did your father ever get to like him?

ES: No! He never liked Red. He accepted him, but he never really liked him.

TB: And this is when? What year?

ES: 1933.

TB: And so now Prohibition is about to be invalidated.

ES: Yes, that's the year Roosevelt took office, but I couldn't vote then. I wasn't old enough.

TB: I couldn't either, but I can still remember the night that it was made official. All up and down Fifty-first Street people were just going wild. You still couldn't buy anything but beer, but around where I was growing up, there were all kinds of places where you could always get bootleg liquor, and on Fifty-first Street there was a place next to the alley where you could go and buy moonshine. I didn't have to do that kind of thing very often because I had an uncle who was on the road a lot, and he would bring back liquor from Canada and be a big shot because he had legitimate liquor!

[*Laughter.*]

Now, you and Red were living on the road during most of this time, weren't you?

ES: Yes, and we didn't come back here until '35. We came back when I found out that I was going to have a baby. If I wanted the baby, I knew that I had to stop dancing, and so my sister, Sue, took my place in the chorus line, but I still continued to travel with Red. I just came back here from time to time so that Mama could take me to see the doctor, and then I'd go back and join Red and travel with the show. We went all the way cross-country: Nebraska, Iowa, Michigan.

TB: Any place farther south?

ES: No, St. Louis was as far south as we went. In St. Louis we played two theaters, one of which was Madam Walker's Theater.

TB: Yes, back then there was a theater in St. Louis that was named for Madam C. J. Walker.

ES: And then, after we played that theater, we played a white theater.

TB: You played in one theater that was for the Negroes and in another that was for the whites?

ES: Yes, and that was the first time that I found that there was a difference even in a place as far north as St. Louis. It surprised me because we didn't have any problems like that around here. You know, something that always makes me angry is when I hear some of our people say, "We couldn't go to this place, we couldn't go here, we couldn't go there"—and that makes me angry because at that time you went wherever your money took you. I knew that this was true because all of my friends weren't fair-skinned people. We had very, very dark-skinned people that were our friends, and believe me, we went all over!

TB: Yes, Chicago was pretty open back then, but sometimes what would happen is that not the management but the other people—the patrons—they would try to make you feel uncomfortable. I knew about that because if Louis or Duke were in town, they were going to play downtown, and I didn't have any choice but to go and see them. I wouldn't wait until they got to the Regal because I wanted to brag to my friends about how I'd seen them already.

ES: My daddy didn't go down there because he didn't have the money. Money— that was the problem. Some people might want to make it appear that they couldn't go down there because of their color, but that wasn't true. At least not here in Chicago.

TB: But in St. Louis you'd run across that. St. Louis at that period was just like a Southern town, and everything was segregated.

ES: While we were in St. Louis, one time Red and I and some of our friends decided we wanted to go and see a baseball game, and so we went.

TB: St. Louis Cardinals or the Browns, which one?

ES: It was the Cardinals, but when we got there, they wouldn't let one of our friends in, and so none of us went—and that shocked me because I had never experienced anything like that before.

TB: My first real confrontation of that type was when I was in the army, and they sent us south to get our training. When I got down there, I didn't know what to do or how to handle myself, but our people down there knew how to protect people from the North, and so we didn't go to the show. When we went to town, we stayed in some neighbor's house. If we wanted to go someplace, they would drive us to where we wanted to go—but even so, at that time I was twenty-two years old, and for me that experience was really very shocking.

ES: It shocked all of us. Red was from the South, but he was only twelve years old when he left, and so he really didn't know anything about it either.

TB: So you came back to Chicago in '35, and that's when you must have decided to settle down because I first met you and Red in '41, and by that time it seemed like he had been the bandleader at the DeLisa for almost forever.

ES: Well, when we first came back here to Chicago, Red couldn't work a regular job. He had a traveling card in the international union, but he also had to join Local 208.

TB: There was no such thing as segregation in the International Musicians Union, which was headquartered out of New York. But, here in Chicago, Local 208 of the American Federation of Musicians was for blacks, and Local 10 was for whites.

ES: That's right, and so Red got a temporary card from Local 208 and then started working with Jimmie Noone at the Annex at Twenty-third and State. That's where he was working when Sonny was born. Do you remember Chippie Hill, the blues singer?

TB: I don't think I ever saw her, but I certainly heard about her.

ES: Well, she had a heart of gold, and she gave us the first baby gift we got.

TB: When did Red go over to the DeLisa?

ES: Red started at the Club DeLisa in '37, just before our son Edmond was born.

TB: Was this at the old DeLisa, which was on the west side of the street?

ES: Yes, Albert Ammons was the bandleader there, and he asked Red to join him.

TB: Who was in the band that you can remember?

ES: Delbert Bright was on clarinet, Frank Owens the saxophone player, Ike Perkins the guitar, Israel Crosby the bass, Albert Ammons the piano, and, of course, Red on the drums.

TB: In '37 I was still a teenager, and I couldn't go into those places—so I would just stand outside and listen. That's how I knew that Red Saunders was such a great show drummer. If ever the singer missed the beat, Red would always catch the beat back for her!

[*Laughter.*]

ES: When Albert Ammons decided to leave the DeLisa, he turned the band over to Del Bright, but Del didn't keep the band for very long because Horace Henderson asked him to join his own band when they left to go to California. So then, when Del left in the fall of '37, he gave the band to Red. He said the band couldn't stay there if Red didn't have it, and so the owner of the place—a guy named Mike—had to accept it, and he did so willingly. You see, by then Red was already very much a family man, and I think that Mike liked that. Mike was a rotten son-of-a-gun, but he was a home man. He believed in his family, and pretty soon Red became almost a part of that family. He would send us big trays full of all this Italian food because he wanted to make sure that we always had enough to eat, but we had to give most of that stuff away. It was just too much food!

TB: Everybody came to the DeLisa, and, if you stayed there long enough, you'd see almost all the celebrities that happened to be in town. I know I saw John Barrymore there at least once.

ES: Barrymore almost lived there. When we were living at Fifty-fifth Place—that's where I first met you—one morning I took my boys over to meet their daddy at the breakfast dance, and who should be there but John Barrymore, and he says he wants to kiss my children, and Edmond says, "No, you're too nasty!" It was so funny: Edmond, a little blond baby, telling John Barrymore he was nasty because he was drunk.

TB: How long was it before the new place opened across the street?

ES: It was close to a year later that the new place opened at 5521 State Street. Mike paid all the musicians half salary during the whole time they were off.

TB: During that period, Fifty-fifth Street was a very exciting place to be.

ES: It was beautiful, and it was very much alive.

TB: Besides the DeLisa, there was the Golden Lily, the Rhumboogie, and after hours, all the musicians used to hang out at a place called Herb's. Art Tatum used to come in there all the time and jam with the other guys. On my way home from the DeLisa I could stop at half a dozen good joints like that where I could drink my beer and hear great music.

ES: Yes, and do you remember that drugstore that was right next to the El and that Chinese restaurant that was right across the street?

TB: Yes, everywhere you went, there was something interesting to see or do or hear—and Red Saunders was well known and respected all over because he was such a fine musician and such a nice person. Most people didn't get to know him as well as I did, and that was my good fortune because you can't understand the history of our community without understanding and appreciating the music that Red and the other musicians were creating during this particular period of time.

September 14, 1992

FRED RICE

· ———

SUPERINTENDENT OF THE CHICAGO POLICE DEPARTMENT

Though we both attended DuSable High School, it was at different periods of time, and so I did not get to meet Fred until the late 1960s through mutual friends. He was and is a jovial person who until his retirement was deeply committed to his work as a law-enforcement officer. Throughout his career he was always very much involved with the prevention aspect of his chosen profession. When he was selected to become the superintendent of the Chicago Police Department by Mayor Harold Washington, the police force was still deeply divided internally along racial lines and tensions. In response to this, in his new position of authority, Fred Rice went to work immediately to confront and resolve those issues. He was always firm but fair in all his decisions for promotions and transfers and, as a result, for the first time blacks and Hispanics were able to rise to positions within the police force to which they were entitled but from which they had been excluded previously.

Though our conversation is not a lengthy one, it should provide the reader with some insight into the life and character of a man who attempted in his professional life to heal some of our society's deepest social wounds.

———

TB: Fred Rice was a longtime superintendent of police here in Chicago, and he is a person whom I have known for many years. Tell me, Fred, where were you born?

FR: I was born in Cook County Hospital here in Chicago on the twenty-fourth of December in 1926.

TB: And where were your mother and father born?

FR: My mother and father were both born in a town called Decatur on the Tennessee River in northern Alabama. It's about seventeen miles from Huntsville.

TB: Is that close to Muscle Shoals?

FR: Yes, Muscle Shoals is about forty miles from Decatur. That's the research headquarters for the Tennessee Valley Authority. When they built those dams there, they electrified that whole area down there and brought it into the twentieth century.

TB: Do you remember your grandparents?

FR: No, but I do know that my mother's father enlisted in the Union army during the Civil War. Evidently they must have come through Alabama and recruited blacks because there is no evidence that he went north to join the Union army. But we are certain that he went into the Union army because we have a copy of his discharge papers.

TB: The army did things like that back then. As they came through, they would give what they called a manumit of freedom to ex-slaves or even to those that were black and not enslaved. My granddad was given one of those in Alabama where he lived, and your granddad was probably given one as well.

FR: That must have been what happened.

TB: Now, tell me what are some of your earliest memories of your experiences growing up here in Chicago?

FR: Back then the area where most blacks were living was concentrated from Fifty-first Street to about Fifty-fifth Street just east of Cottage Grove, but then the University of Chicago was behind a program that they called urban renewal, and they tore all that area out. The blacks called it Negro removal at the time, and now all you can see are athletic fields down there. That was the neighborhood in which I grew up. At that time it was a crowded commercial and residential area, just west of the university along Fifty-fifth Street.

TB: As I remember it, that block was pretty stable.

FR: Yes, Tim, when I was growing up, I think there was only one family on our block in which the father was not living in the home, and that was because of the fact that in that particular family the father had died a premature death.

TB: So as you remember it, in each home there was a father along with the mother to raise the children.

FR: Yes, and you don't see that now.

TB: No, you don't.

FR: And you know something else? I can't remember any crime in that neighborhood. We used to leave our doors open all night long. We had a little latch on our door, and it stayed half-latched most of the time, but, of course, if a burglar would have broken in, there wasn't much that he could get. All he'd get might be a little practice!

[*Laughter.*]

We didn't have much. I think the radio was our most prized possession.

TB: What kind of programs do you remember listening to?

FR: Most of my radio listening as a kid was to the adventure programs that came on right after school: *Jack Armstrong, Superman, Gang Busters*, and programs like that. So we were much less sophisticated than today's children, who see all these examples of violence on television. They don't have to visualize the story in their minds like we used to do. Now they can see it right there in front of them on the television, and I think that all that violence that they see on television is one of the major reasons why we are living in such a violent society. When I was grow-ing up, things were different. Besides the radio, our only source of outside enter-tainment was one of those old Victrola phonographs.

TB: The kind you wind up?

FR: Yes, and every now and then my mother and dad would play some of the old church pieces that they liked to hear. Another thing that I remember is that kids were very inventive back then. We made our own toys. We made kites and bows and arrows. We made our own wagons out of fish boxes and baby buggy wheels. I suppose we were so inventive because our parents couldn't afford to buy us the toys we wanted. I remember that I bought a wagon in a store for myself when I was around eleven or twelve years old, but that was because I had worked and saved my own money to get that wagon. You see, I had a job at a grocery store, and I needed that wagon to transport people's groceries so I could earn a little more money. It also came in handy when I had a paper route when I was around twelve years old. I can still remember that my route was along South Park Way.

TB: So you began to work early.

FR: Very early.

TB: And back then many kids also began to work early.

FR: Yes, out of necessity.

TB: But whatever the reason, you developed an attitude toward going to a certain place at a certain time, staying there for a certain time, and learning to do some-thing while you were there.

FR: Well, I lived a much more disciplined life than what I see these kids do now, because I had to get up at a certain time, go out and work, get back home and then go to school—or sometimes go to school and then go to work. Before I was sixteen years old I had already had about four different jobs. I even worked over there in the 5400 block of Hyde Park Boulevard in a very exclusive restaurant as a busboy.

TB: Were there any other blacks working there?

FR: No, there weren't any blacks at all over there at that time. Blacks didn't start moving in in significant numbers until after the midfifties.

TB: Back then the only blacks that lived in that area were those who were employed as full-time domestics. Who do you remember from DuSable?

FR: We had quite a few good people. Judge Cousins was in my class. Arthur Hines, who went on to become vice president of Meharry Medical College, was also in my class. Gene Ammons, the great saxophonist, was at DuSable at the time.

TB: Was Johnny Hartman there?

FR: Johnny Hartman was there. We had Johnny Griffin in my class. We had an opera singer in my class named Adelaide Boatman. She became really famous out East.

TB: Yes, she did. I didn't know she went to DuSable.

FR: She was in my class, but she died at a very early age.

TB: Who are some of the teachers you remember?

FR: I remember quite a few of the teachers. I remember Ben Mosby.

TB: Everybody knew Ben!

FR: And, of course, Captain Dyett! Back then DuSable was famous for its musicians because of Captain Dyett. Captain Dyett was quite a dynamic bandleader!

TB: To say the least. Do you remember Mary Herrick?

FR: Who couldn't remember her?

TB: She was like Captain Dyett.

FR: I had Mrs. Jackson for French. She just died about two years ago, but there are still some of those teachers who are still living. One is Mr. Woodley. He used to teach chemistry. He didn't teach me because I dodged chemistry, but I got acquainted with him because he was the sponsor of some of the extracurricular activities that I was involved with. He was always a Lyric Opera aficionado, and he is still involved in a Lyric Opera club.

TB: He's continued to remain active.

FR: Mrs. Maudelle Bousfield's daughter Julia taught me botany.

TB: Back then they didn't have a single course called biology. They broke it down into botany and zoology.

FR: That's right—so I took both! But I remember Julia because she was so good-looking. All the boys were crazy about her, especially me, and I've often wondered if she is still alive. After all, she was still a young woman at that time.

TB: I'm sure some of those people are still living.

FR: But she is the one I fell in love with!

[*Laughter.*]

TB: While you were going to school were you still working as well?

FR: I was working all the time. I got a job at the post office, where you could work part-time and still go to school.

TB: Short hours?

FR: Short hours, yes! So I worked the school set down at the post office for seventy-two cents an hour until I graduated, and I continued to work there while I attended Wilson Junior College.

TB: Did you graduate from Wilson?

FR: I didn't graduate because I wasn't taking the core courses which were required, and then I was drafted into the army in 1950 and sent for my training down South.

TB: Had you ever been down South before?

FR: Yes, I was down in Alabama back when I was about eight years old. I will never forget going back to Decatur in the midsummer, visiting relatives that I didn't even know. That was a harrowing experience that I will never forget. This was in the late thirties, and they didn't have any modern facilities. They didn't have electricity or running water. Certainly no air conditioning or inside toilets. They had outhouses, and you had to get your water from a well. It was so hot, and you didn't get any relief at night. You'd look up at the trees at night, and not a leaf was moving. I was glad to get out of there, and I never wanted to go back.

TB: But then you went back South as a member of the armed services?

FR: Yes, after I was drafted, I was first sent to Fort Knox, Kentucky, and then to another camp just outside the city of New Orleans to complete my basic training. After that, they sent me overseas to Korea.

TB: What year was that?

FR: In February 1951 I arrived in Korea, and they placed me into an all-black unit called the Twenty-fourth Infantry. It was all black in spite of the fact that Truman, as you probably remember, had ordered the armed forces to become integrated in 1948, but General MacArthur was the commanding officer in the Far East at that time, and he resisted that order. He refused to integrate any army unit that was under his command, and so the Far East command didn't integrate until Truman fired MacArthur and put Ridgway in as commander.

TB: What happened to your unit?

FR: Ridgway retired the Twenty-fourth Infantry colors and integrated us into other elements of the Far East command. I went into an artillery unit and stayed there until I was rotated back to the States.

TB: How long were you stationed in Korea?

FR: I spent a total of thirteen months in Korea.

TB: Did you have a rank?

FR: Yes, I went over there as a private and came out as a master sergeant.

TB: That's top of the heap in terms of noncommissioned officers!

FR: Well, that happened not because I was so brilliant but because they were having so many casualties that the vacancies kept opening up! That's why I happened to be fortunate enough to be considered for promotion.

TB: The black soldiers were getting hit pretty bad.

FR: Everybody was getting hit pretty bad as a result of the Chinese intervention in the Korean War. So, anyway, after those thirteen months, they sent me up to Camp McCoy in Wisconsin to finish my tour of duty. Then, after I was discharged, I had a six-year reserve obligation. After that, I reenlisted in the reserves because by that time I was raising a family, and I needed that extra money to supplement my meager income as a police officer.

TB: Did you become a police officer right after you came back?

FR: Yes, right after I got out of the army I took all sorts of exams. I took the police exam. I took the fire department exam. As a matter of fact, I was taking every exam I could possibly take in order to try to get some sort of halfway decent job. The fire department called me first, but I kind of chickened out on that when I found out that I was also on the police department's list.

TB: When did they hire you?

FR: The police department called me in May of '55, and I got a job working for the park district police.

TB: That was big-time stuff in terms of policemen in Chicago.

FR: Well, it was a cut above the city police.

TB: And the uniforms looked better!

[Laughter.]

FR: Well, the criteria were higher too. So I worked as a park policeman in Washington Park and Jackson Park, along Drexel Boulevard, and along the lakefront until Daley combined the park district police with the city police.

TB: How many of the park district police were black?

FR: The park district police had about a thousand police officers, and when I left, approximately one hundred of these were blacks.

TB: Only that many?

FR: Actually that was quite an accomplishment because, if you remember correctly, prior to World War II they had only one black, and he was shot at the Thirty-first Street Beach while trying to separate a fight, and they didn't begin to hire additional blacks until after the war. So, when I was hired, blacks were still relatively few in the park district police department.

TB: Did the situation change when the park district police were combined with the city police?

FR: Well, the city has always hired blacks, but when we came over to the city, I think that out of the seven thousand police officers at that time only about three hundred and fifty were blacks!

TB: An even smaller percentage! When you combined with the city police, how many black command officers did they have?

FR: When we initially integrated with the city police, there was only one black commander and about five black sergeants. The park district police didn't have any black command officers or sergeants. Even after we combined, there were so few black police officers here on the South Side that most of the residents around here knew each of us by name—and the fire department was even worse! I think they had only two black fire stations: one on the West Side and one on the South Side.

TB: At Thirty-fifth Street.

FR: So we didn't participate too much in city government in those years in spite of our numbers. Back then we already had close to five hundred thousand blacks, but you didn't see much of any black participation in city politics either. We finally got up to where we had six aldermen, and so we thought we were being well represented, but as it turned out, those aldermen were commonly referred to as the Silent Six.

[*Laughter.*]

TB: So now you were a member of the Chicago city police. Where were you stationed?

FR: At the old Second District Station at Twenty-ninth and Prairie.

TB: Was the Stanton Avenue Station still there?

FR: Yes, the Stanton Avenue Station was on Thirty-fifth Street.

TB: Was Milton Deas still there?

FR: Captain Deas had been in charge of that station, but he was already gone by the time I came over.

TB: So now you are starting as a patrolman in the Second District. Tell me something about your experiences.

FR: At first they had me investigating accidents. As a matter of fact, I was the first black to be assigned accident investigation, and I continued to do that kind of work until I took the detective's exam in 1960. After passing that, I became a burglary detective.

TB: What area did you cover?

FR: We covered an area that went as far south as Sixtieth Street, as far north as the Loop, and from east of the Rock Island railroad tracks all the way over to the lake. Any burglaries that occurred in that entire area we were in charge of investigating, and there were quite a few at that time because, if you remember, in the early sixties heroin was the drug of choice in the black community. Thirty-ninth and Cottage Grove used to be the heroin headquarters.

TB: Which became known as Dope Street, U.S.A.

FR: Yes, because that is where all the dope addicts would gravitate to looking for pushers. So when we were investigating a burglary, we'd usually go down there and invariably that's where we'd find the ones who did it. Heroin is such a pernicious drug because it is very habit-forming and the more you use the more you have to use. So sooner or later, most addicts have to steal in order to support their habit. Most of the heroin addicts, of course, were either shoplifters or burglars. Very few of them were robbers because if you are on heroin for any length of time you eventually lose your nerve, and robberies always require a certain amount of nerve.

TB: The people that came into that area to buy heroin, were they mostly black or were they mixed?

FR: There was a sprinkling of whites that came into that neighborhood to buy, but if you remember correctly, heroin addiction was a black problem back then. Whites weren't into drugs back then to the extent that they are now. You had some upper-middle-class whites who could afford to be on drugs, but they didn't have to steal, and most of them were morphine addicts. A lot of those people were doctors and professional people, but back then drug addiction wasn't much of a problem with white people or with most blacks either for that matter. Of course many of the black musicians and entertainers smoked marijuana, but the rank-and-file black man usually got high off of alcohol.

TB: How long did you stay assigned to the Second District?

FR: Until 1963, when I was promoted to sergeant and transferred to the West Side at the old Maxwell Street Station.

TB: I understand that that's where Two-Gun Pete started his career.

FR: Well, that was before my time, but the old Maxwell Street Station is still there at Maxwell and Morgan. It is the oldest station still operating in the city of Chicago, but now I hear it is going to be torn down because the University of Illinois has bought up all that property.

TB: Soon that entire area will be torn down and changed to fit the university's requirements.

FR: As far as I'm concerned, I'll be glad to see them take all that junk out of there. That entire Maxwell Street area, among other things, was a place for pushers to sell their drugs and thieves to sell the things they'd stolen. So I stayed there for five years as a sergeant detective for burglary. Then I made lieutenant in '68, and I was assigned to Ninety-first and Cottage Grove as a robbery lieutenant in the detective division, and I stayed there for a year before they sent me downtown.

TB: That would be in 1969.

FR: Yes, and that was when the gangs were beginning to proliferate: the Blackstone Rangers on the South Side, the Vice Lords on the West Side, and the Disciples out in Englewood. So they sent me downtown to be in charge of the gang intelligence unit. Our mission was to make solid criminal cases against the leadership of the gangs, and we made a good case against Jeff Fort. In fact, we were the ones that put him and some of his lieutenants into jail. On the West Side we didn't have too much luck in putting the leadership of the Vice Lords into jail because they got out of the gang-banging business and became con men. Remember how they conned Sears Roebuck out of a million dollars by claiming that they were a viable community organization, and then they went out and bought themselves Cadillacs with all that money?

TB: What is your opinion of how they organized these street gangs?

FR: I think that the number one reason for the street gangs starting is that you have an underclass of young blacks that are unemployed, and they have nothing to do to fill that vacuum but get out and organize gangs. They try to make money illegitimately because there are no legitimate outlets for them. Tim, we've got to remember what it was like when Chicago was a leader in meatpacking, a leader in the steel industry, a leader in railroading. Back in those days unskilled and uneducated young blacks could always find employment in one or another of those industries, but then the stockyards left the city, and the steel mills had to close up because they couldn't compete with the Japanese and the Germans, and the airplane industry all but killed the railroads—so the three main sources of jobs that blacks depended on disappeared from Chicago!

TB: That's absolutely true. When your dad and my dad came here, even though they didn't have a great deal of education, they could always find a job and be able to take care of their families.

FR: And after those industries left, we couldn't move into the trades because we were blocked by the unions. Learning to be a plumber, for example, was just an exercise in futility unless you wanted to be a bootleg plumber and take your chances.

TB: So they cut off our ability to get a trade education because they controlled who was hired.

FR: And that knocked us out of the trades, and when you have youth that don't have decent jobs, naturally they are going to gravitate to antisocial activities because they don't have much of anything else to do. Even if one of these young black men does manage to get employed, he usually gets just a marginal job and makes only a marginal salary, which is not enough for him to support a family, and if he can't support his family, then he is going to leave and let welfare support them.

TB: Which leads to the destruction of the basic family structure.

FR: And this entire situation has an economic background. Industry has moved out, and a service type of economy has developed, but these are types of jobs that most of our young people are not considered to be qualified for. Most of these jobs are taken up by people who ride the train into the city from the suburbs, get off, go to work, and then get the hell back out of the city in the evening.

TB: Yes, when you go downtown on the El, as I did this morning, and go down along the Dan Ryan, you can almost have a car by yourself because there are so few people going to the Loop to either work or shop. But now let's get back to your own story. As I remember, you stayed at the level of lieutenant for a little while longer.

FR: Yes, until 1970, when I was promoted to district commander of the Fillmore District on the West Side.

TB: That is a busy district.

FR: It is a very busy district. I was district commander there until '72, and during that time, I also went to Roosevelt and got my bachelor's degree and my master's degree. Then I was transferred to district commander at Fifty-first and Wentworth. That was from '72 to '74, and then I went over to Englewood from '74 to '78, and all of that time I was still going to school. So I was working all day and night, but then in 1978 I was promoted to deputy chief of patrol on the West Side. That meant that I was in charge of four district commanders.

TB: Were you the first black to hold that level of position?

FR: No, the first black deputy chief of patrol was George Sims. I took his place when he was transferred over to Fillmore. I took his place again when they promoted him to assistant deputy superintendent. They made me deputy chief of patrol on the West Side, and I stayed there from '78 to '80, at which time I became the first black that was ever to become chief of patrol, and I stayed in that position until August of '83, at which time I became superintendent of the Chicago Police Department.

TB: How did that come about?

FR: It came about because of the election of Harold Washington. As soon as Harold was elected mayor, the former superintendent of police immediately quit his job. He had prophesied that crime would run rampant in the streets now that Chicago had a black mayor. In fact, he had been openly campaigning for Jane Byrne, who was Harold's main competition, and I thought that for a police official to engage himself in partisan politics like that was denigrating the job he was supposed to be doing, no matter which of the candidates he wanted to support. Anyway, he quit when Harold won, and so the superintendent vacancy opened up. Now, of course, the mayor can't just appoint a person to become superintendent. He has to go through a procedure and search nationwide for suitable candidates. Then the police board interviews the potential candidates and culls the list down to the three most qualified individuals and gives those three names to the mayor, who makes the final choice. If he is not happy with the three names the police board gave him, he can send those three names back and tell the police board to bring him three other names, until such time as he determines the person that he wants to be superintendent. So I went under that process, and I happened to be one of the three finalists. Two of the finalists were black—myself and Rudy Nimocks—and one was Hispanic, Matt Rodriguez, who is currently the superintendent.

TB: And Nimocks is the chief of the University of Chicago Police Department.

FR: When I made superintendent, I made him chief of organized crime. Then I promoted him to deputy superintendent in charge of administration. After that, he retired from the city police and went over to the University of Chicago.

TB: So when Harold chose you to be superintendent, you were up against some pretty stiff competition.

FR: Yes, but by then I had much more experience. I had commanded districts. I had been chief of patrol. I had been deputy chief of patrol. I had more seniority at the time than they did and much more varied experience. Plus there was the fact that I knew Harold Washington personally because he was the congressman of the district that I had commanded out there in Englewood, and I had attended community meetings with him.

TB: So he knew you.

FR: And he didn't know the other two. You always tend to choose the one you know.

TB: Yes, that seems to be the normal practice.

FR: So that's how I got to be chosen superintendent. At that time the Chicago Police Department was deeply involved in politics. If you remember, not only was the prior superintendent engaged in campaigning for Jane Byrne, but he had police officers go out to the black neighborhoods with voting registers, checking the voters' registrations to make sure the people lived exactly at the addresses which were on the lists.

TB: Hoping to disqualify as many black votes as possible?

FR: Exactly. As you know, when Harold Washington ran for mayor, part of his platform was that he would abolish the Office of Professional Standards because all that it did was to function as a washing machine for brutal cops. There was no proper mechanism to investigate police brutality, and so when I became superintendent, there was a certain element in the department that I just had to get rid of. If I was going to effect change, I was going to have to bring in some new faces.

TB: Which means you had to overhaul the whole police department, and you received a lot of protests for doing what you knew had to be done.

FR: Yes, it meant years and years of going to court because every time I moved one of those white guys they sued me. I had to go to court on those types of cases up until the very last year I held that office, but I won every one of them. I doubled the number of black command officers. I doubled the number of Hispanic command officers. I totally revised the Office of Professional Standards and brought in new investigators, all of them with master's degrees. I transformed the top echelon of the police department and took the politics out of it, but that created a lot of opposition.

TB: I would imagine not only from within the department but also from people like Vrdolyak and the other aldermen that were part of the political machine.

FR: Yes, the Vrdolyak 29—Ed Vrdolyak and all the aldermen he had in his pocket! If you remember, I was appointed in August, but it wasn't until November that they finally confirmed me, and even then it took two long days of my sitting there in the hearing room being grilled by those twenty-nine damn aldermen before they passed on me! Those people were accustomed to dictating all that went on in the police department, and they didn't like the idea that I was going to take their bodyguards away from them. You see, previously a policy had been established of keeping the allegiance of certain politicians, such as these aldermen, by assigning police officers to them as their personal bodyguards, but none of them were in any danger of getting hurt. They just wanted to use those guys as chauffeurs and gofers, and when I took away those privileges, I became even more of a bad guy in their eyes.

TB: How did the mayor react to all of this?

FR: He used a hands-off approach. I kept him abreast of all my promotions and appointments—why I promoted this guy and appointed that guy as opposed to someone else—and he never did interfere with any of my decisions. You'd just sit down with him and explain your actions fully to him, and he'd always be your ally and support your decisions. I am not saying that some of his subordinates didn't try to interfere, but the mayor never did, and I think one of the reasons for that is that he didn't want the adverse publicity of anyone saying that he was interfering in any way with the police.

TB: Because he had run for election on a platform of reform.

FR: Yes, I think that is probably one of the main reasons why he stayed as far away from the police department as he could.

TB: So you've spent most of your life as a member of the Chicago Police Department.

FR: At least thirty-three years. That's half a lifetime.

TB: And in that period of time, as you have indicated, you have witnessed a great many changes in the department and in the city as well.

FR: The biggest changes in the department were when O. W. Wilson came here in 1960 and really brought the Chicago Police Department out of the dark ages. He modernized the buildings. He put in new communications. He reorganized the entire department, *and* he stressed integration. That type of thing had never been stressed before in the Chicago Police Department. Prior to that, the Chicago Police Department, like most police departments, had always been very conservative.

TB: They had a right-wing, reactionary attitude toward their responsibilities.

FR: Yes, they tended to resist any form of change. That is just the nature of the business.

TB: Tell me what other social changes you have witnessed during your career.

FR: I was a lieutenant during the 1968 riots on the West Side when Dr. King was assassinated and also during that year's Democratic convention. I was also the district commander in Englewood when the Nazi Party was over on West Seventy-first Street, and it could be rather violent at times when the civil rights group headed by Reverend Dunlap tried to conduct their marches in Marquette Park.

TB: Did you ever meet Dr. King?

FR: I never did meet Dr. King. When he was on the West Side marching, I was still on the South Side.

TB: After Dr. King was killed, how do you account for the difference between the response of the black community on the West Side as opposed to that on the South Side?

FR: A lot of property on the West Side was destroyed because the West Side had many more social problems at that time than did the South Side. On the South Side you saw very little destruction. A few windows broken on Thirty-fifth Street and on Sixty-third Street—and that was it! But on the West Side they burned down miles of Madison Street and Roosevelt Road, and the reason for that was the people living on the West Side had many more social and economic problems than those who were living on the South Side. Many of them had recently come up to Chicago from the South, and they were less sophisticated, less well educated, and many of them felt like they had nothing to lose.

TB: To expand upon the point you're making, have you noticed any significant difference between those of your generation and my own who came to Chicago and those who came here during or after World War II?

FR: I think that the main difference is that the people who came up here earlier got jobs much more easily, and, therefore, they didn't have all of the social and economic problems that subsequent generations have had. They came up here because jobs awaited them—otherwise they wouldn't have come here.

TB: But for this second migration conditions had changed both here and in the South.

FR: Yes, they came here not because jobs were waiting for them but because there were no more jobs for them in the South. Mechanization had put them out of work in the rural areas, and they became surplus in the South.

TB: And now they became surplus here.

FR: Yes, so it was altogether a different set of circumstances, and it creates a different set of problems.

TB: And, as the number of available jobs continues to decrease, these problems are going to grow larger and larger. What is your prediction for the future?

FR: In a capitalistic country such as our own it is to the benefit to a certain element for there to be a mass surplus of labor. They want us to have a reservoir of labor like this that they can draw on and pay cheap wages so they can maximize their profits. If they don't have that reservoir here, then they are going to go to Mexico or somewhere else to get it.

TB: From the standpoint of law enforcement, what does this mean?

FR: It means that law enforcement and the criminal justice system are going to be overworked. You can see that now in the proliferation of prisons. I don't know whether you know it or not, Tim, but in recent years there have been seven new prisons built right here in the state of Illinois, and all of them are already overcrowded.

TB: And the reason for this is?

FR: If you don't provide the populace with a viable method of earning a livelihood, they are going to get in trouble. So the trend in this country is to be tough on crime, and what they mean by being tough on crime is just to build more and more prisons and keep on warehousing people until somebody is astute enough to see that the root problem is economic and addresses that issue!

TB: In the meantime, a young guy coming into the police force, his work is probably going to be much harder for him to handle than yours was.

FR: It certainly will, because the number of crimes—especially violent crimes—just continues to increase, and people always look to the police to resolve these kinds of problems, but, like I've said, these are problems that cannot be easily resolved or eliminated by the police because the source of these problems is economic, and the root of these problems is not being dealt with. Everybody today is crying out for law and order, but what they mean by that is that we should put these people in jail and throw away the key.

TB: But you can't do that. I mean you can put them in jail, but you can't throw away the key.

FR: That's right. All we can do is to get them off the street temporarily.

TB: You can warehouse them temporarily, but eventually they are all coming back to the streets.

FR: Yes, they are all coming back, and they are coming back to exactly the same or possibly even worse circumstances than those that they left behind when they were arrested.

TB: And that won't change—

FR: Unless and until the basic economic problems are resolved.

January 4, 1994

LeROY WINBUSH

GROUND-BREAKING DESIGNER

Roy Winbush and I have known one another for at least seventy years. (Whew, my, how time does fly!) He was at Englewood High School in Chicago, and I had transferred from Englewood to Wendell Phillips and later to New Wendell Phillips (the building that later was renamed DuSable High School), but we continued to stay in touch because we had a number of mutual friends, and so we continued to see one another rather frequently at parties, dances, and other social events.

Very early on it seemed that Roy had a passion and talent for both drawing and singing jazz vocal music. He and some of his more musically inclined classmates formed a singing group and did gigs around the neighborhood. Eddie Johnson, who later became a well-known tenor saxophonist and played with Louis Jordan's band, and Jimmy Jones, who became known worldwide as a pianist and arranger, were both members of that vocal group. In the end, however, it was his talent for drawing that occupied most of Roy Winbush's late teens and early twenties. He immersed himself in his art and was considered to be very talented by his teachers and peers, such as the later well-known artist Charles White.

A little later on, just before, during, and after World War II, because of the need and the demand for more blacks to be employed by the large downtown department stores, Roy Winbush was asked and accepted the challenge of becoming a commercial artist and creating window displays in prominent, white-owned department stores. He was probably the first black in the United States to attain such a position, and he was very, very successful. As a matter of fact, the demand for his talents spread rapidly *across the entire country, but even though he would constantly be traveling to other places, Chicago always remained his home. His talents can be seen in the work he did as exhibit arranger for Chicago's DuSable Museum of African American History, which was founded by an equally active poet-artist, Margaret Burroughs.*

Roy was and is an avid tennis player, skier, deep-sea diver, and at present (at the age of 76) is learning to play the tenor sax!

––––––––

TB: LeRoy, I believe that you and I share some fond memories of Forty-seventh Street.

LW: Yeah, just mentioning Forty-seventh Street brings back a lot of wonderful memories! That's where I met Joe Louis at the Savoy Ballroom. He used to practice there every day. So I would go over and watch him work out on that big, heavy punching bag they had there, and, believe me, when he hit that bag he made a dent in it that was about ten inches deep. That's how hard he was hitting it! Boy, I would *not* want any guy to hit me like that!
[*Laughter.*]

TB: Which reminds me—Joe's first wife is now living back in the neighborhood. She moved back to that house at Forty-third and Michigan where they moved to after he first won the championship. She's had it renovated, and now it has a beautiful garden.

LW: Joe was just a really great guy—and do you remember Floyd Patterson? What was his brother's name?

TB: It was Vern Patterson.

LW: Vern was one and Floyd was the other. Floyd became the more famous of the two.

TB: Floyd became the heavyweight champion of the world.

LW: Another guy that I remember specifically is Austin Powell.

TB: Yeah, the Cats and the Fiddle!

LW: Well, he and I were still selling newspapers together when he first started to get into the music. His first group was called the Harlem Harmony Hounds, and Austin and his group had these white outfits that they wore.

TB: White jackets *and* white pants?

LW: Yeah, and so Austin used to have to press those pants of his every single day. He would always try to put the crease back in where his knee had knocked it out of place the night before. Well, one day I was standing there watching him doing this sort of thing, and all of a sudden, the pants split in half. You see, he had pressed them and pressed them so much that they finally fell apart right at the seam!

[*Laughter.*]

Another thing that I remember vividly about Forty-seventh Street is that when I was just getting into high school I started working at the Rexall Drugstore.

TB: At Forty-seventh and Drexel?

LW: Yeah, and back then at that place they used to serve three meals a day. They had their kitchen upstairs in the hotel, and the lady that was in charge of it, she used to keep this great big can of milk sitting in the refrigerator just for me—so I drank milk all day long! That was my first job as a busboy. I was hired to clean off all the dishes, but I didn't really know too much about what I was doing because, when I saw all the tips that were left on the tables, I thought they were for me—and so I was collecting all of that for myself. The waitresses had to kind of pull my coat and tell me to stop that sort of thing, but then, after that, it was OK with them and me. That was just one of the little jobs that I had.

TB: When did you first start working in design?

LW: Well, not too long later, Parker Jr. and I started working for his dad and doing work for the Savoy Ballroom and for different places like that. Do you happen to remember Curtis Williams?

TB: Curtis Williams was a sign painter, wasn't he?

LW: Well, Curtis Williams and I started doing all of the theater fronts for the Regal Theater. As a matter of fact, we had our shop right under the stage of the theater.

TB: Is that right?

LW: Yeah, and one of the other things that I want to mention is that when I first started out I also did window exhibits for a clothing store that was right there on Forty-seventh Street called the Club Store. It was owned by a fellow by the name of Haberman, and he let me have the run of the whole place. I even had my own individual label that had my signature printed on it. That's a long time before designers even thought of having their own labels, but back then, I didn't make any kind of money from it. All I knew was that I wanted to make the label and put my name on it. Which is what I did. As I think back on it now, I probably should have come along a little later when you could make real big money by having your own label like that. But, nevertheless, all of that is just another segment of what I still remember about Forty-seventh Street. That street at that time was a really big thing for me. It was a big thing in terms of learning, and it was a big thing in terms of doing. All the people that were doing big things at that time were members of the Old Timers' Club.

TB: What was the Old Timers' Club? What was its function?

LW: The Old Timers' Club was formed by Bobby Anderson and some others, and its primary function was the sponsorship of athletes. They sponsored young men like Buddy Young, and wasn't there a runner by the name of Brooks?

TB: Oh, yeah, that guy was a great runner. He graduated from the University of Chicago, but the university did not want to sponsor him to go the places that he needed to go.

LW: Well, that's why the club was formed, and we had a whole fleet of guys and gals like that which we sponsored.

TB: Where was the club located?

LW: It was upstairs over Thornton's place. You know, you would go upstairs to the second floor. We had a pool table up there because it was a social club as well. Do you remember Eddie Plique, who used to announce the fights?

TB: He looked like a white guy but wasn't. He was from New Orleans.

LW: Well, I used to play cards—blackjack—with him up there all the time. Not for a lot of money. Just for the fun. But there were three other people who were very instrumental in terms of guiding me, and they were Bobby Anderson, O. C. Buckner, and Homer Thornton. Actually, what they did was not so much to guide me as it was to give me encouragement in terms of what I was doing. You see, I always wanted to know if I was doing the right thing, and I needed to know if people like them appreciated what I was doing. Every time I would accomplish something, they would give me a little pat on the back, and that was just what I needed.

TB: Those years you spent on Forty-seventh Street, when did they terminate?

LW: Oh, I don't know exactly what the year was, but what happened is that I kind of started looking around at what was going on. You see, I was doing a lot of work for people who were trying to get things started. Everybody had a little extra money back then, and they were trying all kinds of business ventures, and, of course, they wanted artwork and logos and that sort of thing—but there was one big problem, and that was I had trouble collecting the final payments from them. As a matter of fact, the only way I could survive financially at that time was to charge them twice as much as the job was worth so that in case they didn't pay me the balance they owed I already had all the money that I needed! That was the only way I could do it. Then I decided that this sort of thing is really not for me. I am not getting anyplace. What I've got to do is to move downtown. That's when I moved to 333 North Michigan Avenue. The American National Bank on LaSalle Street was one of my first clients.

TB: What year would this be?

LW: Nineteen forty-seven is the exact date. I still have a framed picture of that first exhibit, and there was a write-up about it in a magazine called *Signs of the Times*. At about this same time I met this fellow who was the owner of Consolidated Manufacturing. He had built the Saxony Hotel in Miami Beach, and his latest project was the Exchange National Bank, which was the very first drive-in bank that was ever built. Now, of course, they have places like that all over the place, but this was the first one, and it was considered to be very experimental. After that, I was doing a lot of banks: the American, the LaSalle, and the Harris. One of the reasons that I was picking up all these clients is the man that I worked for at American moved from American to LaSalle and from LaSalle to Harris. So every time he would move, I would pick up another new client. As a result, my reputation just grew and grew and grew. By this time Dackens, Parker, and my brother-in-law Bradshaw are working for me putting in all these displays, and so we came up with the idea that instead of going to an outside company and having them build the displays for us, we should try to build them for ourselves. We knew how to do it. We knew we could do it. So that's when we formed Winbush Associates. We still had our business office at 333 North Michigan, but our shop facility was in a very, very small triangular building at 330 North Milwaukee. Pretty soon we moved from there to 222 South Morgan, where we were able to have a ten-thousand-square-foot facility. We had all kinds of work areas and a spray booth. Each partner had an office of his own. We had vans and trucks, and it was really a very nice operation. Then we moved from there and bought our own building at 806 North Peoria, which was a five-story building with five thousand square feet per floor.

TB: This is before the University of Illinois took over that entire area?

LW: No, that building is still there. Later on I sold it to the Paul Crest Company, but before I could do that I had to liquidate all of our debts. Each of my partners took their money out, but I stayed on in that building for a whole year, until all of our debts had been paid. You see, the name of our company was Winbush Associates, and if we had gone bankrupt, then that would have been like a black mark on me personally, and I didn't want that to happen. So I stayed there by myself for an entire year, until I'd paid everybody off. That's when I moved from there to 540 North Lake Shore Drive. The person that rented me the space told me you have got to pay your rent every month on time. That was the law he laid down, but, well, at the time I got this office from him you could have fired a cannon in there and you would not have hit anybody because nobody else was in there except me! It was just an old terminal building that used to be flourishing with activity when ships and trains were coming in, but then, of course, they put landfill in all that part of the river in order to make the North Pier Terminal what it is today.

TB: By this time you are becoming quite well known nationally as well as locally.

LW: Yeah, by then I had started going to Aspen—I went there eight years in a row, I think—and I became a member of the executive committee of the Aspen International Design Conference, and that's where I met some really famous designers. People such as Buckminster Fuller, Charles Eames, and George Nelson. All the important designers from all over the world were coming there every year, and it was a very exciting place for me to be.

TB: How did you get accepted into that circle?

LW: Well, I first went to Aspen in 1958 in order to learn how to ski, and then I started going to Aspen representing *Ebony* at the International Design Conference, and once I got there, I started meeting all these wonderful people. There would be no way in the world to meet and become familiar with that many important designers unless you were in that kind of unique situation. So it was a great opportunity, and the same sort of thing happened when I became president of my diving club. I was able to build it into one of the biggest and finest clubs in the entire country. When I was running it, we had about two hundred members. Now I guess the membership is down to forty or fifty. It's the same old story once again. People think you can run a club like that without any fanfare, that it's an easy thing to do, but it isn't easy at all. A lot of thought has to go into it. That's what people don't seem to understand. They don't realize that you have to have a concept of how to run a club like that effectively according to just what kind of club it is. That's the way I did it, and I used to think that anybody could do it the same way, but now I realize that they can't. The main thing I would like to mention here is that I have always tried to put forth my leadership ability simply because if I didn't, a person like me would be placed in a position in which I would not be able to accomplish the things which I knew I could do. If you are a black guy, people sort of brand you in a certain way—"What does he know? Nothing."—and so it is a matter of your always being in the spotlight and trying to prove what your capabilities really are. I have been doing that sort of thing all my life, and eventually you either burn out or go into what I term as overdrive, and then you are always still driving and driving, even when that kind of driving is not really necessary anymore. Sometimes you say to yourself, "Why should I be doing this when other people can just wake up in the morning and are already in it, right at the top?" Even now, when you think about the corporate structure, sure there are African-Americans in major corporations and in their own successful businesses, but just look at the struggle it has been! Yes, some of us are making pretty good money, but not too many blacks are making three or four hundred thousand dollars every year. What I am saying is that, no matter how many marches we have had and how many speeches we have heard demanding equal opportunity, tell me, when are we actually going to get this kind of equality? I have been around here all these years, and I still don't see it. All you have to do to give yourself some kind of measuring stick as to where we are and where we are going is to look at the Loop area and notice just how little of that area we actually own. What we are actively involved with is one-tenth of 1 percent or even less. They are still trying to keep us boxed in, and that continues to happen because we cannot seem to learn to think and plan and work together effectively. When we do get together, we only get together and agree about a lot of foolishness like wearing your cap on backwards or having an earring in just one ear or wearing braids or dreadlocks and all that baloney that's going on right now. In other words, it seems that every time some new fad comes along then we can adhere together just like magic, just like a magnetic force is causing us to do all these foolish things. But then when it comes to getting together and using our money, our talent, our intelligence, and our voting power to create a solid power structure, well, we just don't do it!

TB: It is a frightening situation. What do you say to young people today about their futures?

LW: They have got to have dreams, but you have got to remember that you have a lot of young people today who are not capable of dreaming up a meaningful idea. They are just living from day to day. Right now, if you took a roomful of young people—let's say you had fifty people in the room—I will guarantee that you would be fortunate if you could get even ten of them to think of an idea that was a dream that they wanted to work toward accomplishing. You might find ten, and that would be all.

TB: As you were saying, when you were growing up, young guys like you had those older guys on Forty-seventh Street to give you the right kind of encouragement.

LW: Yeah, and they just don't have that anymore.

TB: So what are these young people supposed to do?

LW: Well, I will tell you what they do do. They look to gang leaders for leadership. That's what they do. You have this growth of the gangs because these kids are running around with only one parent or no parents at all. They don't have anybody to look up to but just some gang leader.

TB: They don't have a Forty-seventh Street.

LW: No, but now, even if there was a Forty-seventh Street or some place similar to Forty-seventh Street, it would just be like another no-man's-land because you've got dope and guns and all of that. When I was growing up and starting to think about my future, I don't remember anybody selling dope or anybody carrying a gun.

TB: You could walk to the store any time of day or night. There were no iron bars on the windows or doors.

LW: That's right, and I will give you a good example of what you're talking about. When I first came to Chicago—I can't remember what year it was, but I think I was about fifteen or sixteen years old—there was a boathouse in Washington

Park. You could rent a boat and go out on the water and then come back. The water was relatively clear because I still remember looking in and seeing seaweed. But now, well, shit, you can't even see if there is any seaweed in there because of all that pollution in the water! Back then, in the wintertime the water would freeze over, and you would have ice-skating there. I remember hiding my skates, going someplace else, and then coming back and getting the skates back right where I'd left them. Do you remember Ray Nance? He used to play with Ellington. Well, Ray and I used to like to play tennis together, and sometimes when he was supposed to be on his way for a violin lesson, he would hide his violin in the bushes, and we would go off and play tennis. Then he would go back, get his violin, and go on home. We used to do that all the time.

TB: There was no reason to worry about what might happen.

LW: No, not then. Not back then.

TB: And now?

LW: Now things are different.

TB: And there are a lot of things to be worried about.

LW: And a lot of things that need to be changed.

September 7, 1995

FLOYD CAMPBELL

PIONEER JAZZ MUSICIAN

Back when I was in my early teens, I used to hang out with my best buddies—Carl, Cleo, Bob, and Lester—around the various dance halls and nightclubs so that we could hear the jazz bands that were playing there. One of those bands that we all particularly liked to hear was led by Floyd Campbell. Not only did his band play in the largest and most popular arenas but it was also the favorite of the more exclusive and somewhat elitist sororities and fraternities and other similar social groups. Floyd Campbell was such a favorite because he was a precision percussionist and because of his sweet, gentlemanly ways with the participants in these social events.

Our final conversation took place in a hospital where Floyd was attempting to recover from a serious illness, and unfortunately I did not get to have a lengthy discussion with him because of an interruption created by the arrival of his roommate's relatives and friends. I planned to return the next day, but Floyd passed away that very evening. Even so, our brief conversation provides an interesting and revealing insight into the struggles that beset jazz musicians in their efforts to create a new kind of music.

FC: I guess I'm ready—go ahead and shoot the questions!
TB: We might as well start right at the beginning. Where were you born?
FC: Helena, Arkansas.
TB: When?
FC: September 17, 1901!

TB: That's quite a while ago.

FC: Yeah, come to think of it, I guess that is a few days ago all right!

[*Laughter.*]

TB: Where were your mother and father born?

FC: They were born in Mississippi, but they moved over to Arkansas.

TB: Do you remember how your dad made a living?

FC: My dad was a barber. He had a barbershop and poolroom.

TB: Did you go to school in Arkansas?

FC: Yeah, in Helena. I went to Peabody grammar school and high school. Later on, I went to Philander Smith College in Little Rock.

TB: That's an AME college, isn't it?

FC: It was ME back in those days.

TB: That school had a very good reputation.

FC: Well, at least they had a good choir. That choir is what got them their good reputation!

[*Laughter.*]

Most recently, Bill Clinton really put that choir on the map.

TB: Yes, I saw them at his inauguration.

FC: Well, there was also quite a lot of singing when I was in school there. Back in the summer of 1920 they sent their choir to Columbus, Ohio, to sing on the state fair grounds. But now I see that their choir director is moving to Tuskegee.

TB: Is that right?

FC: Yeah, I got a letter about that from the school just the other day.

TB: So you still keep in touch?

FC: Oh yeah, I send them some money from time to time, you know, and if you keep sending them money, they'll keep on keeping in touch!

[*Laughter.*]

TB: They sure will, but we all try to do what we can because those black colleges did a lot of things for our people.

FC: I still have a lot of fond recollections of what happened when I was in that school. A lot of buddies, a lot of friends, a lot of activities that I'll always remember.

TB: What was Little Rock like back then?

FC: In those days, it was a typical Southern town, and so we stayed in a certain vicinity. We didn't go all over everywhere. Back then it was just like most of those towns down South.

TB: And up North as well. Even Chicago!

FC: Well, when I was at Philander Smith, most of our activities were in the area around West Ninth Street, with a radius of maybe ten blocks either way. There were a couple of ballrooms and a drugstore—

TB: The neighborhood was kind of self-contained.

FC: Yeah, everything we needed was right there.

TB: How long were you there at that college?

FC: Just two years. I didn't finish.

TB: When did you start playing? When did you really begin to get interested in music?

FC: Well, frankly, all of my life I could always sing a little. In high school I sang show songs and always got a lot of applause. After that, I went to college, and on Friday they'd have what they called a literary society, and I heard a fellow that was there try to sing "Till the Sands of the Desert Grow Cold," but he didn't sound so hot!

[*Laughter.*]

So I made arrangements to have a girl I knew play the piano and rehearse a song that I had learned while I was working on a dining car in the summer during the war.

TB: World War I?

FC: Yeah, World War I—so I had this girl play that song for me, and on that particular night a guy in the audience gave me a big hand and said, "That man really sang that song!" So I got to do a couple of encores, and that was what really started me on my way.

TB: Was that the beginning of your career in music?

FC: No, that summer I went back to working on the dining car and was running out of Pittsburgh, Columbus, and St. Louis.

TB: What railroad line were you working on?

FC: Pennsylvania. Then, when my mother took ill in 1921, I quit my job and came back home, but it wasn't too long before my mother passed, and there was this white man that had a drugstore right on the corner across from my dad's place, and he hit upon the idea of playing music on the weekends. So he brought in a piano and a drum and tried to entertain the people on Friday, Saturday, and Sunday nights. The reason he was doing this was because he was selling a sort of tonic drink called Jamaica Gin Gin!

[*Laughter.*]

That Jamaica Gin Gin had a little orange peel in it, maybe some coloring and water, and all the rest—maybe 90 percent—was alcohol!

[*Laughter.*]

So I'd go around there to his place and sing several songs. He had this drummer there, and they called him Slick. He could play the drums all right, but the only problem was that Slick would get so drunk on that tonic that half the time he couldn't even find the drum!

[*Laughter.*]

So one evening George Randolph, who was the piano player, said to me, "Floyd, why don't you get up here and see if you can keep time 'cause tonight Slick can't do it!"

TB: Is that the same Randolph that played with Louis?

FC: Hell no, that's another Randolph. This was *George* Randolph. He played the piano. The Randolph you're talking about used to play saxophone, but he started playing trumpet when he went with Louis. Anyway, what happened to me was that from that point on I was playing the drums, and whenever one of the minstrel shows or something like that would come to town, I'd hang out around the drummer and let him show me whatever he could. Eventually I got so I was pretty good, and a fellow came down from Memphis and said, "You ought to come on up to Memphis and get you some work." So I went to Memphis all alone, and I got a job waiting tables at the Peabody Hotel. As a matter of fact, I served the last meal in the old Peabody just before they tore it down.

TB: Is that right?

FC: We didn't serve breakfast. We only served lunch and dinner, and they had a white band that would come in and play for their cabaret during the evening.

TB: What about you? Did you play any music while you were in Memphis?

FC: Well, I played in two or three other little outfits while I was in Memphis, but all of that was on the side. My main work in Memphis at that time was waiting tables, but then, of course, then I'd also play a job on the weekend if anything was available. One of those times I got a job playing with a band on a boat. We played the matinee, and then between the matinee and the evening session we all went over to the piano player's house to have a little crap game, but the police followed us, and the captain of that boat had to come and get us out of jail so that we could play that night. Well, about that same time, one of those evenings I was working at the hotel, the head waiter came over to me and said, "That man over there wants to talk with you," and it turned out that it was that white guy that owned the drugstore back home, and he told me that some musicians had come to town and that he would like for me to come back down there and join the band. You see, he wanted to start a little band to play at the country club and places like that, and so I accepted his offer. That's when I went back to Helena.

TB: You went back home. Did you have any brothers or sisters?

FC: My sister married, and she passed away while she was living in Chicago. That was in '23 or maybe a little earlier. My brother went to New York and wrote any number of popular songs. As a matter of fact, I'm still receiving some royalties right now from some of those songs my brother wrote. He had a song—"One-Sided Love Affair"—on Elvis Presley's first album. He had another hit song called "Don't Stop Now." One of the songs he wrote wasn't a hit, but it made a lot of money because it was on the flip side of "That Lucky Old Sun"! So every once in a while I'll get a little remembrance of him in the mail.

TB: Well, when you went back to Helena, did you lead the band?

FC: No, and I didn't play in that band for very long. What happened in Helena at that time is that they lynched a young boy. They caught him in some bushes with some old white girl, and that broke up our band. That was more than we could stand, and so we all left and went our separate directions. Three of the fellows went to St. Louis. I went back to Memphis, and I forget where the other two went.

TB: In which year did this lynching take place?

FC: I'd say it was 1922, and you know what? The guy who followed me playing there at that drugstore was a young guy named Louis Jordan!

TB: That's right. His original home was there somewhere in Arkansas.

FC: Louis Jordan's home was right up the road there in Brinkley, Arkansas. That's where Louis's father had a great big brass band. When I first heard them, Louis, who was just a fifteen-year-old kid at the time, was already playing lead clarinet in front of the band, and I thought that was so great. That was what really inspired me to become a musician.

TB: So now you're back in Memphis.

FC: I was pretty satisfied being back in Memphis, but I didn't stay there too long.

TB: Why was that?

FC: It was because of a shirt.

TB: A shirt?

FC: Yeah, you see, where I was working the waiters started playing cards. We'd play at my home one night and at yours the next. Well, one night we were playing at my house, and one of the guys came up there with some marked cards, but the trouble was he couldn't read them, and I wound up winning about eighty dollars. So I had this eighty dollars in my pocket, and because I needed to get a new white shirt in a hurry, I went to a place called the National Shirt Company. They had stores all over the country in those days, but this one was on Main Street, and when I rushed in there, the clerk was just standing there talking to a white woman, and he just ignored me completely. So I stood there and stood and stood, and finally I said to myself, "Well, this just does it. This is enough. I've got some money in my pocket, and my buddies have been telling me there was work for me as a musician in St. Louis. Good-bye, Memphis!" So I went up to the Shrine Room, where I was working at that time, and told the headwaiter I was quitting. "What? You quitting? We were going to make you captain!" But I didn't care about any of that. I had had enough!

TB: So then you went up to St. Louis.

FC: And that's where I got hooked up with George Randolph and that group of musicians once again. At that time they called me the Triple Threat Man because I could sing and play drums and play a kind of little harmonica type of thing that sounded almost like a violin when you'd blow it the right way into a microphone. Next thing I know Fate Marable hired me to work with him on the riverboats. We went down to New Orleans for the winter, and then we'd come back north and play every town along the river all the way up to Davenport, Iowa. Then we'd come back and play St. Louis all summer. In 1927 I left Marable and started my own band with some of the guys that were at Philander Smith College with me. Well, one of the boats on the river at that time had only white bands that played on it, but when the white band they had decided to strike for more money, the company that owned the boat said, "Well, maybe we don't need them white ones. Let's get us some colored band." So they arranged to have Louis Armstrong come down. At that time Louis was already playing here in Chicago, but they offered him a hundred dollars a night to play, and that was *big* money in those days! Well, this guy that hired him thought that Louis would fit in real well with my band, and he got the idea that my band with Louis in it and another band which was led by a guy named Alphonso Trent should have what you might call a musical battle, and they sold five thousand tickets to this event, but they wouldn't let the boat go out on the river because they thought it might capsize!

[*Laughter.*]

But that made a big splash in the music world anyway. We held that battle in a big ballroom on shore, and that other band, they had a bunch of young, good-looking boys who had a lot of stunts and tricks. I mean, they'd jump up and down on their chairs, and they used megaphones and everything. So it seemed like they might be winning the battle, but that's when Louis says to me, "You know we've got a little ole band like that up in Chicago, but when they come to play at the Savoy Ballroom, we know how to take care of 'em and put 'em in their place. So when we go back on stage, let's play the 'St. Louis Blues,' and you make a drum break, then let the saxophone play a riff, and I'll take it from there!"

[*Laughter.*]

Well, he must have hit a hundred of those high notes of his, and when he was through, that contest was over, and we had won!

TB: Louis was already getting quite famous, wasn't he?

FC: Yeah, as a matter of fact, that other bandleader got mad at me and said that I had tricked him, but I had nothing to do with it. I didn't hire Louis, and I certainly didn't tell Louis how to play!

TB: How long did you stay in St. Louis?

FC: I left St. Louis in 1930.

TB: The Great Depression was just beginning at that time.

FC: Yeah, but working out there on the riverboat we couldn't see it coming. I remember when we were in Vicksburg, Mississippi, one of the musicians on a boat that was coming down river from the North told us, "You fellows better start saving some money because something is fixing to hit this country and hit it hard." That's the first inkling we got of a depression. At that time each of the guys in the band was getting ninety-nine dollars a week, but in about six months they would be glad to get eighteen dollars a week. I remember one of the guys in the band was complaining, "Why are we getting eighteen dollars a week?" And someone said, "Benny, stop bragging or they'll cut it down to fifteen!"
[*Laughter.*]
Then I heard that up in Chicago guys like Erskine Tate and Billy Eckstine had big bands and were paying their musicians seventy-five dollars a week.

TB: And that's why you decided to come up to Chicago.

FC: You're darned right. That's why in 1931 I decided to move to Chicago!

December 5, 1996, and March 4, 1997

CLARK BURRUS

—

INFLUENTIAL BUSINESSMAN

Clark Burrus is a Chicago native. Born and raised in Woodlawn, he has distinguished himself in so many capacities that I cannot list all his accomplishments in a brief introduction such as this. Suffice it to say, he was trained to be a certified public accountant and for many, many years has worked both for the government and in private business. Very early in his career he was the accountant for jazz-blues-gospel singer Dinah Washington. Later, he worked as an accountant in Chicago City Hall and became a close adviser to Mayor Harold Washington. He has been an influential member of the Board of Education for the Chicago Public Schools and a senior vice president of the First National Bank of Chicago. At present Clark Burrus continues to be an active board member of many volunteer educational, political, and financial organizations—and, by the way, he still finds time to play golf and always carries the equipment necessary for his favorite sport with him in all of his out-of-town, out-of-country travels.

During this conversation, we were having lunch together, and it seemed to me that everyone who came into the restaurant knew him personally and placed great value on their friendship with him. I was truly grateful for having had this opportunity to speak with Clark Burrus about his life and his many accomplishments.

———

TB: Clark, where were you born?
CB: Here in Chicago.

TB: When?

CB: I was born in 1928 at St Luke's Hospital.

TB: This is the old St. Luke's at Fourteenth and Michigan?

CB: Yes, but the Michigan Avenue entrance was for whites only. So this meant that my mother had to enter through the back doors of St. Luke's Hospital, and so she went in on Indiana Avenue.

TB: Were your mother and dad also born in Chicago?

CB: No, both of them were born in Mississippi. My father is from Jackson, and my mother from Gulfport.

TB: Do you know anything about your grandparents?

CB: Yes, they also were all from Mississippi.

TB: Were they born as free people or not?

CB: I doubt that they were born free because I was a late child, and both of my parents were born in the nineteenth century.

TB: As were mine.

CB: So it would be reasonable to assume that their parents were born during slavery.

TB: Tell me something about your parents.

CB: My father was very dark-skinned, and my mother was very fair-skinned.

TB: What was her maiden name?

CB: Mattie Hall. In those days the Halls were a very affluent and influential family down there. As a matter of fact, the only black undertaker parlor in Gulfport is still owned by the Halls. They also had branches of their establishment in most of the towns from the middle to the southern part of the state, but they did all of the embalming right there in Gulfport. So they would go get the bodies of the deceased and bring them to Gulfport and embalm them there and then return the bodies for display back at the homesteads of the family. They were also very active in education. Both of my parents taught at Alcorn, and right now one of my cousins is the dean of music there. Another cousin is dean of students at Alcorn, and my brother is a professor of history there. My sister is the dean of nursing at Florida A & M.

TB: Do you know what year your parents left the South to come north?

CB: No, they never discussed that with either my brother or me.

TB: What kind of work was your father doing when he got here?

CB: When my father first came up here, he couldn't get into the profession that he wanted for the first three or four years, and so in the meantime he got a job working for the railway mail service.

TB: Which at that time here in Chicago had a lot of status associated with it.

CB: Very much so, but I never knew how important that sort of job was until much later.

TB: What are some of your earliest childhood memories?

CB: Well, one thing that has always stayed with me is how back in those days poor folk always supported one another. I can still remember how my mother used to cook an extra large pot of greens and beans and big pans of cornbread so that there would not only be enough to feed everyone who was already there but anyone who might happen to come by and knock on the door as well.

TB: I imagine she must have been a very good cook.

CB: She most certainly was, but not only could she cook. My mother could also take almost anything that was available—peaches, apples, pears—you name it, and she could can it. There was nothing she couldn't can. So we always had those mason jars sealed with wax that were full of goodies. They were all lined up on shelves in what we called in those days the pantry, and that way she was always ready to feed as many people as showed up to be fed.

TB: Because she had already done almost all of the work.

CB: Yes, all she had to do was to get one of those jars off of the shelf, take off the wax, and there were sweet potatoes, onions, and just about anything else that anybody might want.

TB: Just as fresh as when she first put it in.

CB: She also made her own wine.

TB: Did your mother have any kind of outside work?

CB: In Mississippi she had worked professionally as a teacher at Alcorn, but here in Chicago being a housewife and mother were her primary occupations.

TB: How many children are in your family?

CB: Two.

TB: Just you and your brother.

CB: Well, actually there were four, but one was stillborn and my sister who was the oldest died when she was still very young.

TB: Which grammar school did you attend?

CB: I grew up in Woodlawn and went to grammar school at McCosh.

TB: Who are some of the people that you still remember from those early years?

CB: Earl Neal was a semester ahead of me and a semester behind my brother, but we all three grew up together. Then, of course, there was Buddy Young and his whole family.

TB: He was an outstanding athlete who put Phillips on the map in many ways.

CB: Yes, he was living in Woodlawn while he was going there, but the coach at Englewood wouldn't let him play football, and that's why he went to Phillips.

TB: Is that so? Who are some of the others that you remember?

CB: At that time Archibald Carey was the pastor of the Woodlawn AME, which was right on the corner of Sixty-fifth and Evans. I was baptized in that church. In those days the whites had their service from eleven to twelve thirty, and the blacks had a separate service starting at one o'clock.

TB: Was there any racial friction in the neighborhood?

CB: We really didn't know anything about racial friction except that the area east of Cottage Grove was one hundred percent white. The other boundary was South Park. Woodlawn itself was also somewhat divided: west Woodlawn was where the very affluent blacks were living, and east Woodlawn was considered to be much more blue collar.

TB: I remember that those of us that lived north of there looked upon the folks living in Woodlawn as being kind of snobbish.

CB: Well, that's because they were!

[*Laughter.*]

When I was a kid, south Woodlawn had as many whites as blacks. In my early years I was raised on St. Lawrence at Sixty-fourth Street. That was right behind the old Pershing Hotel, and all of my childhood friends were little Italian kids.

TB: So you went all the way through elementary school at McCosh?

CB: Yes, because we continued to live in Woodlawn. In 1937 my parents bought a place at Sixty-fifth and Langley, and I continued to live there until 1960 when I married my current wife, and then we moved down to Prairie Shores. We lived there for ten years and then moved to Pill Hill, which is where I'm still living. In all my life I have only lived in those four places.

TB: Where did you go to high school?

CB: Well, Hyde Park High School was less than half the distance from where we were living, but I went to Englewood because of the way they had gerrymandered the school districts. They did not want to have any blacks over there in Hyde Park—so they drew the line at Cottage Grove.

TB: And everybody west of Cottage Grove went to Englewood.

CB: That's right, but it was really a changing neighborhood. When I first entered Englewood in '42, it was about 70 percent white, but by the time I graduated in '46, it was already 70 percent black.

TB: When I went to Englewood in 1932, it was maybe only 10 percent or so black, and I just couldn't handle it. So I left in '33 and went first to Phillips and then to DuSable. What year did you graduate from Englewood?

CB: 1946.

TB: After you graduated from Englewood, what did you do?

CB: Well, at first I couldn't do much of anything in terms of completing my education. You see, my father had died when I was still a senior in high school, and my brother was going into the army, and my mother had some problems with her health. So I could not go away. As a matter of fact, I had received a number of scholarships at really good schools to play football, but, until my brother returned, there was no way I could leave home. So I stayed here in Chicago for another year or so and went to Wilson Junior College.

TB: At least you stayed in school.

CB: Yes, then my brother returned, and I got a scholarship from Texas State University down in Houston.

TB: That's now Texas Southern. How big was that school back then?

CB: It wasn't really very large. Maybe about three thousand students.

TB: Was it an all-black school?

CB: Yes, it was.

TB: Were many of the other students from Chicago?

CB: There was a group of about eight or ten of us. We were all athletes.

TB: Football?

CB: Football and basketball.

TB: And you stayed there for how long?

CB: A year and a half, and then I came back to Chicago and finished up at Roosevelt.

TB: How long were you there?

CB: Two and a half years.

TB: And what year did you graduate?

CB: I finished Roosevelt in '53.

TB: I came there in '47, just a year after they opened their doors, and left in '50.

CB: So you were gone when I got there.

TB: Yes, I must have just missed you. Tell me—who are some of the people that you remember from those days when you were at Roosevelt? Was Warren Bacon there?

CB: No, Warren had already graduated. If I remember correctly, Harold Washington was there at more or less the same time I was, but he left the semester I got there or something like that. The same thing with Dempsey Travis. Even so, I knew all those guys back then.

TB: How about Chuck Hamilton? Did you know him?

CB: Well, I was in the business school, and he was in sociology or anthropology or something like that. So he was there, but I didn't know him personally back then. I just knew him as a name.

TB: So you graduated with a degree in business.

CB: The degree I received was called a "bachelor of science in commerce." That's what it was called back then. Now they call it a "bachelor of science in business administration," but, even so, it's really the same degree.

TB: How did you happen to choose the field of commerce?

CB: Well, I certainly wasn't counseled to do so. I took it because I was always good with numbers. As a matter of fact, I already had enough college credits for a minor in mathematics, but there is not very much that you can do with a degree in mathematics—especially if you are a young black guy—other than teach. So I thought that I could use those same skills at something that could be more productive for me. Well, I quickly discovered that in order to obtain a degree in commerce you had to concentrate your studies on accounting or marketing or any one of a number of other specific areas. So I decided to take a course in accounting, and from that point on my concentration was focused on accounting and nothing else.

TB: Most of the rest of us back then had the GI Bill to help us complete our educations, but you had not been in the service. How were you able to finance your education?

CB: Since I had none of those benefits, I had to pay my own way, but that wasn't a problem because I have worked all of my life. As a matter of fact, I've never known how *not* to work. You have to understand, Tim, that I started at the post office when I was just a sophomore in high school. I was only fourteen, but back then they'd hire just about anything that was walking!

[*Laughter.*]

And I continued to work at the post office on a part-time basis from 1944 to 1958, but while I was in college all of those wages went directly to my mother to pay for her expenses. The way I was able to pay for my tuition was by tutoring the other students at Roosevelt with their various accounting assignments. That's how I financed my education.

TB: What did you do after you graduated?

CB: Well, after I got my CPA degree, I applied to all the big accounting firms and then to all the medium-size accounting firms, but I couldn't find a job. Fortunately, the previous summer I had tried to get a job with the city and had taken the civil service exam, but when the time came for me to go back to school, I forgot all about that. I put it entirely out of my mind. Then sometime in December or January they called me in and offered me a job, but I turned them down because I thought that after graduation I was so sure that I was going to get one of those jobs with an accounting firm. Well, when that didn't happen, I went back and took a job with the city government as an internal auditor for a while.

TB: Didn't you go to New York and get involved in the music business just after that?

CB: Yes, that's when I got an opportunity to meet and know on a first-name basis many of the people whom I had grown to love and respect and admire only through their music. All the jazz people: Sarah Vaughan, Dizzy Gillespie, Charlie Parker, Miles Davis, Billy Eckstine . . .

TB: Was Sarah your major account?

CB: No, I also did work for Sammy Davis as well as some work for Sinatra and Nat King Cole, but now let me tell you who was the one person in that whole group that I grew the most to know, admire, and really—as a matter of fact—love, and that was Ella Fitzgerald. She was just such a nice person.

TB: Just a good human being.

CB: That's right.

TB: Why didn't you stay in the music business? After all, it was pioneering work that you were doing by helping all those artists to "professionalize" their careers and prevent the dishonest accounting practices that had become the standard for black artists in the music industry.

CB: Why didn't I? Well, it was because I didn't like the lifestyle that was associated with the music industry.

TB: Couldn't you have separated the business aspect from the lifestyle?

CB: No, you can't separate them because you always have to be at the openings and events like that. That means you have to be out all night, and I was supposed to be at the office by eight o'clock in the morning! So I decided to come back to Chicago after a little more than a year. You see, I didn't really quit the city. I just took a leave of absence, and when I returned, the people that I knew in the city government were willing to accept me back.

TB: That was because they knew that you were a skilled and dependable person. When you returned, what was your position?

CB: I was still an internal auditor, and for the first eight or nine years I continued to work part-time at the post office in order to supplement my income.

TB: And when you finished your many years of working with the city government, what position did you hold?

CB: Twenty-seven years later I was comptroller and chief financial officer for the city of Chicago.

TB: During which years did you hold that position?

CB: From 1974 until 1979. I was appointed to that position by Richard J. Daley, but my appointment was not really a matter of politics. I didn't just go directly from internal auditor to comptroller overnight. Don't forget that I had been there for more than twenty years, and by then I had become sort of an institution there in City Hall. It took such a long time because I advanced my career step by step through a series of seven consecutive jobs in city government, and all of these advancements were the results of competitive written examinations. It finally got to the point where the only further possible advancement I could get was through a political appointment—and that is what I received.

TB: Yes, it is my understanding that the comptroller and chief financial officer is the highest office in terms of handling the city's financial affairs.

CB: No question about that, and I am very proud of the fact that I served as the chief financial officer of this city, but it is a very poor commentary on our society that I am not only the first but also the *only* black to have been of service in that capacity. I left there thirteen years ago, and there has not been another black in that position since then. The irony of it is that I am not just the first black to hold that position. I am also the first person to have held that position that is not of Germanic descent. The reason for that was that a "tradition" had been established of appointing certain offices only to members of certain particular ethnic groups, and, prior to myself, the financial officers for the city had always been Germans, and certain other ethnic groups were always appointed to other positions. So the treasurer was always Jewish, and I am sure that the Greeks and the Scandinavians had positions that were reserved for them as well.

TB: So every ethnic group had their own place within the hierarchy.

CB: Everybody except blacks.

TB: But you helped to change that situation.

CB: It has not changed nearly as much as I had thought that it would by now.

TB: At the present time, Clark, tell me how many positions do you currently hold here in the city and other places as well?

CB: To answer that completely would take a great deal of time. First of all, as you know, I am senior vice president of the First National Bank of Chicago, but I am also head of my own department here. In other words, senior vice president is my official title, but my functional title is department head, which means that I am in charge of copy centers, affirmative action, and public image. There are a series of copy centers that report to me, and I am in charge of my own balance sheets and profit and loss statements. If the revenue generated is not enough to cover all the costs—not only my direct expenses but also my corporate overhead—then we lose money. But, if we make money, that profit is structured to become the source of our compensation from the corporate company.

TB: So those are your responsibilities here at the bank, but you are also chairman of the Chicago Transit Authority, is that right?

CB: That is right, and I have been on their board for a good number of years.

TB: Then, of course, you also belong to many civic organizations.

CB: Yes, here in Cook County I serve on many boards that serve the civic, educational, health care, and private sectors. Let me think what you would be the most interested in. I am the chairman of the Health Care Subcommittee. I am also a member of the Executive Committee of the Board of Directors Committee, and cochairman of the Metropolitan Council. At the CTA I am president of the pension fund, and I serve on the advisory board for all the pension funds for the City of Chicago.

TB: In looking back over your impressive career, Clark, is there anything that you might like to say by way of summation?

CB: Yes, I would like to say that I am proud of the fact that I chose to make my career in the *business* of government and not in the *politics* of government. I could probably have moved up a lot faster by going the other way, but I chose not to do that. That was a conscious decision on my part, and it is one that I have never regretted even for one single moment.

TB: What you're saying is that because you worked your way up the hard way, step by step, you were eventually able to achieve your success solely on the basis of personal and professional merit. That's how you were able to break the mold that had previously held so many others back.

CB: Tim, I did not break the mold. I shattered it from within!

September 23 and November 11, 1992, and July 15, 1993

BURNETT "BO" CARTER

LIFELONG FRIEND

I first met Burnett Carter in 1938 when he was living with his mother, his step-dad, and two sisters — Clotele and Lucille — in a kitchenette apartment building that was located in the block at Fifty-sixth Street and Calumet Avenue in Chicago. Back then I was living on the same floor of that building with my mother and father. (By then my older brother Walter had already gone off to college.) My aunt Georgia with two of my cousins also were living in a single room on that same floor. Living conditions were crowded for all of us, but we got along so well together that we were like loving members of exactly the same family.

Because of the interest that both Clotele and Burnett shared in the show life of that period, as well as the personal connections and friendships that they had already established, I got the opportunity to meet and associate with the jazz saxophonist Lester "Prez" Young and Billie "Lady Day" Holiday. Bo was on the road to play professionally. Unfortunately, it was not very long before he discovered that the income from his musical career was not sufficient to support his wife and children, and he returned to Chicago where he found a steady income as a doorman at some of the posh apartment buildings on the Near North Side of the city.

Bo was born in Florida, where his family fled from the repressive (and often dangerous) conditions of life in Cuba. He spent much of his boyhood in Florida under oppressive conditions before the family finally moved to Chicago, the promised land, where many promises were broken but where hope at least remained on the horizon.

TB: When were you born, Burnett?

BC: On September 1, 1922.

TB: And where?

BC: Near Tampa, Florida, and my mother brought me and my sisters to Chicago in 1933. There was a world's fair here at that time.

TB: You probably weren't old enough to be interested in the fair back then.

BC: Well, I was about eleven. So, of course, that was the one place that I most wanted to go!

TB: Do you remember where you first lived?

BC: Yeah, we first lived at Thirty-fifth and Giles, right next to the Eighth Regiment Army Headquarters.

TB: That building is still there, but now it's in total disrepair. What was the neighborhood like when you first moved there?

BC: Everybody knew each other. It was a real friendly neighborhood. There was one family I remember around there that was kind of rough. I still remember one time when one of their kids caught me going to the movie and took away my fare, but the reason that I can remember that so clearly is because that was an exception. I don't remember anything else like that ever happening.

TB: This was that movie house on Thirty-fifth Street?

BC: Yes, at Thirty-fifth and State. I think it was called the States Theater or something like that.

TB: When your mother brought you all here, did you have any relatives that were already living here?

BC: No, we left my grandmother and an aunt and uncle down in Florida. Those were on my mother's side. My father was from Georgia, but I never knew him or any of his until I was much older.

TB: Is that so?

BC: Yes, you see, I first went out on the road playing my horn when I was about twenty years old, and on my twenty-first birthday, after touring all around Kansas City and the South, I came back to Chicago, and that's when I met my father for the first time. He was at my mother's house, but he was just leaving and going over to where his youngest sister was living. So at least I saw him, and he saw me, and we recognized each other. That's what I remember best about my twenty-first birthday!

TB: Where did you go to grammar school?

BC: Well, I started out at Raymond Elementary School, which was somewhere around Thirty-fifth and Wabash, and then I went over to Doolittle, and from there I went to Phillips High School.

TB: You went to Phillips? I thought you went to DuSable.

BC: I just went over to DuSable to play my horn!

[*Laughter.*]

TB: So you weren't really enrolled at DuSable?

BC: No, I wasn't, but I used to go around there and sit in with the concert band. That's when Captain Dyett took me under his wing.

TB: The great Captain Dyett! Is that when music became your passion?

BC: Yeah, so then what happened was that I dropped out of Phillips after the first year and started going to all the nightclubs just following the musicians and entertainers around and learning as much as I could.

TB: Wasn't there a place at Thirty-second and Michigan where your older sister, Clotele, was working for a while?

BC: Yes, that's the Cavern Inn. That's also where I first met Lester Young.

TB: This was in the late thirties, and the Cavern Inn was quite a lively place.

BC: Right, and that's where I got to be real good friends with Lester Young.

TB: Did you also know Billie Holiday?

BC: Yeah, I was never around her very often, but I met her, and she was a great lady. She and Lester called themselves the Royal Family: Prez named her Lady Day, and she named him the President.

TB: They related to each other so well in their music, but there was nothing going on between them romantically, was there?

BC: No, they were more like a sister and brother because their minds ran in the same direction: his sound, her voice.

TB: When she's singing, she pauses and waits for him to come in with his tenor to fill the space behind her.

BC: And when he would play a solo, he modulated his chords toward the end so she could flow right into the music.

TB: They knew how to listen to each other.

BC: And there aren't even too many brothers and sisters who seem to be able to do anything like that!

[*Laughter.*]

TB: So, now you've left Phillips, and you've met some famous musicians, and now you're starting to earn a living by playing music?

BC: Yes, at first I was just doing little gigs playing tenor in the bands in all the small nightclubs, but then I met this fellow named Charles Taylor that came out from New York every year to recruit upcoming musicians so that he didn't have to pay them much, and he'd take them on tour all around the South.

TB: Where were some of the places you went?

BC: Oh, let's see, Baton Rouge, Memphis, but we ended up in Kansas City. That's where I met Charlie Parker.

TB: Kansas City was his hometown. Was he still playing with Jay McShann?

BC: No, he had just left McShann, and he was just gigging when I met him.

TB: Now, this is in the early forties. As you remember them, what were the conditions like for black musicians and entertainers that were traveling through the South?

BC: Well, I think that black musicians had a little more liberty than the blacks that lived there or just came to visit their relatives. That was because they came down there to entertain, and so at least in the smaller towns and places like that the people that lived there would go out of their way to give them a little slack. Of course that wasn't true in the big cities where we were among the upper class. In places like that we always had to take a back seat or no seat at all! [*Laughter.*]

TB: Did you play mostly for whites?

BC: No, we played for both but separately. When we'd play in a small place, it was usually all right, and we didn't have any problems to speak of, but in the first-class places, you couldn't come in the front door. You had to go in through the back door, and you also had to go to the back to get your food or anything else you needed.

TB: It must have been kind of hard for guys like you from the North to make that kind of an adjustment, or did you just take that sort of thing for granted?

BC: Listen, back then I was just a young guy, and I was just playing and having fun. That's the way it was with me. We were traveling on a train, and Charles Taylor's wife would do most of the cooking for us, so food wasn't really much of a problem for any of us.

TB: You were traveling in your own train cars?

BC: That's right. We'd stop someplace to play every night, and we'd be practicing during the entire day, both before and after. Sometimes I was working so hard and enjoying myself so much that I even forgot to eat!

TB: So you traveled all through the South. Did you ever go East?

BC: Well, let me see, once we got as far east as Buffalo, New York. It was during the winter, and the strange thing about being there was that was where I met my father once again. It just so happened that he was staying there when we came through.

TB: Did you ever get to New Orleans?

BC: Yeah, that's where I met Punch Miller. I hadn't heard anything about him before I met him, but he played just like Louis Armstrong and was a really fine musician.

TB: Did you ever run into Nat King Cole during your travels?

BC: Not in the South or anywhere else but in Chicago. I always used to go and see him over at the Warwick Hall on Forty-seventh Street. We'd go up there on Sunday just to hear King Cole and his band. Well, Prez was in town on one of those Sundays and we talked him into going to the Warwick Hall with us, and Nat's band sounded so good to him that he called over to Oakwood Manor, which was where Basie's band was staying.

TB: Yes, that's where the band would be staying all right, but Count Basie would be staying somewhere else.

BC: And no one ever knew where that was!

[*Laughter.*]

Well, so, anyway, Prez told the guys in the band to give me his horn. So he gave me cab fare, and I went and got his horn and brought it back to him, and—oh, man!—that night Prez must have gone through at least twenty-five choruses with Nat's band!

TB: So you got to know Lester Young pretty well. Just what kind of guy was he?

BC: Oh, man, he was one of a kind! He was just like his style of playing: totally unique!

TB: He set a new standard for playing the tenor.

BC: And his sense of humor was going on *all* the time! I never got together with him anywhere except here in Chicago, but, whenever he'd hit town, we'd always get together.

TB: How long did you stay on the road?

BC: Only for about two years.

TB: And then you came back to Chicago?

BC: Yeah, and I started gigging with the local bands. I played with Gene Ammons for a while over at the Bamboo Lounge at Fortieth and what's now King Drive. Do you remember that place?

TB: Yes, I do.

BC: Then I started playing with the bands at the Rhumboogie. That's where I met that great tap dancer Baby Lawrence.

TB: He was fantastic! I remember one evening when he danced all the way from the DeLisa down to the 'Boogie, and he didn't repeat a single step or rhythm pattern anywhere along the way.

BC: He was one of a kind. You know I also had the opportunity to meet Coleman Hawkins when he was playing at the 'Boogie, and you know something? That Hawk could play so strong and loud that he could drown out their thirteen-piece band!

[*Laughter.*]

You know a lot of famous musicians go commercial or try to put a little show-manship or even some comedy into what they're doing, but guys like Prez and Bird and the Hawk, they were real stars, and they never did things like that. When they played, they meant *serious* business, and they didn't clown around.

TB: Now, you got married about this same time, didn't you?

BC: That's right. I got married in 1950, and then I started to have to settle down and take care of some serious responsibilities of my own. In terms of music, I guess I never really did make the big time, but along the way, I met some great people: all those people we've been talking about and other guys like Dizzy Gillespie and Miles Davis. You name them, and I knew them. Those memories mean so much to me.

TB: Well, thanks for sharing them with me.

BC: Now I know for certain that they won't be lost.

TB: No, they won't. That's a promise.

July 17, 1995

JERRY "ICEMAN" BUTLER

PIONEER OF RHYTHM AND BLUES

It came as something of a surprise to me to discover that Jerry Butler, who is an internationally known popular singer as well as a Cook County commissioner, is one of the most modest persons whom I have ever met. Though I was familiar with his musical abilities (and most especially enjoyed his song "Only the Strong Survive"), I had never met Jerry until Lovana Jones's campaign for Illinois state representative in 1984. We were both at a planning meeting at the home of one of Lou Jones's friends, and she said to me, "Tim, I'd like you to meet Jerry Butler."

At first I did not make the connection between his name and the person whose music I had so much enjoyed until she saved the situation by adding, "You know, Jerry Butler the singer!" I felt embarrassed, but Jerry just smiled and said, "Glad to meet you" in a quiet, self-effacing sort of manner. Later on, our paths crossed again when Jerry was running for county commissioner, as a Democrat, but without party support. He won that election and has been re-elected continuously ever since because his political independence on crucial issues such as health and criminal justice has created a lasting bond between him and the constituency that he represents.

Our recent conversations together were warm, informative, humorous, and insightful in regard to the experiences of a young boy and his family coming from Mississippi to the Near North Side of Chicago and struggling against the odds to find their way to much deserved success.

TB: Jerry, where were you born?

JB: I was born in Sunflower County, Mississippi.

TB: And when were you born?

JB: December 8, 1939.

TB: Well, I'm one day and a few years in front of you. I was born in 1918.

JB: Then you are also Sagittarius, and so is my son. Like you, he was born on December 7.

TB: Where were your parents born?

JB: I don't ever really recall discussing where my old man was born, but my mother was born down around a town called Drew, Mississippi. They were married down there and came to Chicago in 1942. They came on the Illinois Central over here on Twelfth Street. Snow was on the ground, and a big old Yellow Cab picked us up at the station and took us to the eleven hundred block of Sedgwick Street.

TB: That's on the Near North Side.

JB: Yes, we went there to live with my father's sister and her husband, who owned a restaurant right at the corner of Orleans and Oak. It was called Pearl's Kitchen, and it was a place where the all the preachers, all the players, all the police, all the judges would go to meet and eat morning, noon, and night! I mean, everybody who was somebody on the North Side was in Pearl's Kitchen at one time or another. When nobody felt like cooking, everybody would come to Pearl's Kitchen.

TB: It was a solid part of the community.

JB: More than that. It was home, and most of the folks in the family who came to Chicago, whether it might be from my mother's or father's side of the family, started out working in that restaurant until they could get on their feet and move on. There was one fellow that used to come there a lot that they used to call "T-Bone." He looked like an old beggar, and he'd usually come in the restaurant to get something to eat. Sometimes when he got sick and couldn't come in, my aunt used to send him food. Then one day they learned that he had died because it turned out that he had left everything he owned to my aunt for what she had done for him.

TB: Beautiful story.

JB: So when old Uncle John—John Bennett was his full name—died about two years ago, it wasn't surprising that a great many of the people that he had helped through the years—white, black, whatever color—came to his home to pay their respects.

TB: How long did you continue to live with your aunt and uncle?

JB: We lived with them until my father got a job with the Northwestern Railroad. That's when we moved down the street to 1139 North Sedgwick.

TB: What was that neighborhood like?

JB: Wayman AME Church was not too far from where we lived, and Olivet was right there between Orleans and Wells. That is where Ramsey Lewis and his family went to church. That's also where he learned how to play the piano. So it was a marvelous area, that little strip around there where we lived. You know, when I tell most people about where I'm from they all think that I must have come from either the South Side or the West Side because very few people really know anything about that little area north of the Loop, west of the Gold Coast, and east of Halsted Street, but that's where we lived.

TB: That part of town during that period of time was often referred to as "Little Italy" or "Little Sicily" because there was also a sizable number of Italians who lived in that neighborhood.

JB: No question about that. As a matter of fact, there was an Italian family that owned a drugstore down the street from us, and maybe four or five Catholic churches were within walking distance of my house. What later became Cabrini-Green was at that time called the Mother Cabrini Home.

TB: Yes, there was no "Green" back then, and it was a low rise.

JB: Right, they had little townhouses sort of like Ida B. Wells. It was fairly mixed in terms of who was living there. You had blacks, you had Polish, you had Jews, you had Irish, you had Italians—all of them living in that same housing complex.

TB: And there was a hospital close by.

JB: Yes, Henrotin.

TB: So back then the neighborhood was fairly self-contained.

JB: Yes, it was.

TB: Now, going back a little, since you left the South when you were still quite young, you probably don't remember very much about your experiences down there.

JB: Well, my mom and dad had a big fight when I was about eight years old, and she packed up all the kids and went back to Mississippi, and we stayed with her sister down there for about six months. So that was how I got my experience of Southern living! But I also have vivid memories of a time when I was three and my father was going out with an old hunting dog and throwing me up on the back of a wagon that was pulled by a mule. I tell people that, and they tell me, "There's no way you can remember that. You weren't old enough." But I also remember quite clearly that when that old hunting dog contracted rabies my father had to follow him out through the cornfield and shoot him.

TB: That must have been a heart-wrenching experience.

JB: Yes, it was.

TB: Did you know your grandparents at all?

JB: My grandfather, Jerry Butler, the man I'm named after, came up later and lived here in Chicago with us for a long time.

TB: How old was he when he passed?

JB: In his late seventies.

TB: Where did you go to school?

JB: I went to Jenner, which was right across the street from where we lived, all the way through the fifth grade, and then I went over to the Sexton School.

TB: You know, there were two Sexton schools: A. O. Sexton and James A. Sexton.

JB: Well, I graduated from James A. Sexton, and then went on to Washburne in 1954.

TB: How did you get into Washburne?

JB: I just walked over there and applied.

TB: It was in your neighborhood?

JB: Yes, it was at the corner of Sedgwick and Division.

TB: And later that same school became Cooley High.

JB: But then they tore it down.

TB: The reason I was asking you about how you got into Washburne is because back then Washburne was very selective about black students.

JB: Well, you know, Tim, I didn't know that, and because I didn't know that I didn't think about that. You see, my father died in the year that I graduated from grammar school. I was fourteen, and since I was the oldest son, that made me the man of the family. So I wanted to hurry up and learn a trade and get a job.

TB: How many brothers and sisters did you have?

JB: I have one older sister, one younger sister, and one younger brother.

TB: And you wanted to go to Washburne so you could learn a trade and help to support them.

JB: That's right, Tim. Washburne didn't have sports teams or anything like that, and so most of the kids I knew opted to go to Wells or to Wadsworth as opposed to going to Washburne.

TB: How many black students were in your class?

JB: My freshman class had about three hundred students, of which nine were black, and all of those black guys just like me lived within walking distance of the school.

TB: And where were the white students coming from?

JB: They were coming from the suburbs and everywhere else.

TB: What kind of school was Washburne? What was so special about it that made people want to come there from all over?

JB: Well, Washburne was unusual in the sense that it was a very highly accredited place. Most of the unions had an apprenticeship program inside the school. That's why Washburne was what it was. It was because of those trade unions' affiliation with it. As a matter of fact, when I went there, almost 40 percent of the students in the school were there under the GI Bill. Those guys had come back from the war, and they were going to Washburne to learn lithography, cabinet making, carpentry, auto mechanics, and things like that. It was mandatory that you take one of those shops—so I wound up becoming the first high school student ever admitted to the Washburne chef training school, and that was just where I wanted to be because I really didn't much like tinkering with metals and scraping my knuckles and all that kind of stuff.

[*Laughter.*]

All the big chefs in town used to come to our school and give demonstrations. Sometimes they would even hire students right out of the class and give them a job in their kitchens.

TB: So at Washburne, if they were able to get in, there were opportunities in terms of the possibilities for employment for blacks that would not have been available in any of the other schools.

JB: The only other two schools—and I don't think they were as highly accredited— would have been Chicago Vocational and Lane Tech, and both of them were lily white back then.

TB: Let me ask you this question, Jerry. Did you ever take advantage of your training there or did you just go directly into the field of music?

JB: Well, at the time I was going to high school and studying chef's training, I was working after school at the Lawson YMCA, which was right over at Chicago Avenue and Dearborn. My aunt was working in their kitchen, and she told me there was a position open for a dishwasher or busboy or something like that. So I went over and took a part-time job based on her recommendation. Then I worked my way up to being a short-order cook.

TB: How did you feel about doing this kind of menial work?

JB: To tell you the truth, I never thought of it that way. For me it was just work. My father worked two jobs from the time he first landed here in Chicago until the time he died, and he was only forty-seven or forty-eight years old when he died. So he probably worked himself to death, but what that meant to me was that work was a habit in my house. The only person who didn't work was my mom. My father said, "You stay here and cook dinner and raise these kids, and I'll take care of everything else." So I grew up with that kind of work ethic, and for me my attitude toward my job wasn't about it being menial work. For me it was a job, and that's all, but you know, I recall one time my cousin came by the restaurant, and I told him I wanted to borrow some money from him because I wanted to quit my job. So he said, "Why do you want to quit this job?"—and I said it was because they were giving me so much bullshit that I just couldn't take it anymore. He said to me, "Well, it seems that you're too proud to take the bullshit, but not too proud to stoop to borrow money." That statement he made has stuck with me all of my life. Is pride not having to put up with some bullshit on the job or is it not begging for money? Which is it? Where do you draw the line? So, anyway, for me it was never about how menial the task might be. It was about how well you do that particular task and whether you are going to be satisfied doing this sort of thing for the rest of your life. What happened for me was that I got started early in show business and started traveling around.

TB: So you didn't need to develop those skills you had learned at Washburne?

JB: Well, even now, when I cook at home, it's from what I learned back then, but I never actually got a chance to practice my trade.

TB: How did you get into show business?

JB: Accidentally on purpose! You see, at the time I was going to high school all of the kids were not only singing in church choirs and school choruses. They were also singing on the street corners and everywhere they went. So I was messing around with a lot of little groups in town. As a matter of fact, I even wrote a song called "If Love Is Wrong," and one of those little groups I'd been messing around with recorded that song while I was working, and they didn't cut me in on the pay! I was just so upset that I was really heartbroken, but then about a year later a group of guys came here from Chattanooga, Tennessee, hoping to make a recording.

TB: At that time Chicago was the place to come for things like that, especially if you were from the South. What's more, there were really no major recording companies in places like St. Louis or Detroit either. So Chicago was the major recording center.

JB: As a matter of fact, Vee-Jay Records here in Chicago was the company I started with myself, but, anyway, these guys came here from Chattanooga with the hope that they were going to get a recording contract, and a friend told me about them. He said, "You know, Jerry used to be in our group, and he wrote a song for us," and so those guys asked me to come in their group as a kind of substitute for a couple of people who thought that coming to Chicago was just a fool's errand. Well, they still needed someone else, and so I got another friend of mine—Curtis Mayfield—to get involved with the group. About a year after that happened we made a recording, and the song that I composed for that session was called "For Your Precious Love"!

TB: And that song hit the top of the charts!

JB: Yes, it did, and that started my whole career. It was difficult to get a ballad like that on the pop charts, but "Precious Love" stayed there for almost a year.

TB: Do you remember how many copies you sold?

JB: No, I don't. I still get royalties from that song some thirty years later, but the reason I say I don't know how many copies were sold is because Vee-Jay was one of those companies that was not into explaining whether or not you sold a million records. You see, this was during the end of the period of the transition from the 78 to the 45 and the long-playing album, and so the song was released in all those different formats. It was also released on three different labels because Vee-Jay wanted to build a subsidiary company which was going to be called Falcon Records. So they moved it there and then back to Vee-Jay. Because of all that, there was never one single place to focus where all the sales were coming from.

TB: Now, besides Curtis, who else was in your group at this time?

JB: It was Curtis Mayfield, Arthur and Richard Brooks, and Sam Gooden, and myself.

TB: And you called yourselves?

JB: The Impressions!

TB: How long did you stay together?

JB: Well, after rehearsing for about a year in the basement over on Larrabee Street, we recorded "Precious Love" in April of 1958, but then by October of that same year I was out of the group!

TB: Why was that?

JB: What happened was that when we went to Vee-Jay Records, we originally signed a contract as the Impressions, and then we each signed another series of contracts with them as individual artists. Well, the lady who owned the company—her name was Vivian Carter—she also had a record shop in Gary, Indiana, and a radio show of her own. So she took this record we had made over to her record shop and started playing it on big loudspeakers that could be heard out on the street as well as featuring it on her radio program. Now, what she was playing was not really a copy of the record itself but just a test pressing, and when people heard that song, they started asking her who was singing the lead, and she told them my name. So pretty soon they all started asking for the record by using my name, and that's why she decided to release the record as being by "Jerry Butler and the Impressions." That was her business mind working, but, when that happened, all of the other guys in the group assumed that I had cut some kind of deal with this woman in order to get my name out in front. So that's what destroyed the group. Every place we went to perform there was a new fight about that same subject.

TB: So now you decided to go out on your own.

JB: Yes, but that was a painful decision for me to make. You see, I have always been pretty much of a group-oriented person in the sense that I believe that the group is more important than the individual.

TB: And that belief no doubt comes out of your earlier family experience.

JB: You're right. I would certainly agree with that. Well, now I was out on my own for the first time.

TB: Did you have an agent?

JB: Well, I had an agent in New York who was part of a company called the General Artist Corporation, but Ewart Abner, who was president of Vee-Jay Records, was for all intents and purposes my personal manager.

TB: He was the brother of Willoughby Abner, the great labor leader. During the split with your singing group, did you have legal counsel?

JB: Yes, it was the attorney for Vee-Jay Records at that time whose name was Earl Strayhorn.

TB: Jerry, did you know that Earl and I were in the second grade together at Burke School? Now he's a judge.

JB: No, I didn't know that. The only thing I know is that he gave me good advice, and so I left the group. I remember sitting down with Curtis and asking him to go with me, but he said, "Well, Jerry, I think I'm going to stay with the group." You see, at that time Curtis was only about sixteen or seventeen years old, and he had already dropped out of school. So he decided not to go, and, after my leaving, he naturally became the new lead singer. What is interesting is that eventually all of us—Jerry Butler, Curtis Mayfield, *and* the Impressions—went our separate ways, and yet all of us continued to be successful.

TB: Which is very unusual. Do you ever see each other now?

JB: Curtis has been living in Atlanta since about 1965. He no longer travels or performs because he became paralyzed in a freak accident.

TB: How did that happen?

JB: Curtis was performing in an outdoor arena and getting ready to go off stage when a heavy wind blew a lighting scaffold on top of him. It broke his neck in about six places and paralyzed him.

TB: That's terrible.

JB: Yes, it certainly is.

TB: So, when you went out on the road as a solo, did you have to select a new backup group?

JB: At first there was no money for me to hire a backup vocal group or any musicians to go on tour with me. So I went on the road alone and had to suffer at the mercy of whatever band I might happen to run into wherever the gig was being played. Eventually I saved enough money to be able to afford an accompanist, and things continued to get better from then on.

TB: So now you were traveling around the country and trying to build what would become a highly successful musical career. What are some of your memories of those days?

JB: Well, my first solo venture took me to New York, Philadelphia, and Washington, D.C. From there we headed south, and most of the gigs were not in major cities but in small towns where the folks didn't get to see much entertainment.

TB: Were the performances you gave before segregated audiences?

JB: Yes, the audiences were segregated in the early days, but blacks and whites attended the same performances. After the civil rights movement, the audiences were either all black or all white. You would have thought that integration would have brought all the people together, but that just isn't the way it happened. As a result, a lot of black promoters went out of business because when the audiences were segregated they were able to sell to both the blacks and whites who wanted to see the show, and now those days were over.

TB: How were entertainers like yourself treated in terms of accommodations during those early days?

JB: Well, by the time we'd reach southern Indiana, we'd start to see separate bathrooms for colored and white people, and there were no restaurants to speak of where we could get something to eat. So we had to stop at grocery stores along the way and buy some bologna and crackers and stuff like that. When we got into the really Southern cities, unless someone happened to know a family living there, invariably we had to rent a room in one of those "transient hotels" which were usually just flophouses or places where you could go with a prostitute. Those were the only kind of places where you could get a room, and sometimes even those kinds of rooms were hard to get because there was so much demand. Truck drivers, travelers, minor league baseball players—anyone who was black—would have to vie for those same accommodations, and sometimes the competition was really fierce! Conditions were much better in the large cities such as Atlanta and Birmingham because there at least they had fairly decent separate hotels that we could stay in. Even so, I loved what I was doing, and, on top of that, it was educational for me. I'm fifty-two now, but can you imagine what it was like for someone who is eighteen or nineteen years old to be going to all of these cities? Just tell me what town you want to go to, and I can probably tell you exactly which highway to take if you want to drive there!

[*Laughter.*]

What's more, I made friends in all these different places. So now I've still got friends from Greensboro and Birmingham and Nashville and Chattanooga that were all the direct result of performing in those towns—and the stories those people would tell me! They were just wonderful.

TB: What about some of the other entertainers and musicians that you met during your travels?

JB: Well, it was a marvelous period. We had the Apollo Theater in New York, the Regal Theater here in Chicago, and the Howard Theater in Washington, D.C. The house band at the time we played those places might be Red Saunders or Buddy Johnson or sometimes Count Basie or even Duke Ellington. As a matter of fact, I recall doing a show at the Howard Theater when Miles Davis was on the bill.

TB: That must have been a thrill.

JB: It most certainly was.

TB: And it seems that your early experiences here in Chicago prepared you rather well both personally as well as professionally for all of those both positive and negative experiences that you were to encounter in your travels.

JB: You know, I've always viewed New York the same way that I now view California. Sure, you've got all the best cats out there, but, believe me, they weren't all born in those places. Most of them migrated there from someplace else.

TB: Yes, and much of that talent was nurtured right here in Chicago. Performers became seasoned here so that when they arrived in New York, they were polished and ready to go!

JB: That's right, but now hardly any of those venues that we used as our training grounds are still in existence.

TB: How long did you intend to stay on the road?

JB: Well, sometimes I'm *still* on the road, but back then it was like being in the army! I got married when I was nineteen, and I would be gone for three, four, five, six months at a time because it was too expensive to come back home, but we worked things out and my wife and I have now been married for the last thirty-four years!

TB: You also performed overseas. How were the audiences in England or France different from the audiences we have here?

JB: First of all, let me say the reception from young African-Americans in this country was greater than anywhere else, but what I found in Europe was that people in the audience tended to know more about you. They would come not only to see the performer and hear them perform a hit song. Over there they would also know who played on the recording session. They would even know in what studio the song was recorded and who the songwriters were. Over here all they seem to care about is the hit song that they want to hear. They don't care about any of the interesting stuff that made the hit happen.

TB: Did you ever work with Curtis again?

JB: Yes, years later Curtis came back to work with me, and we formed a company to publish the songs we were writing together, but then on his own Curtis wrote a song called "Gypsy Woman" and that catapulted him into an exclusive contract with ABC-Paramount Records.

TB: Now, in reviewing your own life, most of it lived here in Chicago, what changes have you seen positively or negatively in regard to your profession or as they might relate to your current work as a government official? In particular, what are some of the challenges that you see for the young people of today?

JB: All right, first of all, let's deal with the changes that I have seen take place. I have seen middle-class and working-class neighborhoods that were once stable and family-oriented almost totally wiped out. They were destroyed primarily by the advent of public housing. In those high-rise buildings there are just too many people per square foot! I suppose there were always problems before any of those places were constructed, but those problems are nothing like the kind of problems you get when you concentrate ten or fifteen thousand people into a couple of blocks of real estate.

TB: Especially when you add to that the present level of poverty and the breakdown of the structure of the family.

JB: And it's not just the breakdown of the nuclear family. It's the breakdown of the entire community. In those twenty-five-story buildings, the guy who lives on the twenty-fifth floor probably hasn't ever even met most of the people living on the floors below him.

TB: And that same level of anonymity causes people to become much more apprehensive and suspicious of one another.

JB: I find that to be true, Tim, even here in this building where I live. When I say good morning to someone, I often see them tense up a little because they are not quite certain whether they should say good morning to me or not. "Why is he speaking to me? What does he want?" That sort of thing really troubles me because the way I was raised you don't ever walk past anybody without saying good morning or something like that.

TB: Your attitude comes from a sense of community that is part of a tradition that's been handed down from your own family, but today most people are quite literally living in a community of total strangers.

JB: Yes, where are the "Pearl's Kitchens" of today? They have all been replaced by the McDonald's and the Kentucky Fried Chicken type of places where you just go in, grab the food, and take it on out. People used to sit down in the places where they ate and have conversations there. You know, the most wonderful thing about Pearl's Kitchen was that you'd hear all sorts of people speaking with each other. You'd hear preachers talking to gamblers. There was a mutual understanding that even though I can't convince you that my philosophy is right or that your philosophy is wrong, we can still have an interesting and informative conversation with each other.

TB: People were able to communicate with each other like that because there was mutual understanding and respect.

JB: Yes, and parents would bring their children with them into those places, and the children would listen to those conversations and learn from what was being said. I miss all of that, but you know, I think that if there is one thing that I miss the most about the good old days, it is that doctors used to make house calls. You could lie in your own bed, and the doctor would come in and take care of you. "All right, Mrs. Butler, now your son's going to be sick for a couple of days. I'll give you these pills for him to take, but you better be sure to give him some of that homemade soup that you've got because that will probably do more good for him than what I'm giving him." Back then doctors were people that we knew. They weren't just somebody that walked into the room where you were waiting so they could stick something up your behind!
[*Laughter.*]

TB: And when they'd leave, they'd pick up their bag and say, "Just call me if you need me."

JB: But all of that got wiped away by the violence that exists out in the streets. Now it isn't safe for a doctor to come to someone's house carrying any kind of money in his pocket.

TB: Or any kind of drugs in his medical bag.

JB: The more civilized we become, sometimes the more uncivilized we become. It didn't used to be the way it is now because people had more respect for each other. To the people who lived in our neighborhood, my father's name was *Mr.* Butler, and *Mr.* Laverty who owned the grocery store down the block always referred to him as *Mr.* Butler. That meant that *Mr.* Butler could always send one of his kids to *Mr.* Laverty's store and get anything that was needed from that store and sign for it because *Mr.* Laverty knew that *Mr.* Butler would die before he would leave that bill unpaid.

TB: But unfortunately that degree of trust and mutual respect just does not exist anymore.

JB: You know, I can also remember that once I stole some comic books from the drugstore around the corner, but the man who owned the store waited until my father came in with me to buy something, and then he said, "Mr. Butler, your son is stealing comic books." Well, of course, my daddy started to get pretty upset, and so the man said, "Now wait a minute. I don't want you to get so angry about what I just told you. Your son didn't know that I've been watching him take them, and he thinks he's getting away with it. So the reason I want to speak to you about this is because I'm worried that he just might start stealing bigger things some day and get himself into trouble." So my father took me back home, beat my ass, and made me pay for those comic books, but you know something? I never hated that man for telling him, and I never hated my old man for whipping me.

TB: Because you knew there were rules.

JB: Yes, and those were the rules I had broken.

TB: Those same rules are what some of us crazy fellows in the social sciences call "barometers of behavior," and back when I was growing up every kid in the neighborhood knew exactly what those boundary lines were.

JB: But now most of those lines have become nothing but gray areas.

TB: Yes, now it seems that the only boundary lines that are truly respected are those that define "turf," and, as a result, most of our young people have become more isolated than ever before.

JB: And Chicago is more deeply segregated now than it was when we were young.

TB: That's right. If you are caught up in the Cabrini-Green community, you know very little about the Gold Coast that exists just beyond the "gray area" where you live. If you are caught up in the Robert Taylor housing complex, Michigan Avenue seems to be a great distance away from you. King Drive—and the Grand Boulevard that it once was—is even further away. A place like Hyde Park is another world entirely.

JB: And you can't even dream about places like that—not even for your kids!— because you hardly know that places like that really exist or that you might have any possible means of access to them.

TB: What is there that we can do to connect our young people with the positive possibilities and opportunities that exist beyond their awareness?

JB: Well, first of all, I think that the black community needs to get back together and find a way to help these young people. Now, by "getting together" I don't mean any kind of a racist sort of thing. To be "pro" ourselves doesn't mean to be "anti" anyone else. Once we are able to get our own piece of society together, then all the other pieces—the problems, the pieces that don't quite fit—will fall into place. You know, what we're talking about reminds me of something that happened to me once. My wife and I were standing in line at the Stage Delicatessen in New York trying to get in and order ourselves a corned beef sandwich. You know that place? It's where all the performers that are working on Broadway go to get something to eat after the show. So, anyway, we're standing there right up next to the door waiting our turn, and the guy behind me steps on the back of my shoe. Well, when he does that, naturally I move up just a little bit, and, just as soon as I do that, the guy behind me also moves up a little more. In fact, the whole line, they *all* move up a little, and when that happens, this same guy steps on the back of my shoe again! So I start to get angry, but then my wife says, "You know what? You have just proved an important point about America, and that is that when a *black* man moves up in the line, everybody else moves up too!"

[*Laughter.*]

TB: Yes, and if we *don't* move up, then nobody moves. They stay right where they are, and these problems we're talking about will just continue to get worse instead of better.

JB: That is absolutely true.

January 30 and February 3, 1992

MATTIE BUTLER

WOODLAWN COMMUNITY ACTIVIST

I first made the acquaintance of Mattie Butler through my friendship with her brother, Jerry Butler, the well-known singer who is also a Cook County commissioner. The two of them are very close, and she is a star member of his singing group. Mattie Butler is an energetic, vivacious, aggressive social activist as well as an artful entertainer. She was and still is the vigorous proactive leader of a community organization in southeast Woodlawn whose primary mission is to save existing affordable housing for the lower-income families in that community. She is a feisty, outspoken, knowledgeable, and courageous little woman who does not try to avoid letting friends—and opponents as well—know just how passionately she feels about the ongoing attempts to displace these people from the homes where they have been living for the better part of their lives. The fact that the opponents she has squared off against are quite formidable (and include both the University of Chicago and the Woodlawn Organization) does not seem to matter very much to her. She just goes on fighting for justice for all of those whom she believes are being treated unfairly.

In this conversation Mattie Butler tells me about her experiences growing up on the Near North Side of Chicago and the forms of racial prejudice she had to endure and fight against in the public schools that she attended. The most important (and thrilling) aspect of this conversation for me, however, is that it serves to reflect the moral strength and fighting spirit that have defined her life and still enable her to continue the struggle for the kind of social justice in which she so fervently believes.

TB: Mattie, are you a native of Chicago?

MB: No, I was born in Mississippi in April 1943.

TB: Was your brother Jerry already born by then?

MB: Yes, he's the oldest son. My sister Dorothy is older than Jerry. The three of us were all born in the South. Our younger brother Joey was born here in Chicago. We are the four that survived.

TB: There were others that didn't.

MB: There were two that died. Both of them were born in Mississippi—one of them between my oldest sister and Jerry, and one between Jerry and me.

TB: What did your parents do to make a living?

MB: My father was a very special man. He was legally blind, but that didn't stop him. But because he was handicapped, people often tried to take advantage of him, and that was hard for him to bear.

TB: What about your mother? What sort of background did she have?

MB: My mother had a very different sort of background. She was the first-born granddaughter of a Baptist minister, and so she was educated to the point where she got at least an eighth-grade level of education.

TB: Which for black people of that generation from that region was highly unusual.

MB: It was, but my mother was very intelligent. She probably had an IQ that was stretching over to the other side of the planet somewhere. If only she had been born in another time in some other place, she probably would have been a professor or something special, something really great.

TB: So in spite of not much, if any, formal education, both of your parents were intelligent people.

MB: Very intelligent, and they knew a lot of things and developed a lot of skills. "Necessity is the mother of invention"—so they became great inventors of how to survive.

TB: And for that they had to be creative.

MB: Yes, they did. They had to be *very* creative.

TB: So, by the time they decided to leave Mississippi, your parents already had three children. Why did they decide to come to Chicago?

MB: They wanted a better life for themselves and their children, and they decided on coming to Chicago because my Aunt Pearl, who was my father's sister, and Uncle John, who was her husband, were already living in Chicago and had established a successful restaurant business on the North Side. They had a place called Pearl's Kitchen, which was famous throughout the city for serving Southern soul food.

TB: Yes, I remember that.

MB: And they were the ones who provided the gateway for the rest of the Butler family to come up here to the big city.

TB: When did they first come here?

MB: They came here about ten years before we did. My uncle was originally a navy man, and when he got out of the navy, he took the little money that he had saved and took his wife up to Chicago and opened up a little neighborhood restaurant.

TB: And that became Pearl's Kitchen?

MB: Right, after they'd saved a little more money and expanded it some more.

TB: When your family first came to Chicago, where on the North Side were you living?

MB: At first we lived on Sedgwick, and then we moved into one of those cold-water, four-flat walkups on Wells near Division. From where we were, we could actually watch all those other cold-water flats being torn down and Cabrini-Green being built. Later on, we were one of the first families to move into those new towers when they got built, those same ones that are being torn down right now. Curtis Mayfield's family also lived there back then.

TB: And Ramsey Lewis's family lived there as well. Did you know them?

MB: Yes, we knew the Lewis family.

TB: One of the authors of *Black Metropolis*, St. Clair Drake, also lived in Cabrini back then. His wife was white, and they both said that they liked living there. So in many ways back then that neighborhood was intellectually, culturally, ethnically a very diverse community.

MB: Yes, there were still a lot of Italians living in the neighborhood, but there were also quite a few Chinese and Japanese people as well a lot of Jews. We were within spitting distance of the Gold Coast area and also within walking distance from the Oak Street Beach.

TB: So how well did you all get along with each other?

MB: You mean our relationships with the other ethnic groups? Well, the Chinese and Japanese were real quiet people, and they just kind of blended right in with the African-American people who lived there. The Jewish people owned and operated most of the stores, but they kept mostly to themselves on any kind of social level. There were even some Hawaiians and Indians living there. So I guess we were all living together in what they now would call a "multicultural" neighborhood, but we didn't mix it up together very much, and so it still seemed sort of segregated.

TB: So there wasn't much socializing. Was there ever any trouble between the various groups?

MB: The only trouble came when we got Polish people coming into the neighborhood.

TB: Which school did you go to?

MB: I went to James A. Sexton, which is now a museum, and then I went on to Edward Jenner.

TB: After Jenner, where did you go?

MB: I went on to Wells High School.

TB: Where was that located?

MB: On Ashland near where it crosses Milwaukee Avenue.

TB: What was your experience like at that school?

MB: Well, let me tell you, going there was a whole different kind of experience for me.

TB: How so?

MB: That was the first time I had ever run smack dab into redneck racism. That school was in an all-white Polish and Italian neighborhood, and so right away I ran into all that stuff my mom had talked about having run into down in the South!

TB: How were the teachers?

MB: It wasn't just the students. The teachers were also extremely prejudiced. They acted as if they really thought that black folks were subhuman and didn't deserve anything of value, especially a good education.

TB: How did you handle that kind of situation?

MB: Well, I was a moody kind of child—very introverted—and so most of the time I would just sit there quietly and let the anger build up inside of me, but then when I got all the way filled up and I'd had enough of what was going on, I'd stand right up and cuss them out!

[*Laughter.*]

That's right. I'd just explode to get it out of me because I couldn't hold it in me any longer. That's still true, but now that I'm older and have more self-confidence, I don't hold it in for quite so long. These days I've learned how to do that sort of thing much quicker!

[*Laughter.*]

That's how I got kicked out of high school!

TB: Kicked out?

MB: Yes, I was a high school "kickout," not a dropout!

TB: How did that happen?

MB: Well, I was assigned to a history class, and the subject of this history class was the "Cradle of Civilization." So in the textbook they had a special section on

Egyptian culture, and the teacher kept referring to the people that were described in that section as if they all were white, and that troubled me because I knew my history or at least I knew what my mother and dad had taught me. So I knew full well that Egypt was on the continent of Africa!

[*Laughter.*]

You know, as I look back on it, that class was really just a class for the basketball team and the football team so that they could get good enough grades to stay on the teams. Myself and another young lady by the name of Juanita Armstrong were the only two females and the only two African-Americans in that entire class. The rest of them were all Italian and Polish kids who were playing on the teams. Now, in the seating pattern of that school, usually when you have a last name like "Armstrong" or "Butler," you are placed in seats that are in the front of the class, but when that teacher saw us there in his classroom and realized that most of his other students had names that began with an S, a T, or a Z, or something like that, he immediately changed the established seating pattern and placed the two of us way at the back of the room!

TB: So all of the X, Y, and Z's were up front, and the A, B, and C's were seated at the back.

MB: Yeah, and that pissed me off, and it pissed off the Armstrong girl as well.

TB: Was your brother Jerry in that school at that time?

MB: No, he was over at Washburne—so I didn't have a big brother at that school. I was the only one there, and Armstrong didn't have any relatives at the school either. Her sisters went to Waller. You see, during that time that's when they were changing all the boundary lines: if you live on this side of the street, you go to that high school, and if you live on that, you go to that other high school. So we got caught up in that boundary line changing, and that's how we found ourselves up at Wells High School in this very foreign neighborhood with a bunch of foreign people who didn't like us because of our color.

TB: I imagine that many of them still spoke with foreign accents.

MB: Absolutely, and some of them couldn't speak English at all.

TB: So most of them were first generation and yet they had already assimilated the bigotry of the established American culture.

MB: Well, I think most of them must have come here with those sorts of attitudes already in place. So, anyway, even though we were seated way in the back of the class, we tried to participate in the classroom discussions, but, because we were so short and all those ball players in front of us were so big, that teacher could never see us raise our hands and let us join in on what was being said. So, at the end of our first marking period, we both got bad grades because that teacher claimed that during the discussions we didn't ever answer any of his questions, but the only reason we didn't answer those questions of his was because he never saw that our hands were up.

TB: Or, perhaps, he chose to ignore them.

MB: Well, you might very well be right, but when I went home with that bad grade, my mama really kicked my butt!

TB: That was because she knew you could do better than that.

MB: That's right, and so she thought I must have been messin' around more than I should have.

TB: Didn't you try to explain the situation to her?

MB: Yes, I did, but my mother would not listen to any of that "it's the teacher's fault" sort of explanation because she was taught you should always show your teachers respect because they are adults and they know more than you do. So, although by now I am furious with this teacher, I decide that I'm not going to get any more bad grades from that man because I don't participate in class. If he can't see me raising my hand, then that means I've got to find a way to make him see me. So I worked it out in my head that the next time we'd have one of those quizzes and he starts asking questions, I am going to stand up in my chair and raise my hand. That way maybe I would be tall enough for him to see me and call on me. So that's just what I did!

TB: What did the teacher do?

MB: He turned his back on me. That's what he did, and then he turned around and bellowed at me, "Armstrong, sit down!"

TB: He called you "Armstrong"?

MB: Yes, so that pissed me off even more because Armstrong was very light-skinned and I was very dark. Ain't no way for anyone to mistake us because, you know, we were looking like chocolate and vanilla sitting there next to each other!
[*Laughter.*]
So I told him, "My name is not Armstrong. It is Butler." "Well, what do you want?" he says, but by this time I am so angry that I've forgotten exactly what his question was. So instead I ask him, "Isn't Egypt on the continent of Africa?" "Yes," he says. "And isn't Africa the home of people who are black in color just like me?" "Yes, but what difference does that make?" "Well, if it don't make no damn difference, then why are you always trying to make it sound like they must have all been white?"
[*Laughter.*]
Oh, that was just the start. I really went off on him. I said, "You redneck son of a bitch, I hate you!" Yes, I did, and then I talked about his mama . . . and his daddy!

TB: You got into the dozens?

MB: Oh, yeah, I played the dozens with him real good, and I told him, "You are do-ing your own kind more injustice than you are doing to me because at least I know my history, and you are teaching them a bunch of lies. How do you think they're going to feel when they get out of this class and grow up believing all this bullshit and then some day they go to Egypt and find out for themselves that the people in Egypt are black? And when they go to college, the anthropologists there are going to ask them just who the hell their history teacher was, how are you going to feel about that? You know, if you cared anything at all about *any* of your students you would be telling them the truth and not just lies." So he told me, "Butler, you are not the one teaching this class," and I said, "And you ain't either, you stupid son of a bitch!" So he said, "Butler, you're suspended!"—and I said, "You can't suspend me because you don't have the authority to suspend me. Anyway I quit. Fuck you!" So I walked out of there right down to the princi-pal's office, and that's when I got kicked out of school.

TB: What happened then?

MB: They put me directly into a school for "bad" girls. I was in there all day until two in the afternoon, and then they'd let you go home.

TB: Did they try to teach you anything?

MB: All they were doing in there was teaching you how to sew, and all you were do-ing was waiting until you got to be seventeen and you could get out of there. It was like I was in jail. They weren't teaching shit in there.

TB: At least you were able to go home at night.

MB: Yes, but once you got in that place, they locked the doors. Then at two o'clock they'd unlock those doors and let you out.

TB: Meanwhile nothing much of an educational nature is happening.

MB: Zero formal education, but a lot of informal education was going on there.

TB: Such as?

MB: An introduction to lesbian culture and information about how to become a successful lady of the night working out on the streets!

TB: How long did you have to stay there?

MB: Only about two months, because I turned seventeen and then I was a legal age where I didn't have to go to school anymore.

TB: After leaving school, what did you do?

MB: I went straight downtown and took the GED test so I could get a high school diploma.

TB: Did you pass it?

MB: Of course, but they wouldn't give me my diploma until I got to be to be eigh-teen. They told me they would send it to me on my eighteenth birthday. So that's when I started working at the Lawson YMCA. I got that job because I had two aunts—my mother's two sisters—who were working there in the cafeteria. One of them was the head cook, and the other was working her way up from being a carver or something like that. So I started working there as a busgirl.

TB: That was a residential YMCA, wasn't it?

MB: Yes, I thought it was some sort of a men's club where they had exercise rooms and stuff like that and where some of them were also living.

TB: How long did you continue to work there?

MB: Until the late fifties.

TB: By then your brother Jerry had already joined a singing group.

MB: Yes, they had already started their group.

TB: And the rest is history! Were you doing any singing with them at that time?

MB: I was singing by then, but not with them. I was with a trio singing jazz in the nightclubs up on Rush Street on the weekends.

TB: Really?

MB: Yes, I was the baby of the group, and those older jazz guys thought they were my chaperones or something and made sure I would dress in a manner that they thought was appropriate for my age. I mean, if I had on something that was too revealing, they would take me back home and make me go into my closet and get something else to wear. Those guys were almost like my brothers or my uncles. It was almost like we were some sort of extended family or something. So, at the same time Jerry was starting out, I was doing more or less the same sort of thing.

TB: So now you are singing professionally on the weekends, and you've left the Lawson Y.

MB: No, I was still working part-time as a busgirl at the Lawson Y, but then I had my first child when I was twenty. I was lucky because I had just given birth to my daughter at around the same time that the War on Poverty with all its massive training programs was coming into the city of Chicago, and I was recruited into their clerical jobs training program. What happened was I got about six months of training, and then they hired me as a clerk. They were just amazed at how quickly I could learn something like that and be able to do it so well. As a result, it wasn't very long before I moved up from that position to become an office manager.

TB: How did you like that kind of work?

MB: Well, I was working under a white guy in the Jobs Now program in a branch office in a Hispanic neighborhood. That guy was a relative of somebody who was a really powerful person, but I was responsible for writing all their checks and balancing their checking accounts and stuff like that. Then one day this guy tells me to write a check for him and to sign it, but somehow what he is saying doesn't sound quite right to me, and so I ask him a few questions about what it's for, and he says, "Don't question me—just do what I say!" So I say, "Hey, wait a minute. It's *my* signature that's going on this check. Now, if *you* want to be the one who signs it, then I'll be glad to type it up for you to sign, but don't you just tell me to sign some shit without answering my questions about why the hell I should do something like that!"

TB: How did he respond?

MB: Well, he said, "You're fired," and I said, "Fuck you," and I got up and packed up all my shit and I left and went straight downtown to the main office, which was in the YMCA building, because at that time the Y was acting as their fiscal agent and controlling all the financial aspects of this federal program on the local level. So I went right in and asked to speak to the top director, and I told him what had happened and why I'd been fired. Well, he said something crazy to me that got me mad—so I got up out of my chair and stepped up on top of his desk!

TB: You did what?

MB: I stepped right up on top of his desk, and the reason I did that was because he was this big, tall white guy, and I wanted to look him right in his eye when I told him that those people I was working under were stealing money from the program and putting it into their own pockets, and that I was not about to go along with anything like that.

TB: The federal money never dripped down to the level it was supposed to.

MB: That's right, because at the upper levels they were all in cahoots. It wasn't just the local people stealing money. They were stealing money right at the top executive level as well. That's why it makes me so mad when I hear that the Jobs Now program failed because black people were the ones who were stealing from white people. That's absolutely untrue. Black people were the ones who were trying to make that program work, and when the top people over them told them to sign this, that, or the other thing, they didn't usually question it, and because it was their signatures that were on the checks, they were the ones that got all the blame.

TB: The money got stolen over them.

MB: Yes, they were the fall guys, and all of the top people were mostly crooks. I mean, they must have been teaching them how to be crooks from the very first minute that they walked in the door!

TB: And blacks usually can't even get in that door, and yet they're usually the ones to get all the blame—

MB: —when the shit hits the fan!

TB: *If* it hits the fan!

[*Bitter laughter.*]

And about the same kind of thing is still going on in the world today. The people who are making the real money are almost always white, and the folks who get the crumbs also usually get all the blame, and they are most usually black.

MB: Sad but true.

TB: So what happened next in terms of your career?

MB: Well, they transferred me to another office, and I became a counselor for people graduating from the job training program.

TB: Exactly what kind of counseling did you do?

MB: I was dealing primarily with those banks here in Chicago that were taking federal money but were *not* hiring black people. You see, in order for them to keep that federal money coming into their banks, they needed to hire the people that were coming out of our job training programs. So this young man who was my partner and I would go in as a team and talk to the white managers of those large banks and try to get them to hire our graduates after they had completed their training.

TB: Did you have to tone down the kind of language you used when you were talking with those guys at the banks?

MB: Hell, no! A lot of those people cursed worse than we did, but they didn't know how to take a breath every once in a while and let it build!
[*Laughter.*]

TB: They didn't have the right beat.

MB: That's right. They just let it all out without pausing—and, by the way, what's with all this "gee," "golly," and "wow" kind of thing they were always saying?
[*Laughter.*]

TB: At this point, had you transferred your residence to the South Side?

MB: No, I was still living in Cabrini.

TB: All right, but tell me this. We've always had this kind of breach in the relations between the black communities on the North Side, the West Side, and the South Side. How did the young people like you relate to those kind of divisions? Did you have any friends who lived on the South Side?

MB: Of course I did. I had friends and relatives who lived all over the South Side, and I also had friends and relatives on the West Side. So I never got caught up in any of that kind of crap! I've always been of the mind that if you are my color I don't care what side of town you're coming out of. No matter where you're living, you've got the same kind of problems that I've got. You know what I mean? We've got more in common than we have that isn't common, and geography doesn't make much, if any, difference! So when people start talking about how on the South Side they do this and on the West Side they do that, I always say, "Is you black or ain't you?"

TB: So for you there never was a barrier of any kind. Your feelings transcend—

MB: They transcend geography.

TB: Well, I have been fortunate in that same way, but for other people there has always been a social distance between those three geographical areas.

MB: All of that is superficial and artificial.

TB: But it's also a class thing. People on the North Side and the West Side think that those who live on the South Side think that they are of a higher class.

MB: Well, all I can say is that for me and my brothers and sisters, we never saw the point of any argument about people of our color being any different from each other no matter what side of town they happened to live on.

TB: So when did you move to Woodlawn?

MB: We moved to Woodlawn in '69.

TB: Your whole family, including your mother and dad?

MB: No, my father was dead by that time. He died when I was only eleven.

TB: Now, when you moved into Woodlawn, you also started to become active in community organizing. Did this come naturally out of your previous experience?

MB: I really don't know if it comes naturally or because of the fact that when I was a counselor I somehow managed to develop some skills that I didn't even know I had, but what happened was that I got involved because at that time in Woodlawn we were being burnt out of our homes. I mean, every weekend there was another fire!

TB: Arson?

MB: We knew that all these fires were set by outside arsonists, but the fire department kept trying to convince us that it was members of our own community that were trying to burn us out. Somehow they expected us to believe that we all were so messed up and suicidal that we would actually be setting ourselves on fire!

TB: Fires were also being set in North Kenwood and Oakland during that period.

MB: What was happening was that they were trying to burn us out of our homes, and so every week we'd be fighting fires and sometimes being shot at while we were trying to put those fires out.

TB: And this was in 1980?

MB: Yes, and then in the fall of '80 there was this house two doors away from my own house that got burned down. It used to be one of those big, old houses that had been cut up and turned into a two-flat. There were two women living in that building who were sisters, and each of them had five kids. Although those women survived the fire, each of them lost four of their five kids. One of those children only survived because he was out getting McDonald's for the other kids. When he came back, the building was engulfed in flames.

TB: Where was that building?

MB: On Sixty-fifth Place between Blackstone and Stony Island. Now it's just a vacant lot, but when I start to talk about what happened, every time I close my eyes I can still see the devastation of those families. So it ain't over for me yet. It ain't over at all.

TB: Did this happen in the morning?

MB: No, in the evening, and so, after the firemen put out the fire, we took what was left of the families over to their aunt's house because she happened to live in the next block. Then we found some people in the neighborhood who had a car and sent them to go get the mother of one of those kids that had survived. You see, she had just started a job out in the western suburbs, and so she didn't yet know that four of her babies were gone. Then, when they brought her back, that's when those guys from the television station came in with their cameras and everything. Well, when those guys came busting through the door, what they found were those two devastated black women and myself because I was sitting quietly over in a corner of that house holding onto one of the babies that was left, trying to calm that baby down. Now, this was the Channel 2 News team, but they were led into that house by two of the organizers from the Woodlawn Organization who were so eager to help these reporters get their story that they started shouting at those women and clapping their hands at them and telling them where to stand and what to say and what to do. Well, what was happening was making me so angry that I put the baby down in the crib, and I got me a great big sheet from out of that crib, and I hung that sheet over the cameraman's head and the camera that he was holding, and then I told them, "Get the fuck out of here!" Yes, I did. That's what I told them because this was not the time or place for any of their kind of nonsense. If these had been white women who had lost their babies, they would have brought a medical person along with them to help those women with the trauma they were going through. There would be doctors there to help them deal with what had happened and not some cameraman flashing lights in their faces. There needed to be someone there to say to those guys, "You can have your story a little later, perhaps, when these people are ready to talk to you," but nobody was there to say that except me—so I became that person, and I said, "Get your monkey asses out of here!" Well, when I did that, one of those organizers from the Woodlawn Organization kind of looked at me in surprise and started to say something crazy to calm me down, and so I said to him, "You better not say any more shit, my brother, or I will move some niggers in here to kick your ass!" So they all backed off, but I stayed angry, and, looking back, I think that what happened that day was what led me toward becoming more active in the community. I mean, it was almost like I had lost part of my own family, and so from that point on I started asking questions about what was really going on. Why are we having these fires? Who is setting them? Is it someone inside the community or is it someone coming in from outside? Who has something to gain from all these buildings burning down? So, on my own, I became a sort of one-woman research team for the next two years or so.

TB: All by yourself?

MB: Yeah, until I ran into Arvis Arverette.

TB: Tell me about him.

MB: Well, Arvis is a young man who came here from Ohio to go to the University of Chicago School of Social Work to get his master's degree. During that period of time, he was also an intern at the Woodlawn Organization and actually was writing his thesis paper on those fires that were being set in Woodlawn. His paper documented the fact that those fires were set by outside owners and not by the people inside the community. So he was well aware of what was really going on, and when he saw how angry I was, he told me, "Well, if you're so upset about what's happening, then do something about it!"—and I said, "Listen, Arvis, I'm just four feet eleven inches tall, and I only weigh ninety-eight pounds. Just what the hell do you think I can do?" He told me, "Well, you might be surprised at what you'll learn once you start talking to the neighbors that live beyond your own street. Just ask them what's going on, and see if somebody can answer those questions you're asking." So that's what I did.

TB: So now you're reaching out into the wider community, and you develop an organization called WECAN. How did you come up with that name?

MB: Well, that was Arvis's invention. He knew we were looking for a name, and he said, "Well, first of all, let's look at what your group is doing and where it is located." So that's how we got the first letter: W for Woodlawn, and because we were located in the eastern region of Woodlawn, that's how we decided on the second letter, which is E for Woodlawn East. The C, the A, and the N stand for Community and Neighbors because now we were reaching outside of our immediate area to gather information from the people who used to live in the community but had recently moved away.

TB: Yes, we're talking the early 1980s, and by that time probably about a third of the population of Woodlawn had moved out of the community. At that time were the gangs still active here?

MB: Well, the gangs were still active, but they were going through some kind of internal metamorphosis, and now they were operating more like some kind of a major corporation with various departments and heads of those departments and things like that.

TB: Where did they learn those organizing skills?

MB: I would imagine from the Woodlawn Organization and the University of Chicago. They even got money from the politicians because they were such a major force to be reckoned with in this community at that time. What I mean is when Jane Byrne was running for mayor, she had all of them knocking on people's doors in the community in order to tell the people inside to vote for her instead of Harold Washington. She gave some of her campaign money and dressed them up in suits and sent them out with handbills in their hands that said, "Vote for Jane"! Can you believe it?

TB: I can because I remember it happening.

MB: Well, when one of those brothers came knocking on my door, I let him in and sat him down and gave him a little history lesson. I took that campaign literature right out of his hand, and I told him, "You can take that money from those people if you want to because that is money that they have taken away from you and all of us, but, when you go into that voting booth, my brother, and get behind those closed curtains, you had better vote for somebody that looks like you and me, because if you vote for that woman, the minute she's elected your mama's going to be sitting on the sidewalk and you all are going to be going to jail!"

[Laughter.]

TB: So now you've organized WECAN and are getting actively involved in the affairs of the community.

MB: Yes, I was organizing people around the issue of maintaining safe and affordable housing for the low-income people who were living in our community, but what I discovered was that it wasn't just the outside white landlords that were ripping people off and trying to "gentrify" them out of their homes. What surprised me most was that black people were also involved in doing those same kinds of things. I mean, it's not just a matter of white folks kicking our ass. It's us kicking our own ass. It's our own ministers kicking our ass. It's our own leaders knocking us down. Why are we doing this to each other? So I've searched for the answers, and the answers I've found are troublesome for me. It seems that we no longer have the sense that we are all responsible to and for each other, and what's more, we don't respect each other the way that we should.

TB: And once did.

MB: You know, it makes me physically and emotionally ill to go up to one of our ministers and tell him to his face, "Shut the fuck up and sit back down," but that's what I've had to do because now I can see that these issues aren't just a matter of us being black and them being white. These are economic and class issues that I'm fighting.

TB: So now that you're beginning to uncover some of the root causes of the problems in the community, what is the nature of your relation with the Woodlawn Organization?

MB: Well, at first I wasn't much concerned with them. I mean, I was still pissed off about the way those two women had been treated, but I wasn't really against them or for them. I guess I was just sort of indifferent to them. I remembered that they existed, and that it was good to have them in the community to do what they were doing. If they needed support on an issue that I felt was correct, I would always give it to them freely. Actually, my brother gave them a fundraiser one time. So I wasn't fighting with them until we started to organize people at a deeper level, and that's when I found out some real ugly stuff about them and how the people in the community believed that they had been sold out by them.

TB: It was about this same time that you came up with the idea of restoring the extension of the Jackson Park El to Stony Island.

MB: Yeah, and the Woodlawn Organization was ardently against anything like that happening. At first I couldn't understand why they would react that way. It seemed like it was out of character for them to take that position. I mean, all that we were trying to do was to make affordable transportation available for people who couldn't afford to drive to and from their jobs. So at first I couldn't understand why they were on the other side on this issue.

TB: What do you believe was the reason for such strong opposition to what you were trying to do?

MB: Well, I have come to believe it was because they wanted to have control over what type of people were going to live in this community. They wanted to bring in people who could afford to buy ninety-thousand-, hundred-thousand-, two-hundred-thousand-dollar homes. They wanted to attract people who could pay seven or eight hundred dollars a month for the places that they would rent.

TB: To the best of your knowledge, would there be any space reserved for the poor in these plans of theirs?

MB: Not that I know of, to any great degree. Most of the people who are not at least middle class or above just wouldn't be able to afford to live here.

TB: Has the University of Chicago had any role in helping them to develop these plans?

MB: A major role.

TB: So then it seems that this time the university was able to accomplish what it has always wanted to accomplish without even having to use restrictive covenants in the sense of enforceable legal restrictions.

MB: Yes, they have just let the economics of the situation fall into place and drive out the people they don't want to let back in.

TB: What do you think they'll do with that lower-economic-scale black population that they are displacing?

MB: Well, they will probably do with them just what they are doing with them now. They are putting them in jail, putting them in foster-care homes, and putting them in the ground—and what's more, they're making money off us again by doing all those things!

TB: Nevertheless you keep on fighting.

MB: Yeah, I keep on fighting because things are getting worse instead of getting better, and what I'm talking about is not just about what is happening here in Woodlawn, because I think that what is happening here will set the stage for what is going to happen in every other black, urban, inner-city neighborhood all over this entire country unless we as a people can get together and turn things around.

July 11 and 18, 1997

JESSE BROWN

WOUNDED VIETNAM WAR HERO

The late Jesse Brown was a former student of mine at Hyde Park High School and later served honorably and was wounded in the Vietnam War. Upon returning to the United States, he became the executive director of Disabled American Veterans, before being appointed by President Bill Clinton as secretary of veterans affairs. His personal experiences in Vietnam led to his deep and ongoing concern for the welfare of all veterans and their families.

These conversations took place outside Washington, D.C., where I was his honored guest at the Marine Corps headquarters in Quantico, Virginia. It was an occasion that I will never forget, but it was just one of many examples that could be quoted testifying to his graciousness and thoughtful consideration to everyone he met. Jesse Brown was just that way! He always seemed to know how to link the past in a meaningful way to the present. I am so proud of my relationship with him, both as a student and as a deeply respected friend.

TB: Well then, let's start at the beginning. When did your folks first come to Chicago?

JB: We came here in about '53 from Selma, Alabama.

TB: I helped free your town! That's why I went there in '65 with Dr. King. You know my family is from Birmingham, and when I was growing up, my dad used to talk a lot about Selma because sometimes he used to go over there and play baseball. Is that where you were born?

JB: No, I was born in Detroit.

TB: Quite a few folks from Alabama went directly to Detroit or Cleveland.

JB: That is exactly right.

TB: A few stopped in St. Louis but not for very long!

[*Laughter.*]

When were you born?

JB: On March 27, 1944, but my mother and I only lived in Detroit for about two years. She separated from my father, and so she decided to go back to Selma.

TB: And she stayed there until when?

JB: I don't know exactly how long she stayed there, but after a while she left and went to Chicago to find work. So we stayed there in Selma with my grandmother until we were able to join her in Chicago, and that was in about '53.

TB: Where did you all live?

JB: At 6424 Ingleside.

TB: What was the neighborhood like back then?

JB: It was all black. There were no whites at all in the community when we moved there, but it was not like it is now. It was much better. It was not a middle-income community, of course, but at least it was a neighborhood where all the people knew each other on the street, and it was a stable community. We did not have a lot of the problems that you see now.

TB: It was not only stable. It was safe.

JB: On school days I used to have to walk from Sixty-fourth and Ingleside all the way down to Hyde Park High School, and you know something? That whole street on both sides was lined with parents watching their kids going off to school.

TB: Yes, there was quite a bit of home ownership in that neighborhood back then.

JB: At that time, although most black people who were our neighbors owned the buildings in which they lived, we were renters, but the lady who owned our building lived right next door. Her name was Mrs. Summers. She still lives there, and she still owns her own building, which is 6422, and our building, which is 6424.

TB: What grammar school did you go to?

JB: Wadsworth at Sixty-fourth and University.

TB: And then, of course, you went to Hyde Park High School. That's when I first met you.

JB: And I graduated from there in '63.

TB: That was a good class, but then, as I remember it, all the classes were good during that period.

JB: The thing that I most remember about you as a teacher was that you made us feel proud of ourselves. You brought a new dimension into our lives because you taught us to have self-respect and helped us to learn that we as a people don't have any reason to be ashamed of who we are or apologize to anyone for the way that we look. You know it really bothers me today when I see these young boys with their hair all processed and all that stuff because it suggests to me that they want to defy nature in order to look more like someone that they can never ever or should never look like. For example, take Michael Jackson. He is all screwed up trying to look white. He has messed up his hair, his skin, his facial features, and everything else in order to look like something that he can never be. What a lot of people like him don't seem to understand is that we don't need to be running around trying to look or act like somebody else. We need to be proud of who we are.

TB: It's like Elie Wiesel said when somebody said to him, "You are white. Why don't you just become a gentile? Why don't you just stop being Jewish?" His answer was, "What? Betray my ancestors, my great-grandparents, my whole history, betray all of that? No, I can't do that. I don't need to be a gentile. I need to be Elie Wiesel." Of course I take that same position. All of my grandparents were slaves. My mother was kind of fair-skinned, but none of my relatives ever professed to being anything but black. My daddy was a strong black man. He is my hero. I don't need no other hero to be my inspiration. All the rest of the heroes have to ride on his back! My mama was a strong black woman who carried us in comfort through the Depression. For me to try and transfer my allegiance to some other group would be like Elie Wiesel deciding not to be Jewish. Being who I am is my foundation, and I will go down in defeat, if it is necessary, proclaiming the legitimacy of that heritage!

JB: What's more is that if you attempt to deny your heritage, you will automatically fail in whatever it is you have chosen to do.

TB: And the reason for that is that once you have decided that you want to look like someone else or act like them, then you are also going to try to think like them and accept their limitations as your own. You are going to think that they have all the answers, but the answers for you are not out there. Those answers are in you! Once you get that straight, your confidence level moves up, and then the sky's the limit!

JB: Everything is a challenge from that point forth.

TB: Yes, but a *meaningful* challenge! That's the reason I enjoyed teaching so much.

JB: That's what young black people need to recognize.

TB: Yes, but I've also taught in schools where all of my students were white, and my message is always the same. I remember one time when the principal of one of those schools decided to put me to the test. You see, in the yearbook for that school, they had a place where they indicated which teacher and which subject the students liked best. Well, about 80 percent of the students said Mr. Black and chose either history or social studies, which were the classes that I had been teaching. Now remember that at that time I am the only black person in that entire school, including the janitors! So some of the white teachers got jealous, and, as a result, one day the principal came into my class unexpectedly to check out what I was doing, and my kids caught the signal and really showed off what they had learned. They really went to town naming and explaining various dates and events. I really didn't have to do anything. They did it all, and so this principal comes over to me and asks me what it is that I think I am teaching. I say, "American history," and he says, "Well, this is not the way we've been teaching it." So I say, "Of course not. This is *corrective* American history," and I ask him if he wants to see my course outline, declaring, "If you doubt any of the things that I have been helping these students to find out, then check it out, not by what I say, but by what three hundred respected historians have said, and if what I've been teaching does not jibe with what they have said, then I will alter what I've been teaching, but otherwise I won't."

JB: How did he respond?

TB: Well, he just couldn't handle that. Here was a black man talking to him like another man on an equal basis without any form of compromise and acting as though keeping his job was not the most important thing in the world, which, of course, it isn't.

[*Laughter.*]

JB: For the past several years I have been giving a lot of talks to both white and black people. Recently I made a speech out in Kenosha, Wisconsin, and there was also a parade. About forty thousand people were there, but, you know, as you ride along those parade routes, you can see that there are always little pockets of black folks, and, by and large, you can see that they are not doing very well. Everywhere you go you see black people that stand out in a way that clearly brings to focus the fact that as a people we are not doing nearly as well as we should. Now, of course, there are a number of us that are doing just fine, but that is not good enough. None of us can ever claim to be really successful until we as a people are no longer regarded as always being at the bottom of the fold.

TB: Yes, and even if we are successful, very often we are not perceived as being successful.

JB: Let me give you an example of that sort of thing. Not so long ago I was in France, and I went to this official luncheon. The queen of England was there, as well as Prince Charles, Prime Minister John Major, and various high-ranking representatives of our own government. I was the only black person there, and I didn't have my security people with me. So I told the maitre d' that I needed some assistance in finding out which table I had been assigned to, and he asked me if I was with the technical staff. I said no and that I was the secretary of veterans affairs. Well, then he looks at his schedule and escorts me directly over to where I needed to be. It was already all set up with my name and the whole works, of course, but the point I want to emphasize is that because I was black he had immediately decided that I must be part of the technical staff, which is another way of saying that I am only there as one of the servants or something like that.

TB: How do we eliminate those forms of ingrained prejudice?

JB: Well, this is my own philosophy, and it has nothing whatsoever to do with attempting to make a point that would reflect the current administration's point of view. It is my own, and it is this. We talk a lot about empowerment zones and so forth, but I think, quite frankly, that we are headed in the wrong direction. We continue to look for outside resources to revitalize our own neighborhoods, but if you look at the histories of other ethnic groups, they have been able to revitalize their neighborhoods from within. You see that in the Chinese community, the Polish community, the Jewish community, the Korean, the Hispanic, and so on. That is the secret of their success.

TB: And meanwhile we continue to look outside our community for what already exists inside.

JB: During the civil rights movement, looking outside our community for the solution to the problems that existed inside might have been an effective and necessary strategy. As a matter of fact, at that time it probably was correct, but now we need to completely rethink our situation. It seems to me that our neighborhoods are never going to be stable and productive unless we tie people down to them, and what I mean by "tying them down" is so that they can once again have their own businesses, their family units, their houses and buildings, and so forth. Tying them down so they can control the education, control the police department, control the flow of economic resources that already exist within these neighborhoods. If we depend on someone to bring a new business into the community from the outside, the problem still remains that, even though this new business may generate a few new jobs, a substantial part of the income from this business will always flow back out of the community and back toward the source from which it came.

TB: And those new jobs may also replace a lot of the old jobs that were the backbone of the community.

JB: Do you remember Eighty-seventh Street back during the early seventies?

TB: Of course I do.

JB: All those stores from Stony Island to the Dan Ryan were owned by black people, and all those black people lived right there in the community where they were working. That means they had a vested interest in keeping the streets clean. They had a vested interest in preventing crime. They had a vested interest in maintaining the infrastructure of the community. They bought and sold from each other, and, as a result, they brought wealth and vitality and energy into the community. What's more, they stabilized the community because they lived just down the street, and they saw to it that you did not act up on the street where they lived.

TB: Johnny *got* to be good!

JB: Yes, Johnny *got* to be good because otherwise we are going to get Johnny out of here! But now it seems that we have lost all of that. Now that these second and third generations have come on board, they seem to be obsessed only with getting something that somebody else already has.

TB: Just giving you some support for the ideas that you are saying, according to the best figures that I have been able to obtain, the black community of Chicago has a spendable income of approximately twelve billion dollars—and that is just in Chicago! Now, if that twelve billion dollars were properly invested *within* the community, it would create not only a lot of jobs but also the conditions for increased stability.

JB: Yes, the money would continue to circulate around and around within the community and not be drained into the pockets of outside investors. In the Jewish community they say that the dollar circulates at least three and a half times because they make sure that it stays in their community, and the Chinese do the same thing. I saw statistics that show that if all the black people in this country were to pool all of their economic assets they would be the sixth wealthiest nation on the face of the earth! But do you know how the white man looks at that? He looks at that as a market, and rightly so, because he is a businessman. He is the one that is producing almost everything, retailing almost everything, and distributing almost everything—and so that means that when we make the money that we spend we turn around and give most of it right back to him. This is a marketplace that has that sort of advantage built right into the system. What we need to do now is to take that same principle and make it work for us.

TB: Just turn it around and make it work for us for a change!

June 18 and 21, 1994

DR. EMIL HAMBERLIN

INSPIRING TEACHER

Because of his educational and scientific skills and creativity, Dr. Hamberlin is much sought after by many prestigious institutions at the levels of both secondary and higher education. At the time of this conversation, however, Dr. Hamberlin had been teaching at DuSable for thirty-one years, and he vowed that he would not leave: "These children need me and love me, and I love them too. Why should I leave?"

To walk into his classroom and to visit the horticultural garden that he has created at DuSable is to be suddenly thrust away from the artificiality of the urban landscape into the naturalness of a quiet but vital and complex countryside. This is his laboratory, where he has created an ecosystem of flora and fauna that is no less than a living work of art.

It is people like Dr. Hamberlin at DuSable and others at Phillips who continue to give vision and inspiration to the new teachers and the attending students. It is inspired teachers like him that help to keep hope alive so that their students can move on and fulfill their dreams. In that well-organized building, shutting out the dismal conditions that exist outside, Dr. Hamberlin and other teachers that are like him—young and old, black, brown, and white—continue to prove that the impossible is possible for anyone who is willing to learn.

TB: Would you tell me where your mother and father were born?

EH: My mother and father were born in Mississippi. They still are there today. My father's ninety-five and my mother's seventy-eight years of age. I lived in Mississippi until I was twenty-one, and then I started teaching here at DuSable High School.

TB: Did you know your grandparents?

EH: Yes, I knew my grandparents on both sides—my maternal as well as my paternal grandparents.

TB: Where were they from?

EH: They were also from Mississippi.

TB: I can guess they were of mixed parentage, weren't they?

EH: Yes, right. Absolutely. On my mother's side the whites were acknowledged, and that was a very interesting relationship we had with our white relatives that are still in Mississippi and how we lived with that relationship with my aunts and uncles and all.

TB: *They* knew and *you* knew.

EH: Yes, on my mother's side it was recognized and accepted.

TB: And what about on your father's side?

EH: Well, on my father's side, the Hamberlins were originally of German descent. We went back and we traced all that. That's how we got our name because my great-grandfather was a slave.

TB: And the assumption is, therefore, that he came from Africa someplace in that era.

EH: Right.

TB: Now, when did you leave Mississippi to come north?

EH: I visited here in 1960 and stayed with my sister, and I got odd jobs to earn enough money to pay tuition back at Alcorn State University. Later, after finishing at Alcorn State University, I had planned to go into the Peace Corps, but my brother said, "While you're waiting, why don't you come to Chicago and teach for a while until your assignment comes?"

TB: Your brother was already living here?

EH: Yes, my brother and sister were both living here.

TB: Where were they living?

EH: They were living on the South Side at 215 East Fifty-fourth Street at the time.

TB: Between Indiana and Prairie.

EH: Absolutely.

TB: All of that area's torn down now.

EH: Yes, the building is no longer there, but, of course, back then it was a really incredible experience for me, coming to Chicago, because of Forty-seventh Street and the Regal and all of the shops! It was just another world to me. There was a city on the South Side as well as the city that was downtown in the Loop, and so

TIMUEL D. BLACK JR. AND A. PHILIP RANDOLPH, 1961

Protesting what they called "racism within the house of labor," African-American union activists founded the Negro American Labor Council (NALC) in 1960. The legendary leader of the Brotherhood of Sleeping Car Porters, A. Philip Randolph, was its president; Timuel D. Black Jr. served as president of the Chicago chapter.

PAUL ROBESON, 1950s

Actor, singer, and political activist Paul Robeson began visiting Chicago in the 1920s. Timuel D. Black Jr. remembers hearing him in concert as a child in 1932. Robeson's prominence in labor, civil rights, and radical movements resulted in confrontations with the FBI and other federal agencies from the late 1940s into the 1950s.

BEN WEBSTER AND JOHN YOUNG AT THE BEE HIVE CLUB, circa 1953

Chicago's jazz scene was one of the most varied and influential in the nation beginning in the 1920s. Here saxophonist Ben Webster, who spent three years with Duke Ellington's band, joins forces with pianist John Young at Hyde Park's Bee Hive Club.

NATIONAL CREDIT CLOTHING STORES

4608 So. ASHLAND AVE.

SAM SCHNEIDER

YARDS 2072

OFFICIAL BOARD

EBENEZER BAPTIST CHURCH

DR. J.H.L. SMITH

PASTOR

OFFICIAL BOARD, EBENEZER MISSIONARY BAPTIST CHURCH, 1935

Ebenezer Baptist Church, located at Forty-fifth and Vincennes, became one of the early centers of the gospel music revolution in the 1930s. Reverend J. H. L. Smith also involved the church in support for Ethiopia against Mussolini's invasion. With a gospel chorus directed by Theodore Frye and featuring Roberta Martin, church membership soared above three thousand.

ARNA BONTEMPS WITH A CHILDREN'S SUMMER READING GROUP,
1941

The George Cleveland Hall Library, at Forty-eighth and Michigan Avenue, was the first full-service branch of the Chicago Public Library to open in Bronzeville. It became a magnet for prominent black literary figures such as Richard Wright, Langston Hughes, and novelist and children's book author Arna Bontemps.

AVIATORS' TRIBUTE TO BESSIE COLEMAN, 1935

Chicago was the center of early African-American achievement in aviation, beginning with Bessie Coleman. After Coleman's death in 1926, black aviators held an annual tribute to her. This 1935 event, organized by Pilgrim Baptist Church pastor Reverend J. C. Austin, included aviators Will Brown and Cornelius Coffey.

CAPPING EXERCISES, PROVIDENT HOSPITAL NURSES TRAINING SCHOOL, 1952

Provident Hospital, with one of the oldest and most respected African-American nursing schools in the country, was a source of pride in Bronzeville. Capping exercises marked the completion of a nursing student's first six months of academic and clinical training. Undergraduate nursing students were housed in a dormitory at Fiftieth and Vincennes, behind the hospital.

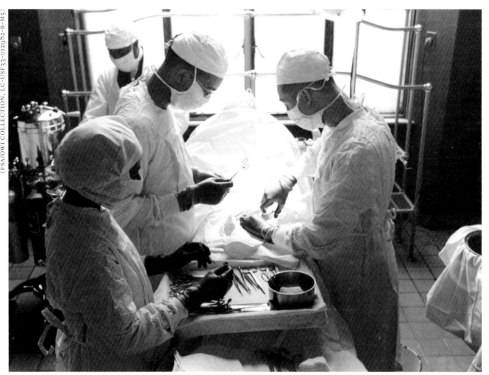

OPERATION, PROVIDENT HOSPITAL, 1941

CHICAGO DEFENDER ATTORNEY NATHAN K. McGILL SR. AND SON
SIMUEL McGILL II, 1934

In the crowded space of Bronzeville, with African-Americans hemmed in by restrictive covenants, wealth and poverty often resided only blocks apart. One of Bronzeville's most influential citizens was attorney Nathan K. McGill Sr., here seen in front of his home at 4806 South Park Way (now Martin Luther King Drive). McGill's new Pierce-Arrow stands behind his son's miniature Packard.

FAMILY IN A "KITCHENETTE" APARTMENT, CHICAGO, 1941

This Farm Security Administration photograph was used by Edwin Rosskam and Richard Wright in the searing book *Twelve Million Black Voices*. "The Bosses of the Buildings," wrote Wright, "take a seven-room apartment, which rents for $50 a month to whites, and cut it up into seven small apartments, of one room each. . . . The kitchenette is the funnel through which our pulverized lives flow to ruin and death on the city pavements, at a profit. . . ."

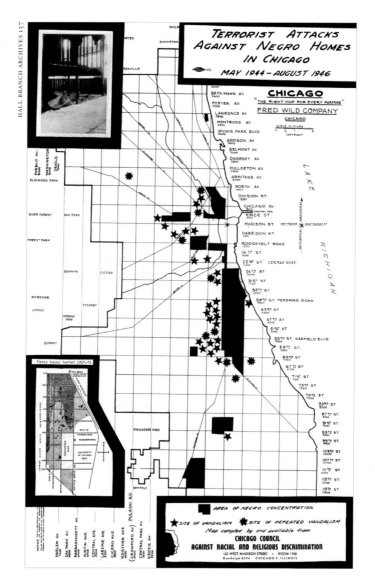

MAP, CHICAGO COUNCIL AGAINST RACIAL AND
RELIGIOUS DISCRIMINATION, 1946

For the first two-thirds of the twentieth century, African-Americans who
resided on Chicago's South Side were largely confined to a narrow corridor
between the Rock Island railroad tracks and Cottage Grove Avenue. Segregation was enforced not only by restrictive covenants but also by terrorist
attacks against those who dared to move into white neighborhoods.

MARTIN LUTHER KING JR. IN MARQUETTE PARK, 1966

Through much of 1966, Martin Luther King Jr. lived in Chicago, working with a broad coalition of civil rights organizations to protest ghetto slum conditions. On August 5, 1966, King was hit by a rock as racists attacked a fair housing march in the Marquette Park neighborhood. Frank Mingo is the man trying to protect Dr. King; Jesse Jackson Sr. is seen in the background.

MARCH ON WASHINGTON PLANNING MEETING, 1941

The March on Washington Movement, led by labor union president A. Philip Randolph, called on President Roosevelt to hire African-Americans in all war-production industries. This Chicago planning committee met in the Englewood home of journalist Ethel Payne and included Clementine McConico Skinner and Rita Baham.

FLYER, 1960

When black students in the South began sit-ins at lunch counters in February 1960, support demonstrations broke out in Chicago. A movement was formed to present civil rights demands to the Democratic and Republican conventions. This poster advertised a march on the Republican convention held in Chicago in July 1960. Timuel D. Black Jr. was cochair of that march and cochair of the Chicago contingent of the March on Washington in 1963.

BUD BILLIKEN PARADE PASSING IN FRONT OF THE REGAL THEATER,
1948

Launched by the *Chicago Defender* in 1929, the Bud Billiken Parade grew to become the largest annual event in Bronzeville and the nation's largest African-American parade. The route ran past the Regal Theater on South Park Way at Forty-seventh Street. This Madame C. J. Walker Beauty College float was among dozens in the 1948 parade.

UNIQUE BEAUTY SCHOOL, circa 1947

Unique Beauty School, founded in 1934 by Helen Graine-Faulk, was one of more than forty African-American cosmetology schools in Chicago from 1920 to 1945. The United Beauty School Owners and Teachers Association sponsored styling competitions among the schools.

WOODSON'S SHOE STORE, circa 1933

Many small black-owned businesses sprang up in Bronzeville in the 1920s. Among them was this shoe store at 3222 South State Street, operated by William and Elzata Woodson (shown in front of the door). "You could buy anything you needed in our community," Timuel D. Black Jr. was quoted as saying in an exhibit on his life and work at the Chicago Public Library's Vivian G. Harsh Research Collection of Afro-American History and Literature (2005–6). "You didn't have to shop downtown."

I fell in love with Chicago. Then, after staying here for a while and teaching, I got an assignment at DuSable High School, and I became very attached to it through my experiences in teaching—and that was it for the Peace Corps! I've been here at DuSable ever since that time—1965 until the present.

TB: When you first came to DuSable, the neighborhood was entirely black, but I suspect in most other aspects it was somewhat different from the way it is today.

EH: Very much different. There was a tremendous amount of pride in the neighborhood at that time. There was a tremendous amount of peace at that time. I can remember going to the Robert Taylor Homes—

TB: They were there already?

EH: Yes, they were already there, and I would say to my sister, "Gee, I love these apartment buildings. Why don't you move there?" I said that because back then the neighborhood was so peaceful, so quiet, so serene. It was similar to Lake Meadows but with a different color of brick.

TB: At that time the ambience surrounding the Robert Taylor Homes was great.

EH: And the neighborhood itself was good. Families were there. There were lots of moms and dads at home, and so there was a different kind of attitude among the young people.

TB: What about the rest of the students? Those who were living over east of the school?

EH: Yes, at the time there were quite a few kids growing up whose parents were living east of the school on Michigan or Indiana—and so we had quite a heterogeneous grouping of kids—socioeconomically speaking. We had middle-class and upper-middle-class students in the school at the time, and, of course, that made a difference.

TB: Yes, now, who were some of the people on the faculty that you remember from those early years?

EH: Well, when I first got here, there were some incredible educators here. Captain Dyett was still here. Julie Graham was still here. Mr. French was still here, and Mr. Mosely. Now, these teachers—to me—were like pioneers. They were *great* educators, and there was nothing else anyone could do but to respect them. They handled themselves so well at the time. I can remember all those individuals very well, and I would observe how they would present themselves in the meetings we had after school.

TB: Do you remember the "Hi-Jinks" shows when Captain Dyett was in charge?

EH: Yes, I certainly do. I remember that coming to the "Hi-Jinks" at that time made me think that I was over at the Regal Theater! The kids were just totally professional.

TB: Miss Clark was here also, wasn't she?

EH: Miss Clark was also here—Irma Clark, the librarian. And there was another Miss Clark that was in mathematics. Oh, another great name was Mr. Woodley. Nelson Woodley was still here in chemistry. And another woman—a fantastic counselor—Miss Bogan.

TB: Yes, Kate Bogan. You know, her father had been a superintendent of schools for the City of Chicago when I was a kid, and he was what you might call a political operator inside the system—so when Miss Bogan came to DuSable, at the beginning, when I was here, she had to kind of live down her father's reputation because her father was not the best-liked type of person, but she was so strong and so determined that she accomplished just that, and people included her as part of the family of DuSable High School.

EH: Yes, and I think also here at that time was DuSable's first black principal—Mr. Minor.

TB: Yes. Byron Minor.

EH: And during that time—in the early sixties—I don't think there were very many black principals in the city of Chicago. There was only a handful of them, if even that.

TB: Yes, but could students distinguish that Byron was a black principal? That he was actually a black man?

[*Laughter.*]

EH: No, it would be rather difficult. Someone would probably have to actually tell you that he was black because at first glance there was hardly any way you could actually tell.

TB: And yet he *never* pretended to be anything but a black man as far as I can remember.

EH: Yes, from the texture of his hair to skin color and eye color he appeared to be white.

TB: That's true. As a matter of fact, I was in Africa with his widow this past year, and she continually talks about her late husband because he in his own way was a pioneer. When he went to Northwestern University, there were very few people of color there, and he never denied his color. What that meant was that there were just certain things he couldn't do as a student—as a black man.

EH: And yet he could have easily passed.

TB: Oh, yes, he could have just not said anything, but he always let folks know who he was.

EH: He was proud of his heritage.

TB: Now, the students here at DuSable, as you remember them during that early period, were quite a bit more aggressively academic, weren't they?

EH: Yes, many of the kids at the time were very aggressive toward education because they realized that education was their way out.

TB: What about the students at DuSable at the present time?

EH: Well, today we have kids that are much, much brighter, but most of them do not put as much emphasis on education as they actually should. When I first got into DuSable High School, kids had pride in answering all the questions. At that time there were course books, and every kid wanted to have an excellent course book with the best grades in it.

TB: But they don't have course books like that any more, do they?

EH: No, they do not have course books.

TB: What do they use?

EH: They have a copy of their academic records that they give kids, but it's just a sheet of paper, and that's all that you get.

TB: I remember those course books! I've still got mine at home, and I go back sometimes and look them over for the memories they bring back.

EH: When I was coming through school in Mississippi, there was a report card that was sent home, and you got to keep your documentation, but you don't have that sort of thing anymore. Nowadays kids just get a slip of paper that tells them what their grade is for the first semester or the second semester and that's it. That's all there is. There's no accumulation.

TB: Where do they keep the continuum?

EH: The continuum is kept in a vault in the main office.

TB: But the students have nothing like a booklet that they can keep? It would probably be easy to lose a piece of paper.

EH: And they do, but the course book was something solid that reflected your growth as a student, and with that you could easily turn back to look at your grades and chart your success. You did not tamper with your course book. You had the privilege of taking that course book home every semester or every marking period and having your parents sign off on it, and then you'd have to bring it back to the division teacher, who would keep it for the following marking period, but when you got to be a senior it was yours to keep.

TB: Yes, yes!

EH: And even if you lost your course book—and that did happen—your division teacher could go back and put your grades in a new copy so you would be able to monitor your progress.

TB: Yes, and I can go back even now and look at the signatures of all the teachers that I had. After they put the grades in, then they had to sign it to verify it, and so when I look at my course book now, it gives a history of *those* people as well as of my own progress.

EH: Yes, and what is remarkable too is the amount of school pride that the students had at that time. Kids enjoyed wearing the school's red and black jackets. They wanted to be seen wearing a sweater or something that reflected the school, but, of course, those days are now gone.

TB: During that same period, I believe, you also had some outstanding students. Who are some of those students that you remember—whether they were in your class or not?

EH: Oh, I remember lots of them! James Bronson, who is a doctoral candidate now at the University of Chicago; Ward Graham, a very outstanding architect who works for several firms here in the city; Kathleen Patterson, who's doing very, very well. But really, so many of those kids are doing very, very well. All they wanted to do was to get their foot in the door of a university where they would excel—as well as they did at DuSable High School. They took that same talent with them, and many of them have become police officers, teachers, and doctors.

TB: So there is a sizable segment of the students who graduated from DuSable who went out into the world and managed their lives very well.

EH: Oh, yes! There's Glenn Johnson, who has an outstanding, award-winning, championship football team at Dunbar High School today. He graduated in the early sixties, and one of his mentors was, of course, Coach Bonner.

TB: Yes, Bob. You know, those Bonner brothers—they have their own reputation!

EH: Absolutely!

[*Laughter.*]

TB: They went to Phillips. Of course, I am older than they are, but when I met them, they were already legendary in terms of their achievements because most of them became teachers and coaches.

EH: Well, during that time the best you could be was a teacher or a social worker, or perhaps, one or two of them might have become doctors.

TB: The period, then, that you're talking about for these young men and young women—the first ones that you've had as students—begins to be the period of not just educational enlightenment but also opportunity because the civil rights movement was going forward at this same time.

EH: Right, and it was opening doors then that had been closed for many, many years. I still remember that when I got here in the early sixties what was amazing to me coming from the South was that when I went with my sister to places like Marshall Field's or to the First National Bank, there were no black women working there! None at all, and so I asked my sister where all the black ladies were! It was just amazing to me not to see any black people working in places like that.

TB: Especially seeing that you were coming to the promised land.

EH: Absolutely, and, since I didn't see them, I asked my sister, "Where are they?" I didn't realize that they were not welcome or ever hired to work in places like that back then.

TB: Now, in relation to the civil rights movement, what was happening back in Mississippi during that period?

EH: Well, as a child growing up in Mississippi, I was devastated when I saw on TV what had happened to Emmett Till. It was 1955, and so I was fourteen or fifteen at the time. We had a television, and it brought those events right into our living room. I just could not believe—well, I *could* believe—that this had actually occurred, that a child was lynched like that. And so, during that time with Martin Luther King and the civil rights movement, it was only then that things began to change for the better and that we began to have higher aspirations, but back in 1957, when those kids were going to Little Rock Central High School, I was still in high school myself.

TB: One of those young men at Little Rock Central, Ernest Green, had an uncle who was teaching here at DuSable at the time, and now Ernest's son is at Northwestern University doing his doctorate.

EH: Isn't that incredible?

TB: And now there are more black students in the University of Mississippi than there are in the University of Illinois.

EH: Yes, and there are more black kids at Alcorn State University, at Mississippi Valley State University, at Jackson State University than there are at Ole Miss.

TB: Now, by the time you came up here to teach, the civil rights movement was really getting into high gear. Wasn't that the same summer that the civil rights workers Goodman, Schwerner, and Chaney were murdered in Mississippi?

EH: Yes, 1964 is the same year that those civil rights workers were murdered. At that time I was doing student teaching in Marks, Mississippi. We had the sit-ins, the walk-ins—all of that. So that was a very dangerous time because many blacks at the time were used as examples, and we were boycotting stores and things of that nature.

TB: Back in 1965, all of those things were happening throughout the South, but Mississippi was kind of targeted by the civil rights workers—particularly the young civil rights people, both black and white—and some of us would go down there, and then we'd come back home on the weekends. But when we got there, we quickly discovered that we had to find a way to get *into* the community. People can't just come from the outside, even if they're black, and say, "I'm going to come in and tell you all what to do." So the thing that was really inspiring and awesome—to me at least—was that these young men and young women from the small Mississippi towns and hamlets would pick us up in the dark of the night and drive us out on those dirt roads to a destination where we would meet some indigenous person who knew all of the rest of the folks around there and who was the person you'd better give your respect to or otherwise you weren't going to get anywhere! It was amazing for me to witness the courage of these young people. In fact, I really believe that the bravest people I have ever seen in my life—and I went through World War II in France—were those young men and women that I met in Mississippi.

EH: Yes, the courage of those young people—white and black—and what they did in the state of Mississippi when I was coming along—well, there's no way to compare their bravery with anything else because at any time their lives could have been snuffed out, and there was no law down there that could actually protect them. There was no law for blacks! It was amazing. There was no *law*! There was no one to go to for help!

TB: It was only last year that Mississippi ratified the Thirteenth Amendment. Only last year! I guess it was an oversight, but anyway that was when it happened! Now, back here at DuSable, what was the feeling among young people, because many of these young people at that time still had relatives in the South?

EH: It was only later than that, in 1968 and the early seventies—during the time that Martin Luther King was assassinated and when we had the black revolution—that the kids at DuSable really came into play. In the late sixties and throughout the seventies, they would not stand for the national anthem, and they protested in order to have black history taught and to have black subjects taught in the schools. So the kids really stood up then. During the time of Angela Davis, then there was a big rebellion, but not back in the early sixties. And then, of course, there really was a total disruption at the time of Dr. King's assassination because by then the kids here had become very alert to the things that they had been denied.

TB: How did the administration here react toward that?

EH: They tried their very best to contain it, but the spirit of the individuals—the students, the entire environment—at that time throughout the United States—especially because all of this was enhanced by television, because all of this was happening right in your living room—that spirit spurred things on and kept pushing forward. There was no way that anyone could hold it back any longer—so the kids actually changed things around here quite a lot, and those of us who were teachers, we resolved some of the inadequacies of the Chicago Board of Education in terms of teacher assignment and in terms of teacher certification.

TB: At that time you had to go down to City Hall and get a picture taken, and it identified who you were, and, of course, they didn't certify you if you were black.

EH: Yes, it was *very* difficult for me to get certification as a teacher when I first started here. You had to pass the test.

TB: But you passed it.

EH: Yes, I did.

TB: Both the written and the oral?

EH: At that time I only had to take the written.

TB: Well, there were a lot of black teachers who had passed the written test but couldn't get past the oral because the testers who were white would fail them, blaming their accent or their use of grammar or making some other kind of excuse.

EH: Absolutely, and there were many other ways to weed you out. They were going to let only so many black teachers become certified teachers, and that meant that you could keep on teaching as a substitute teacher for your entire career. It took three years to become a full-time substitute, but even then, you were still a substitute, not a teacher.

TB: What was the usual freshman enrollment at DuSable at this time?

EH: At that time there were close to fifteen hundred kids in the freshman class. In fact, the enrollment was so large that when they graduated there had to be two graduation ceremonies. As I remember it, there were close to six hundred kids graduating in June, and then another three to four hundred were graduating in January.

TB: When you're talking about fifteen hundred, you're talking about both the A and the B classes.

EH: There you are. That's right. They had both A and B groups. Nineteen sixty-seven was the last group we had of January graduates.

TB: Now, you're saying that if about one thousand of those fifteen hundred graduated, then it is quite likely that approximately five hundred of the others in their class did not.

EH: Yes, but you must also remember that back then the community was much more mobile than it is today. Many times kids would leave DuSable High School, but they didn't drop out. They just went to another school, but it looks like they're dropouts because they're no longer on the school records.

TB: So what you're saying is that a very large percentage of those young people who started at DuSable would finish, if not here then somewhere else.

EH: Yes, but, of course, I'm not saying that there weren't kids that were dropping out. By the way, when I first started teaching here, there weren't very many social programs available for kids.

TB: What do you mean by social programs?

EH: When I first started here, for example, I don't think there was any free lunch. Later we got President Johnson and the War on Poverty, and during that time, lots of money came in to the kids for enrichment programs and Head Starts and things of that sort.

TB: Now, the stability of the neighborhood that allowed for a socioeconomic integration in the school in those late sixties and maybe early seventies, when does all of that begin to change?

EH: I would say that sort of change started after 1975. After 1975, we were beginning to get more and more of a homogeneous grouping of kids.

TB: Did you begin to get a change in the community population about this time, or was it just a change in the school population—or was it a combination of both?

EH: I think it was a combination of both factors. The community began to change, and as a result, many parents began to move their kids away because of the gang activity.

TB: So the gangs by now have become a strong force?

EH: Very much so. The Blackstone Rangers and that group of people were very prominent, and kids were being shot, and so people started moving their kids away from here. Some actually started sending their kids away to boarding schools.

TB: Yes, I know.

EH: And, of course, the inner city at that time became a very hostile environment instead of a friendly place. That's when the students enrolling here at DuSable changed to a very low socioeconomic grouping, and then we started to get the one-parent families, and you would notice that instead of being able to talk to a mama *and* a daddy, you were mostly talking only to mothers.

TB: And those mothers were relatively young, I would imagine.

EH: Yes.

TB: And growing younger as time went on.

EH: Yes, because when I first started working here at DuSable High School, girls that were pregnant couldn't come to school. Then things changed, and when they changed, pregnant girls could stay in school.

TB: They didn't have to go to special schools because they were pregnant?

EH: No, and now we have a clinic for them here in the school.

TB: How long has that been here?

EH: The clinic has been here for close to twelve or fifteen years.

TB: Is that right? What is its purpose and what does it do?

EH: Well, the purpose of the clinic, basically, is to provide kids with services—shots and whatever other health needs they might require. But for some reason or another it was generally believed that the real purpose of the clinic was to cut down on the number of girls that were getting pregnant, but, as you know, whatever its intentions, the clinic has not been very successful in reducing the number of pregnancies.

TB: Have you had a chance to read Leon Dash's book *When Children Want Children: The Urban Crisis of Teenage Childbearing?*

EH: No, I haven't.

TB: Leon Dash is a young—well, not that young anymore—his dad was in the service at the time that I was—but, anyway, he is now writing a book about Rosa Lee, a woman who died recently of AIDS. He made a documentary about her. She was living in Washington, D.C., and she was smart, but she got caught up in the situation where she couldn't read or write, and she was unable to solve that problem because she just kept on having babies—so she asked him to write her story. Now, Leon is a staff writer for the *Washington Post*—a black guy—but he had to prove to that community that he was *their* kind of black guy when he started to do this work. He thought that being a black guy, he could just walk on into this neighborhood and everything would be all right and that people would start telling him the truth about their lives, but that's not the way it is, and so after becoming accepted, that's when he discovered that most of those girls like Rosa Lee get pregnant by choice and not because they don't know any better. They *know* how to not have babies, but they decide to have them anyway.

EH: The problem that needs to be solved is a matter of both economics *and* culture—and not only for black girls but also for many other poor young people—because by now it has become socially acceptable for them to have out-of-wedlock children. In the former days, marriage was an institution, and you had a family only within that context. Of course, outside the family it also might happen but not nearly so frequently.

TB: There has been a breakdown not only in terms of the family structure and values but also in the structure of the community itself. In relation to their present environment, one of the few places where the young people of today can find a haven from the dangers of the outside is here in this school. The outside is no longer safe for them.

EH: Right, DuSable High School is one of the few institutions or buildings in this area that is still here. It has stabilized itself, and with the exception of a few churches, DuSable is all there is. DuSable is an oasis, and because of the way we have it here at the school—because of the administration and especially because of the dedication of the teachers—the kids feel very, very safe here. This is a place where they can enjoy themselves. Not only do the kids get their education here, but they also get a social outlet. This is where they meet their friends, their buddies. It's not easy for them on weekends—or even during the week—to walk around outside from one place to another in peace. The minute many of these kids leave DuSable they go *straight* back to their apartment buildings! And that's where they will stay until the next day because it's not safe for them to be anywhere else.

TB: And during that time when they're out of school, there's nothing for them to do recreationally.

EH: No, not now, but we're hoping to develop an educational park where the kids would be supervised in basketball, dance, volleyball, and tennis.

TB: Another idea might be to rehab and use the Hayes Center across the street as a recreation center for young people—and for older people as well—from Robert Taylor Homes. Would a facility of that nature add any advantages if it were properly done?

EH: Yes, it might, but because of the hostility of the environment itself—and believe me, I hate to be negative about things like this—but because of the possibility of a drive-by shooting or some other form of violence, most of the time the parents would not give permission to their children to come over to a place like the Hayes Center. We find it very difficult even for us to have the social center here at DuSable, and that's obviously because of the danger for the kids in getting from DuSable back to their own homes. That's why only rarely do we ever have any after-school dances here anymore. After the dance, a girl must still get back from the school, down the street, across the way—and that can be very dangerous!

TB: Yes, yes.

EH: The kids, therefore, live a very sheltered life because of the hostility of the environment. It's not a friendly place to be. Outside the school, there may be people all around, but you're still alone and unprotected.

TB: And now I understand that here at DuSable you are the sponsor of a program called the Future Teachers of America?

EH: Yes, we have about thirty kids in the program at the present time.

TB: Tell me about what you are trying to do.

EH: Well, it is a group of young people that serve as tutors to other kids in the school. Even though those who are in the program are not necessarily the most academically advanced children, we've discovered that being tutors puts a lot of pressure on them to become more academically secure in themselves. It means that they have to try harder and learn more, and that's why I picked them to participate! You see, I believe that everybody is a teacher in some way. Everybody can teach something. Whatever you know, you can at least pass that information along to somebody else.

TB: And you've been here thirty-one years?

EH: Yes, that's correct.

TB: How many teachers—or administrators, for that matter—have been here as long as you have?

EH: There's probably a nucleus of about three or four.

TB: Is that right? Who are they?

EH: There is Sarah Dickens, the music teacher, Connie Montgomery, and Vonteil Jones—those are the ones that I can think of.

TB: So there has been a great turnover of teachers since you have been here?

EH: Yes, many of our teachers end up being administrators or are transferred to other schools, and there are some that have retired early. So I have seen a tremendous change in teachers as well as administrators since I have been here.

TB: Without prejudice, tell me which one of the administrators do you feel has been the most seriously productive?

EH: During his time, Byron Minor was a *fantastic* individual who really knew how to delegate responsibility. After him, Mr. Frank did very well in trying to come up with new approaches and new techniques, but he wasn't able to accomplish as much because during that time he had to handle the transition of social unrest. Then, I suppose, Miss Steinhagen did the best she could, but as a Caucasian female she just really never knew what the students needed. What they actually needed at that time when she came here in the 1980s was to have a strong male as a role model. That image is so important in the lives of so many of our young people. They needed somebody to fill the image of a strong male, and now they have it. Mr. Mingo is a great person. He presents very innovative programs that try to meet the real needs of the kids.

TB: And he's strong!

EH: Yes, he's strong, and he has also inherited another thing that DuSable has, which is a solid nucleus of dedicated teachers that want to keep the school intact. So it is not just the administrator by himself that makes a difference but also the very dedicated group of teachers who are still here. We have a group of teachers who may not have been here for thirty years, but many of them have been here for at least twenty years. A great percentage of them have been around for that entire length of time, and they are very committed to their jobs and careers as teachers.

TB: What has kept you here?

EH: I *enjoy* doing what I'm doing here. I enjoy teaching, and I enjoy young people. Another thing is that I've been able to adjust to the times. I've not stayed stagnant. You see, I realize as an individual and as a biology teacher that my students stay the same age, but *I'm* the one that gets older, and so I must always learn to adjust to *them* rather than expect them to adjust to me. So I adjust with the times, and what I teach reflects the attitude and the behavior of the children that I am teaching, and I never forget that these children are a reflection of their environment and the society that they were actually born into. So I'm not burned out because I'm not doing the same thing over and over again, and my work always continues to be very exciting and challenging.

TB: If you had the power, what things would you recommend and try to acquire for a school like DuSable?

EH: I would start with what I already have and then add some of those things that we really need. I like the concept of schools within a school. I would like to take all the kids who already have the right attitude toward learning and put them all in one school. Then I would have another school for the kids that need help in developing that kind of attitude and the type of behavior that goes with it—with, of course, the plan that in response to that kind of help, they would move on to that other school. I would give those kids a tremendous push to help them catch up with the things that they need in order for them to excel in that other school. The idea is never to keep them in that one track but to do everything in our power to make them progress over to the other school. And then there could also be a third school for the kids that are academically broken, that are really and truly far behind, that need some kind of a handle to catch on to. By that I mean the kids that are coming into high school reading at third- or fourth-grade level, for instance. Those kids need help. They often have problems in the home, and they need a tremendous amount of counseling. So basically what I am saying is that instead of teaching a subject, we should also focus in on teaching the child. That's the basis of my philosophy. Teach the subject but also teach the child. If you think that way, then you're going to be coming out with kids that are able to excel.

TB: And your hope is that at each level of school the teachers will be attuned to this series of objectives, and as a result of this, you could make the majority of these children become educationally well.

EH: Yes, and even beyond that—if I could have the power—I would see to it that each parent must also become involved *directly* with their children. When you save the parent, you save the child.

TB: What devices can you think of that would get the parents—many of whom are young themselves—to become involved directly in the schools and their children's education?

EH: This is a generation whose spirits have been broken. Welfare has not been successful. There has been a war on poverty, but poverty has won—so now there's *got* to be a sense of responsibility of parents toward their children. They must learn that they have the responsibility to learn the skills of parenting in order for things to be better for themselves as well as their children.

TB: You have, conceptually, tried to do some of that sort of thing here, haven't you?

EH: Yes, by setting up programs that bring the parents into the school building along with their children, but so far we're not getting enough positive response.

TB: And most likely the reason for that is, as you mentioned, the fact that the community outside is so hostile. How would you try to remedy that?

EH: Well, when you ask the children, "Name me three places in the community that you feel good about, that you really like," only rarely can they ever come up with any names. So, first of all, you've got to have a secure community, and that means you've got to have jobs. You know, when I first started here thirty-seven years ago, there were plenty of jobs right here in the neighborhood that the kids were taking after school and during the summer, but now there are no jobs like that they can walk to. When a kid is working in a job, there are things they can buy with the money they make. In the past not just a few kids but many of the kids found jobs on Forty-seventh Street or Sixty-third Street and places like that. There were businesses here. There were opportunities right here in the community for the children, but to have those, you need to have a working class of people making money *above* the poverty level. Then, when you have that, you're going to get a different kind of attitude and a totally different kind of behavior—but now you're dealing with kids who reflect back at us their hostility because they're just living from month to month with no hope.

TB: What percentage of these young people come from the Robert Taylor Homes?

EH: Well, I'm not sure, but let's say at least 85 percent of these kids are at poverty level. That's how many qualify for free lunches.

TB: And a large number of those come from Robert Taylor?

EH: Yes.

TB: In your opinion, what is the remedy for these high-rises that have become almost like prisons for the people who live in them?

EH: What you say is true. When the students leave the school, they're going back to a kind of jail. To put that many individuals with the same low socioeconomic background into buildings like these is a travesty! One of the better things to do—and that should have been done—is you've got to have scattered housing.

TB: Scattered sites throughout the city would help, but you must also give individuals some type of support on how to maintain the place where they live. Don't just give it to them but teach them how to maintain it, and then give them enough money to maintain it properly. And then in that more diversified environment in which they would be—as a result of scattered-site housing—they would begin to see some examples of other ways that they might be living.

EH: Yes, they would begin to see better examples. Kids would get to see that things can be better. There's a lot that you can learn from just observation—and if you know better, you can do better!

TB: Some philosopher said that education is caught, not taught. That means that when I can see what you can do, I can learn from that because I can imitate that which you have done.

EH: Absolutely true!

TB: As a teacher here at DuSable, apparently you have gotten a great deal of satisfaction, but today at the entry level—which is different now than it was when you first came here—what would you advise a young person that is an African-American like yourself about going into the field of education?

EH: In my experience in this field I have found a great deal of fulfillment, and my sons have also gone into teaching, and they have found a great deal of fulfillment as well, but you always have to keep an open mind and recognize the fact that technology is changing so fast that it's going to be reflected in the specific needs of the current generation. They want to be able to obtain immediate information. They want quick and instant gratification. If you watch children watching TV and they have remote control, they are constantly turning the channel—"I don't have time to wait for action. I want to see it now. Where there's action—that's what I want." So the kids resent any kind of lecturing. They want to talk awhile, and to act awhile, and to write awhile. But they have too short an attention span to sit still for long periods of lecturing.

TB: Everything's fast for them, but I suppose that now that's the way it has to be.

EH: Yes, they want to have things very, very fast. They've got to have it—whatever it is—right now, right away! But if you learn to be tolerant of that attitude and try to understand what it is that they need, then you will discover that you are able to teach them quite effectively.

TB: But that also means that now teachers will have to have even more personal discipline and dedication than ever before.

EH: Yes, they have to understand that the children that are coming to them very often don't know where they are or even who they are. Those children are damaged and may be broken. You must learn to have empathy for each child and not get carried away by an established routine or any set way of doing things. Teach the subject, but please also always remember that you must teach the child as well!

TB: And it helps that child if you are able to be optimistic about his or her potentiality.

EH: Absolutely.

TB: Well, this has been indeed a pleasure. I've taken up all of your time—but I don't care!

[*Laughter.*]

EH: That's fine for me! I'm glad to be part of your project.

January 29, 1996

DILLARD HARRIS

—

RETIRED TEACHER, ADMINISTRATOR, VOLUNTEER

—

Dillard Harris is one of those rare individuals who, whenever he has nothing to do with his time, always does something useful—such as after his retirement, becoming a full-time volunteer at Wendell Phillips High School. His memories of the glory days of the Ida B. Wells housing development and of his experiences at Phillips and in the surrounding neighborhood reveal a love and affection that would be hard for anyone to match. Our conversation took me back to the time of those astonishing athletes of his generation, such as Jim Golliday and Ira Murchison, many of whom had been coached by my childhood friend Henry Springs.

At the present time Phillips is located in a rougher and tougher neighborhood than DuSable High School, but both of these schools continue to have unselfish individuals like Dillard Harris who remain steadfast in their efforts to give back to the community some of the good that their community had given to them. I would like to thank Alice Crawford, assistant principal at Phillips, for suggesting that I have the following conversation.

—

TB: I'm here speaking with Dillard Harris. Where were you born, Dillard?

DH: I was born in Little Rock, Arkansas, but I grew up here in Chicago.

TB: When did you come to Chicago?

DH: In 1939. I was six years old.

TB: Were your mother and dad born in the South?

DH: Yes, my mother was born in a place outside Little Rock called Bigelow, Arkansas, and my father was born in Taylortown, Louisiana.

TB: Why did they come north?

DH: Like so many others, they were looking for a better life, better work, and an opportunity to raise their family in a better manner.

TB: So when you first came here, you were already school-age?

DH: Yes.

TB: Where did you go?

DH: I went to Douglas first, and then I went to Doolittle.

TB: So you have been in and around this neighborhood almost all of your life.

DH: Correct.

TB: And then you came here to Phillips for high school.

DH: Yes, I came here in September of 1948.

TB: Was Ms. Bousfield still here?

DH: She was the principal for a year while I was here, but she left in 1949, and then Virginia Lewis came in as her replacement.

TB: When you came to Phillips in September of 1948, World War II was over. What was the neighborhood like and what are your memories of the school?

DH: Well, I grew up in the Ida B. Wells housing project. Back then many of the people who weren't able to get in were very envious, if you will, of the people who actually lived there. They would have given their right arm to get in there because at that time this was a *beautiful* facility. They had rules and regulations as to how you had to maintain and support the community—and if you didn't, then you were subject to being removed. So we all did our job to keep it up, and we loved living there.

TB: Who was the manager? Oscar Brown Sr.?

DH: No, Billy Cole was the manager at that time.

TB: And they still had rules and regulations and an established selection process.

DH: Absolutely.

TB: So you couldn't get in there just because you wanted to get in. You had to meet certain requirements. As I remember it, there was a sense of pride.

DH: Oh, yes.

TB: The lawn had to be kept up and things like that.

DH: Yes, and one of the things that I want to mention about Ida B. Wells is this. I married a girl from Phillips who didn't live in Ida B. Wells. She lived down on Forty-fourth off of Vincennes. But at any rate, one of the things that she remembers most vividly about that time is that she would have liked to have lived in there. She is still a little bit jealous because my old friends that came out of there always refer to each other in terms of what backyard you lived in! "Oh, yeah, he lived in so-and-so's backyard!"—and that's a way we relate to one another that's precious, you know?

[*Laughter.*]

Well, I don't know if you know the name, but Troy Yates lived right down by Madden Park, and so still we refer to that as Troy's backyard!

TB: There were also community activities for the young people over in Madden Park, weren't there?

DH: Right. As a matter of fact, many of my friends credit Madden Park with much of their subsequent success. If you recall, there was a building over there that had been converted from a living facility into a park district facility. They had a girls' gym and a boys' gym. They had shop classes where you could learn to make different kinds of things. They had places where you could play recreational chess or pool. They had a myriad of things like that—and then in the summer they had the outdoor bands come there to play for us. It was just a wonderful place to be, but then they tore that place down and put up another one— a little bitty place—on Thirty-seventh Street to replace it. But while Madden Park existed, we had a wonderful opportunity to improve and develop, and we had some marvelous people who were there running that facility.

TB: Who are some of the people whom you still remember?

DH: The one that I remember most was A. Wesley Ward. He just had all the confidence in the world in us and our future!

TB: His father was a prominent minister, and Wesley and his brother went to Du-Sable. As I remember it, back then you had some softball players at Phillips.

DH: Oh, yes, they were marvelous! One of the ones that I remember most was a guy whose last name was Cole, and he could hit a softball over the fence almost at will. He was just a wonderful player and a beautiful personality. Always very easygoing and cooperative.

TB: Did you participate in the sports activities at Phillips?

DH: We had all of our sports activities in the park that was near there, but Phillips also had after-school activities—a social center and things like that—that we participated in. In addition to that, though, we also had the Wabash Y.

TB: So the neighborhood was vibrant.

DH: Yes, it was full of people and fun.

TB: In that neighborhood there used to be a place on the corner of Thirty-ninth and King where they had a lot of jazz. I saw Joe Williams perform there, and there was another guy who was the forerunner of what later became Elvis Presley's style of performing—and that was Dr. Jo Jo Adams. You are too young to know him, but you might remember the name. He did all the gyrations and twistings that Elvis did, and many of the same songs. So a little later those things are stolen from our culture and called *their* culture!

[*Laughter.*]

While you were going to school did you work any jobs?

DH: I always had to have a job to help out my family. As a matter of fact, I worked at five jobs when I was in school. I made beds in the dormitory every day. I worked a board of education job. I worked for two professors cleaning their homes and things like that. I refereed games on the weekends. Then through the football season I sold programs and parked cars, and on Sundays I swept out the stadium.

TB: Who were some of the people at Phillips that you still might remember?

DH: Al Pritchett. He was on our track team in 1950 that won the state championship.

TB: Oh, yes, yes.

DH: We set a record in the half-mile relays that lasted ten years.

TB: Who else was on that team?

DH: Jim Golliday, Willie Burks, and me!

TB: Oh, yes! I remember those names well, but I didn't know you were a part of that team!

[*Laughter.*]

DH: Oh, yes, and the next year we won the state championship again with Ira Murchison, Willie Stevens, and that group.

TB: Yes, I went to Ira's funeral service about two years ago. It was a beautiful service. People came in from all over the country to pay tribute to Ira because they still remembered that little guy who could run so fast. Was Henry Springs your coach?

DH: Yes, he was our coach. Now, whenever I get a chance to talk to young people—and I always mention this because it was so prevalent back in our time of growing up—a guy like Henry Springs instilled in us a belief that we were well qualified, that we were trained properly, that we were the best—and that nobody could beat us! We believed that in our hearts. So, when we went to Champaign, we believed that we were going to win. I remember we were in the shower room that morning before the game thinking about all of that, and when Mr. Springs approached us about going out and practicing, our immediate response was, "Don't worry, Coach. It's in the bag."

[*Laughter.*]

And so we went out there and set a record!

TB: Yes, yes, yes! I remember it very well! Phillips turned out some really fantastic track teams.

DH: Well, as I mentioned, Willie Stevens was a world-class hurdler who came out of Phillips with us—and then, of course, there was Booker Rice!

TB: Oh, yes. Did you know that Booker's in New Jersey now? He's an executive with Prudential. I met him because he heard I needed some insurance, and he came by, and he was such a nice guy, but I had no idea that he had been a great athlete here. Of course, having spent some time here at Phillips, I always had dual loyalties: Phillips and DuSable! I'm sure that you agree with me that the histories of both Phillips and DuSable should not be lost and forgotten. In fact, that's one of the major reasons why I've got to get this book finished. There's really nothing that I know of to compare with their combined history in any other American city, but, of course, the reason for that may very well be because here in Chicago we were so completely segregated.

DH: That's right. We were completely boxed in, and you know something? That reminds me of one of the things that our coach said when we were going into the semifinals for the city championship. He thought that we weren't practicing like we should, and so our coach sat us all down on a bench said, "I have something that I want to tell you. Now I realize that all of you think that you're really something that's pretty great, but I want to tell you guys that unless you practice you are less than a pimple on the ass of progress—so you might as well get yourselves in check and come on down and practice and do what you're supposed to do." Now that stuck with me, you know? It made all of us come down to reality. You're not as great and as high-powered as you think you are, so get with it and do what needs to be done.

TB: In a little environment like this you were sometimes prone to think that way, and therefore you might begin to actually believe that you were the king of the hill, but, of course, then when you got out into the outside world, circumstances forced you to discover that sort of perception might not necessarily be entirely true!

[*Laughter.*]

So when did you graduate from Phillips?

DH: 1952.

TB: What did you do then?

DH: I went to Northwestern University.

TB: Did you run track there?

DH: Yes.

TB: Well, you guys did some stuff at Northwestern that was pretty exciting too.

DH: Yes, we had a pretty decent team. While I was there, I was a roommate of Jim Golliday.

TB: Did he play football out there too?

DH: He played a little but not much. He stuck primarily to track.

TB: Did your team go to the Olympics?

DH: No. I would have been eligible for the 1956 Olympics. Jim Golliday would have been eligible for both the 1952 and the 1956, but in both cases, right before the Olympic trials, he pulled a muscle, and that's what kept him from going even though he was a world-class sprinter. He had beaten all of the major guys.

TB: Tell me about your other experiences at Northwestern.

DH: Well, I majored in physical education, but at the same time I was also enrolled in the ROTC. So upon graduation, I was commissioned a second lieutenant and went directly into the service, where I was trained as a navigator and where I spent the next three years.

TB: Where were you?

DH: Basic training was in Texas, down by Brownsville, but then I went to Sacramento for advanced training at Mather Air Force Base.

TB: You didn't go to Korea, did you?

DH: No, I was still in school at the time.

TB: How long did you stay in the service?

DH: Well, after I got out of active duty, I made the decision to continue in the reserves and the National Guard, and so I spent part of my time instructing in the advanced air program, and that way I eventually managed to finish twenty-eight years' total duty, which allowed me to retire from the military as well as my teaching career, and so now I'm eligible for all of the benefits that go with retirement.

TB: So you retired when you were quite young?

DH: Well, I retired from the military in 1984.

TB: What rank?

DH: Lieutenant colonel. I can get on any plane now and go to Europe or Japan or wherever free of charge.

TB: Can you take the family?

DH: Yes.

TB: Oh, man! I think I'll go back and reenlist!

[*Laughter.*]

Well, in my opinion, people who spent a good part of their younger lives in the service deserve every one of those sorts of benefits.

DH: I agree.

TB: But when I finished up my military service, a guy asked me, "Do you want to volunteer?" And I said, "I wouldn't volunteer for the Salvation Army!"

[*Laughter.*]

But that was because I had been in Europe through all that bad stuff—and also because at that time the army was still segregated. Incidentally, I remember having a meeting in this very building when Mr. A. Philip Randolph and some of us were protesting the continuation of segregation in the armed services. You see, when we came out of service we were determined that the next group of young black men and women would not have to go through that same kind of racism. To give you an example of that type of thing, during my tour of duty, we fought four major battles, and we were awarded the Croix de Guerre by the French — and you know you don't get that for just hobnobbing around — but then when we got ready to come home and we got on the boat that would take us back, they let these white guys who had just gotten there and who hadn't been in any action get on that boat, and they took us off! We had already loaded up our belongings, and one of those white guys came up to me and said, "Do you mean you're going to just let them put you off this boat? You've been over here all this time, and we just got here. Why should we go home before you? I wouldn't stand for that kind of treatment, man." And so I told him, "Well, you wouldn't because you're white, but I can't because I'm black." You see, essentially, even the most liberal or radical white person cannot fully understand that there are adjustments and adaptations like that which we as blacks have to make continually on a practical, daily basis — and one of the things that these kids of today have got to begin to understand is that all of these little adjustments and adaptations generate a lot of genuine anger and that although you can carry that anger around with you for a long time, it will continue to build up, and if you do not learn how to use it creatively, if you just let it blow off without the proper perspective and self-control, you will eventually destroy yourself, and nothing will ever change for the better.

DH: Well, what you just said is certainly true in the military. The type of attitude that you carry will be what determines how successful you are going to be or not be in that kind of environment. If you have the proper attitude, you can move upward through the system and do very well for yourself, but if you go in there fighting the system, the system's not going to change, and eventually it's going to get the best of you.

TB: Yes, because you can't beat the system until you can get yourself to a position where you can *change* the system.

DH: Another one of the things that our coaches taught us — and which some people still don't appreciate fully — is that you're not going to win any close games away from home, and so in situations like that, if you really want to win, you'd better be out front from the very first and stay there until the very end.

TB: That's right. Back when I was in school, we also recognized the fact that when we sent our teams out to play at other schools they had to believe that they would win because if they didn't they would be sure to lose. "There's no way those guys can call a close one on us because this game's not going to be close!" That's the story of how we managed to survive—and not just in athletics!

[*Laughter.*]

Now, comparing the days of your years when you were in service, even in the reserves, were you still teaching?

DH: Oh, yes. I taught at Doolittle for five and a half years, and then I went to the West Side to Manley, and then I went to the district office, where I worked with Mr. Springs after he became district superintendent and some other people. My job was to make educational programs for parents to help them maximize the use that they could get out of the system on behalf of their kids, and so I took that job of mine very seriously. But prior to Springs's arrival, what I was trying to do was not looked upon favorably. They didn't like or want to support what I was trying to accomplish, and so they said, "We want you to just relax and don't make any more waves," and so forth. Well, anyway, I went on ahead and continued to do my job as best as I could. So eventually the lady who was my boss got promoted because of all the good things that I had been able to accomplish there even without her support, and when she left, she said, "Well, Dillard, I got my promotion, and so I'm going downtown, but I want you to know that there's nothing more I can do for you." So I said, "Well, OK, whatever"—and I just turned and walked away. But then when I got to the door, she said, "Wait just a minute. Don't you want to know why?" So I said, "OK, why?" And she said, "Because, although you did a masterful job, you didn't do what I told you to do!"

[*Laughter.*]

So I knew that there was no future for me there. Mr. Springs recommended that I look at a job in Saginaw, Michigan, which I got, and so I left the state, and that's the last time I was in the Chicago educational system until I came back here this September.

TB: Did you stay in Saginaw very long?

DH: No, and after leaving Saginaw as an assistant superintendent, I went to Rock Island, and then I came to Lockport at Fairmont School as superintendent, and I worked for fifteen years out there in that school district.

TB: Well, you've certainly had a great deal of administrative experience.

DH: Oh, yes, and then, after that, I went to Ford Heights for one year as superintendent, but then that's when I retired.

TB: And you were still quite a young man!

DH: Well, sort of.

[*Laughter.*]

TB: So, when did you start teaching here at Phillips?

DH: I just started this September. My wife and I came over here to bring some scholarship money. You see, my wife and I have established a scholarship for the students here.

TB: It that right? Well, that's wonderful!

DH: And so, when we came here, my wife said to Ms. Tucker, "My husband retired in 1992. Don't you have something he could do?"

[*Laughter.*]

And she said, "Oh, yes!"—and so I've been here ever since!

[*Laughter.*]

Well, at first I started off as an assistant principal, but then I just reverted to becoming a more or less full-time volunteer.

TB: So you're not on salary anymore.

DH: No.

TB: Looking back, the new world that we're living in now is quite different from the one you lived in when you were growing up and is certainly even more different from the one I grew up in. What are some of the comparisons that you see here in Phillips in terms of the changes that have occurred sociologically, economically, educationally? For example, the atmosphere, how would you describe what it *was* like when you were here and what it *is* like now, and how can we make this current situation the best that it can be?

DH: One of the differences that I see that is most glaring is that when we were coming up, we always had older adults and young adults who were ahead of us that took time to share with us their experiences and show us by their examples what was possible for us if we went through the system in a reasonable way. That sort of thing meant an awful lot to us because it prepared us to take advantage of what was out there—and I don't see that sort of thing happening to any noticeable degree right now.

TB: Yes, also back in my time and in your time as well, whenever there was a problem of any kind you always had folks at home to help you. You could just pick up the phone and call Mama or Daddy or a neighbor or somebody, and they would come right over.

DH: For most of these kids that kind of support no longer exists.

TB: And what about the teachers then and now?

DH: When I was a student here, the teachers seemed not only to demand but also to receive more respect from us than the young people are giving to them now. You know, I remember that sometimes when we were getting ready for a meet or something, some of the young men who were on our track team who didn't quite have the guidance that they should, they'd be off at the pool hall, and so Mr. Springs would say to the rest of us, "Well, let's go get them!" He literally went to people's homes or wherever was necessary, and he picked them up and brought them back here to school so that we could get on about the business of doing what we had to do—but, sad to say, we don't see quite that same kind of concern and reaching out going on around here today.

TB: Not that same level of commitment.

DH: Right, but back then I had teachers who not only were concerned about me but also looked after the kinds of programs I was taking in order to help me maximize what I could get out of the educational situation. Let me give you an excellent example. My division teacher was Mrs. Bush. Now, I don't know if you ever met her, but believe me, Margaret Bush was a wonderful person, and she said to me when I was a junior, "Dillard, I want you to take a year of typing." When I said, "No, I don't think I need that," she said, "Yes, you need typing, and I want you to take it." Then I said, "No, no, I won't do it because typing is just for sissies." Well, she kept on insisting, and so eventually I listened to her, and I went and took a year of typing so that when I finished, I had a certain level of skill, which I discovered was absolutely essential once I got to college. You see, I had to keep my grade level up so that I could compete in track, and I was able to do that only because I was able to type my own term papers and class assignments. Then, later on, when I got to be a superintendent, if my secretary was missing, I could always type my own letters and send them all out. Nothing ever had to stop. There was never any unnecessary delay. So that advice she gave me was the best advice that I could have received at that particular time, and I'm glad that I finally accepted it. That's the difference between then and now, and I don't see people being that concerned anymore about where their students are headed or what it is that they really need in order to succeed in the future.

TB: And what about the students? How have they changed?

DH: Well, I don't believe that the average student that was coming along when I did believed that they were smarter than their teachers or their parents. They were willing to listen to the advice that they were given.

TB: Yes, the roles back then were much more clearly defined. There was an adult, and there was a child.

DH: Right.

TB: There was a teacher, and there was a student. All of those roles were very clear. There was no confusion whatsoever as to what those roles were. You might not have liked the fact that one had power and that the other one didn't, but those roles were known and accepted, and if there were any abuse of power, that sort of thing would only happen so seldom that you couldn't even recall too many incidents of it. Sometimes there might have been an incident that occurred along racial lines, but situations like that were very rare even though most of the teachers here at Phillips back then, as I remember, were white.

DH: Right, and you know one of the things that I remember most vividly from that time in my life is that people would sometimes raise the question of whether or not I thought that going to a predominantly black school—back then Phillips was about 99 percent black—was a good thing or if it would have been better for me to have gone to an integrated school. Well, my response was always immediate, and I always said that I thought it was definitely in my best interests to have gone here because being here gave me so many more opportunities to develop my skills and obtain information that I would not have had if I had gone to, say, Evanston Township High School or someplace like that.

TB: What about the social life here at Phillips?

DH: If I had not attended Phillips, I would never have been able to be head of the ROTC. I probably never would have been president of the student council. There were just so many things like that which were open to me here and which gave me experiences that I wouldn't have had otherwise because this was a place where I could compete on an equitable basis with all the other students. Out there in another sort of environment I probably wouldn't have been able to do that.

TB: Also in a more integrated situation if you got shut out, you would always be able to tell yourself that this had happened to you just because you were black. Even if that might not have been the real reason, that would always have been an excuse you would have been able to use. But you couldn't use that kind of excuse in a place like this because everybody else here looks more or less like you! [*Laughter.*]

So, as you've been saying, today there is a difference in the attitude of the students toward their teachers and each other. The result of this is that many of our young people today are not doing as well academically as we once did. Now, of course, there were always those of us who didn't do so well back then either, but they were the exception to the rule. What's more is that even though today there are greater opportunities in many ways for these students, and now the world is much more open to them than it was even when you were going here, there seems to be a distinct reduction in the aspiration level of the majority of these students. The only ones that seem to have definite aspirations want to be another Michael Jordan or Oprah Winfrey, and for them there are no steps in between.

DH: Right, they want to go straight to the top.

TB: But they don't have the necessary role models to show them the steps along the way and keep them on the right path. In addition to which they are confronted with outside dangers that are now a part of this world that were not a part of this world when you were going here.

DH: Well, you know we had gangs at the time that I was here, but there was a different level of respect that existed between the gangs and the portion of the student body that was doing well academically. They respected those people, and they didn't bother them, but the way it is now if you're not a part of the gang, they will do whatever they can to hinder your progress. Back in those days when I was here if you were a scholar or an athlete, you got a pass, and you just went on your way without any trouble whatsoever.

TB: Also back then the level of violence was not as great as it is now. When the youngsters come here now, they have to figure out exactly how to get here safely and then how to get back home. So they can't have the kind of stimulating cultural and athletic after-school programs that I imagine they used to have when you were here. For example, do they still have night school here?

DH: No, but they're talking about reinstating it in the near future.

TB: Well, historically, Phillips had one of the first night schools in the country. This was created to enable people who had left the South without much education to return to school and get the credentials they needed in order to get better jobs. I know the positive results that those classes had because I've taught night school here myself. Now tell me what you think are some of the potential remedies for closing the gap that exists between what these kids are getting and what they really need.

DH: Well, certain efforts are being made to reduce that gap. As you can see, we are in the process of redoing the physical facility here to make it more operable as well as more pleasing to the eye, and that's important. We are also revising the curriculum so that it is one that is more challenging and meaningful so that it will stimulate the students to want to work harder. For instance, when we went into one class of juniors and observed that these kids were being given work at the sixth- and seventh-grade levels, one of us raised the question, "Shouldn't they be doing sophomore- and junior-level work?"—and their teacher replied, "Well, yes, of course, they should, but these students can't handle it." So we said, "Well, let's give it to them, and let's see what happens." Well, what happened was that once they presented the higher level of work to those students and started challenging them, the students were, in fact, able to do that level of work. As a matter of fact, they were able to move from reading at the fifth- and sixth-grade levels to reading hundreds of words a minute with comprehension. The problem was that those who were responsible for their education had sunk to the level of believing that their students were not capable, and so they didn't try to challenge them. But once these students were challenged, they rose right up to the mark that had been set.

TB: At one time some years ago I taught in Gary, Indiana, in an all-black school. When I first went there, I was low man on the totem pole, and even the kids were hostile to me because I was new. They had decided that they were going to run me out because they didn't know me! So we played that little game for a little while until one day I said, "Young people, you may have fooled everybody else, but you're not going to fool me. You may act like you're dumb, but you aren't going to get away with that with me." "Yeah, Mr. Black, but everybody else thinks we're dumb." You see that type of negative attitude and self-image had gotten so deeply ingrained through the years that they had developed a sort of vested interest in being dumb and staying that way!

[*Laughter.*]

What those kids needed was a challenge of the kind that you're suggesting in order to change and eliminate that negative type of self-image—and that's what, as their teacher, I tried my very best to provide for them.

DH: Kids like that are going to start to feel better about themselves once they are taught how it is possible for them to succeed. Just yesterday I went and talked to some kids that they call second-chance kids out there in Markham, and one of the main things that they didn't have was a vision of themselves as being successful, and they had absolutely no idea as to how to start to approach that kind of concept. First of all, because they didn't believe that they were capable of success, I started them on the road to understand the concept that you can do almost anything you want to. Like Jesse Jackson said, "If you can conceive it and believe it, you can achieve it."

TB: Yes, but only if you believe in yourself, if you eliminate that negative type of self-image.

DH: That's true, but, you know, one of the things I still remember is that when I was a student here, very often our counselors used to counsel us out of believing that we were capable of moving on and becoming successful. For example, I remember that a guy who is now president of an important corporation—J. T. Jones— was a classmate of mine, and he was told by his counselor that he was not college material. Well, J.T. went on over to Illinois Institute of Technology anyway, completed his degree, and now runs a most successful company.

TB: Well, I certainly hope that those who are in a position to counsel these students of today have learned to be more careful and positive in what they say.

DH: And that's true especially because of the vast variety of offerings that are available to the students of today.

TB: So right here, right now, in this school you are currently developing some challenging new programs that are specifically designed to improve the learning skills of the students.

DH: Right, and some of these teachers are completely astounded by how well it's taking effect. They expect that when these kids take their IGAP tests next time around, about two weeks from now, they are going to do so well it's going to shock the community in general.

TB: Is that right?

DH: Yes, and, you know, I had this same kind of experience when I was superintendent down in Fairmont. I organized my kids in such a way that they could get the best instruction possible. What I did was I had them stay with the same teachers for four years, and it worked out to the point that when our third graders took their tests in 1989, they scored higher in math and language and reading than 98 percent of the third graders in the entire state of Illinois!

[*Laughter.*]

But some people were so upset about those scores that they just couldn't believe they were true. The *Chicago Tribune* even demanded that there be an investigation. So they carried it out and got the tests back from Iowa City and went through them meticulously, but then they had to write a letter to the school board stating that these were indeed legitimate scores and that there was no evidence of any impropriety. But they were still upset, and so they came back when those kids were in fourth grade and tested them again. Well, their scores were still up there, and what that shows is the level of achievement of which they are capable *if* they have been given the right kind of instruction.

TB: They meet the challenge and rise to the level of demand.

DH: Yes, and now let me give you another little example. Not long ago I was at a meeting with the superintendent, and we were discussing the athletic program at Phillips in comparison to the other schools out there, and I said, "Part of our problem here is that we don't have enough students that are able to try out for the team. Most of the other schools will have sixty or more kids that come out for football, but we're lucky if we get even twenty." So that guy said to me, "That's not your real problem. As a matter of fact, I could take your twenty and beat sixty from any of those other schools every single time!" So I said, "What are you talking about?"—and he said, "Your problem's coaching." So I went back and called an assembly of the whole school—staff, students, everybody—and, in a sense, I read the riot act to them. I said, "I don't want anyone ever again to tell me that we're not getting the proper coaching, and that's the reason why our students aren't succeeding." Well, they didn't like to hear that, but afterwards some of the students came up and said, "Mr. Harris, don't worry. Next year we're going to do much better." So next year when they came back, our football team, which normally would win maybe one or two games a year, went undefeated and won the conference! In basketball there were two levels, and our teams went undefeated at both levels. In baseball, well, in the past if we won one game we celebrated because it was a great thing, but that year they won thirteen in all! That was because we told them what we wanted and that we believed that they could do it.

TB: That's why they succeeded.

DH: But now, getting back to something you said earlier, you said you had some kids in Gary that didn't believe that they were capable of success. Well, I had the same sort of thing at Doolittle. I had been assigned to what they referred to as the dummy room. These were kids with behavior disorders and all of that, and they kept them separated from the other students and wouldn't even let them participate in the class assemblies. So I told those kids, "You're going to perform in the next assembly that's coming up, and you're going to do well"—and they said, "Oh, no, they're not going to let us in the assembly." But I said, "Oh, yes, you're going to be in it, and we're going to be ready to do it the right way." So we spent time rehearsing and made sure that all of those kids were dressed properly, and when those kids went out on that stage and performed flawlessly, the whole auditorium gave them a standing ovation. It did so much for those kids' morale for them to be able to be successful and accepted like that.

TB: Building confidence is always a necessary part of the learning process. I'm sure you've seen that same sort of thing happen in athletics. When you have a whole series of successes, then one defeat doesn't really mean much of anything. But the way things are today so many of our youngsters have already had so many defeats—social problems, breakdown of the family, fears of all kinds—that then when they go to school and somebody tells them that they are nothing but a failure—no matter what their potential might be—it becomes almost impossible for them to move ahead. The result of this is that they may then decide that they have to do some "undesirable" things in order to have any degree of success at all. You can be successful by having a baby. You can be successful by hurting somebody with a gun. And the consequences of these actions don't even begin to get into your mind because you want so badly to achieve that success that you think those actions will bring.

DH: That's right. Developing an expectation of success is absolutely crucial when it comes to working with our kids, but if you expect them to do well, they'll step up and do well. But now let me give you another example from Doolittle. I always used to say to my kids, "Listen, when you go out there, I expect you to win." "But we can't win all the time," they said, and so I replied, "Oh, yes, you can. You can always win if you want to. Now here's what we're going to do. If you lose, I'll be standing here waiting for you, and I'll want every one of you to drop a dime in the kitty." So the first time they went out, when they came back they all had to drop a dime in the kitty. But the next time they didn't want to put a dime in there, and so they played hard, and they won! Then there was one time I had to go away on a mission for the principal, and when I left, they were going to play a baseball game against another team. Well, when I came back, they were losing that game 17–1, and the gym teacher, who was a fraternity brother of mine, was teasing me, "There's no way they can win this one." Well, I just looked at him, and I said, "Don't worry. When they see me, they'll win!"—and they won, 18–17. [*Laughter.*]

TB: The kind of human capital that you represent in many ways is even more important than all the scholarships and other opportunities they have because what these young people really need is to see a live body offering service to them and to realize that he or she doesn't have to do this. It's not a job. It's something that a person like you is doing because you want to do it, and you want to do it because you believe in them and in their future.

DH: That's right, but to put it a different way from a somewhat different perspective, over there in Bosnia, I've heard about all these problems they've been having with land mines that have been left behind after their recent war, and now things can't go on their normal way until all of those land mines have been cleared away. Well, we have things like that over here in our own society as well, and one of the things that most of these young people of today don't fully appreciate—and something which many of them don't seem to appreciate at all—is the fact that the Tim Blacks of the world came along and cleared away most of those land mines of ours before those kids were ever born! They tend to think that the road for them has *always* been clear.
[*Laughter.*]
But, of course, it hasn't. They just don't seem to realize that somebody came along before them and did the job that needed to be done.

TB: Well, listen, I have taken up more of your time than I deserve, but I've enjoyed this conversation very, very much.

DH: I appreciate it. I'm really glad we had this conversation.

March 5, 1996

ROGER SALTER

LEADER AND ENTREPRENEUR

Roger Salter, who was a student at DuSable High School in the class of 1958, has gone on to become the founder and president of Sanmar, a financial investment corporation that handles millions of dollars annually for its investors.

When he was in high school at DuSable, he was very well liked and was a natural leader. Although his class, like all the classes during that period, was filled with a wide variety of soon-to-blossom future leaders, Roger Salter always stood out from all the rest. His self-confidence, his manner of dress, his humor, and his smile, as well as his seriousness, made his teachers admire and even coddle him. Not only Roger but his entire family were very well known and highly respected throughout the community.

After graduating from high school, Roger went to college and then worked for a brief period of time as an insurance agent before he decided to go into business for himself as an investment broker. In order to ensure that his business will continue and stay within the community, he already has his own children working with him in his office. It is his hope that his business will become even more successful when it passes from him into the hands of this next generation. Unfortunately, so many enterprising black businesses do not outlast the visions of their founders—and so Roger's commitment to the future should be a genuine source of inspiration for many who continue to live in our community.

TB: I'm here with Roger Salter, who was a student at DuSable High School, from which he graduated in 1958. Roger, where were you born?

RS: In Chicago, Illinois, on July 15, 1940, at Cook County Hospital.

TB: And your mother and dad, where were they born?

RS: My mother, whose maiden name was Frances Pugh, was born in Quitman, Mississippi, on, I think, June 25, 1906, and my father was born September 8, 1902, in Clarksdale, Mississippi.

TB: Did you ever know your grandparents?

RS: Well, yes, my maternal grandparents, but I never met my father's parents.

TB: Did you ever have a chance to talk to your mother's parents?

RS: Oh, yes, I knew my grandmother, and I knew my mother's father, who was actually her stepfather.

TB: Did they ever talk about their early life in Mississippi?

RS: Not to any significant extent. He was a minister, and she ran a local grocery store. They had ten children—four sons and six daughters—a big family.

TB: Where did you visit them?

RS: In Quitman, Mississippi.

TB: As your memory goes, what kind of town was it?

RS: It was a small rural town, but my recollection was that they didn't go wanting for a lot. They were very proud people. I think a lot of them graduated from high school there in the South. They were a close family. Very God-fearing. At least that's what they passed down to us!

TB: Your religious values were handed down from that generation?

RS: Handed down by a very proud grandmother. I remember her to be that, and she was very well recognized in the community—kind of like my mother! My mother became a precinct captain in Chicago. She was with the Eastern Star. She was her block club president. She was the president of her choir. In most ways she was probably the more active one of my parents. My mother was more brown-skinned than my father, who had very fair skin and very sharp features. He looked like a white man, really. Straight hair—the whole bit. His mother also looked like a white lady, and, in fact, for a time I thought she was, but she had to have been a mixture, white and Indian, because all of her sisters looked like Indians.

TB: What about your father's side of the family?

RS: From what I gather, my father's brothers and my father were very different in their personalities, but I never got a chance to meet my father's brothers. One of my father's brothers was kind of like a wild guy, you know, but in his early years my father's claim to fame was as a baseball player. That's when my mother met him.

TB: They met in Mississippi?

RS: Yes, they met in Mississippi, and all of his friends said that George was the best pitcher in town, and so his team would go from city to city—

TB: They would go barnstorming?

RS: Right, they'd travel the local circuit and play for money.

TB: He was a semipro because in those days black players were not allowed to play pro league ball. Many of them were certainly qualified to be pros in terms of their ability, but they were just shut out, and so they became pros outside the system.

RS: Yes, that describes my father exactly.

TB: Now, after your mother and dad met and married in Mississippi, when did they decide to leave Mississippi and where did they go?

RS: Well, they first were going to go to California.

TB: Did they go there?

RS: No, they came here to Chicago and moved in with my aunt!
[*Laughter.*]

TB: When was that?

RS: This has to be around 1937.

TB: So they already had relatives here?

RS: Yes, my mother's sister was already living here at Forty-third Street and Prairie, and then they moved—prior to my being born—to Forty-fourth Street and Wabash Avenue. Joe Louis lived right around the corner, on Forty-third Street and Michigan!

TB: His first wife has moved back into that same building, and she still lives there.

RS: Right, Marva Spaulding. Her name used to be Marva Louis. We used to play with their sons.

TB: Oh, is that right?

RS: Yes, but we didn't play a lot with them. They would just barely come out of their yard, but that's where they lived, and Ralph Metcalfe lived on Wabash or Michigan down in that same territory. We lived a block from Reverend Cobb's church. I was a Cub Scout there at that time.

TB: His church was the First Church of Deliverance.

RS: Yes, and I remember very clearly that his church was where we had our Cub Scout meetings.

TB: You remember Reverend Cobb then.

RS: Oh, of course! Everybody remembers him.

TB: A very charismatic man!

RS: Yes, a real leader! When I was in the Cub Scouts there, that is where I had my first experiences in leadership. I was the den leader or whatever you called it back then. It was very rewarding for me because I used to like to do all of the things that they were teaching us to do. I was only about nine years old at that time.

TB: But you already had good discipline?

RS: Right, and we also went to the YMCA down there on Thirty-seventh Street.

TB: I was there just last night!

RS: Is that right?

TB: That's become a landmark, and now they're going to restore it and fix it up like it was when you were a kid.

RS: We used to play basketball there. We swam there. There were a whole lot of activities. Ping-Pong and things like that—so that's where we hung out.

TB: Now, as you remember it, what was the rest of the neighborhood like back then?

RS: I don't have a lot of bad memories. I don't remember any hard times.

TB: You could go out into the streets?

RS: Yes, and in fact, that's what we all used to do. We used to go out and play baseball in a lot—we called it the big field—but it was really just a cornfield. The people in the neighborhood used to grow vegetables there. We had our little gangs, I suppose, but they weren't any big deal.

TB: They didn't frighten people off the streets.

RS: No, not like these gangs nowadays. They weren't the dominant thing in the neighborhood. You know, I've had a job all of my life. In fact, my first job was when I put up my little shoeshine stand on the corner of Forty-fourth Street and Wabash.

TB: So you were starting to become an entrepreneur even then!

RS: Oh, yes, that was the way to go! That way I didn't have to ask anybody for money. My father and I got together and built a stand that I could sit on and another little stand that my customers could put their feet on, and all I had to do was buy my paste and my polish and my brushes and my rags and take those wooden stands, and I would be ready to make my little dimes and quarters! Yes, that was my first taste of entrepreneurship! And it was all right! My second job was selling papers. In fact, I was the leading newspaper salesman in my neighborhood. My paper route ran from Forty-third Street and Wabash Avenue around the corner to Forty-seventh Street and State Street.

TB: How was delivering papers in those days? Did you get your money?

RS: Oh, yes, I always got my money!

[Laughter.]

We were raised not to steal, you know, but I could have collected even more than I did because I knew all of the tricks and techniques, but remember, I had already become a leader! So I was an example, and the last thing I was going to do was to consider stealing. The way it worked we would make a commission selling papers, and every paper that I sold I made money off of—so I'd just be stealing from myself because you had to account for all the papers that they gave you. Very simple! Whatever number of papers you took out, you had to bring back that much money or return the papers!

TB: That's right!

[*Laughter.*]

Which papers did you sell?

RS: The *Sun-Times* and the *Herald-American.*

TB: Did you deal with the *Defender*?

RS: I never sold it. At that time I think they were beginning to sell the *Defender* mostly out of the stores.

TB: Yes, maybe so, but I used to sell the *Defender.* In my days we'd go pick our copies up on Friday right after school, and I would take my *Defenders* up to the El station at Fifty-first Street, and I'd sell out every time!

RS: Is that right?

TB: We sold it for a dime, and I think we got to keep four cents for ourselves. Maybe later they changed their policy, but I'm talking about when I was the age you were when you were a paperboy — so there's at least a twenty-year difference.

RS: Right, and I didn't even know what the *Defender* was back then!

TB: Do you have brothers and sisters?

RS: I *had* three brothers. George just passed last year.

TB: Now, George was a doctor, wasn't he?

RS: Yes. George was a doctor, but George had many different jobs throughout the years, and he excelled in practically all of them. He was one of the early guys in advertising, and he also did a little stint in the insurance business. At the time he died, he was developing software for computers, but he was also a musician from day one. I remember when he first learned how to play the piano, and I would sing. Well, actually we both could sing, but I never could learn to play the piano!

[*Laughter.*]

Learning to play the piano just didn't hold my attention long enough for me to develop the proper coordination. But since George could do it, it was fine with me because then I could sing. I would write the music, and he would play it! That was George. He was also a very spiritual guy. He even became a minister for a while. He just continued to add different dimensions to his life all the time. Then there's my brother Ronald, who has also become very spiritual. He's the one that's a CPA. We both went to Southern Illinois. Then he went into the service, and after that, he went on to get his CPA. That's what he has been doing for the last twenty-four years. He's been involved with several different firms. He was with A. B. Dick for a while. He was head of accounting for DePaul University.

And then there's my youngest brother, Phillip, who is the artist. He is the vice president of Brainstorm.

TB: That's the one I know! We've done a number of things together in the voter registration area. He did all the ads when Harold Washington was getting ready to run. Whenever we needed ads and things like that, Phil was the guy we went to!

RS: Right, he also did the Jolly Green Giant and Pillsbury Dough Boy ad campaigns.

TB: Now, you also have a nephew, I believe, who is a psychologist?

RS: That's right. My cousin, Lonnie Salter.

TB: Yes, yes.

RS: Lonnie and Edna are my cousins. My father and their father were first cousins. *Their* fathers were brothers.

TB: Well, through the years I've met lots of Salters!

[*Laughter.*]

That's why in my getting around, whenever I bump into a Salter, I always say, "Well, I think I know some of your relatives!" Now, when you were living at Forty-fourth Street and Wabash Avenue, which elementary school were you going to?

RS: Coleman School.

TB: How did you like Coleman?

RS: I was an excellent student. I did well because I was trying hard. I thought that education was cool. I was number two in my class. I don't remember why I was just number two, but I do remember I didn't particularly like that.

TB: So it sounds, from what you're relating here, that the period of your life that was spent in that community, in those schools, in the Scouts, and all the various activities that you did—all of that was pretty enjoyable.

RS: Yes, for the most part it was very enjoyable, but during those same years I was hit by a truck and also hit by a car. Another time I got badly burned, and once I had my wrist cut so badly they thought I was going to lose my hand. It seems that I always had some kind of perilous type of accident, but I would always recover!

[*Laughter.*]

TB: Only a series of temporary disabilities?

RS: But never defeat. I would always keep going. So then I went to DuSable.

TB: What year was that?

RS: In 1954.

TB: Then you were there when they had that great basketball team.

RS: They were leaving as I was coming in. I entered DuSable in the September class, and by then they had already graduated.

TB: I had been there as a sub for a semester, but at that time I was leaving to go to Gary.

RS: Right, and then you came back.

TB: Oh, yes, I came back and was very happy to do it. I enjoyed the students over there, but even so, I was very happy to leave Gary. So when you came to Du-Sable as a freshman, what was that experience like? Did you take a lot of your Coleman friends with you?

RS: I guess I did, but high school's like another dimension altogether because it's a melting pot of everybody coming from everywhere. So this was a new kind of challenge for me because I might have kind of got lost in the shuffle in a place like that. Well, not lost per se, but you begin to go different ways from your old group of friends because of the divisions that separate you.

TB: Which division were you in?

RS: I was in Miss Gallagher's division.

TB: Oh, so you were in Miss Gallagher's division! That's probably because she stole all of the best students. She and Mary Herrick would battle for the best students. A little later I came to DuSable and took Mary Herrick's place when she left and went to help organize the teachers' unions in the South. So I took her division, which by then consisted of sophomores, and I followed that division all the way through.

RS: Well, we had our own little world there in the Gallagher Division, and, of course, we were known as the smartest—at least we believed that we were! [*Laughter.*]

TB: But the Black Division gave you a challenge, didn't we?

RS: Yes, but well, you know, we thought that we were tops! And when you really think about it, maybe we were! Of the top ten in our class when we graduated in June of 1958, we had, like, seven or something like that from our own division.

TB: Well, the most important thing to remember about that period of time is that when you and your friends were there, DuSable took second place to nobody.

RS: Oh, yes!

TB: Nobody!

RS: There wouldn't even be a discussion!

TB: On any level!

RS: All the way from the choir to the band to the scholastic scene to athletics—I always felt *very* proud to be there.

TB: Did you have any jobs after school or during the summers?

RS: During the early part of my high school days, I shined shoes at Lydel's Barber Shop at Forty-fifth Street and State Street. Then I worked with some Jewish guys on Forty-third and Prairie at a place called the Food Store or something like that. After that I worked for Hi-Lo Food Stores over on Seventy-first and King Drive. So throughout high school I was working all the time.

TB: Tell me what you remember about Forty-third and Forty-seventh streets in that period of time that we're talking about. What do you remember?

RS: Well, I remember the Woolworth store that was right there on the corner of Forty-third. I remember Forty-seventh Street also was a pretty brightly lit-up street.

TB: Everybody remembers that!

[*Laughter.*]

At that time you were still living at Forty-third and Prairie?

RS: Yes, but every day I'm also going all the way back over to Wabash, going east past State Street. I didn't go past King Drive that much because, you know, I didn't have a car, and I didn't have anything to go over there for. There wasn't any show or anything over there that I can remember. The show that we used to go to was the Indiana.

TB: Yes, down on Forty-third Street.

RS: And there was another show we went to called the Owl over on Forty-seventh Street.

TB: What about sports?

RS: Most of my days after school were spent playing baseball and basketball and all of that. I also used to sing. I was in the DuSable choir. In fact, I was the assistant choir director there for a while. I even had a singing group called the Cupids—and believe me, we could jam! So we became pretty darn popular around there. But most of my activity was with my jobs. I'd get out of school and go directly to work. After I'd get off work, sometimes I'd go out to play, but I always really enjoyed going to work because I felt if I was going to go to work, I was going to be the *best* worker they'd ever had! Of course, I also liked the money, but I always felt that if I was going to do the work, I was going to be the best they'd ever hired. That's kind of the way I was cut out. I'd be the fastest stock boy! I'd be the best cleaner!

[*Laughter.*]

And I was always popular. The ladies liked me. I dressed well, and I could get pretty much whatever I wanted. So that was kind of a nice life for me. Then in 1955 we moved to Seventy-first and Champlain.

TB: Which means that your family was moving into Park Manor. That neighborhood was just changing. Why didn't you transfer to go to the school out there? After all, Hirsch was much closer than DuSable.

RS: Right, but I didn't want to transfer—so I'd get on the Seventy-first Street bus, ride out to State, and then ride down. That's what I used to do every school day for three years.

TB: So you didn't ever transfer?

RS: Oh, no! Where was I going to transfer to? Hirsch?

[*Laughter.*]

Please! Parker?

[*Laughter.*]

I was really enjoying myself at DuSable! I loved the teachers, and I liked the atmosphere, I liked what was going on, and I never got in any trouble there.

TB: Between the white teachers and black teachers there, did you find any distinctions among them? Along race lines?

RS: Not really. They were just teachers, and all of them were concerned about their students. I had a lot of wonderful teachers, but I didn't have any classes with you.

TB: No, but I guess I had the rest of the clan at one time or another!

RS: Yes, you did! You were always very well respected. Everybody always liked you. I wasn't surprised when you went on to become politically involved. You were always a stand-out cat.

TB: I was a DuSable-ite!

RS: You had your own presence. We thought that you were real cool!

TB: When did you graduate?

RS: I graduated from DuSable in June of 1958. In January of 1958, I had gotten married, and so I was married when I graduated.

TB: Which was not so unusual back then. People could get married at eighteen because the economic outlook wasn't so bad in those days. There was usually an opportunity to work somewhere and earn a decent living.

RS: I graduated number nine out of my class of about three hundred people. So I got a scholarship to go to Chicago Teachers College, and I did well there in the beginning, but I was working nights in the post office, and that first year was a challenge! There were a lot more whites over there, and I did very well, but then I could not really see myself as a teacher. What happened was I began to lose interest. The greatest motivation for me, Tim, was that at the post office I was kind of a popular guy, but I guess I was going through some changes. My wife and I separated for a while, and then we got back together. So, you know, there were a lot of things happening during that period in my life. But the biggest thing that was happening was the contradiction that I saw between people graduating and teaching school and earning forty-nine hundred dollars a year, and postal supervisors who had two years of college and now were earning fifty-six and fifty-seven. That's why all of my frat brothers were working at the post office! I just could not see myself graduating and teaching and making only forty-nine hundred dollars a year. So in about the middle of my third year—in about 1961, when I had only one year to go—I said, "I'm going to drop out of school." What had happened was I had met some friends that were in the insurance business at Metropolitan Mutual Insurance Company of Chicago. I had seen, for example, Gaylord Smith had gone with Western and Southern, and he had been written up in *Ebony* magazine as a new leader in the insurance industry. So I began talking with the fellows over at Chicago Met, and their checks were bigger than any principal's! You know what I'm saying?

TB: When was this?

RS: This was in November of 1961.

TB: So you weren't wasting any time.

RS: No, there wasn't any time to waste, but my mother would say, "Hey, all you've got is a year to go. Stay on in school there." And I'm like, "This just isn't turning me on. I'm getting bored with all this singing, "B-I-N-G-O, B-I-N-G-O, B-I-N-G-O, and Bingo was his name, oh!" Boring! And so I got into the insurance business with Chicago Metropolitan. They started me off with sixty-five dollars a week.

TB: Was Blackburn there still?

RS: Yes, Leo was about to be the agency director. He was the head of the Ordinary Insurance Department.

TB: You know he went to DuSable too?

RS: Hey, of course I know. He and I worked together! I was the vice president of his organization. I worked for him for ten years. Before I opened up this company of my own, he and I opened up the first black insurance agency in the history of the United States! Back then an African-American-owned agency was like having a black Cadillac dealership, but Leo and I, we're the ones who did it! [*Laughter.*]
But that's the way it was. They started me out with sixty-five dollars a week, and all of my frat brothers told me I was crazy! They said, "What's he doing?" But they always knew I didn't care what they said. I was always my own cat, you know? And in the first three months I was making one hundred and sixty-five dollars a week, which was more than eight thousand dollars a year!

TB: Can you translate that into today's dollars?

RS: Well, in today's dollars that meant I was making more money than baseball players by the end of the year. So whatever people like Ernie Banks were making back then, that's less than what I was making. If I had to translate it into today's dollars—and we're talking about thirty-three years ago—I'd have to put on a 5 percent inflation rate on thirty-three years, and so I'd guess it would have to be equivalent to a thousand dollars a week or something like that.

TB: It would probably be closer to sixty thousand dollars a year.

RS: Yes, in today's dollars.

TB: And you were on your own most of the time?

RS: Yes, I was out there selling.

TB: Were you in Ordinary?

RS: Well, I sold a *lot* of Ordinary, but I didn't want to just stick with that. I wanted to sell the bigger policies as well.

TB: People like Langford Spraggins had already set the pace. He was a contemporary of mine.

RS: Right, I'd already heard about him. Well, I was the third black in the world to make the Million Dollar Round Table. Cirilo McSween was the first. Then Langford Spraggins and I made it in the same year, but I was the baby in that group. Langford was about your age, and I was twenty years younger. Cirilo was somewhere in between, maybe about fifteen years older than me. So I was like the baby of the group, and they wondered where I came from! It surprised them, and I liked that! After six months, I was making about two hundred and sixty-five dollars a week, but by the end of the year I was making close to four hundred dollars a week. Well, by that time all of my frat brothers had changed their attitude because when we came to talking about what the real deal was, they noticed that my check was about four times bigger than theirs!

[*Laughter.*]

And the next year I was fortunate in that I learned a couple of things that allowed me to make even more than I did that first year! Then in the third year I went into management, and I'll be very brief with you, but I became disenchanted with management, even though I was the youngest in their history, because no matter how hard I tried, I couldn't motivate the guys to do what I knew they could do.

TB: Where were you doing your business?

RS: Right here in the black community.

TB: You were getting all the business that you were making this money on right here in the community of which you were a part?

RS: Oh, yes, and I was always a student. You see, I went *back* to school, and I graduated from LUTC.

TB: LUTC is what?

RS: Life Underwriters Training Council, and that's where I met Leo Blackburn. Leo, of course, was already a legend. He was a real sophisticated cat. I was younger than him. He's twenty years my senior, and at that time he was ready to leave Chicago Met because he felt he was being unfairly treated. He had thought that he was going to become the agency director, but they gave that position to someone else, and so then he went on to get the first general agency in America with a major life insurance company, Mutual Benefit Life out of

Newark, New Jersey. That was a first, and I was his first recruit. I was the first recruit because when we were sitting there talking I had told him, "I'm ready to make some changes." So he invited me to come down with him to his agency. I actually worked next door to him in my own office on 100 South Wacker Drive. So I'm down here with my white secretary and all of that sort of thing, and suddenly it's a whole new world!

[*Laughter.*]

So that began a whole new chapter in my life. That was the year I made the Round Table for the first time.

TB: Which year was that?

RS: That was 1965. When you make the Million Dollar Round Table it means that you have sold at least a million dollars worth of life insurance coverage in a twelve-month period.

TB: Yes, I know.

RS: My annual earnings at that time were probably about twenty-five thousand dollars.

TB: When you left Chicago Met to go with Blackburn, what was the name of the firm?

RS: It was called the Gerald Griffith and Associates Agency of the Mutual Benefit Life Insurance Company.

TB: And you said that Mutual Benefit Life Insurance was headquartered out of Newark, New Jersey.

RS: Yes, it had been established there in 1845, and they are the ones who hired Leo Blackburn as the first black general agent in America for a major life insurance company. I was his vice president, or assistant general agent. Like I said, a general agent is like a Cadillac franchise owner because if a person wants to write business with Mutual Benefit, they have to come through one of their general agents. Since I am what is called a master general agent with American General, it means that if you want to have a contract with American General in this area, you've got to come through me. So anybody—whatever color: pink, black, green, Chinese, whatever—will have to come through me, and when this happens, I will make a portion of the money.

TB: In commissions?

RS: Right, they pay a certain amount, and of that amount I get a portion because I am the one that screens everybody before the policies can be written.

TB: You seem to enjoy your work!

RS: I do! I really do! Well, let's go back now to 1965. When Leo brought me to 100 South Wacker Drive to the Mutual Benefit Life Insurance Company, he was my coach. He was my mentor. I was a young whippersnapper just twenty-five years old. I had been one of the leaders in sales of the Metropolitan Mutual Insurance Company, and then I was one of their leading managers. But the prospects of my hitting a limit were there, whereas Leo had then gone into the bigger world with the bigger policies—the higher-quality product that until then very few blacks had ever had access to. So now we had an opportunity to bring to the black populace a high-quality, first-line product.

TB: And at this time you were still with the Gerald Griffith Agency downtown?

RS: Yes, but then we spun out of there to open up our own general agency, which we opened up officially in 1968, and we moved from 100 South Wacker Drive in the Hartford Building over to Dempsey Travis's new building, called the Seamark Building, on Eighty-seventh Street.

TB: Dempsey had just bought that building?

RS: Yes, he had just put it all together, and we were among his first tenants in there. We were probably the first ones under contract. So we stayed there, and we had some very prosperous years. Now we were back out on the South Side, and it was a historical first because we had finally broken the ice and had a black general agent in the United States representing a major life insurance company. So we started hiring black folks to develop our market with black professionals. That was our marketing strategy!

TB: What was your estimate of the potential of the black insurance market?

RS: I thought it was so far-reaching that we hadn't yet even hardly scratched the surface of it.

TB: It was relatively untapped.

RS: Right. Before then, blacks were doing all their business with whites. It was considered to be fashionable to have a white New York Life policy or a Metropolitan Life policy, and then we came in with a company that they knew very little about—Mutual Benefit—but which had a *quality* product that was better than the others, and now we were the people who were going to introduce this to the black population!

TB: So now you have a policy that you can offer which is superior to the ones that they already had?

RS: Right—well, don't get me wrong because the quality was so close, but, as a matter of fact, we were just a *little* bit better than the rest of them.

TB: And what you were offering far outpaced anything that the other black companies could offer?

RS: Oh, there wasn't even a discussion in that area because all of our competition had a fee for the agent selling the product and another fee for the agent collecting the premium. So the premium had to be fat! Do you know what I'm saying?

TB: Now, you and Leo and the other agents stayed awhile in Dempsey's building, and then you moved again, didn't you?

RS: Yes, I moved over here to where I am now. Leo and I stayed together for nine years, from 1965 to 1974. They were great years. We had a great time together, but I was thirty-three years old and feeling my oats once again. I felt that I wanted to own part of the agency as compared to just being a hired employee. His goal was for me to take over the agency after he retired, but I couldn't wait. I knew I wanted more than I was getting, and, more important than that, I really felt that I could do it by myself. I figured *I* could own it and get a bigger piece of the premium and also do some creative things I wanted to do that were different from what he wanted to do. It's like the child that grows up and says, "I want my own house." So he said, "No problem. Go on and get your own house, but you can't have this one." Which is cool. So I said, "OK, I'll pack my stuff and leave," which is what I did, and I moved here into this building in 1974. I moved upstairs into just a small space, and then I went to recruiting. That was the key. To recruit people to market your product to the public. I was already fairly good at marketing, but I was still learning even more because I always stayed in school—all during this time I was always in school. Back then many people of color knew *nothing* about the field of insurance. Well, maybe they thought they knew something, but they really knew very little. You see, most blacks thought that the few blacks they saw were the ones who were running the business, but the fact is that the insurance business was predominantly run by white folks, and right now, even *now*, I would say that we have no more than 10 percent of the business that we own, or even less. Maybe 7 percent, if that!

TB: Of the business in the black community? Or the total community?

RS: Of the total insurance business. In terms of agents in this business, I would say only 7 percent of them are black. The rest of them are white. What was happening was that black folks didn't know the magnitude of this business. They didn't understand the various uses of the product. The estate planning. The business planning. The partnership arrangements. The retirement plans.

TB: So now you found yourself tapping into a gold mine in a certain sense.

RS: Yes, because I was approaching this business altogether differently—and by that I don't mean I'm better than everybody else. It happened because I got a chance to talk to these guys at the Round Table early on, and because by then I was already doing the amount of business that I did do, they were looking at me like I was some sort of a novelty. I was the third black guy in the world to make it to the Round Table! So while I was at those meetings, I was like one of maybe two black people out of two or three thousand people from all over the world.

These guys were from England, Canada, Africa, Panama, Germany. So when they converged in this meeting and they see this one black guy—the only guys from Africa were the white ones, not the black ones—that's when I got a chance to see a whole new world. They had guys there that were making hundreds of thousands of dollars, and at that time we had no idea that sort of thing was what was going on—nor did we know the concepts to use to tell the people what they need. One of the reasons I do a fairly substantial amount of business is because I introduce people who have never bought a million dollars of insurance to that concept. Just to give you an idea, right now I have a proposal that I expect to write that is for five million dollars of business, and my commission on that will be a fairly large amount.

TB: I would imagine! Do you operate on 10 percent, 15 percent?

RS: Of the million or of the premium?

TB: Of the premium.

RS: You get 50 percent of the first-year premium on the policy I'm talking about, but on some products you only get 40.

TB: And then it continues to go down?

RS: Right, it jumps all the way down. The next year there's a service fee up to like 5 percent or something like that—so it changes drastically, but it's still OK.

TB: So you then come to this building on your own as what?

RS: As a general agent for Mutual Trust, another insurance company—and I was their first person of color. They had never even done business with blacks before. The only blacks they had were some blacks down there in accounting—maybe one or two. This was in Oak Brook, Illinois, in 1974, and that was twenty-one years ago. When we came here my goal was to lead the company—to lead all the white guys all around the country—and that's what we did! We led them every year. Year after year. Back then I was like Muhammad Ali. I'd tell them I was going to kick their butts, and then I'd kick them!

[*Laughter.*]

But just think what was happening *inside* me, Tim. One of my passions happened to be public speaking, but the real reason why I would go around and speak—you can see all those different plaques on the wall over there saying "Speaker at the Million Dollar Round Table," "Speaker Here," "Speaker There"—was that I was trying to make my mark in terms of educating white folks as to who we black folks really were. That was the path that I wanted to take. I wanted whites to see that blacks were just as intelligent—and more intelligent in many cases—than whites were. That we could make just as much money as whites could. That we were just as articulate, dressed just as well, and all the rest of that.

TB: Well, at DuSable you never were bashful!

RS: Right, I was not! And what I was doing was my own way of carrying my sword. For me it was just as if you went into politics or education—you were carrying your sword and saying, "Hey, black folks, we are who we are. We are *somebody*! Just look out over here, and see who we are. Look at what we're doing!"

TB: And so you were expanding all this time?

RS: Oh, yes, I've got pictures here of the operation. We started out with two people and wound up with thirty-five.

TB: So your company has expanded to over thirty, and you are still running it. Is that the continuum you are on now? Have you altered anything along the way?

RS: Well, the entire industry has changed. After the government got involved and cut the margin of profit out of our products, insurance companies began to look for new ways to invest their money.

TB: Yes, I know that, for example, Lake Meadows is a product of New York Life's having so much surplus that they could even deal with what one might loosely call risk capital.

RS: Right, right, but there's very little like that now in the insurance business in terms of investment in real estate. In their portfolio they have bonds, stocks, and more bonds! OK? That's what it's all about.

TB: Is the competition also keener now?

RS: Yes, because everybody is trying to get their market share, and, as a result, now the consumer's attitude has changed as well. Consumers have become much more intelligent about what insurance is all about, and now they want insurance that covers more and costs less.

TB: They demand a much better product?

RS: Yes, and so now when any of these companies hires a new agent, they always pick the candidate who is the smartest and the best educated, and it really doesn't matter anymore whether that person's black or white or whatever. What they say is, "Let's get a smarter soldier. Not just a soldier that goes out there to get hit in the head. Let's get one that can shoot missiles, lasers, and all of that kind of stuff." What these companies are really saying is, "Give us a smart agent so he can bring our average-size policy up from a twenty-five-thousand-dollar policy to a quarter-of-a-million policy!" That's what is happening in the industry today, and that's why there's an educational requirement. That's why we have the CLU, the CFP, the CHFC, the bachelor's in financial services, and all of these other kinds of courses. For years I was taking management courses like those in order to have the specialized education that I knew was going to be necessary in order for me to continue to be successful in the future.

TB: But it seems that now the insurance company begins to diversify so much that it's almost like it's no longer an insurance company anymore.

RS: Well, it's still an insurance company, but now we also have other products. Most insurance companies want to be known as financial institutions with insurance as one of their major products. Take American General. They diversified, and now they have mutual funds, stocks, and bonds—so that when a person looks at an insurance company like that it doesn't have that old stigma that it once had. People no longer believe that the insurance person is slick and uneducated. There is still only a little bit of that attitude. Well, maybe there is a little bit more of that attitude in the black community than in the white. In fact, maybe there is a lot more of that attitude in the black community, but that's why I love this work! I'm still here at the forefront. I'm one of the top financial planners in the country, and I know exactly what I'm doing. I am designing financial plans for the future for myself and for the members of this community.

May 16, 1995

PROFESSOR
WILLIAM DANIELS

DEAN AT ROCHESTER INSTITUTE OF TECHNOLOGY

In 1956 I returned to teach at DuSable High School at the specific request of Miss Mary Herrick, who had been my civics teacher back in 1936. Miss Herrick was going on a two-year leave of absence in order to do union organizing in the South for the American Federation of Teachers (AFT), and she prepared the way for me to take over the responsibilities for her homeroom and academic classes. I agreed to do so, and thus began one of the most beautiful experiences of my life.

During this period (1956–58), Bill Daniels was one of my students. At that time he had already developed a very well-planned agenda for his future, and it was my privilege to help him make those plans a reality. At graduation he received many awards and was offered several scholarships. He chose to attend Upper Iowa University, where he was the second black student ever to have been enrolled and where his subsequent achievements set the pace for those who were soon to follow. The realization of his well-planned goals next took him to the University of Iowa, where he obtained his master's degree and Ph.D.

Back during the time he was an undergraduate at Upper Iowa, he met a young lady named Fannie Pearl Hudson, who was also a DuSable-ite. They have a daughter who is now in college.

In terms of setting career goals and determination to achieve them, Bill Daniels is one of the most well-organized persons I have ever met. It was an honor for me to converse with Bill. I am so proud of him.

TB: I'm here with Professor William Daniels. We use to call him Willie when he was a student at DuSable High School, but now I call him Bill. What do you do now, Bill?

WD: I am presently dean at the College of Liberal Arts at the Rochester Institute of Technology, a position that I've held since July of 1988.

TB: What are your area and level of training?

WD: After I graduated from DuSable High School in Chicago in January of 1958, I went to Upper Iowa University and, as is the practice with many undergraduates, I changed my major two or three times, but I ended up with a major in history with a certificate in high school teaching. I went from there in January of 1962 to the University of Iowa, where I earned a master's and a Ph.D. in political science with a concentration in public law, or constitutional law, as we call it.

TB: I understand that you were a Woodrow Wilson Fellow at both the master's and the doctoral level. What exactly does that mean?

WD: I was awarded a Woodrow Wilson Fellowship to begin my graduate training. I got a Pullman Foundation scholarship when I went to Upper Iowa, and it's my understanding that they funded several other students that left DuSable and went on to college during those years. The Woodrow Wilson was limited to one year, but quite frequently, if you performed well enough, the custom was for the university you were attending to pick you up as one of its own fellows. So my first year was as a Woodrow Wilson Fellow, but then the University of Iowa continued to offer university fellowships throughout my entire graduate career.

TB: Which meant, of course, that you had to maintain certain high standards—but let's back up a little here. As you may remember, you were in my homeroom at DuSable.

WD: Oh, yes.

TB: With all those smart kids!

WD: I still have the scars!

TB: That was a great place, an excellent class!

WD: You know, I remember one thing that happened in that class when I was a freshman, and it's something silly, but it's kind of funny. At least it made an impact on me. I first started school in January of 1945, finished grammar school in January of 1954, and then went to DuSable from January of 1954 to January of 1958. I remember that when we went over to our first assembly at DuSable, all of the freshmen got assigned seats up there in the back of the assembly hall, and somehow I got assigned a seat near a window that had a hole in it. Well, it was January, and I got cold—so every time we had an assembly I'd balk, and Miss Herrick would say, "You've got to go!" But I would say, "It's too cold! I don't like these assemblies."

[*Laughter.*]

Another thing I remember is that toward the end of the first year, after we had gone through and taken all of these history tests, she said, "OK, now you've got to study for your final exam." And I said, "No problem," but then she said, "Of course, that means you've got to read the whole book over again." So I said, "You mean *everything* is going to be covered on the final?" And she said, "Well, of course it is!" After that, all of the other teachers told me the same sort of thing, but Miss Herrick was the one that first broke the news to me that I had to study *everything* for the final exam!

TB: Yes, well, you know, when Miss Herrick went away on leave, she asked me to take over her division—which I did. It was a great experience for me because it was so well organized and everybody in the division was like my daughter or son. All of you were college-bound, and, as I remember, when you were getting counseled during that last semester as to where you should be going, you were working after school at Sears Roebuck on Sixty-third Street in their auto repair section, and after you went to get counseled, you came to me almost in tears because your counselor had said something that was very discouraging. So I said something to you like, "Listen, she can't tell you what you want to do. She can tell you whether she thinks you can do it, but she cannot make an accurate prediction about what your capabilities are. She can only tell what she *thinks* they are." Then you got encouraged again, and you got the Pullman interview. Your interviewer happened to be a black guy, and he looked at your complete record—your academic performance as well as your test scores—and then you went on ahead. After that, there was no stopping you!

WD: Well, that was a significant scholarship for me. It was a hundred and twenty-five dollars, which, as I recall, at Upper Iowa was a full scholarship. At least it was at that time. Let me tell you a story about when I was working at Sears. This is something that I will always remember. My friend Melvin Duncan and I went out there together to get a job. Well, Melvin is very light-skinned, and so when we went to the personnel department, the white guys there took a look at us, and I could tell right away that something was wrong, but I didn't know what it was. Then they went out, and I overheard one of them say, "Well, they were supposed to send up *two* light-skinned Negroes, weren't they?" It seems they were going to have to desegregate the store, and so they'd sent them Melvin—who was very light—but they also sent me, and these people were somewhat unhappy with my complexion. So they put Melvin to work in the elevators, and since they were obligated to keep both of us, they sent me off to the garage! But, as it turned out, that was one of the best things they could have done because my father was an automobile mechanic, and I was happy to be working out there in the garage.

That happened in 1956, and, although I took a couple of summers off to become a lifeguard, I continued to work at Sears nearly every summer and every winter during the break between semesters for at least eight or nine years. As a matter of fact, anytime I was in town I'd go out there. You see, they'd always be short of somebody—somebody was always sick or on vacation. I'd go on in and get my little uniform on, and I could do everything that needed doing: tires, batteries, mufflers, seat covers, whatever.

TB: That's very interesting because I suspect that in that period of time a lot of young men and women who would go away to school could come back during breaks and find some employment that was temporary, and they knew it was temporary, but you had done your work well before, and so they would always welcome you back. That way you could make a little extra money for the little things that, I suspect, were very important to you.

WD: That was *good* money. They started me out at a dollar and fifty cents an hour, but just a little later I was making well over two dollars.

TB: Translated into today's dollars that would be about what?

WD: Oh, well, translated into today's dollars, that would be hard for me to say, but let me put it this way. On the campus the jobs were fifty cents an hour, and even that was considered to be good money! If somebody left his position, word got around that campus, and there'd always be somebody there who'd want to get that job, but now with the way things are, students can't pay for their room with the money they make.

TB: No, they can't.

WD: Part of the reason is that I don't think that back then they had the regulations they have now that require them to give you benefits, but anyway, during those breaks, I could work forty hours, and that seemed like a lot of money to me.

TB: At least that would cover the extras you might need at school. Now let's look back a little further. Bill, where were you born?

WD: I was born in Chicago on March 7, 1940—at six thirty in the evening, as a matter of fact. It's five thirty now, and so almost fifty-six years and one hour ago from now was my birthday!

[*Laughter.*]

TB: Where were you born?

WD: I was born on the North Side at 2931 North Marmora Avenue. I know this for a fact because I got it from my birth certificate, which also states that my father's occupation was unknown. There were some other children born to Alice Daniels, and my father was named Roland, but I don't know anything about my mother or my father because at the age of two, I became the child of William and Ethel McCoy—my foster parents, who brought me up until their deaths. My mother died in 1981 and my father in 1983.

TB: As far as I could see, they were great people.

WD: Well, they were my real parents as far as I was concerned. I've never really had any burning desire to go back and look up more information about Alice and Roland.

TB: I remember talking with them on a number of occasions. Particularly I remember that last year at DuSable when I visited everyone who was graduating and asked their parents about their plans for their child's future. Well, your parents had very definite plans that you were going to continue in school, and you also wanted to do that. But do you know that Miss Stack tried to prevent me from doing things like that?

WD: Eileen Stack?

TB: Yes, but I felt that what I was doing was an essential part of my job, and so I said to her, "All right, but you can't tell me how to do my job after I leave work."

WD: She discouraged you then?

TB: Yes, and not just me! Did you ever notice that when they used to have those big assemblies, she would get only polite applause, but Mr. French would get a roaring ovation?

WD: Oh, yes! You know Mr. French lived right across the street from me on Champlain Avenue. I lived at 4814, and right next to him was Mrs. Hudson, the math teacher. So both Mr. French and Mrs. Hudson lived right there on my block. Then down the street was the sixth-grade teacher from Willard School, Mrs. Caldwell.

TB: Now, that neighborhood you lived in at that time was popularly known as Grand Boulevard. Describe growing up in Grand Boulevard as you remember it.

WD: Well, I really had a somewhat atypical childhood, I think, in many respects, but let me give you an aside: I went back there not long ago and it's all gone! All the houses and everything are gone. It's all vacant land. It really affected me when I realized that now my whole childhood was *gone*.

TB: Physically wiped out.

WD: Yes, physically wiped out. Totally gone unless there are some photographs, but kids don't go around taking photographs of the neighborhood they live in. They don't ever even think about it. But anyway, I was sort of atypical in the sense that not only was I working at Sears but I also had a paper route, and that was unlike any of the other kids in those days. For them, it wasn't quite the thing to do, but that didn't bother me, and because of delivering all those newspapers, I knew I'd say about 70 percent of everybody that lived between Forty-seventh and Fifty-first, and between Cottage Grove and what was then South Park. I knew just about everybody!

[*Laughter.*]

I even had one route across Forty-seventh Street up as far as the Ebenezer Baptist Church, and so I just *knew* everybody. I knew their professions, their occupations, and you know, you also had to collect, and so every week I'd have to stop in and talk to people and get to meet their lovely daughters—but, well, that's another story!

[*Laughter.*]

And then again, of course, there was the social life of that area. There was the Regal Theater, and then every Friday night there was an activity right there at DuSable. There'd be a dance one Friday, and the next Friday we'd have roller-skating. We'd roller-skate around the whole place, but you know, it's hard now to remember all the details about my childhood. Not much goes on for you as a kid except that you meet a lot of people. You know that there's a book called *The Promised Land* in which the author writes about blacks coming up from the South.

TB: Yes, I know it very well.

WD: Well, I had a chance to read it a couple of years ago, and it was kind of interesting for me to read about the place where I had lived. For example, the author talked about the train station out there at Sixty-third Street. Well, I used to date a girl who lived on Sixty-fourth, and you could look right out of her dining room window and you could see all of the blacks coming up from the South carrying their boxes and suitcases with all their possessions in them, and when we saw that, we used to sit there and say, "Here come some more folks." But, you know, I didn't really understand the significance of all of that until much, much later. Even so, for me it was a very exciting time. There was community. There was cordiality. There was friendship. There was also some crime. I'll never forget that once when I was riding a bus on Madison I saw a man get shot. I saw what happened through the bus window. A fellow got shot on the south side of the street, and the bus just kept on going. That's when I first realized what a bullet could do. I'd seen movies where you got shot and just went down to the ground, but when the bullet hit this guy, it threw him six feet! It just blew him away, and the bus never even stopped! It seemed sort of surreal to me until I realized that it was real—that it had actually happened.

TB: But back in the neighborhood where you lived, people could still walk the streets and be safe.

WD: Yes, my mother could walk down to Forty-seventh Street and walk back without ever being afraid that anything was going to happen to her. Besides, one of the things with me was that when I would walk down the street, I knew the people who lived in every other house! I could tell you exactly who lived there. If I could take the time, I could still probably show you house by house whether I had delivered a paper there or not!

[*Laughter.*]

TB: If you went out to a dance or something and stayed late you'd walk home.

WD: Of course you'd walk home! You know I bet I didn't ride to DuSable more than three times in all those four years. Every morning we walked down to Forty-ninth Street on Champlain, and then there'd be St. Lawrence, there'd be Forrestville, then Vincennes, then South Park, then Calumet, then Prairie, then Indiana, and then Michigan—and on all these blocks all these kids would be accumulating together as we walked to school. And if you got tired of those people, you'd walk straight down Forty-eighth Street, and you'd walk with a different group of kids. We'd always walk to school. I went to Frances Willard School from kindergarten on, but since that was right at the end of the block where I lived, I always went home for lunch. My mother was always home. So I had lunch and then went on back to school.

TB: Tell me something more about Willard.

WD: Well, maybe I'm a little strange, but I still remember my kindergarten teachers. I had two of them. One of them was Miss Lewis and maybe the other one was her helper—I'm not sure—but I considered them both to be my teachers. Then in second grade I had Mrs. Coffee, I think. Mrs. Ross was my third-grade teacher. She walked with a limp because I think she had had polio, and Mrs. Lemon was my fourth-grade teacher. Mrs. Anderson was my fifth-grade teacher. Mrs. Malone was my sixth-grade teacher, and Mrs. Sportsman was my seventh-grade teacher. Then I had Mrs. Turner for eighth grade. The interesting thing about this is that I can still remember all of these teachers as individuals. I can even remember specific episodes that happened in each of their classes. As a matter of fact, about five or six years ago I scared Mrs. Lemon almost to death! I think she lived up in Lake Meadows, and because I frequently go to Michael Reese Hospital to visit somebody that I know, I had stopped at the Walgreens drugstore near there, and I saw a lady in line, and I said to myself, "I know that lady!" So I walked right up to her and said, "How are you, Mrs. Lemon?" Well, she was a very frail lady, and to have this big black guy come running up to her just scared her until I told her, "I was one of your students. I was your student in the fourth grade over at Willard School." So then she said, "Oh, it's so nice to see you again," but she was really surprised that I still recognized her after all these years.

TB: Now, back then did most of the students from Willard go to DuSable? Or where did they go?

WD: As I remember it, it was necessary to take a test to get into Tilden Technical High School, and so most of the students that I'm aware of went to DuSable.

TB: Now, when you got to DuSable, you must have met quite a few new people.

WD: Yes, of course, I met some new people. It seemed like they were coming there from almost everywhere.

TB: From other schools such as Burke, Coleman, Forrestville. You came in right on the heels of that great 1954 basketball team.

WD: Yes, I experienced that, but remember I came in in January, and the season was half over, as I recall, but even so, that was one of the most exciting times. The school spirit in January of 1954 is very difficult for me to capture fully with a succession of words. We had all those pep assemblies. We danced, and we clapped, and it was just such an exciting time to be there! The other team never had a chance. We were undefeated until Sweet Sixteen. We went all the way to the finals, but we lost that one game, and then on the heels of that we came back, and we played one more game—the City-Catholic game—down at the Chicago Stadium.

TB: The stadium was completely full.

WD: I didn't go down to the stadium, but I still remember that game. I watched it on television, and I was just glued to the set.

TB: That team was not only so good at playing the game but their style of life was such that it created for DuSable a great deal of good feeling and goodwill all over the entire state. It was really remarkable.

WD: Yes, I remember that we all had civic pride. If someone dropped a piece of paper in the hall, we'd say, "Hey, we've got some paper over there." That school was spotless. You didn't trash the building you lived in, and there was not a mark on that building. They had a custodial staff that continually shined up the floors. Each week they'd do one of these long corridors, and you'd come in there and that thing would be shining, and then the next week they'd do the next corridor. That way they went around the whole building and then started the whole process over once again.

TB: What about your teachers? Were they predominantly white at that time?

WD: Yes, and I remember one teacher who took a dislike to me for some reason. I don't know, but I think it was my last semester, and I believe it was a woman named Mrs. Duffy. She taught French, and I had done all the work that was required for her class. Now, I don't think I earned an A, but clearly I had done enough work to meet the requirements.

TB: It seems to me that we had a different kind of grading system back then. We were dealing with Superior, Excellent. We weren't dealing with A, B, C, and D at that time.

WD: Oh, that's right: S, E, G, F. Anyway, she wouldn't give me my E or whatever it was. She gave me a G—so I asked her about it, and she never did say what the reason was, but I think I figured it out. If I'd gotten an E, I would have been in the National Honor Society because I'd have been in the top 10 percent. But with that grade of G, I got moved out, and that was that! I don't like to dwell on things like that. As a matter of fact, I haven't thought about it for a long time, but this lady for some reason didn't like me. I think she had in mind a person to move ahead of me into the National Honor Society.

TB: Who were some of the classmates that you remember who may have done well besides yourself?

WD: Since moving away, I got isolated, you know, and unfortunately, although I can still see pictures of so many of them in my mind, I can't quite remember their names right now. You see, after I graduated I went right off to Iowa and only came back for the summers. So my only real connection was when I'd come back during the breaks, but then I'd go to work, and I never had much of any contact with my high school friends ever again.

TB: Meanwhile, while you were in college, the neighborhood began to change more rapidly.

WD: Yes, that's when they built those Taylor Homes.

TB: That's right. They weren't there when you graduated.

WD: No, they weren't.

TB: And there were several people in your class who lived over on Dearborn and Federal.

WD: And they got moved out when the Taylor Homes were built.

TB: They used to have a really nice little community there. Good people with stable families. Some of them owned their own places. They might not all have had central heating, but the atmosphere in those homes was nice and warm.

WD: That's the way I remember it.

TB: So the environment in that community began to change when you went away—and by the way, was that the first time you'd ever been away?

WD: Yes, I'd never even eaten in a restaurant!

[*Laughter.*]

Now, if I can just go back, you were asking me about the integrity of the neighborhood. Well, when I had the paper route, one of the things that the folks would always ask you was, "What are you going to do with your life? Are you going to get an education?" That was a constant refrain, and somehow I think we might have gotten away from that kind of attitude now. I don't know, but back then *everybody* talked to me about things like that.

TB: It was as though you had a personal responsibility to them to do something more with your life than just have a paper route.

WD: Oh, yes, you had to tell them what you were planning to do—and if you changed your mind, they wanted to know about it!

[*Laughter.*]

TB: Later you married Fannie Hudson. When did you first meet her?

WD: Well, she was also at DuSable, but I never knew her there.

TB: She was behind you, wasn't she?

WD: Two years. I had already been at Upper Iowa for two years when she and her good friend came on the scene: Fannie and Annie! Fannie was the tall one, and Annie was the short one. They're still good friends, and Annie Odom is now an assistant principal somewhere in Chicago. I met them both at Upper Iowa. I was the second black at Upper Iowa, but the first one that graduated.

TB: What size school would that have been?

WD: About three or four hundred at that time in January of 1958. Upper Iowa is a small private school in Fayette, Iowa. That's about sixty miles west of Dubuque and fifty miles from Waterloo and a hundred miles or so from Iowa City. It was an interesting place. When I first got there, I found out that in the dorms somebody had called a meeting and said, "You know, we're going to have a black fellow here. Who wants to room with him?"

[*Laughter.*]

And so one guy—Bob Ricks—says, "I don't care." He was from Blue Island, Illinois, and he was one heck of a football player. Hell of a temper, though. Tackle—big guy. He was muscular, strong. No fat. On the team in those days they had a bunch of these guys like that who had just come back from Korea, and they all played ball. There were a lot of friendly people, but I'd never been away from home before, and there I was out in the middle of a cornfield with a bunch of people like that! What's more is that I came there a little late because I had just graduated, and so the classes had already started, and I wasn't sure I could catch up, but I knew I had to because, you know, people back home were always asking me what I wanted to do, and then they told me I had to do it!

[*Laughter.*]

And I was from a family where I was with five foster brothers, and none of them had ever finished high school, much less gone to college. So what I'm saying is that there was quite a little bit of pressure on me, and so I spent a lot of time working to catch up and do well, but I also made a lot of friends because in the winter there were basketball games. Within fifty miles of that place, there must have been thirty colleges—practically a college in every town—so we'd go over to these other towns to have a basketball game, and I remember a fellow said to me after we'd won a game, "Hey, we're going over to get something to eat. Do you want some pizza?" And I said, "Yeah!"—even though at that time I didn't know what a pizza was! So when they brought this stuff out to me, I just looked at it, and I said, "Lord have mercy, what is this?" But then I took a bite out of it, and that's how I was introduced to pizza.

TB: So you were having a series of new experiences. What kind of social life were you having?

WD: I had a small group of people there that were close friends. We all studied together, and then that following September the school went out and recruited a lot of people, and I got a black roommate named Frank Lipscomb. Frank had graduated from Farragut. Jim Neeley came in there from the West Side, and another fellow came in from Toms River, New Jersey. So all of a sudden they brought in about a half dozen blacks, and then we palled around together. Then the following September after that they brought in some female black students. So I would say that by the time I graduated we must have had about thirty or so blacks on campus. A very nice group of people, and, of course, I also had all the friendships that I had made earlier. So I could have forgotten about work and just had an interesting social life.

TB: So you didn't have the racial tensions that you might have found on some of the other campuses.

WD: No, not at all. I was on the swimming team at DuSable, and I had flirted with football, but at Upper Iowa what I probably did most effectively was debate. I was on their debating team for several years. Then, in addition to that, I flirted with indoor track. That was the second thing I did for more than one season, but I never earned a letter because I didn't care about that sort of thing.

TB: So it wasn't all just books?

WD: Oh, no, it wasn't. I had no time on my hands even though I was in the middle of a cornfield!

[*Laughter.*]

TB: So now you get your B.A. and you go to University of Iowa for your advanced degree.

WD: Yes, that was in January of 1962, but at this point I didn't know I was going to have the Woodrow Wilson for which I had interviewed in the fall of 1961, and then I got a very nice letter from Vernon Van Dyke and John Schmidhauser at Iowa, and they said, "Look, let's put a package together for you." And I said fine, because by then I'd exhausted all the money that I had that I'd saved up from Sears. Then one thing led to another—it all happened so quickly—and they said, "Why don't you come down here in January. We can give you a scholarship, and later on we'll see what happens with the Woodrow Wilson. Meanwhile we'll give you some tuition." I didn't really even know how much money they were going to give me, but before I knew it, we were shaking hands, and I was already a week late for classes in their graduate school!

[*Laughter.*]

TB: Now you are at the University of Iowa in Iowa City at the master's level. How long did it take for you to get the master's?

WD: Well, because my major was history, I had to do a little backup work in political science, and so it took me from January of 1962 until June of 1964 to get my master's degree.

TB: Well, that wasn't so much longer.

WD: And meanwhile, I was a grading assistant as well, but now let me tell you the story about my interview for the Woodrow Wilson. It's a funny story. A member of the panel was Donald Johnson, who taught presidential politics at the University of Iowa, and it turned out I became his grading assistant. He was also a member of the committee that awards the fellowships, and, mind you, they had been bringing in people all day to interview for fellowships from that region. Well, as luck would have it, Hans Rosenhaupt, who was the executive director, just happened to be sitting in on the session when I came in. Now at that point, although I was a seasoned debater, of course, I was a little bit scared, but then once I got into a discussion with the committee, things started going well, and then Rosenhaupt said to me, "Well, what is it you want to study?" So I told him I wanted to study public law. Now, mind you, I had already taken a constitutional law course from Charley Clark, and so I got into a spirited debate, and I guess I must have overcome my nervousness because we were really going at it! You see, I had some very firm views on certain subjects, and I remember that during that debate we were going back and forth, and at one point Rosenhaupt said, "Daniels, I dispute that statement you have just made." And I said, "I beg your pardon? If you will recall, I was only quoting you. *You* were the one that said that." Well, then everyone in the room stopped talking, and I said to myself, "Oh, Lord have mercy! I just put my foot in my mouth." Later, of course, I found out that I had received the fellowship, but it wasn't until I'd been in Iowa for a few months that Don said, "Let me tell you something about your interview. Do you remember that?" And I said, "Yes, I remember that, but I don't want to remember it." And he said, "When you left the room, they said, 'Well, that guy's pretty spunky,' and the chair of the committee said, 'How do you want to vote on this guy?' But before they could vote, Hans Rosenhaupt said, 'We don't have to vote on a guy like that. We'll just give it to him!'"

[*Laughter.*]

TB: One thing's for certain: DuSable guys of that period didn't run away from a fight!

[*Laughter.*]

So it took you two years to get your master's, and then you went straight into the doctorate.

WD: Yes, and I took my qualifying exams a year later and started my dissertation a year after that.

TB: What was your dissertation?

WD: "Public Perceptions of the United States Supreme Court." I used survey data out of the Survey Research Center at the University of Michigan to examine attitudes about the Supreme Court, which was making extremely important decisions at that time. It was largely a methodological exercise where you used a lot of statistical analyses such as multiple linear regression. So then I stayed there until 1966, and meanwhile we got married.

TB: Was Fannie still at school at Upper Iowa?

WD: Yes, and isn't that the craziest thing you ever heard? She's still in school, and I'm down there at Iowa City, and so we got married in the summer of 1963. As a matter of fact, it was on the Sunday before the March on Washington.

TB: Is that right?

WD: So we had a choice. I said, "We could go to the March on Washington or we could get married." And every once in a while I still tell her, "You know we could have participated in history if we had just gone on the March."

[*Laughter.*]

And so we got married the twenty-fifth of August, 1963.

TB: That's now almost thirty-three years ago. I was the March organizer from Chicago, and, of course, that was a mammoth event. Spiritually, I have not experienced anything like that except when I was in France during the liberation of Paris, when everyone was on the Champs-Elysees with de Gaulle singing the "Marseillaise," and people made us stay on the outside of Paris because the French wanted to believe that they had freed themselves. You know that's what they wanted to believe!

WD: And guess what? The French still believe that!

[*Laughter.*]

TB: So when did you get your doctorate?

WD: Well, it took me a while to finish my work because I went off and got a job and didn't do anything for about three years, but then, when I started doing it, it took me only four months to finish it, and I said to myself, "I finished in 1969 but I got my master's degree in 1964, and I could have done this three years ago!" At that time I was only the second black on the faculty at Union College, Schenectady, New York. It was all male at that point. Then I got involved with the NAACP, and you know how it is, one thing just led to another.

TB: Yes, I know very well. When I got involved in the civil rights movement, I was in a doctorate program as well as teaching at DuSable.

WD: And the rest is history.

TB: When you were at the University of Iowa, how many black students were at the graduate level?

WD: When I got there, there was one in our department. That was Joe Penson. Then we started getting a few more in. We got Ed Jackson, who now teaches at South Carolina State, and Alex Willingham, who is now at Williams College. Now, mind you, it was not as bad as it might seem, because the University of Iowa has always had black students—and when you say you've only got three black graduate students, it's not like you've got three out of two hundred, you know, but three out of twenty-five.

TB: So then you had gone off to a teaching position in Schenectady, New York. What was that like and how long did you stay there?

WD: Oh, I stayed there a long time. I was there twenty-two years. Here again I came to a campus, and there was one other black faculty member. He was in biology. They had a faculty of one hundred and thirty or forty. There were very few black students, and those were mostly Africans. The student body at that time was about twelve hundred—all male. The town was about seventy thousand, with about 5 percent being black. But Vietnam was heating up and also the civil rights movement—so it was an interesting time to be there and to try to talk to those students about all the things that were going on.

TB: When did Union College start admitting women?

WD: We started to admit women in 1970, and they hired a couple more blacks for the faculty, but that was about it as far as any changes were concerned.

TB: And you were teaching what?

WD: Political science, American politics, judicial politics, presidential politics, and other courses that I'd created, like Court Watchers!
[Laughter.]

TB: During that period of time, you received an appointment to do something at the Supreme Court, didn't you?

WD: Well, that was sort of toward the end of my career there. The first thing that happened at Union was in 1970, when I got an Alfred E. Smith Fellowship to work with Governor Rockefeller. And so I worked with him on that from 1970 to 1971 at the Division of the Budget in the educational unit.

TB: Were you still teaching?

WD: No, I took a year off, during which time my colleague Jim Underwood and I wrote a book on the Rockefeller administration. Then, when I got a Fulbright in 1973, Fannie and I went to Japan.

TB: Did you learn to speak Japanese?

WD: The period leading up to going there was so hectic that I didn't have time to learn it. We were there for one semester, and then I got the Fulbright people to extend it for another month along with my stipend. What happened is that I must have spoken to every Rotary Club and Kiwanis Club within fifty miles of Tokyo! I mean, I was on the road *all* the time. So I told them, "I've come to this country and the only things that I've seen are the subway and the trains," and so they gave me an extra month, and we spent that month traveling around Japan. We didn't get back till February or maybe March because we didn't come straight home. We went to Hong Kong. At that time Bruce Lee had just died, and to be there and see how much they revered him—well, you'd have to have been there to have believed it. As a matter of fact, I had taken up karate myself by then. Then we went to Indonesia—Bali—Bangkok, and Singapore, and we spent our last two weeks in Hawaii before we finally came home.

TB: In Japan, particularly, what was the reception to you as a black scholar?

WD: That's an interesting question. Obviously the Japanese had not seen many colored people in the flesh, and, of course, the Japanese are *very* good at not disclosing what they think, but I discovered when I walked into a room that the most important thing was not that I was black, but that I was a professor, that I was at the Foreign Service Training Institute, and that I had a Fulbright. I mean, to them that's powerful stuff! You've got to go all the way down there past all of that before you get to skin color, and by then, they're already bowing down because in Japan professors are respected. They may not pay them very much, but at least they are genuinely respected, and so I found that the treatment that I received there was almost reverential.

TB: I found it to be that way in Germany as well. When we were there at the end of the war, I'd walk into the room, and they'd stand up.

WD: Well, that's what the students also did in Japan.

TB: And for them color . . . ?

WD: Was subordinate.

TB: Over there, yes, but whenever I was teaching in a predominantly white school in the United States, I always had to prove that I could teach, and I did that! But the level of my education wasn't that important to them. Race was much more important. "We're going to run this nigger out of here." But they didn't know the type of person they were messing with!

[*Laughter.*]

So in 1974 you came back to the States and back to Union and continued to teach there. How did you get to the Supreme Court?

WD: Well, in 1977 I launched an internship program at Union in which I took twenty students down to Washington for ten weeks. I took those students down there for the first time just after Jimmy Carter won. Well, he was an alumnus of Union, and so we got invited to go to the White House. I say that because I was down there the following year when I applied for the Judicial Fellowship. Chief Justice Burger had initiated a program in 1973 in which he would bring in two nonclerks to work on the administrative side. One of the nonclerks typically was an attorney-at-law. So I applied and got interviewed while I was in Washington with another group of students in the winter of 1978. When I was interviewed by the Judicial Fellows Commission, it was chaired by Judge Walter E. Hoffman from Virginia, but on the commission was Edwin Griswold, the famous dean from Harvard, and I could tell that that guy really didn't like me. I found out later from Judge Hoffman that the reason Griswold didn't want me interviewed was because he thought that I was too old. I was thirty-eight. Anyway, as it turned out, after my interview, they outvoted him!

[*Laughter.*]

And so I got the Judicial Fellowship and started the first of September, 1978, with Justice Burger. One person who receives this fellowship is designated as being a Tom C. Clark Fellow, and so they gave me one of Tom Clark's bow ties in a frame! So that was a good experience because, as I'm sure you know, Tom Clark, whose grandfather was a slave owner, was a previous justice on the bench, and he was replaced by Thurgood Marshall, whose grandfather was a slave!

[*Laughter.*]

And, as you know, for many years I have been interested in Thurgood Marshall.

TB: Didn't you write a book about him?

WD: No, I never wrote that book, but I did write several articles, and one of these years—the good Lord willing—I might still get that book completed. You know, in the past the Supreme Court has sometimes been referred to as the Last Plantation—nine men in black who think white—because that's what it was until Marshall got there!

[*Laughter.*]

But you know, being there, you begin to see the Supreme Court as a group of individual justices who wrestle with certain specific issues. As a matter of fact, when I would take my students down there, it was always Potter Stewart that would meet with them and not Thurgood Marshall. He was always too busy, but he had a very good friend in Anthony Lewis, who was teaching a course at Harvard, and when Tony Lewis would bring his students down every year,

Thurgood Marshall would find the time to meet with them. The important thing for me is that every time Mr. Marshall would have an interview with anybody, they'd tell me, and I'd always sit in. So I have notes from some of Marshall's interviews, and that way I learned a lot about the making of law, as well as the quality of judges as people. As a result, I became a trained mediator, and when there were feuds going on, particularly in terms of issues involving race, I mediated the squabbles between whites and blacks in the Supreme Court. When there were problems, I was a troubleshooter. I also wrote a lot of letters. The chief justice of the United States doesn't read all of that mail that comes in. So I read it, and I wrote all of the letters of response for him. Not all of the personal letters he got, of course, but the letters to people he didn't know. When there were bills that were introduced into Congress, I read every bill that was introduced and wrote weekly summaries. Although Jeffrey Morris was Warren Burger's chief speechwriter, when he got overwhelmed, we would work together on sections of them, and I would travel with him when he gave those speeches that we had written.

TB: Were you able to transfer that level of work you had accomplished to your students back in the classroom?

WD: Yes, I did, and, even now when I speak with African-Americans who we're trying to convince to go to graduate school in political science, I always use what I learned from Thurgood Marshall and some of the experiences that I myself had at the Court to shape the remarks that I make on the way in which the law has developed and been interpreted.

TB: You are currently involved with an organization which is called the National Conference of Black Political Scientists. Tell me a little about its origin and purpose.

WD: Well, I wasn't in it the first year, but I got in on it very early because, as a black political scientist, I always attended the meetings of the American Political Science Association, and in 1970, in Los Angeles, on my way to give a paper at a meeting, I believe, I became aware that there had been a heated discussion earlier that day about the relation between black political scientists and white political science, and they told me, "You can't go. You can't give that paper." And I said, "Why not? I came all the way across the country to do it." And they said, "Because now blacks are holding their own meeting." So that's when I got involved in some of the discussions involving whether we were going to continue to work within that organization or whether we should establish another organization of our own, and so that following year at Spelman—this was in 1971—we had a series of discussions about how the black experience was being interpreted by white political scientists and the fact that there was a void that needed to be filled. Prior to that time, as a matter of fact, I hadn't really given a lot of thought to this issue. As a matter of fact, I was a black political scientist who was teaching, basically, *white* political science, and so at that point I began . . .

TB: Without mixing up or diluting the facts.

WD: Right. Up until then I hadn't read a lot of our own literature because I hadn't been expected to, and so, for me, that was another part of my educational process. Eventually I became the third president of this new organization, and you know I've discovered that quite frequently even black political scientists have to be reminded, intellectually, that there is a racial ingredient in most of our social problems.

[*Laughter.*]

TB: Well, let me ask you something that's related to what we're talking about. How do we provide proper education for all these bright young black kids who live in the mixed suburban areas and who will be the ones shaping public policy for blacks in the future?

WD: The point that you raise is a serious one, and although I can't prove it to you conclusively, I like to think that we've got materials out there that will provide these students with the kind of training and insights and perceptions that just weren't there for people like myself when I was in their . . .

TB: And those questions always involve power and the acquisition of power.

WD: Yes, the acquisition of power and the retention of that power.

TB: But also the *use* and abuse of power. There may be an undercurrent of economics, but the decision about how you use *whatever* power you have is always a political decision.

March 7, 1996

WILKS BATTLES

SUPPORTER OF DUSABLE HIGH SCHOOL

Wilks Battles is a product of the Chicago public school system who graduated from DuSable High School in 1954. While a student at DuSable, he witnessed the development and eventual successes of one of the greatest high school basketball teams in the nation, many of whose members went on to break the racial barriers that still existed in American athletics. He is a veteran of the Vietnam War and is a retiree from the Chicago Transit Authority (CTA). In recent years he has become a regular volunteer at DuSable High School at many different levels. In this conversation he shares his observations about the changes in our community, to which he has been a perceptive witness.

TB: We are here at historic DuSable High School and about to have a conversation with Wilks Battles. Please tell me where were you born?

WB: In Pine Bluff, Arkansas, in 1935.

TB: And your mother and dad, where were they born?

WB: They were also born in Pine Bluff.

TB: Did you know your grandparents?

WB: My grandfather was also named Wilks Battles, and my grandmother was Rose Battles, but I never got the chance to talk with them. My grandmother passed when I was very young, and my grandfather passed in '57 while I was in the service.

TB: When did your parents leave the South?

WB: They left in 1942 and headed directly up to Chicago.

TB: Did they ever talk about why they left Pine Bluff?

WB: Well, I don't know exactly how they were making a living down there, but whatever it was that they were doing it wasn't very profitable, and so they decided to move up North because back then everybody thought that they'd find the land of milk and honey!

TB: Yes, the promised land. So, when your family came here, do you remember how old you were and where you lived?

WB: I was maybe seven or eight, and we lived at 4610 South Calumet.

TB: And World War II just had started.

WB: Right, and I can still remember that there weren't too many radios, and so everybody would raise up their windows so they could listen to Joe Louis on the nights when he was fighting.

TB: Joe was the champion of the world at that time.

WB: And he was living right here in our own neighborhood!

TB: Forty-sixth Street and Calumet, where you were living, was a very busy and exciting area back then. What do you remember about that?

WB: Well, one thing I remember quite fondly was that Joe Williams the singer used to live at Forty-fifth and Prairie, and sometimes he would come out on his back porch to rehearse, and we'd all stop what we were doing just to listen to him sing. At that time Al Benson had a radio show, and Joe was a regular on that program, but a lot of people don't remember that because there were very few radios in our neighborhood, or later, televisions. I remember that we were living in one of those kitchenettes at that time, and the lady that was living in the two rooms at the extreme back of our apartment floor, well, she had the first television on the block. In fact, I used to babysit for her just to get a chance to look at her television!

[*Laughter.*]

TB: At that time what were your mother and father doing?

WB: My father was working in the stockyards at Campbell Soup, and my mother was also working in the stockyards at Libby, McNeil & Libby.

TB: What school were you going to?

WB: I went to Forrestville Grammar School, and then, after graduating from there in 1950, I came over here to DuSable.

TB: Do you remember any of the people at Forrestville? It must have been pretty crowded.

WB: Yeah, it was! The school had triple shifts because it was so crowded. I went to school from 8:00 A.M. to noon, and then they had another shift from 9:00 A.M. to 3:00 P.M., and one from noon to 4:00 P.M.

TB: As a matter of fact, Robert L. Ripley wrote in one of his "Believe It or Not" columns that Forrestville was the most densely populated elementary school in the entire United States at that time.

WB: But that didn't stop us from having fun!

TB: No, I didn't think it would.

WB: When I was coming up, our area was south of Thirty-fifth Street, north of Sixty-third, and went all the way over to past Federal and the west side of Cottage Grove. That was the area that we were able to go to because everywhere else was all white back then. The only movie show we were allowed to go to was over on Forty-seventh, and the pictures there were changed every day. To be able to get tickets we would go and find empty bottles and then cash them in for a few cents, but I think the show fare was only six cents, and so we were able to have a lot of fun and see all the movies we wanted most of the time.

TB: Was the Willard still open on Fifty-first Street?

WB: The Willard was still there, but we never went there.

TB: What about the Regal?

WB: The Regal was there, and later on, when I was here in high school, I was in the ROTC, and once or twice a year the Regal would have Kids' Day where they'd just show cartoons, and we would go over there in our ROTC uniforms and act as ushers.

TB: Did you and your friends ever go dancing?

WB: Yeah, we went to the Savoy and Parkway ballrooms, and we had skating over at Park City, which was at Sixty-third and South Park. Back then we had curfew which was strictly enforced, and kids couldn't be out after 10:00 P.M., but that skating rink was an exception because they gave you a stamp on the back of your hand, and if you got stopped, you would just show the man that you had that stamp, and then everything would be OK.

TB: When you graduated from Forrestville and came to DuSable in 1950, what was DuSable like?

WB: Well, unfortunately the first thing that I remember is that when we came here the older kids would try to get us to buy elevator tickets from them so that we could get to our classes on the second and third floors. Of course that was just a way for those older kids to get a little money, but we didn't know that. We thought that what they said was true, and so we paid them whatever they were charging until we learned the ropes and knew that we didn't have to do anything like that.

TB: Who was the principal then?

WB: Joseph Meagan.

TB: And Mary Herrick was here.

WB: Yeah, she was the history teacher.

TB: And Captain Dyett was still here.

WB: He certainly was!

TB: Who was the coach of the basketball team?

WB: From '51 until I graduated, Coach Brown was the coach of both the football and the basketball teams.

TB: Those were powerful teams.

WB: But the 1954 basketball team is the one that all other teams since then have patterned themselves after. They would have been the state champions, but one of the officials admitted later that he made a false call against them because he didn't think that the state was ready to accept a championship team that was black. People from all over the state wrote to the newspapers with angry comments because they realized that the best team had not been allowed to win.

TB: That was a great team and a great year. That was also the year that DuSable sent its first graduate to Harvard University.

WB: When I graduated from DuSable in 1954, I didn't go to college. I went over to the CTA and got a job. Then I went into the army, and, after I was discharged, I went back to work for the CTA. Altogether I spent thirty-one years working for the CTA, and then I retired in 1988 at the age of fifty-two. I have been retired for seven years now, and, during that time, I have become a volunteer back here at DuSable, and now I am the alumni coordinator.

TB: What do you do in that capacity?

WB: When people call to the school to find out if any of their classes are having a reunion, it's my job to go to the computer and pull up that particular year and send that information to the person who had requested it.

TB: Do you have access to all the names from the various classes?

WB: I have approximately thirty-two hundred names in the computer from all the classes from '35 to '89, and I can bring them up alphabetically anytime I want to.

TB: What are some of your other activities here at DuSable?

WB: Well, I was one of the founders of the Alumni Foundation, which was organized to help with some of the emergency needs of the kids in the school. We work with the counselors, and they identify for us the needy students. Kids like that can come to the foundation up to twice a year and get up to a hundred dollars each time if there is some sort of an emergency need that we can help them with.

TB: Now tell me how would you compare the period when you were at DuSable with what we have here now?

WB: Sad to say, but between the kids of today and the kids of my own generation, there's very little comparison to be made because back then the conditions of the world were so much different. Back then we were all striving to graduate and trying to do our best to help our families, but now for these kids coming here is more like a job, and they don't have any commitment or real school spirit like we did. Yet they have opportunities that we never had.

TB: Such as?

WB: If they come to school and graduate, the kids of today can get scholarships to go to college just about anywhere in the world. When I was here, those sorts of opportunities were almost nonexistent because we didn't even know about them.

TB: Most of those scholarships were available back then as well, but the politicians were getting all of them for their own sons and daughters.

WB: But now you can bypass all those people and go directly to each institution on your own *if* you qualify.

TB: That's true, of course, but a lot of these young people can't qualify because they drop out before graduating.

WB: That's true.

TB: And so now you don't have as many kids here in this building as compared to when you were here as a student.

WB: I think that in the building now there are only about fourteen hundred kids, and the enrollment is still continuing to decline. Even now, a lot of the classrooms are vacant.

TB: What about sports?

WB: When we were here, we always had so many kids going out for sports, but the last two years we only had sixteen players trying out for football. We get a few more players for baseball.

TB: What about basketball?

WB: Well, for basketball we usually have an abundance of players because everybody thinks they're already good enough to get into the NBA.

TB: And become another Michael Jordan.

WB: Without having to practice very much.

TB: Well, the times have changed. The world has changed, and the neighborhood has changed, but tell me—what can the older generations do for these young people of today?

WB: Well, we tried to start a program here at the school where some of the big hotels and restaurants would take some of these kids and show them how to cook and do different things like that, but most of the kids in the program didn't even want to eat any of the food that they'd cooked because they didn't know how to use the proper utensils, and they felt ashamed about that. All they felt was embarrassment because the only food they'd ever eaten was fast food. Just hot dogs, hamburgers, and pieces of chicken!

TB: I imagine in your high school days you would go downtown sometimes and get something to eat or see a show. Are these kids of today so bound to this neighborhood that they don't go out into the bigger world, that they don't ever get to see the larger picture?

WB: They don't because they are afraid to go out into the world. In fact, some of them are deliberately failing their classes so they won't have to go out of here and confront what is on the streets. They start with good grades, demonstrate that they have good skills and abilities, and then they realize all of a sudden that they don't know how to be successful or sometimes even to survive beyond these boundaries that we've established for them. Some of them have never been off the block where they live except to come to this school.

TB: That is a tragic situation.

WB: I have a friend that works in the CHA, and he says that sometimes he has to go into some of the apartments in the projects and what he sees is maybe four or five generations of people living together in that one small apartment.

TB: And that's all that many of these kids have to go back to.

WB: Yeah, that's right. We are lucky because we have sixty years or more of wonderful memories that will last us for the rest of our lives, but most of these kids of today will never be able to have memories like ours because the majority of them won't even be able to live that long!

May 17, 1995

MILTON DAVIS

SOUTH SHORE COMMUNITY LEADER

At the time I talked to him, Milton Davis was the retired president of the pioneering South Shore Bank in Chicago, but when I first met him in 1965, he was a leader in the civil rights movement and the president of the local chapter of the Congress of Racial Equality (CORE). He was always aggressive and creative in his role within the struggle for racial justice. As an officer in the South Shore Bank, he was a leader in the successful effort to save and restore that bank, which had been one of the cornerstones of the community but was quickly falling into decay as the result of the types of landlord and city neglect that had brought an increase of drugs and gang violence into the area. Having accomplished this, with the consent and cooperation of the South Shore Bank's board of directors, he was able to help other banks to survive in several of the city's most threatened neighborhoods. These successes encouraged other banks to make similar efforts, and by now this sort of involvement has become a nationwide phenomenon. In recognition, a few years ago former President Bill Clinton publicly cited the South Shore Bank (later to be renamed ShoreBank) as an outstanding example of how local banks could and should act to preserve and stabilize the communities in which they are located. By the time Milton Davis retired as the ShoreBank's chairman emeritus in 2002, ShoreBank had invested more than two billion dollars in previously underserved communities not only in Chicago but across the country.

Milt is in frail health at present, but he keeps on going and retains his optimism about the future. It was an honor as well as a pleasure for me to have this particular conversation with him because he is a man whom I admire who also happens to be my friend.

———

TB: I have known Milton Davis for at least forty years. Tell me a little about where you were born and the background of your family.

MD: I was born in 1932 in a little town called Jacksonville, Alabama. It's about forty miles north of Birmingham. A lot of the people living in Jacksonville had something to do with the coal industry.

TB: I was also born in Alabama in a little town called Pratt City. The house where I was born is still there. Do you remember your grandparents?

MD: I remember my mother's parents because they lived in Birmingham, which was close by, but I never knew my father's father. I knew his mother quite well, though, because she lived with us for a while.

TB: What kind of work did your father do?

MD: My father was the principal of the high school, and my mother was a housewife. There were seven of us in total. I had one sister who passed at birth and four brothers. I was born smack dab in the middle.

TB: And you went through school in Jacksonville?

MD: Yes, I finished high school in May of 1949, and then in the middle of September I left for Morehouse.

TB: What was Morehouse like back then?

MD: Well, the famous Benjamin Mays was president of the college at that time, and he had attracted some great teachers.

TB: While you were at Morehouse, was Lerone Bennett there?

MD: Lerone had already graduated just ahead of me.

TB: What about Martin Luther King? Was he there?

MD: No, he also had graduated, but obviously his name was still spoken all over the place.

TB: I always remember Morehouse as being a school where almost all of the students knew one another.

MD: That's true.

TB: What did you major in?

MD: A combination of sociology and economics.

TB: Morehouse historically has been famous for producing lawyers and doctors.

MD: Yes, and so most of the names that I heard about on campus were those of people who had left there and gone off to med school or law school.

TB: Because back then Morehouse didn't have a grad school of its own.

MD: Yes, now it has a medical school, but back then the University of Alabama was the place where most of the graduates went to complete their education.

TB: So what did you do after graduation?

MD: Well, I went into the army. Actually I got drafted. Fortunately the Korean War was just ending. When I first went in, the army was still highly segregated, and I didn't make a good soldier. I was in the medics, but I got out early because I had been accepted at grad school at Washington University in St. Louis. I often tell people that the path I was taking was not unlike that which was taken by those that left the South through the Underground Railroad because I was steadily making my way up North just as several of my ancestors must also have done in the past.

TB: What was your field of study at Washington University?

MD: I was getting a master's degree in sociology, but that is also when I started to get involved in the civil rights movement. I was constantly thinking about the issues concerning social justice. Those issues become ingrained in your mind.

TB: When did you first come to Chicago?

MD: I first came to Chicago in '57 because I had some friends who were living in Woodlawn. So I came here and stayed with them for a while.

TB: What were your first impressions of the city?

MD: Well, I didn't like Chicago when I first got here, but later on I changed my perspective and grew to really like this town.

TB: So now you've come to Chicago and are living on the South Side. When did you first become actively involved in the struggle for civil rights?

MD: Well, you know, you never know the exact point at which something like that actually happens. You just knew that things were going on and that you were part of what was happening.

TB: As I remember, I first met you in '58 or '59.

MD: That's right. I had become friends with some people who were involved in the Chicago chapter of CORE. Actually what had happened was that I had gone to look for some housing in Hyde Park and had gotten the same old routine that they usually gave to blacks back then. You know what I mean? There's this big ad in the newspaper that says, "Apartment Available," but when I get there, it's already gone, right? Well, in those days CORE would send a white person right behind you, and, of course, that white guy would be told that the apartment was still available. So that experience made me more determined than ever to do whatever it was that needed to be done to correct that type of situation. Now discrimination wasn't just something that I was reading about or hearing about. It was something that stabbed me squarely in the face, right between the eyes. So I became more and more active in CORE and eventually became chairman of the South Side chapter.

TB: Did you ever meet Jim Farmer?

MD: Yes, of course. Jim Farmer was the national head of CORE at that time, and we used to have long discussions about the civil rights movement and where it was going and what needed to be done.

TB: Before the war, Jim was a student on the University of Chicago campus, which is where CORE originated, but then all of us got drafted and went into the army. When he came back, he picked up the mantle once again and helped them to establish their national office, which was located in New York.

MD: At the same time, as you probably remember, I was also getting involved with the Coordinating Council of Community Organizations.

TB: That was when the CCCO invited Dr. King to come to Chicago for a rally at Soldier Field and then issued an invitation for him to return to focus on the issue of fair housing. Do you remember those events?

MD: Of course I do. I was down there with everybody else at that rally, and I still remember those taunts and the rocks that were thrown at us when we marched through Marquette Park. I had said that if you want to raise the issue of housing discrimination to the forefront, then that was the logical place to have a demonstration because that was where that type of discrimination was the worst. But that was an explosive situation, and those were really difficult days.

TB: That was the time I decided that I could not take this kind of abuse anymore. I had heard threats and taken abuse in Birmingham and small towns in Mississippi and other places when Dr. King led the charge. But I couldn't stand for that same sort of thing to be happening right here in the city where I lived, which was my home! I mean, there was something about what happened in Marquette Park that changed the whole nature of the struggle for me.

MD: And for others as well, but by now Dr. King was being persuaded by some of his mentors to slow down the confrontational aspect of what he was doing.

TB: Andy Young told me that one of the main reasons for that was that Dr. King's supporters could no longer afford to pay all of the court costs and fines that were being levied by Daley's judges. Then, of course, Bob Lucas went off and led a group of protesters over into Cicero. Were you with that group?

MD: No, I wasn't.

TB: Well, Dr. King didn't want to have that kind of division, but even so, there was beginning to be a split between the members of the older organizations such as the NAACP and the younger membership of organizations such as SNCC and CORE—and then, of course, there were also persons like yourself who were beginning to say that we had to find some way to take the energy and momentum of the movement and transfer it into the economic arena in order to make a more permanent and stable form of social change.

MD: That made perfect sense to me because I've always thought the main problem for African-Americans is an economic one. We just don't have a proper, proportional share of the money that's available. This is a capitalist society, and if you don't have money, you just got nothing! If we are ever going to get out of this hole that we're in in this country, it's got to be the result of our own greater economic movement and development.

TB: And this sort of insight has been the blueprint for your future activities.

MD: Yes, it has.

TB: Milt, could you explain the basis for your involvement with the South Shore Bank?

MD: Tim, when we first bought this bank in '73, there was not a single financial institution in Chicago which was willing to make a mortgage for anyone living in the South Shore community. What's more, you could find a great many other neighborhoods in the city—all over the country, as a matter of fact—and all of them were like that. The reason for that was not the fact that black folks were moving in. It was the fact that the resources that any neighborhood needs were being systematically withdrawn from these communities and that no new investments were being made to replace them. Here in South Shore we have one of the city's highest densities of population because of all of these large multifamily apartment complexes. The owners of these buildings were not putting any kind of maintenance or rehab into these structures, and so the neighborhood was a prime candidate for becoming a massive urban slum.

TB: Previously this had been primarily a middle-class Irish and Jewish community.

MD: That's correct. Very middle-class: Irish, Jewish, *and* German, but now that blacks were starting to move in, the bank saw itself as a potential victim of this racial change process, and like so many other white-owned businesses, they decided, "We better get out of here while there still is time."

TB: I remember the swift deterioration of that community. Drugs and prostitution were rampant. Gangs had begun coming into South Shore, and many of the longtime residents—even many of the newcomers who were black—were very worried about what the future might be like.

MD: So, as the result of all of that, the South Shore Bank applied to the federal controllers to move the bank from the South Shore community to the Standard Oil Building in the Loop. But fortunately for us banks are highly regulated in this country, and you can't just pick them up and move them anywhere you want. You have got to get approval from the federal regulators to do something like that.

TB: That's when the South Shore Commission got involved, isn't it?

MD: Yes, Barbara, who was very active in the commission at that time, went before the federal regulator for the bank and said, "We don't think that this bank should be allowed to move."

TB: So they mounted a protest against that application for the South Shore Bank to move, and this was in the early seventies.

MD: Yes, and, as a result of those efforts, the Board of Governors of the Federal Reserve System ruled that the bank had not shown sufficient reason for them to abandon service in the area. As a matter of fact, they went even further than that and said that in their view a bank holding company such as this one possesses a unique combination of the managerial and financial resources which are necessary to address the problems of a community such as South Shore.

TB: Is that right?

MD: Yes, and you know something? Before this happened, there had never been another case in this country where a bank that was trying to leave a racially changing neighborhood had been denied permission to leave! Well, this decision set off a kind of lightbulb in my head and also in the heads of those people with whom I was working.

TB: Now, at that time you were working at Hyde Park Bank, weren't you?

MD: Yes, with Ron Grzywinski, Mary Houghton, and James Fletcher. Well, the four of us were the people who put this concept together that there had to be a better way to address neighborhood problems in this country than just continuing to remain active in all these small, not-for-profit, local community organizations. There had to be something beyond the sit-ins. So we talked at great length about what kind of things we all really wanted to do in the future, but our focus was still in the arena of civil rights and social justice. Well, one day our discussions were given focus by the fact that Adlai Stevenson III, who had been elected as state treasurer, called the Hyde Park Bank and told us, "I'm getting all these calls from African-Americans who own their own businesses in inner-city neighborhoods but can't get their local banks to even talk with them." You see, they wanted Adlai as state treasurer to loan them money to run or expand their businesses, but it was illegal for a state treasurer to do anything like that, and so he said, "As you know, I can't lend them any money directly, but legally I can put additional money in banks, and I'm willing to work with you guys and put money in your institution *if* you're willing to see what we can do about solving these sorts of problems." So out of that grew this continuing discussion between Mary, Ron, Jim, and me about the need for us to form a bank holding company of our own. That was the beginning of it.

TB: But you started with a development program at Hyde Park Bank.

MD: Yes, it was called the Urban Development Division of Hyde Park Bank, and its entire program was to try to see if it could successfully make loans to African-American businessmen in the inner-city neighborhoods who had been unable to get credit from the other banks—and, believe me, that program proved to be highly successful! But then one day, as we were sitting around and talking as we often did, our conversation got around to the fact that although we were doing a good job of funding businesses, there was a much bigger job that also needed doing. If we are really going to do our job, we ought to look at what we can do to save the neighborhoods in which those businesses function. So we came to the conclusion that we would form a bank holding company that would own a bank and also a real estate firm and a venture capital firm and that we would establish our own not-for-profit organization as well. That way all these corporations working together in unison would be able to deal with the full range of problems that you'll find in a changing neighborhood such as South Shore—and so in August of 1973 we bought this bank. You see, we thought that if we could obtain control of a bank like South Shore National, we would be able to reverse that downhill trend by making the appropriate new investments that the situation required.

TB: So then you left Hyde Park Bank and made the purchase of the South Shore Bank, but did the holding company come first or later?

MD: ShoreBank is the holding company, and it came first. So we had to raise the capital that was necessary to set up ShoreBank, and then ShoreBank bought the South Shore Bank.

TB: And the major objective of this holding company was salvaging and improving the neighborhood in which it was located.

MD: Precisely. Tim, what we said to ourselves was that we've got to get out of this mindset in which whenever we talk about problems that have to do with African-Americans we expect the government to find the solution. What we thought was needed—and, of course, we weren't absolutely sure of this because something like this had never been done in this country before—was to establish a privately capitalized investment corporation which would have two objectives. The first of these was that this corporation needed to make money so that it could stay alive to fight another day, and the second was to do community development. If it did one and not the other, then it would fail and deserve to fail. Now, at that point in the early seventies, you couldn't have found even six people in this entire country who would think you weren't crazy if you were talking about buying a bank for the purpose of making investments in changing urban neighborhoods. As a matter of fact, we had a whole lot of people who looked at what we were doing and told us that we were just as dumb as rocks. But even so, fortunately we were able to find enough people who believed as we did that it would be worthwhile to put their money behind testing out this idea of ours. Like I just said, we didn't really know for sure that it was going to work, but we knew we had to try to do something different that had never been done before. We certainly didn't need to have more public housing spread throughout this area because we knew that was part of the problem and not part of the solution.

TB: Now, at about this same time, I was on the board of a not-for-profit that bought into this concept after you all had launched it. It was called the First National Bank Corporation, and it helped to do some of the development that was done in the northeast section of South Shore. Do you remember anything about that?

MD: Yes, the First National Bank also eventually formed a development corporation of their own which was patterned after what we had so that they could also invest in urban development. As a matter of fact, they formed a partnership with our own for-profit real estate division, and working together, they acquired and rehabbed some five hundred apartments in the northwest section of the neighborhood that we're talking about.

TB: And so today that neighborhood has become very, very stable. They have a shopping center and a shopping strip as well.

MD: The shopping center is very successful, but the shopping strip is much less so, and that's because of the change that has occurred in the shopping pattern of the people in this country. When South Shore was in its heyday, the people who lived in this neighborhood, right after we bought the bank, during that same period, these people started jumping in their cars and went sailing off to some new shopping center where they had hundreds of stores for them to do their shopping. So now they don't do much of their shopping anymore up and down these streets—but this isn't just something that's happened to South Shore. More or less the same thing's happened to every neighborhood in the city which formerly relied on strip shopping. Tim, although we tried when we first got here to make loans to those small businesses up and down Seventy-fifth Street, they all went down the tubes because there just wasn't enough to continue to attract people to do their shopping there. So we said we've got to abandon this idea because we're doing nothing but losing money. That's when we developed our concept of establishing a shopping center that would be anchored by a large food store which would draw in thousands of people every day, and as you can see, that concept has worked out quite well.

TB: What's worked out quite well is that you and your partners at the South Shore Bank have managed successfully to stabilize a changing community. Looking at South Shore today, it is quite an impressive community with nice-looking, well-maintained homes.

MD: And that's because we fashioned another innovative program at the bank which we called Ma and Pa Rehab. This program was designed to make credit available primarily to African-American married couples who wanted to buy a home, but we set as a matter of policy that we would not make a loan to people just to buy a property unless they were also willing to put rehab into it.

TB: So you were willing to make them a loan for the acquisition and a loan for rehab as well.

MD: Yes, and what that means is that by now we have somewhere from about 70 to 75 percent of all the large multifamily buildings in this neighborhood owned by African-Americans. Probably for the first time in this neighborhood, the majority of the people who own these buildings are African-Americans and not whites. We are no longer the beneficiaries of any government-supported projects, which can always move African-Americans out whenever they choose to do so. The way things used to be, urban renewal meant black removal, but all of this rebuilding and restoration that has taken place in South Shore has been done without any significant degree of displacement. By and large, the people who were living here when all of this started are still living here. We didn't gentrify the people out of the neighborhood, which is what has happened in so many other communities.

TB: Well, so now that the neighborhood has become successful and stabilized, now that your bank has created a new way of thinking about the banking business, what about our young people? What do you see as the future for them?

MD: Well, I see a mixed bag, Tim. A very mixed bag, because I see so many of these kids who are really out there trying to accomplish something, but then I walk out the door of this building and go down Seventy-first Street and all I see are just these kids hanging out on the corner, coming from nowhere, going nowhere, with nothing to do and no plans for the future.

TB: What about education? What has happened in regard to the education of the children of this community?

MD: Well, unfortunately, Tim, education is one area in which we haven't had anything like the same degree of success that we've had with businesses and housing. The schools in South Shore are probably on the average about like the others that you'll find all over the city. Some of them are bright spots, but most of them are not. If they have school-age kids, most of these families send them to private schools. They either go to the Lab School in Hyde Park or to parochial schools.

TB: You just mentioned the social distance that exists and has increased between the young people that have managed to get an education and have definite plans for their future and those others that you said are just hanging out on the corner.

How does this compare with the time when you yourself were young and were able to bring both those groups together to work for a common cause?

MD: Yes, back then there wasn't that sense of separation. You know, I'll never forget that when I first started working in CORE one of the best kids that we ever had working with us lived in the Robert Taylor project. He told me that he and his brother had been told by their mother all along while they'd been growing up that they were never to go into Hyde Park because black people were not welcome there and something bad would happen to them if they went there. So they were told never to cross Cottage Grove! But as I said, this kid turned out to be one of the very best organizers we ever had because through the movement he got exposed to other people who had different ideas and a wider frame of reference.

TB: But now that this social distance has once again increased, how do we bridge that gap?

MD: It's hard to answer that question because the situation in this society has become very complicated, but, you know, what you just said reminds me of something. Just the other day I became very unpopular at a discussion because people were saying how great Michael Jordan was and how wonderful it was that he was building this million-dollar house up there in Highland Park, and I said that I thought that he ought to be moving his ass back to the South Side of Chicago where he could do some good!

[*Laughter.*]

But then I stopped and thought about it for a moment and said to myself, "Well, a guy like that ought to be able to live wherever the hell he wants. After all, that's what we've all been fighting for, isn't it?"

TB: Yes, but no matter what, part of you must always remain in the place where your roots are or your success will bear no fruit.

MD: That's true, and you know I think a lot about those kids who were in SNCC and CORE and what they wanted to achieve and what we still need to achieve at the present time.

TB: So do I. Thank you, Milt. It has been a pleasure.

September 21, 1997

DORIS SMITH

HOME ECONOMICS TEACHER

I first met Doris Smith when the principal of Wendell Phillips High School, the late Juanita Tucker, insisted that I should meet her and arranged our meeting, and I am so glad that she did so! At that time Ms. Smith was the head of the Home Economics Department at Phillips. However, that title only indicates a very small portion of the work that she was actually accomplishing. In what had become a gang-ridden, violent neighborhood, Ms. Smith was still able to inspire her students with a sense of peace and harmony and a vision of the possibility of a better future. Good character, self-discipline, and the importance of making specific plans for the future were all essential components of the home economics classes that she was teaching.

In our conversation she related to me her memories of growing up in the South as well as her experiences when she came to Chicago and became a teacher. In those early days she witnessed and participated in what were much better times for the students and faculty at Phillips. Later on, when the going got rough, with the sudden outflux of entire families—both students and their parents—who previously had demanded the highest educational standards, Ms. Smith hung in there despite the dramatic physical, cultural, and social changes that had occurred, and she expanded and deepened her educational emphasis in order to include training in those humanistic skills of patience and understanding that are so necessary to keep on keeping on in difficult times and situations.

I enjoyed and also learned quite a lot from this conversation with Doris Smith, and I am certain that the reader will as well.

TB: I have been recording people who have been teaching at Phillips and, of course, at DuSable. Ms. Crawford said that Doris Smith would be an excellent person to talk with and that you have quite a wonderful reputation. What do you teach?

DS: Home Economics and Adult Living.

TB: Adult Living—what exactly does that mean?

DS: We teach the children necessary survival skills. They get child development, consumer economics, some parenting, and also some finance.

TB: You teach them how to handle their money?

DS: As best I can.

[*Laughter.*]

During the first marking period, all of the students must get a credit for Consumer Ed because that's one of the requirements for graduation. Then, of course, we also teach social skills and help to prepare some of the students for teaching careers.

TB: Do they go out and do a practicum of any kind?

DS: No, not really, but with Fashion Merchandising, we first do personal summaries, and then they learn how to shop: how to select clothes that are most appropriate for their body build, how to dress, and how to do modeling. They also learn how to construct garments in both individual and group projects. They learn how to use a home sewing machine like the ones you see here, and then we also have industrial machines. I've just gotten a new monogram machine so that they'll be able to monogram initials and symbols and so on. So, over all, I consider it to be a very good, well-equipped class.

TB: How many students do you have per class?

DS: For the Fashion Merchandising we have at least twenty students that come in every day, but now I have ten new machines and that will cut down on the frustration. Because of the Carl Perkins program, I've been able to get some of this equipment that I would not normally have gotten.

TB: What is the Carl Perkins program?

DS: It's funded from a grant which is supposed to integrate academics with vocational education. We're blocked off in a team with English, science, math, and social studies coordinated with a vocational plan in which the government pays for updating the equipment. The person who is in charge of it gets an additional salary for coordinating the program, and the teachers involved in the program get the experience of doing integrated lessons.

TB: How long has this program been in effect?

DS: For three years, but this year the program is supposed to be phased out. We are hoping we'll still get some funding so that we can buy some more new equipment and continue with the integration of the curriculum, but right now we have a problem. Integrating the curriculum was supposed to improve attendance and increase the reading scores. It was supposed to raise the school academically, but in a situation like we have here, where our kids have a problem with coming to school on a regular basis, we just haven't been able to get the kids blocked properly. The plan was that all of the teachers of math and science would have the same group of a hundred or a hundred and fifty students, and you'd be able to follow the progress of each of those students from one discipline to another. That way, if you had anything specific you needed to tutor someone in, you could always pull that student out and tutor them before they fell any further behind.

TB: It would seem to be that that kind of team-teaching approach would be very effective in the long run.

DS: Yes, but the bottom line for this program right now is to raise the level of the academic scores and achievements of the students.

TB: Are you succeeding?

DS: Yes, because now it seems that our students are becoming more conscious of the importance of tests, and they're much more concerned about raising their scores.

TB: Are they really?

DS: Oh, yes, for sure! Now they recognize that there's nothing wrong with being intelligent because everybody knows that that's the key to their future.

TB: Are most of the students in your classes girls or are they mixed girls and boys?

DS: With Living Environment, I have a balance, sexually, but with the Clothing, the boys seem to think it's only for girls, and with Fashion Merchandising, I have mostly girls, only a couple of guys.

TB: Have any of the young men ever noticed that some of the successful fashion designers are black males?

DS: Yes, but you know how it is. Even so, the guys will still come by the room and make jokes, saying, "That's just for girls."

TB: Like typing was thought to be when I was going to school. But the worst thing I ever *didn't* do was to not learn how to type because when I got to college I couldn't type. I had to write everything in longhand and give it to somebody to type for me! And in graduate school I didn't have time then. So this labeling things as male or female can sometimes really be a handicap.

DS: At one time we taught a class called Boys Clothing, and we did get a better response by putting all the boys in that one class, but back then the young men had pride in how they dressed. They didn't just wear gym shoes and jeans. Now it's just not the same thing, and that makes a difference.

TB: Many years ago, historically, when Phillips had a great football team and Ms. Maudelle Bousfield was the principal, I understand that she took all of the football players—Buddy Young and all of those guys—and they agreed to be in the cooking and sewing classes. That made everybody want to be in them! She de-feminized those two areas, and the guys really liked it!

DS: Well, you know, some of the best cooks are men.

TB: Oh, yes.

DS: For example, my husband does an excellent job of cooking.

TB: And I do too!

DS: My husband makes a pecan pie that really should be on sale! I think he could sell it anywhere. He thinks it's the best in the city. So really and truly, cooking is not just a woman's thing.

TB: And for men it can be a form of therapy. When I have to cook, I've discovered that I can't do anything but be there cooking. I can't answer the telephone, I can't read even a little bit, because I've got to be watching and smelling, and I know that if the smell's just right then it's about time for me to do this or that or some other thing. So it's fun, but it also takes my mind away from a lot of other things.

DS: And it's something you can share with other people.

TB: How long have you been here at Phillips?

DS: Since 1969.

TB: Then you've been here twenty-seven years. Where were you before you came to Phillips?

DS: Well, before I came to Phillips, I worked at Senn High School for a couple of months. I also worked at the Gregory School over on the West Side. I was the only black teacher there. Then I taught at Bass Elementary School for a couple of years, and I was at Lucy Flower for four years, but then I got pregnant, and I was out for a while. When I came back in again, I came to Phillips, and I've been here ever since!

TB: Where are you from originally?

DS: Mississippi.

TB: Where in Mississippi?

DS: Tunica, Mississippi. Right now, they've got all of these casinos there.

TB: Yes, and I suppose that they're making a lot of money there now.

DS: Well, maybe so, but back then it was one of the poorest towns in the state, and I think most of the people there are still poor.

TB: The casino operators are the ones who are making all the money.

DS: There aren't too many of my people still left there, but my uncle who's still there said that the casinos didn't hire very many of the local people.

TB: And that same sort of thing is true in New Jersey and other places as well.

DS: Even if local people are working at places like that, they're not doing anything that requires much education. They mostly get hired for just sweeping up or picking up paper, and you don't have to know very much to do that kind of thing! Most of the people that are working there come from Clarksdale and other larger places like that.

TB: So you were born in Tunica. Where did you go to school?

DS: There was no high school in my hometown. So I lived in a dormitory in Clarksdale, and I went to Coahoma Junior College and Agricultural High School. It's still in existence. For me it was either go there or not go to high school at all. When I became a junior, they finally built a local high school, but it was just freshman/sophomore. Then the next year it went to junior/senior. So I never really had an opportunity to attend high school in my hometown because the school was built a year too late! I graduated in 1954.

TB: That was the year of the Supreme Court decision in *Brown v. the Board of Education.*

DS: That was the ruling that segregated schools were unconstitutional.

TB: Yes, at that time I was teaching at DuSable.

DS: Well, that may have been the law, but I know that all through my college years we'd still have to go to the back of the bus — or at least go back beyond the center line. I rode Greyhound buses like that to my classes at Alcorn State University.

TB: When did you graduate from Alcorn?

DS: In 1958. You see, you couldn't afford to stay very long in school. You had to get right in there, get your education, and then get out.

TB: Are your mother and dad still living?

DS: Well, my mother is still living, but my father died back in 1968. They moved to Chicago after I graduated from college.

TB: In 1958?

DS: No, my parents came here a little bit later, probably somewhere around 1960. You see, I got married right after I graduated, and I went farther south and started teaching back down in Mississippi. I didn't earn very much there in Mississippi — thirty-four hundred dollars a year wasn't much of a salary — and it was a hard living working in a place like that, but even so, you could always get anything you needed because everybody knew you. So it wasn't a problem having conveniences, but you just didn't earn very much. They wouldn't even let us have a charge card at Sears! So when my sisters graduated and went up North, and we heard that they were making twenty-five dollars a day — "Whew, twenty-five dollars a day!" — we all eventually decided to come here, and we've all been here ever since.

TB: Where did your mother and father live when they came here?

DS: They lived at Seventy-third and Kimbark. They lived over in Park Manor, but then, like I said, my father passed in 1968.

TB: What did he do?

DS: He worked at a factory out in Niles.

TB: Oh, is that right? He had to drive all the way out there?

DS: Yes, but he thought nothing about it. He just saw himself as a man who worked. He drove, and sometimes they would have a carpool. But he had arteriosclerosis, and he died of a heart attack. They called us and told us he had just come out of the bathroom, and then he slid down the wall and died. He hadn't even been sick, and so I said, "Well, maybe they made a mistake"—so we all dried our tears and called back to make sure it was true, and it was!

TB: Yes, I know that feeling. You never want to let go because it's someone that is near and dear to you.

DS: He had always wanted all his children to have an education, and now all four of us are teachers. Two of us teach in elementary schools and the other two teach in high schools.

TB: And your whole family still lives around here?

DS: Yes, we're all here, and I've got two sons and a daughter. They all went to Catholic schools. One of my sons finished at Morehouse and the other at Howard. My daughter attended Tennessee State and Jackson State, and she ended up graduating from Northeastern Illinois University here in Chicago.

TB: So you came to Phillips in 1968. What was it like then and who was the principal?

DS: When I came here Mr. French was the principal. Back then things were different. Altogether we had about three thousand students, and the graduating class was maybe four or five hundred kids. The enrollment was so large that we were on shifts, but the kids were different then. We wouldn't even allow the girls to come in the building with pants on, and young people were apologetic if they accidentally said a bad word. So it was totally different back then.

TB: Was Mr. Ellis the assistant principal here?

DS: Oh, yes, Mr. Ellis was also my husband's assistant principal. My husband worked at the branch over on Wells Street. My husband took early retirement just last year. You know five plus five?

[Laughter.]

TB: Yes, nearly everybody took that five plus five.

[Laughter.]

DS: Well, you know, people thought I was out of my mind for not taking the five plus five, but I said, "Well, the problem is that I *do* like what I do, and I'm not quite ready to give that up quite yet."

TB: When you retire—particularly if you liked what you were doing—you'll probably just keep on doing it in one way or another anyhow, and you'll be doing it for free!

DS: That's right! I'd probably be doing it for free!

TB: So, stylistically speaking, when you first came here, these youngsters were pretty much in what we might call a traditional, conservative mode, and through the years you have seen that mode of behavior change, haven't you?

DS: Yes, but you know, I do not allow certain things to happen in my classroom. I mean, I know what's happening in their homes, and the kinds of things that go on, but I don't tolerate any of that, and now the kids pretty well know what they can get away with but also what they can't.

TB: And they know that you're the boss here?

DS: Well, I think I am!

[*Laughter.*]

You have to have some rules and make sure that the students understand them. That way in the long run I think they also learn to respect you a little bit more.

TB: I'm certain that they do.

DS: But the morality has changed, and now the parents are tolerating more. One of the other teachers and I took a group of kids the week before last to the ETA Theater and saw a play called *The Positive Evolution of Bongo Baker*, which was an excellent play. In this play the parents were away on vacation, and the kids were taking over and making all their own decisions. Well, I think that's happening a lot in real life. That's why kids are the way they are today.

TB: When you first came here, I imagine there were many more two-parent families?

DS: That's right.

TB: And the parents probably were older and more mature?

DS: Yes, they were definitely more mature. Now we have another generation of young people who don't quite know what they want to do, and they don't have anybody at their homes to help them to make those important kinds of decisions.

TB: They don't have those mature parents.

DS: Right, their parents often act like kids themselves.

TB: Where are your students from?

DS: Well, most of our kids are from the projects: Stateway, Ida B. Wells, Wentworth Gardens—and *everything* is going on in places like that. Some of these children already have babies of their own when they get here, and not just one—I mean these children have *children*—and so they have problems getting sitters when they come here. That's why we felt that having a child development program was so important—even for the ones that don't already have kids—because they need to know how to train their children when they do come along. Most of them, they just don't know what to do.

TB: And they missed what they think might have been a whole lifetime of fun and experiences in their teenage years.

DS: Yes, and so now they're trying to make up for it. One of the best basketball players and his sister are in my class, and one day we were talking about the way they lived, and the young girl said, "I don't have no curfew." So I said, "What do you mean you don't have a curfew?" And she said, "My mother is out with her boyfriends, and I can go out whenever I want." She just happened to be one student who was willing to volunteer that information, and I am certain there are many who live just like that. I think she told me her mom was barely thirty years old, and since this girl is now a senior, that means that she was born very early in her mother's life.

TB: Yes, when her mother was probably only twelve or thirteen.

DS: And so now her mother's probably trying to play catch-up. You know people are quick to think they've missed something, and if Mom is someplace else, then it's left up to the kids themselves to do whatever they want.

TB: Without any rules or regulations.

DS: Yes, but at least both of these kids have good minds, and they are actually doing pretty well. Even so, it's hard to be a good student when you've got a parent that's only interested in going about and doing their own kind of business.

TB: And also usually without any male parent that will give any kind of support— and I don't mean just financial! That sort of situation is a big handicap for any young person who is trying to learn how to grow up.

DS: The other day in class we were doing something on inherited characteristics and physical features, and I asked this young man I was just talking about, "Who in your family do you resemble?" He said, "Well, people say my face is like my daddy's," but he said he had never seen his father, and then he said, "But I've got his name on my arm," and he pulled up his sleeve and said, "I've got *this*." Well, I said, "Oh, that's great!" Now, this is a kid who wants to be a doctor. He told me he wants to go to the University of Massachusetts, and I asked him, "How did you select that school?" But he didn't really have an answer.

TB: Well, I guess he sees that as being the best place to be, and so, in his mind, that's where he is going to go.

DS: And perhaps he will. I certainly hope so.

TB: Now, you were saying that when you first got here there was somewhere around three thousand students. About how many are here now?

DS: Well, maybe twelve or thirteen hundred. That permissive transfer is what caused that decrease. Without that, we would still have all our neighborhood kids right here in this school. A principal from Mather explained to me why all of this happened. He said it was done to save the jobs of the whites. They came up with this sixty-forty concept so that you've got to integrate the staff but you don't have to integrate the student body. Well, we always think that if we go where there are whites, then we're going to learn more, and so our parents took the kids away from the neighborhood. They took them away even from grammar school! What's more, some of the elementary teachers actually encourage students to go to other schools and not to go to Phillips. Well, so now we're getting the students that maybe nobody else wants. We're getting the leftovers. You know when I was talking to this same young man I told you about, I said to him in order to encourage him, "If you try, I'm sure that you can get your scores up above the fiftieth percentile!" And he said, "Yes, and when I get my scores up, I'm going to transfer over to Curie High School." So I said, "Well, you've got your nerve. Why not stay here at Phillips?" I don't know if that young man has ever even been over to Curie. Maybe that's just something in his mind, but even so, he shouldn't say that. This is his school!

TB: Where is Curie High School located?

DS: It's on Archer at Forty-ninth Street. It's a nice building, and they have air-conditioning and carpets and all that sort of thing.

TB: And that sort of thing is probably what appealed to this young man.

DS: Well, you know now, some of the kids have started calling this school *old* Phillips because of the way that it looks, but once we get the windows and the lockers taken care of and improve the appearance, their attitude will be improved. I paid to have this room painted myself.

TB: Well, it certainly looks very warm and attractive.

DS: And when the kids come in here, I say to them, "Please don't write on these painted walls," but because they think about this place and the walls here as just being old, they don't seem to care very much.

TB: When you first came here, what was the graduation rate of the ones who entered as freshmen?

DS: Oh, I don't know the exact percentage, but we would have at least five or six hundred kids graduating each year, and now you usually have only a hundred and fifty to two hundred. The dropout rate was lower back then.

TB: Some outside factors must have also come into play that were not there when you first came here.

DS: Yes, drugs! Back then, if the kids were doing anything, they might have been smoking a little marijuana—and you could always tell the ones that smoked that stuff because their eyes would change color! Well, I don't know what they've done to that stuff to change it, but now they can smoke and their eyes don't turn red anymore.

TB: Maybe that's because they're doing some other things than just smoking marijuana.

DS: If you mean hard drugs, well, to be honest, I don't have any children that I can say are on drugs who come to my class on a regular basis, but in the school I'm sure there must be kids that do those kinds of drugs because you've got these kids around here who are known to be drug dealers.

TB: You have established a new intervention program for drugs and guns, haven't you?

DS: That's right. One little girl was arrested this week because she had a knife, and one little boy in the division that meets in here was also arrested because he was caught with a gun. When that happened, his mother came here and said, "Oh, my poor baby!" But that woman should be happy they got her "baby" with that gun before he got involved in serious trouble. You can't have guns in school!

TB: But outside you have the gangs.

DS: Yes, they have gangs, but I don't know anything about them. All I know is sometimes I hear them calling each other Folks. Anytime you hear them calling each other Folks, that's referring to a gang that they're a member of, and there's another name I've heard, but I can't remember what it was.

TB: GD?

DS: Yes, that was it.

TB: GDs—Gangster Disciples—of course, come out of the Blackstone Rangers. You know, when I was teaching at Hyde Park, I had Jeff Fort as one of my students. He was this young tough guy, but he would talk with me. He was just another kid as far as I was concerned, and we had a good relationship. There were two or three of us black male teachers whom he respected, and so we had him under control. In fact, we had them *all* under control. But Hyde Park High School was snooty-tooty at that time. It was considered one of the great public high schools in the country, and they didn't want these snotty-nosed troublemakers. So every time they'd get a chance they would throw them out and put them out on the street. Then one day I got two phone calls. One was from the late Bernadine Washington, who went to school here, and she was telling me that Nancy Wilson wanted to do a concert at the school. Well, the principal and I went around and around on that one, and while I was talking to him about that, I got *another* call, and it was from the office of the president of the United States.

DS: Oh, really!

TB: It seems that there was an upcoming conference that they wanted me to be a part of—so I had to leave, and while I was gone, they put Jeff out and put those other guys out on the street. I tried to get them back in, but they said, "Mr. Black, they don't want us in." That's when the explosion began to take place. That's when the rivalry began. At one time the Rangers controlled it all, but after they had done their damage, Jeff and those other guys were all put in jail. They were sent to prison, and the younger guys coming up copied these older ones, and they started to let the drug dealers push their stuff into the community. So our kids are in much more danger now than they were when you first came here, and that, I imagine, accounts for at least part of the dropout rate.

DS: I'm sure you're right.

TB: Now, the neighborhood in general when you first came here, what was it like?

DS: Well, it probably had a few more businesses, but not a lot.

TB: So even then it wasn't a very prosperous neighborhood?

DS: No, and not a lot of businesses were owned by blacks.

TB: And now there are even fewer businesses, and the quality of life, I would guess, has deteriorated visibly?

DS: Well, the ages of the parents are certainly different. The parents are younger, and at open house we don't have as many people coming up to check on their children as we used to.

TB: And now in the streets, is it less friendly?

DS: Well, I always keep my car door locked when I drive down the street. A police officer told me to do that. You see, one day I was just driving along, and they had just put this stop sign out here, and I really didn't notice it, so I ran the stop sign! Well, this officer was sitting there, I guess, just to catch people, and I told him where I was going, and he just gave me a warning, but he said, "When you drive around there, would you please always lock your doors?" So I figured if he told me to do that I would do it, but I don't fear for my life here. I wouldn't work here if I did. Nothing bad has really happened to me here. It may be a little bit naive on my part, but when I come here I don't feel that I'm endangering myself either with the students or with the people in the neighborhood. Whenever I see people in the neighborhood, I always speak to them because I'm from the South—or maybe that's because I don't have any better sense!

TB: I've noticed that this neighborhood is starting to change.

DS: Yes, it is changing. They're rehabbing and redoing.

TB: Well, my guess is that ten years from now there will be no Gateway, no Ida B. Wells, no Wentworth Gardens, but then the problem will be, Where are you going to put all those people who are living there now?

DS: And also just how much destruction are all these people going to cause us when you throw them out on their own into the neighborhood? Some of them, they're not accustomed to taking care of anything for themselves.

TB: Well, that means that there will have to be a lot of training programs available for these people.

DS: Yes, but who will train them? Do you think the city would try to train them?

TB: They're going to have to. In fact, I know of some cases in the suburbs where they're encouraging home ownership at almost no interest. You know, when I was a kid, we walked from Thirty-first Street Beach to Fifty-seventh Street Beach, and I can still do that from where I live now. So this land around here—right next to Washington Park and Jackson Park—is some of the most valuable land in the city, and that's why they try to discourage good people from living here. They make it hard for you to stay here and live in this neighborhood. They take away all the businesses so you have to go outside to shop. They do everything they can to discourage stable black folks from staying, but even so, some stable black folks are staying in spite of having to go somewhere else to shop! They just refuse to give up, and I glory in their spunk! As you know, Ms. Smith, education is even more important for the youngsters of this new generation than it was for my own.

DS: Right.

TB: And maybe also for yours. What changes would you like to see happen here at Phillips—this school, where you've been such a long time—that could improve and enhance the quality of education and modernize it for these kids so that when they go out in the world they can compete? The world that these youngsters have to go out into is much more competitive than it was for me and you. What are some of the things that an educational system or an educational institution like Phillips can do? What can be done by the school for the students that come from these unfortunate backgrounds to help them get ready for this world that they are going to have to face?

DS: Well, right now, high tech is very important, and we need to upgrade our labs. Also there wouldn't be anything wrong with trying harder to involve some of the parents! I have an evening program now. It started maybe a month ago, and I've already got five parents enrolled in it, but you know, there used to be night school here, and there wouldn't be anything wrong with trying to get that night school going again!

TB: This school established one of the first night schools in the country.

DS: You see, parents need to be educated too. Maybe some of these parents dropped out as freshman, but you know, as one woman said to me, "Well, this time we're not going to drop out *again*." So now some of them are coming here for a computer class, and some of these young parents may not even know how to prepare a good meal or even how to plan a balanced diet. I drink pop too, but most of our kids are eating out of those machines down the hall, and only a very few of them will ever sit down and have a real meal with their parents. Their parents only cook on holidays and things like that—and if our people have gotten to the point where they will say, "Oh, I don't cook. I don't do that," then how are they going to be healthy? We also need to have some involvement on the elementary level with curriculum in order to let the elementary school people know what it is that we expect of them. We've got kids that get sent here that are still at second-, third-grade reading levels, and we've got to bring them up to the fiftieth percentile! We can't say it's impossible, but really it has to start someplace before they get here. The principals at each level need to change the schedules. Right now, you've got them doing this so many minutes, and then you've got them doing that so many minutes, and doing too many separate things, and they're not doing what they should be doing! Maybe they need to concentrate more time on math and reading and on some of those specific areas. Maybe we can have some more involvement with that! Maybe they could even set up some of those exchange programs, and some of our high school teachers could go over to the elementary schools and help. Something has to happen. My grandbaby's in school now. She's in first grade, and she's already reading everything, but that's only because we're helping her. She's got all of this readiness, and most of the rest of them, they do too, but they're just not getting the right kind of help.

TB: You have to do more outreach.

DS: Right, that's part of it, but it has got to happen before we get them here.

TB: It has to start earlier.

DS: But you know what? If the proper funding comes through, and if we do what we're all supposed to do, we'll find a solution to these problems. If people see this school with new tuck-pointing and all the windows fixed, and if they get the lockers repaired, then this place will begin to look like a school again and not like a dungeon, and all of that will encourage students to come here. Then when the curriculum is properly aligned, they can start to see some real progress. Of course, we're going to have to put out some flyers and some brochures and try to let them know what's happening, but when they know what's happening, they'll want to be part of it too, and then things will really start to improve!

March 26, 1996

BETTY STELL

VETERAN TEACHER AND ADMINISTRATOR

Betty Stell grew up on the South Side of Chicago, where she went to public schools and graduated from Hyde Park High School, before attending Roosevelt University and the Chicago Musical College (where Ramsey Lewis was a classmate and where she met her future husband, Roy).

Her late husband was a friend and teaching colleague of mine, and so I have known Betty Stell for at least thirty years. She has been at DuSable all of that time and has seen two generations of students graduate as well as witnessed the deteriorating conditions of the neighborhood that exists just beyond the classrooms. Despite other professional opportunities and offers of early retirement, she has remained steadfast in her determination to give to DuSable the best that she can in art, in music, and in guidance. By her very presence she creates an atmosphere of stability, dignity, and wisdom. That portion of our conversation which follows is at least sufficient to disclose those qualities which I have just described. What a gentle and dignified lady!

TB: Betty, please share with me your observations concerning the flow of change that has led to the situation that we now have here at DuSable.

BS: All right, well, in terms of the changes I have witnessed here, number one is the fact that when I first came to DuSable, by and large, the students had parents who were serious about parenting. Those parents might not have been that well-off economically, but people can be financially poor and yet rich in other ways.

As a result, there was a certain degree of respect that the students would give to an adult just for being an adult, and that kind of attitude is something that has been lost. Of course there have always been certain kids who were only interested in doing their own thing, but not to the extent that we have now.

TB: Is that because these children are children who have raised themselves?

BS: Actually these young people today are already the second generation of children of children. Most of their mothers had these children while they were still babies themselves, and sometimes their grandmothers are even younger than I am.

TB: You're still in your fifties, and I've heard that there are some *great*-grandmothers that are younger than you.

BS: Yes, and so in some cases we are dealing with three generations of children that are raising children of their own. That kind of mother is much too young to have any degree of control, and there is seldom any father around except on the first of the month, when the checks come in.

TB: Please explain exactly what you mean.

BS: What I mean is that the men show up only when the women get their welfare checks, and then they just disappear. I've heard about that from a lot of these kids, but then, of course, there are other kids who don't even know who their father is because their mother has *refused* to tell them! She doesn't want them to know because she is so angry with that man that she doesn't have enough sense to understand that it's important for these children to know who their father is.

TB: So there is an increasing lack of connectedness in terms of the structure of these families.

BS: Yes. So now you've got these kids who have no family of their own but who still need to have a family, and for them the only family that's available is the gang.

TB: To them that's a logical progression.

BS: Yes, and within those gangs are the only role models they respect.

TB: How does that affect your own relations with these students?

BS: Well, when you've been at a school for as long as I've been here at DuSable, you develop a certain kind of reputation. You may even have had the mothers of some of these young people in the classes that you've taught. So, as a result of all that, I can do certain things that other people can't do. You know, I can walk down the hall and tell one of these boys to take off his hat, and if he doesn't, another boy will punch him and tell him, "Do what she says. Take off your hat!" You see what I'm saying? That is an advantage of being at one school for a certain length of time.

TB: When you first came here, in your judgment, what was the percentage of pregnancies among the young women?

BS: It was seemingly unusual for one of our young women to get pregnant, but it's hard to tell because so many of them, when they first discovered that they were going to become mothers, just left the school.

TB: What would be your estimate of the percentage of young women presently entering the freshman class that will become young mothers?

BS: The number of pregnancies seems to have decreased. It's maybe about 5 percent now.

TB: It used to be much higher?

BS: Yes, in this past year or so the percentage has dropped—probably because of the AIDS situation—but for a while there it seemed like at least two to three out of every five of our young women were either pregnant or would eventually get pregnant before they graduated. It really became a kind of crusade for me to try to make sure that some of these girls got through their four years here without getting pregnant!

TB: So for the girls the primary problems were involved with their not getting pregnant, but for the boys the main problems were with the gangs and violence.

BS: Yes, the boys' main problems are the problems of gangs and violence, but we also had a situation here two years ago in which the girls were very aggressive toward the boys.

TB: What was the cause of that?

BS: Well, you might think it was the result of the feminist movement or something like that, but in my opinion things like that have started to happen since cable came in. Now these kids are coming to school sleepy because they've been up all night looking at cable, and what you see late at night is nothing but pornography and violent stuff. So a lot of these kids have seen and been exposed to things that they cannot handle either intellectually or emotionally.

TB: What do you think would serve as a remedy for this sort of situation?

BS: What I would do is I would say to the parents, "Why would you buy cable when you already can't control your children?" I'd say that because these children have not been taught anything about personal dignity and self-respect by their parents. They are a bunch of lovely girls, but they just don't know what to do or how to behave because no one has ever taught them.

TB: I have been told that before they went to the senior dinner someone had to instruct them in how to use a knife and fork.

BS: Yes, that's true, but this is not just a lower-class or racial sort of thing because there are also a lot of middle-class white kids with the same kinds of problems. Their mothers and fathers are so busy getting their extra degrees or whatever that their children do nothing but eat fast foods, and those are the kinds of food that you eat with your hands. You learn by what you do and not by what you don't, and so now you have to teach these kids certain basic things that you would not have had to teach kids previously.

TB: What you're saying is that what we've been talking about is not particularly and exclusively restricted to young *black* people.

BS: No, this is something that runs through class and race.

TB: So at this time and in this school you are in the process of stimulating and educating these young people so that eventually they can enter the mainstream of society and become successful, but in many ways your job is now much more difficult and you have to be much more creative than when you first came here thirty years ago.

BS: Yes, in some ways it's different, but the challenges remain the same. It's like my grandfather used to say, "Things may change, but man does not"—and the same human needs still need to be addressed, but maybe even more so now than back then because in the past there were more supportive factors available than there are at present. What makes this situation even more poignant is the fact that today almost everything is filtered through technology.

TB: So the intervention of technology is an additional complication.

BS: Yes, although technology in itself is a wonderful, marvelous thing, it does not take the place of direct human contact. It can help facilitate learning, but the downside is that it can only accomplish part of the job that needs to be done.

TB: If you were totally in charge of the situation in this present environment, with AIDS as well as all of the impediments that we've been talking about, what would you do to prevent these young people from dropping out of school and to help them prepare for a successful future?

BS: Well, first of all, we have to remember that there were always a whole lot of dropouts. The public education in this country has never been as good as it should be, but the problem for these kids of today is that the jobs that those dropouts used to be able to get are no longer available. It used to be that if you dropped out of school, you could always find a job and make a good enough living to be able to raise a family of your own.

TB: Yes, the steel mills, the stockyards, even the corner grocery store—somewhere, wherever.

BS: Right, but, as higher levels of skill have come to be more in demand and common unskilled labor jobs have more or less disappeared, it becomes the task of education to prepare these young people to participate in a much different type of society.

TB: What should be done?

BS: Well, to tell you the truth, I think that DuSable has been very lucky to get Mr. Mingo as the principal because he came here with a vision. He really did, and this has provided us with a very different type of leadership.

TB: He is a visionary, and that is what you think is needed.

BS: Yes, the first thing he did when he came in here was to say, "These children can learn. They are no different from anybody else. What those schools can do with the kids that live in the suburbs we can do here just as well!" That was number one—and number two was, "I don't want to see any teachers just sitting down behind their desks. I want to see them walking around and interacting with their students. I don't want to see our teachers giving these kids seat work. That kind of work should be homework. I want to see *active* teaching happening around here!" Now, of course, the truth is that he hasn't been as successful as he might have expected, but at least the culture of the school has changed and is starting to move in the right direction. It's becoming much more academic in its focus.

TB: What stands in the way of the implementation of his ideas?

BS: Well, it's not so much the attitude of the students as it is the attitude of the faculty, and so he's had to start a program of what he calls staff development. He brought in the district superintendent, who said to our teachers, "I know many of you have been working here a long time, and you've been working hard. No one is saying that you're not working hard. What we're saying is that—even though you are working hard—you are not working effectively. These kids aren't learning—or if they are, they haven't shown it in any demonstrable way. So what this means is that whatever you're doing, you're going to have to try some different kind of approach." What he was saying is that if this isn't working, why are you holding on to it? Try something different! But I suppose that this was just *too* difficult for some people, and so there has been a large turnover in the staff here at DuSable since Mr. Mingo arrived.

TB: What you're saying is that these young people here at DuSable are basically no different from any other children in any other school, and that what really needs to change is the attitude of their teachers toward them.

BS: That's right. The other day some boys were fooling around and making a lot of noise, and so I walked over to them and said, "Why are you wasting your time this way? Don't you know there's nobody anywhere who's any smarter than you?" Well, I got their attention when I said that! So what I'm trying to say is that you have to find some way to get through to these students—and if you do, they will be responsive in a positive way because they are good kids, and all they really need is to believe that the reason you are trying to teach them is so that they will be able to succeed.

TB: But, first of all, you have to believe that these kids can learn and not lose sight of that belief.

BS: Oh, yes, if you truly believe that, you will always be able to find a way!

TB: And one of the best ways to reach them is to teach them social skills that will be immediately useful to them. You know, when I was teaching high school I used to have a section in one of my classes called How You Manage a Teacher, because if you *mis*manage your teacher, you are not going to be able to succeed.

BS: Teacher management—oh, that's wonderful!

TB: I used to say to my students, "Listen, your goal here is to graduate. So when some teacher comes up and tells you to take your cap off, he's not challenging you because he thinks he's better than you. He's just trying to teach you something that he thinks you need to know. If you want to succeed, you have to know how to dress, how to behave, even how to speak." I also used to say to my students, "You've got *three* different languages that you speak, but you're only going to use *one* of those languages here in this classroom. The one that you use in the street you cannot use here, and—unless you have a very unusual home—the language you use in the streets you cannot use at home either! But you also cannot use the kind of language that you speak at home here. This is a school, and this is a place where you have to speak a *third* kind of language. So now let's keep these three languages straight and get down to what needs to be done!"

BS: That's really wonderful!

TB: Betty, this has been wonderful. Thank you for sharing your time and your wisdom.

March 1, 1996

STANDISH WILLIS

ATTORNEY FOR THE DISENFRANCHISED

Stan Willis is one of the most honest and courageous fighters for social justice and fairness in the criminal court system that one could ever hope to meet. His unique combination of honesty, courage, and unquestionable integrity has probably cost him lots of financial and career opportunities because, I suspect, he believes that many such offers would violate or compromise the basic principles by which he lives. He often takes on new cases not knowing when or even if he will ever be paid, and he is willing to take these sorts of risks because of his determination to bring to the criminal courts fairness and equal justice for everyone.

I first met Stan Willis when he was a student at Crane Junior College. At that time he and other young people were leading coordinated protests demanding that more black faculty and administrators be hired in the city colleges of Chicago. These protests opened the doors that previously had been closed to those of us who were qualified but systematically had been denied our rightful opportunities.

Since that time, I have followed Stan's civic and legal activities closely and with great interest—and I have come to the conclusion that one could correctly say without fear of any contradiction that if there is racial or criminal injustice to be found around the criminal courts, Standish Willis will always be there attempting to correct the situation.

TB: I'm talking with Standish Willis. His primary interest as an attorney is to be an advocate—a legal representative—for poor people whose misfortunes have brought them into trouble with the law. Stan, clarify things for me. I'd really like to know a lot more about the kind of work that you are doing.

sw: As you know, I do primarily civil rights litigation and a fair amount of criminal defense in the federal court, but I don't do any legal work in the state court anymore.

tb: So all of your current work is at the federal level?

sw: Yes, now almost all of my work—I would say 95 percent—is in the federal district court. My civil rights work is primarily focused on police violence, although on occasion I've also represented some elected officials and church groups and other kinds of community organizations.

tb: Why did you change the emphasis on where you would represent your clients?

sw: It was just a matter of being burned out. You know, when you're doing state court work, you've got to go to Markham, you've got to go to Skokie, you've got to go all over the place, and most of my getting around was on the bus. We didn't have but one car. We couldn't afford but one car—and so I decided to try to shift the whole practice to the federal court so I wouldn't have to spend so much time just running around. Now when I come downtown, I pretty much stay downtown, and so my work is a lot easier on me. I guess I must be getting old.

tb: Is that right?

[*Laughter.*]

Well, you don't look so old to me, Stan.

sw: It must have been all that running around I was doing!

[*Laughter.*]

tb: So now, just how long have you been practicing the law?

sw: I started in '83.

tb: Is that right?

sw: Yes, I'm sort of a latecomer. I had been teaching at various colleges. I taught at Roosevelt for about ten years in the economics department. I also taught at Malcolm X City College. I taught in the prisons, and during that time, I also drove buses for several years—so I came into law school much later than most. By then, I was already in my forties.

tb: Is that right? I thought you were still in your forties right now!

[*Laughter.*]

Tell me, Stan, were you born in Chicago?

sw: Yes, I was born here in Cook County Hospital in 1941, and Mom always reminds me of that date—my mom still lives on the West Side—because they bombed Pearl Harbor only a few months after I was born. That was something that almost scared her to death!

TB: Scared her to death?

SW: Yes, you see, my folks were from that second generation that had come up from the South. The first wave, of course, was just after World War I, but there was another wave a little later who were mostly sharecroppers. For the most part, they didn't know anything about the city. They just came up here to find work, and so for my mom to hear about that bombing and about how the United States was getting ready to go to war, all of that scared her because she was so far from home, and, after all, she was only eighteen when I was born. She was scared to death because she didn't know what was going to happen to her baby or even what was going to happen to her.

TB: She could probably almost see the bombs dropping from the sky!

SW: That's right.

[*Laughter.*]

TB: Where did your folks come from?

SW: Oh, a little town called Madison, Arkansas, which was about thirty miles away from Memphis, Tennessee. Mom and Dad grew up there together and got married when my mom was fourteen.

TB: Why did they decide to leave and come up to Chicago?

SW: It was for the same reason that so many left. There was a change in the economy in the South because the technology had changed and cotton picking was no longer quite so labor-intensive. So a fair amount of those unemployed workers in the South just were sucked right up into the military industry that developed in the North during the early years of the war.

TB: That was what the economists used to call a push out of the South and a pull to the North as the result of the war economy.

SW: Yes, but they started coming here earlier than that because, even before Pearl Harbor, the United States was already supplying materials to Britain that were necessary for its own war effort.

TB: And so many of those people chose to come here to Chicago because of the attraction of work opportunities.

SW: Yes, but there also seems to be some sort of determining relationship between certain urban areas and the train routes coming up from the South. Wherever the train stopped first, if that place was a major industrial hub, then that's where the people got off—and when people from Arkansas got on a train, that was a train that went right to Chicago!

TB: That was the old Illinois Central! You know, when my folks left Birmingham, they just got on that same train and came directly to Chicago, and when they got off at the station at Twelfth Street, right away they were met by some of their old friends who had arrived here before them.

SW: That's right, and pretty soon my daddy got his job out in Cicero in the metal-works, and he stayed there working at that job for almost thirty years.

TB: Why did your family choose to live on the West Side rather than on the South Side?

SW: Well, my family started off living on the South Side—as many did—because for us, just like so many black families, there was already someone who had come here first and set up a place to live where the rest of the folks coming up could stay until they were able to get a place of their own. In our case, we had a cousin whom we always called Aunt Olive, and she already had an apartment, so whoever came and didn't have a place of their own to stay, they could stay with her. As it happened, she lived on the South Side, and so my folks moved into the Ida B. Wells area at first—I was about two or three years old at the time—and then they moved over to the West Side and stayed in an apartment with another relative. That is where we lived until I was about nineteen.

TB: How many brothers and sisters?

SW: I've got one sister and two brothers—all younger. One of my brothers is still living at home, helping to take care of my parents.

TB: Tell me about your educational background.

SW: I went through public schools and graduated from Crane High School.

TB: And that's on the West Side.

SW: Yes, I grew up on Thirteenth Street near Ashland. That area, it's not far from the big housing project over there and not too far from what we used to call Jew Town. Of course, we don't call it that anymore.

TB: We call it Maxwell Street.

SW: Well, that was my stomping ground. They had a public swimming pool down in that Maxwell Street area, and I used to go down there and swim and then walk back home through what would now probably be where the projects are. I guess they must have built them sometime in the late fifties or early sixties. As a matter of fact, after I graduated from Crane in 1960, I went into the military, and while I was in the military, I got married to a local girl. Then, when I left the military and came back here, we lived for a while in the projects, there at 1410 West Fourteenth Street. Even back then it had its share of problems, of course, but at least the organized-crime element wasn't in existence yet. All you had were some young men who were selling drugs on the q.t. I mean, right from the beginning drugs were always there, but the problem existed on only the individual level. That same sort of thing was probably going on in most communities by then, but you were more vulnerable to acts of violence if you lived in one of those high-rises because of the staircases. What those crooks would do would be to turn off the power and cause the elevators to stick so that you had to walk up the stairs, and that set you up as a perfect victim for robberies or rapes. As a matter of fact, my wife at that time, she was attacked while she was trying to walk up to the fifteenth floor where we lived, but she was smart enough to always carry some of that spray stuff. So she sprayed that chump, and he let her alone.

TB: What about the gangs?

SW: Back then, we had gangs who had territorial fights, but, as you know, in those days when you grew up and became an adult, you kind of transcended those territorial fights, and you could go wherever it was you wanted to go. So when I came back from the military and was driving a bus, I left all of that behind me, and none of that was any kind of a problem for me. The only real danger was for the women or anybody who happened to be staying out real late at night, but at least we didn't have to contend with organized violence and high-powered weapons or anything else like that.

TB: When did you decide to go back to school and get a college degree?

SW: Well, I was still driving a bus when I came into Malcolm X. That was 1965. I joined the Negro History Club that was there and which later evolved into the Black Student Association.

TB: When did you first begin to be politically active?

SW: I started organizing sometime in 1966 or maybe 1967. I was still working as a bus driver out of Kennedy Station. Together with my real close comrade, Robert Clay, who was also working out of there, we organized a couple of wildcat strikes. The one we organized in 1968 was a historic event. We stayed out a whole summer!

TB: And during this time you were still living in the housing projects?

SW: Yes, right off of Ashland and Roosevelt. Most of us were already married, raising families, working, *and* being activists all at the same time! All of which gave us a certain connection and credibility with other workers. We didn't recognize any significant division between the clerical workers and the janitorial staff at the school. It was just a matter of working with all of them and trying to help all of them as much as we could. So what we were developing was a kind of working-class consciousness, although nobody had really studied anything. I mean, we hadn't studied Marx or Lenin or anything like that. For us it was just our community. I mean, that's the way we were.

TB: Wasn't this about the same time that Fred Hampton came into Malcolm X?

SW: Yes, most of the people on campus that we had organized were students aspiring to go into the various professions, but when Fred and the Black Panthers came in, they reached out to a different constituency than just the campus. Right away they started reaching out to the brothers in the neighborhoods, some of whom had been gang members. They actually reached out to Jeff Fort and the members of his gang!

TB: What I remember most about that period was that there were a lot of young, vigorous, and intelligent young men and women who seemed to have a real sense of mission and purpose. It seemed to be so much easier to organize young, professional aspirants during that period of time.

SW: Well, like I said, I was a member of the Black Student Association, and we devised the idea of taking over the student government so that our ideas would be much more broadly exposed. What happened was that I ran for president of the student government. It was a tough race, but I won!

TB: What were the racial proportions within the college at that time?

SW: Probably less than 5 percent were white. It was a black college, and I was president of the student government. Henry English became the vice president, and when they killed some black students down in South Carolina, we decided to lead a demonstration carrying an actual coffin box through the city streets!

TB: This is not long before Dr. King was killed.

SW: Yes, this was February 8, 1968, and the student newspaper at that time was controlled by a little old white lady that didn't understand or have any sympathy with what we were trying to do. So she wrote an article asking what this black nationalist stuff was all about, but that article that she wrote eventually turned into a personal attack on me and was not about the issues at all.

TB: It wasn't very long after that when you went over to the University of Chicago, was it?

SW: No, as a matter of fact, I went over to the University of Chicago in 1968, and that's when I first met you. You probably don't remember this, but there was the Black Student Alliance at the University of Chicago in those days, and you came over and spoke with the students one day.

TB: I was over there many times during those days.

SW: Well, I graduated from there in 1971 with a B.A. and immediately went into their Ph.D. program in Latin American studies. I got my master's degree and stayed there until 1975, but then I just kind of bailed out. Even though I had done all the class work for the Ph.D., I never did the actual dissertation because it just wasn't practical for me to continue any longer. At that time I already had two children to support, and my wife wanted to go to medical school—so I started driving a cab.

TB: Yes, I know that story. That's the place where my own academic career ended. That's where I left it when I became more active in the struggle for civil rights. But then you went on to get your law degree.

SW: Yes, as a matter of fact, I applied for law school while my wife was in her last year of medical school.

TB: What law school did you attend?

SW: I went through the law school at the Illinois Institute of Technology.

TB: In what area did you specialize?

SW: I thought I wanted to do labor law because by that time I had become very sensitive to labor issues, and I did an internship with a labor lawyer named Ryan Irving, who had represented my father when my father got fired at the steelworks, but I didn't like doing that type of work very well. It was too confining. Too much of it was administrative, and then, near the end of my last year in law school, I met three guys from the People's Law Office who were lawyers that specialized in doing police cases and criminal defense work. They represented the Panthers and all of the radical political groups. At that time there were no black lawyers that were organized to do that kind of work.

TB: The only ones doing that kind of work were white lawyers?

SW: Yes, there were seven of them, and they asked me if I wanted to join, and I said yes. It was a good decision. I'm glad I went over there, and I stayed with them from 1983 until about 1989.

TB: What kind of work did you do?

SW: We continued to do police cases and criminal defense, trying to protect people that we thought should be protected, but from almost as soon as I started with them, we all got involved in Harold Washington's campaign for reelection. We weren't talking to the mayor that much directly, but things would come down from the mayor to us that he thought were important, and so we had some input on his decisions and strategies, but we were just independent lawyers, not getting paid anything, who would go out and gear up and file lawsuits and fight it out for what we believed in!

[*Laughter.*]

TB: So young professionals like yourself in that period just jumped in pro bono and helped out. You played an important part in that struggle because at that time Harold could not have afforded to pay for that kind of expert advice.

SW: That's right.

TB: So then some time later you left the People's Law Office, and now you're in private practice.

SW: Well, I was always in private practice because the People's Law Office was a private kind of collective. We were not a funded group. We were just a group of private lawyers. The only reason that I left was that for a group of lawyers doing exclusively progressive work, there just wasn't enough to sustain us economically. We missed paydays, and, quite frankly, we weren't always able to feed our families. So one day I said to myself, "The time has come for me to start out on my own."

TB: And you've been out on your own since . . . ?

SW: Since about 1989 or 1990.

TB: And your practice has been primarily what?

SW: Well, I'm doing pretty much the same things that I was doing at the People's Law Office, except in those days I would do more state criminal cases.

TB: And, as you mentioned, now most of your work is at the federal level.

SW: Yes.

TB: Because there was too much travel?

SW: Well, to be frank, I didn't like the courts either. They were very political in all the wrong senses of the word. Many of the judges were just political hacks, and I didn't feel that as a lawyer in private practice I was organized and funded well enough to fight them—so I shifted my practice.

TB: You mentioned that at this point in your career you are still dealing primarily with cases in which people's civil rights seem to have been violated.

SW: Yes, that's true.

TB: Then please tell me if—in your experience—you believe that justice is distributed equally within the existing legal system.

SW: No, absolutely not!

TB: Not?

SW: Never has been, never was meant to be, never will be!
   [*Bitter laughter.*]

TB: And where do you find this injustice being meted out most *un*equally? Who gets the brunt of the injustice that exists?

SW: Well, of course, black people but also any people of color and generally any poor people. But it's quite clear that from the very beginning people of color in particular weren't meant to get an equal form of justice. What I mean is that the U.S. Constitution included very specific provisions that made it impossible for a person of color to obtain equal justice.

TB: And yet the Constitution was considered to be a revolutionary document.

SW: Yes, the Constitution was a very revolutionary document for its time. There's no question about that, but at the time it was written the slave system was still recognized in the United States, and we were written into the Constitution and only given recognition as slaves.

TB: Not as humans.

SW: Yes, and so we weren't *meant* to get equal justice right from the very beginning!

TB: And now tradition has sustained that original intent?

SW: Absolutely.

TB: Despite all the agitation?

SW: Well, the agitation itself, I believe, is suggestive of the fact that we still have to fight for our citizenship rights even as we're going into the twenty-first century. It suggests quite plainly that we were never given those legal rights that we should have.

TB: Now that we are getting so many people from India and Southeast Asia coming here and becoming citizens, do these new citizens have to contend with the same kind of problems?

SW: Not really, because the problem is even deeper than the color of the skin. It is the result of the legacy of slavery, and this legacy is not of just any kind of slavery but of *chattel* slavery, which is very different in certain specific ways. Slavery has existed throughout many cultures many times in history, but chattel slavery— being slavery which is based on the principle of private property and which is peculiar to the capitalist mode of production—was different from other forms of slavery in that it made us, as people, into just another kind of property.

TB: Like this desk.

SW: Or this chair—and it made us just as dispensable as this desk or chair because it took away all of our humanity. We are still living with the burden of that legacy, and nobody else coming to this country has that same kind of baggage to carry along with them.

TB: So then, coming out of your experiences and vision and training, your commitment has been as much as possible to alleviate some of that bias and burden which the legal system still imposes.

SW: Yes, as best I can, but, you know, to some extent the system co-opts you. I mean, just the fact that you agree to function within the existing system can be considered to be a form of compromise. But even so, I still believe that a person like myself can use his legal skills in this constitutional democracy in order to advance the cause of our people. You know, sometimes legal skills can be used to help to clarify the inequalities so that people can understand them better and more clearly.

TB: Yes, for the past forty-four years my own job as a teacher has been to enlighten young people and to prepare them intellectually as well as emotionally to understand the system as it exists and to be prepared to accept some of the roles which it defines but not to accept these roles in such a way that they believe in them and they go unquestioned. I don't want anyone to say, "You picked on me because I am colored." I want to hear them say, "I've got everything that the system demanded. I went to the schools. I got all the best grades. I've stayed out of trouble, and *now* you won't let me have that job! Now you've got to tell me— what is your excuse?"

sw: That's when their legal rights enter the picture.

tb: Yes, but in your legal work you're usually at the opposite end of the process because you are dealing primarily with those who have failed to accomplish certain things and have fallen into a position where they have been accused of violating the mandates of the system. Your job is to see that they get equal treatment under the law.

sw: That is true in the criminal defense area, but with the civil rights cases, quite a different manner of approach is required. In cases concerning civil rights it is the government that is doing something that violates the legal rights of a given person—not just criminal defendants necessarily. In cases of this kind our job is to challenge the government when the rights of a citizen have been violated by its action. For example, when the police are brutal to someone, then we challenge that representative of the government by going after that police officer whose brutality violated someone's civil rights.

[*Willis hands a photograph to Black.*]

tb: Is this one of your clients?

sw: Was—yes!

tb: Oh, my Lord, what happened to him?

sw: He was shot in the back by a police officer.

tb: Where did this happen?

sw: Down on the South Side. At Seventy-seventh and Damen, as I remember it.

tb: And this picture, is he in the morgue here?

sw: Yes. He was just a kid—fourteen or fifteen—and the police shot him in the back. They shot him down, and he was unarmed. The police who killed him, all of them are back out on the street. Two of the four officers who were involved were suspended for fifty days, but now they're all back on the force.

tb: How did this happen? Tell me the specifics.

sw: Well, this youngster had stolen a car, and the police chased him. So he abandoned the car, and the police chased him into an alley. He ran up on a porch, and then, according to the police, he came down off the porch and attacked them with a screwdriver.

tb: Were there any other witnesses?

sw: No, and a policeman claimed that this kid lunged at him with the screwdriver, and so he pulled out his gun and fired in self-protection. What he claimed to be true, however, was nothing but a big lie because the kid was shot in the back.

tb: That was the point of entry?

sw: Yes, but not only was it the point of entry. This was a contact wound, which means that the gun was pressed right against his back when the policeman pulled the trigger.

TB: The officer that shot him, was he black or white?

SW: As it happens, both of the officers involved were white.

[*Willis hands another photograph to Black.*]

SW: Now, here's a photo of another young black man. He was riding along in a van with a friend of his, and the police suspected that they had stolen some walkie-talkies from the local radio shop. They claimed that they had traced radio waves coming from these walkie-talkies to their van, and so they stopped the van somewhere near Seventy-ninth Street, and they jumped out of their white sedan with their guns already drawn.

TB: They were traveling around in an unmarked car?

SW: Yes, and so one officer runs around to the passenger side and the other one runs around to the driver's side. The young man in the picture, he gets out of the van with his hands in the air and so does the driver, but, according to the police, it seems that when the driver was getting out he forgot to shift the gear into park, and so the van jerked forward a little, causing the officer to "accidentally" fire his gun. He claimed that his gun was pointed up in the air and that he did not even realize that he had shot and killed this young man until he saw him fall to the ground. At the trial, expert witnesses testified that for that caliber of weapon, which has three safety devices and which has a trigger that requires twelve pounds of pressure to activate, there would be no possible way that it could have gone off as the result of the officer's hand being bumped by accident.

TB: So you believe the officer shot this young man intentionally.

SW: Yes, and he shot him right in the temple. He was the father of three children, and once again nothing happened to the police officer. The police department basically ruled that it was an accidental shooting, and that officer, he's still out on the street.

TB: And those officers involved in this were also white?

SW: In this case both of them were white, but I can tell you that there are black officers that also commit these same kinds of violent acts. In my experience, I find more white officers that might say something that would suggest some sort of preexisting racial animosity, but there are black officers that would also just as readily commit these violent actions against black people. It seems to me that it is the race of the victim that is the determinative factor more than anything else. These acts are committed against black people and Hispanics. I don't see corresponding kinds of attacks against white people. You don't see black officers attacking white women, for example, but you do see black officers attacking black women, and you also see white officers attacking black women, and what's more, they continue to get away with it.

[*Willis hands another photograph to Black.*]

TB: This is a photo of a young Latino woman.

SW: Yes, a Hispanic woman about thirty-five years of age who had five children and had never been in any kind of trouble before. When this happened, she wasn't doing anything criminal. She was just talking too much. She had a big mouth. You know how it is? The police would say something to her, and she'd say something back. They don't tolerate that kind of thing, and so they beat her. They beat her to make an example of her.

TB: That sort of thing is not unusual. Where did this particular instance happen?

SW: On the North Side, in the Twenty-fifth District, near Foster and Damen.

TB: What charges did they make? What violation of the law did they claim had occurred?

SW: Well, like I said, she had a big mouth. Earlier in the evening on the day that this happened, when she was coming home from church with two of her children, the police ordered her off the street because they claimed that there was some sort of gang-related activity going on. They told her that she was in violation of curfew, and she told them that she didn't have to leave the street because she was an adult, and "I don't have a curfew!" So they told her she had a big mouth, and then later on there was a confrontation in front of her house, where they were in the process of arresting some kids, and they called her over, and once again she mouthed off—so one of the officers grabbed her and threw her on the ground and then arrested her. They told her that she had been identified as a person who made a mark on a police car, and they charged her with criminal damage to public property. So they handcuffed her and took her to the station, and when they got there, of course, she continued to mouth off, and so they beat her.

TB: Inside the station?

SW: Yes, inside the station, and she was handcuffed!

TB: Were these black cops or white cops?

SW: There were three white officers and one Chinese officer, and they said that her injuries were sustained because she had tried to kick one of the officers and then lost her balance and fell against a file cabinet in the station. What they claimed was ridiculous, but usually they'd get away with an explanation of that nature. The only reason they didn't get away with it this time is that we were able to organize the community to put pressure on the police force. We had a series of demonstrations and all the rest. Otherwise it would have been just a routine kind of thing. I mean, they do something like that and usually nobody goes after them, and so it becomes almost a matter of routine to beat up people and violate their civil rights. That's the scary part about it.

TB: And that sort of violence is usually directed toward black and Latino women?

SW: Most of the death cases are men, but the beat-up cases are both men and women of all ages. Age doesn't matter.

TB: But skin color does.

SW: Yes, and because I am the only black full-time civil rights lawyer in the city, I get a lot more cases than I can possibly handle. The typical person that calls me will talk to me for at least half an hour or forty-five minutes—so you can imagine that it would literally take me a couple of months to give all of these people the amount of time that they feel they deserve—and which I also feel they deserve—just to try to talk through and analyze their particular problem. What I could do, I suppose, is to say, "Don't talk now. Come over to my office and bring a hundred dollars with you." That would solve the problem. Either they would go away or I would have some money! But I can't do anything like that, and so I try to talk through their problems with them, and very often my best advice to them is to get together with their neighbors and start to organize their community.

TB: And the ones that you actually get involved with are . . . ?

SW: The ones that persist.

TB: At the present time it seems to me that the laws themselves are increasingly criminalizing young black men and women.

SW: Yes, there are laws that are being passed now that are directly designed to ensure that certain young black men and women will end up in prison—there's no question about it. In Chicago the city passed an anti-loitering bill that was designed to allow the police to arrest young black men just for being out on the street, and that's just what they did for about two years, until we organized against that law and got it declared unconstitutional.

TB: There's also been an attempt by the city police department, backed up by the mayor, to reinstall the Red Squad or something very similar to it.

SW: Yes, they're claiming it would be easier for them to prevent crime if they were allowed to infiltrate certain organizations which they perceive to be subversive, but beyond that, it would also provide a way for the police to basically ignore the Fourth Amendment and allow them to infiltrate groups that are exercising their First Amendment right to freely associate.

TB: What you are saying is that they can use the fear that people have in relation to street gangs to provide an excuse to move even further into the surveillance of normal political activity.

SW: I think that's correct. What they have done quite effectively is to use gang hysteria—gang equals enemy, enemy equals young black men and women—in order to gain further power for themselves.

TB: Yes.

sw: They start this process off by using terms like *war on drugs*, and so, in a sense, they are able to demonize a certain sector of the population and call that sector the enemy.

tb: And people usually are inclined to let the police get away with certain things during a time of war.

sw: Exactly. What happens is that they use these labels in order to obtain the necessary level of consent that will allow them to go in and eradicate or at least gain complete control over that sector of the population which has been defined as a detriment and a danger to everybody.

tb: And that sector happens to be perceived as being black.

sw: Yes, as a result, in certain suburban communities they are already starting to pass laws that would not normally be passed. These laws are directed at preventing certain forms of established legal activities, such as carrying beepers or wearing particular kinds of clothing and things like that.

tb: And in that way they are trying to criminalize noncriminal forms of behavior.

sw: Yes, the Fourth Amendment doesn't exist out on the street anymore! And when you give the police that kind of power on the street—and not just on the street but in the City Hall and in the halls of Congress—then you are giving the police an increase of power that can be used not only against blacks but also against the trade union movement or against any of the progressive movements that will soon be developing in response to the lowering of the standard of living for all the people in this country except for those that are living at the very top of the heap.

tb: What you are saying is that when the white trade unions try to organize because of a lowering of the standard of living for their members, then the police can bring in all those laws that they've already used against blacks and use them to cripple the trade union movement.

sw: That's the real danger. They test those laws on us, and those laws are accepted when they're tested on us, but those same laws can also be used against any progressive movement that they target in the future.

tb: But because of the indigenous racism of our society, the white population is not likely to see that this impending danger applies to everyone and not just blacks.

sw: That's right. That is why not just the white reactionaries but also the white progressives just sat back quietly and let the police sweep the housing projects clean of "undesirable" elements. That is the sort of thing that leads to grandmothers being pulled out into the hallways and having these marauding groups of police go into their apartments and take their sugar containers and dump all their sugar on the floor because they think they've found a stash of drugs! Things like that are happening all the time, and the courts uphold a lot of what's going on, and all of that will eventually infringe on the rights of anybody who might want to assert their Fourth Amendment rights in the twenty-first century.

TB: The assumption is that because I am a black man the police, without warrant, should be granted the legal right to search me on the street or to break into my house on the pretext that I might have some sort of contraband in my possession.

SW: Yes.

TB: And you believe that this extension of police power breaks down not only civil rights but also civil liberties just as well.

SW: You can't allow the civil liberties of *any* part of the community to be attacked, because an attack on any part of the population is really an attack on the entire framework of civil liberties. Being in a gang in itself is not unconstitutional because gang members are exercising their First Amendment rights to assemble. What *is* unlawful is when you are in a gang and then that gang commits a crime. But membership in a gang does not always imply being involved in criminal activity. As a matter of fact, most gang members are not necessarily drug dealers, and except for the gang-bangers, most gang members don't commit crimes. These kids are members of gangs because that's their way of associating with each other in certain communities.

TB: Much of our rhythm and blues came out of guys just like that who were just hanging out with each other on street corners. They didn't have any instruments, and so they just sang together!

SW: Well, they can't do that kind of thing around here anymore.

TB: What can they do? Where can they go?

SW: You know the answer to that as well as I do. The other side of this equation we're talking about is the prison system which has developed. Nowadays we have a prison-industrial complex composed primarily of black young men and women which generates twenty-two, twenty-three billion dollars every single year! The arrest and conviction rates are astronomical, and, as a result, now we have this huge industry, and so the big corporations are now eager to invest in these prisons. Recently I was reading an article about how the legislators have issued one of these education bonds to Illinois residents in which you can buy these bonds to fund your children's education. Well, what they don't say is that over half of that money that is going to be paid for those bonds has already been earmarked to build additional prisons. So what they're doing is they're trying to lock people economically into the further development of this prison-industrial complex which they have created.

TB: Yes, but what's even more significant is that so many of our young people—the ones who are not behind bars involuntarily—are now working as prison guards or correction officers.

sw: That's right. When you talk to many black kids now and you ask, "What's your major?" they say—

tb: Criminal justice.

sw: Yes, criminal justice, and that means that they are already planning to become prison guards.

tb: So it seems that half of us will be prison guards, and the other half will be in prison!

[*Bitter laughter.*]

sw: And because we have so many of our people that are not coming out of the auto factories or out of the steel factories but out of this prison-industrial complex, we can expect for them to have quite a different social outlook.

tb: A dramatically different perspective.

sw: So I expect that this new generation will be in opposition to all sorts of progressive reform.

tb: Yes, and the incarceration of so many young black women will also have a deep and lasting effect on the structure of our community.

sw: That's right. The incarceration of black women in prison has increased almost 300 percent over the past ten years. Something like 67 percent of these women are mothers and about 10 percent are pregnant when they go into prison—so now you've got these kids whose mothers are in prison for long periods of time because most of them have been given mandatory sentences which are related to drugs. So these mothers are snatched out of the community, and if they are convicted within the federal system, many of these women are not necessarily incarcerated in their own state anymore but are shipped out to prisons all over the country.

tb: And the generation which is specifically targeted for this mass incarceration is from about eighteen to twenty-nine, which is generally the most productive time in a person's life.

sw: And also the most rebellious.

tb: What do you see as some of the possible remedies for this situation?

sw: How can you have a stable family structure if both mom and dad are off in prison? We no longer have the same kind of family structure that we had in the 1930s and 1940s, when the care for that baby could be passed on down to Grandma. You know, the way it is now, Grandma herself might be strung out someplace. So these kids may very well end up in a state institution or might not wind up anywhere at all.

TB: Stan, we don't make the drugs.

SW: No, we don't.

TB: And we don't make the guns.

SW: That's right.

TB: Those people who are in charge of this country are probably at least as smart as I am. Why do you think those people who are in charge don't go to the source of these problems? Especially the drugs. We have a president that endorses open trade with Mexico in spite of the obvious fact that Mexico is one of the major sources of the cocaine that is finding its way into this country.

SW: And, of course, a good portion of that cocaine ends up with various distributors right here in the black community. As you know, some of them mix it with baking soda and convert it into crack cocaine before they distribute it, but they couldn't do that unless that white powder came here from someplace else—and you ask me why haven't they targeted the place it's coming from? The answer is because they are the ones who are doing it. They are intentionally letting it happen, and I think that it is by design that they are letting that stuff flow into our community—and to push that stuff into a community is to destroy the very fiber of that community.

TB: And that's what it does. How does this impact what you were referring to as the prison-industrial complex?

SW: I don't think it will have nearly as much impact on the prison-industrial complex as it does outside here in our community, and I say that because the crack cocaine laws are being selectively enforced. There's a recent study that shows that in the last two or three years almost all of those who were convicted on charges involving crack cocaine were black, and yet the majority of users of crack cocaine are white.

TB: That's because they are primarily the ones who have the means to buy that stuff. Blacks are only serving as couriers to satisfy the demands of the larger white community.

SW: But the police are going after blacks and not going after whites. That's what I mean when I say they are selectively enforcing the law.

TB: What do you see as a possible answer to these dire social and economic problems that are confronting such large portions of the black community?

SW: I don't know what the answer is. I'm basically a socialist, particularly in terms of economics, and I still tend to believe that we are not going to solve the problem as long as we live under a capitalist mode of production in which decisions are based on profitability and not necessarily on the best interest of the society and of those communities from which that society is composed. But I would also argue that one thing that we can do even now to alleviate the source of so many of the problems is to take the profit out the drug market.

TB: Do you mean decriminalization of drugs?

SW: Yes, decriminalization of drugs on the one hand and starting to treat drug problems as health problems on the other. Most of the people that are locked up—particularly the women—are not locked up because they committed some violent act. They are locked up because they're either using or selling small quantities of drugs, and those who are using drugs have health problems that need to be addressed. So, in my opinion, one thing that we could and should do is begin to fight an ideological struggle to redefine the war against drugs as a health problem and at the same time fight an economic struggle to obtain the financial resources that are required to establish adequate treatment centers.

TB: But, of course, any form of effective rehabilitation also requires the creation and availability of jobs for these people.

SW: Yes, but I'm afraid I don't see any of that happening within the context of the way society is moving right now. I think we're going to have to have a whole new kind of struggle in order to really solve any of these problems.

December 5, 1996, and March 4, 1997

SYLVIA WALTON

LIFELONG RESIDENT OF BRONZEVILLE

Sylvia is a lifelong resident of the Grand Boulevard and Douglas community. She is one of the few who have remained residents of this neighborhood as it went through dramatic negative social, cultural, and economic changes. She has always been a consistent and persistent educator and activist in her efforts to improve the educational opportunities as well as the housing, safety, and recreational conditions of the community where she and her family continue to live.

She and her children are graduates of DuSable High School. Later on in her life, Sylvia returned to DuSable to become a library assistant, and at the time that I am writing this, she is just retiring from that position after more than thirty years of service. She still continues to be active in the best interests of her community and is an inspiration to those of us who are privileged enough to know her.

TB: How long have you been the library assistant here at DuSable?

SW: About six or maybe seven years.

TB: Where were you before?

SW: At Richards, Spalding, and Dunbar high schools.

TB: How long have you been working?

SW: Twenty-six years, almost twenty-seven years.

TB: Has all of your professional activity been here in Chicago?

SW: Yes.

TB: And where were you born?

SW: Chicago. Where else?

[*Laughter.*]

TB: When? Or maybe I shouldn't ask that question!

SW: I'm not ashamed about things like that. August 30, 1944!

TB: Where were your folks living?

SW: When I was born, they were living at 6340 South Michigan.

TB: Well, back then, my own family was living at Fifty-first and Michigan. They lived there for years and years.

SW: When I was about seven, my family moved to a building at 4603 Vincennes. That building was later turned into a hotel.

TB: Yes, but now it's just a vacant lot.

SW: Then, when I was about eight or nine, my mother got remarried, and we moved to 524 East Forty-sixth Place.

TB: Where did your mother originally come from?

SW: My mother was born in Napoleonville, Louisiana, about eighty, ninety miles from New Orleans.

TB: And which was the first school that you went to?

SW: Later on I went to Forrestville Grammar School and DuSable High School, but I started out at Burke.

TB: At that time Edmund Burke was one of the best schools in the city.

SW: Yes, well, like they used to say: "You gotta work, work, work for the Burke, Burke, Burke! Yea, Burke! Yea, Burke!"

TB: I graduated from Burke, but before that I also went to Forrestville when I was just a tot. We were steadily moving south, you know? So you went to Forrestville? Who are some of the people you remember?

SW: I remember teachers. I remember Mrs. Posey. She was the eighth-grade teacher. Mrs. Williams, the seventh-grade teacher. Mrs. Ramsey, my third-grade teacher—she was just so sweet. She turned my whole life around.

TB: And there was one of those teachers who looked like she was white, but she wasn't, and she would let you know that very quickly, but I forget what her name was.

SW: Oh, I know who she was. She was short? Real short. I had her as a teacher. She was a little bit loony, and so we used to throw her off track all the time and ask her to tell us about the time when her family got captured by the Indians and about that other time when the grizzly bear came to their cabin, and she would start into telling us about all those things, and then she'd start crying—and after that we didn't have to do any more school work!

[*Laughter.*]

TB: So I suppose that you'd get her to tell those stories just as often as possible!

SW: Yes, that's what we would do, particularly during spelling tests. You know, she could never understand why everybody would get 100 percent every week on the spelling tests, but the reason was because each week she'd test us on twenty words, and those words would be in exactly the same order on the test that she'd give us. So, just before the test, we would make her stop and tell us about what happened back in her childhood, and then everybody was able to just copy down all those spelling words correctly, and that way everybody in the room—every week—would get 100 percent on the spelling test!

[*Laughter.*]

TB: Was Forrestville pretty crowded while you were there?

SW: The entire neighborhood was pretty crowded. When I was there, there were over three thousand kids in that school. When we came in here to DuSable as freshmen in September of 1958, we were the largest freshman class that Du-Sable had ever had.

TB: At that same time I was just leaving to take a teaching job at Farragut High School. Tell me what the neighborhood was like back then.

SW: We were all like a family. Most of my childhood was spent on Forty-sixth Place, which was a small block just between Vincennes and St. Lawrence, and every-body knew everybody. Because my mother worked during the day, I wasn't allowed to come outside unless my girlfriend's mother said it was all right. The way it was, you know, we all had these extended parents, and they were parents true to form. I mean you had to obey them because they might whip you—and then when your mama came home, you might get another whipping!

[*Laughter.*]

TB: Because she had been forewarned!

SW: That's right, and the friendships that we developed there on Forty-sixth Place—the majority of the kids that grew up there—we are all still very close friends. We have never lost contact with each other. All the way from eight years old to fifty-two and yet still be in contact with all these people and know how to pick up a phone and call them—that is really saying quite a lot!

TB: Back then the neighborhood was stable.

SW: Of course, the neighborhood was stable. Most people didn't move around very much—and if they did, they didn't move very far.

TB: They just moved around in more or less the same area.

SW: Right, and back then people had pride. I mean, if one of my friends was on welfare, we'd never know it because it was not something that people let other people know.

TB: So the neighborhood was stable, and you weren't afraid of violence or anything like that.

SW: No, of course not! I remember when I was in high school, about sixteen years old, and I was a real skinny, tiny thing—but I had a job downtown at Henry C. Lytton's.

TB: That was a clothing store.

SW: Right, and I worked in their will-call department, and on Monday and Thursday nights the store stayed open late, but my mother had no fear of my riding the El, and if the bus at my stop wasn't coming, she didn't have to worry about my walking from the El station to my home all alone at night. My mother never even thought twice about it. Sometimes we would be sitting up late watching TV in the summer, and someone would say, "Oh, I sure would like some ice cream," and so we would just get up and walk from Forty-sixth and St. Lawrence to Jack and Jill's to get us some ice cream. First of all, there was always going to be somebody outside that knew us, even if it was one of the winos on the corner. Those guys, they knew all the kids, and they watched after us, and so one of them would say, "What are you doing up this time of night? Where you going?" And you'd tell him, and he'd say, "Well, come on. I'll walk back with you." And so there were just no problems, you know? That's just the way it was, but right now I have a seventeen-year-old daughter of my own who is a senior here, and she works at Burlington's at Forty-seventh and Damen. She doesn't get off until nine o'clock at night, and she should be able to catch the Forty-seventh Street bus and come home from work, but there's no way I'm going to let her ride public transportation because of things like this killing they had the other evening at Forty-eighth and Forrestville. With things like that happening around here, I have to go and pick my child up at night after her work because I am afraid for my child to be out alone at night. Even if she were a seventeen-year-old boy, I would still have to be out there and pick him up in order to bring him home safely.

TB: Just one generation, and there's been such a tremendous change!

SW: Right, you know, the way it is now it's not safe for anyone. Even in a car you're not safe anymore!

TB: But at least that block you still live in has remained pretty stable?

SW: Yes, Forty-eighth and Forrestville has remained a very nice place to live, and the reason for that is that we only have, maybe, four or five three-flat buildings on the whole block. The majority of the buildings are single-family homes—and not only that, but even in those other buildings the owners are still living there. As a matter of fact, we have only one building that has an absentee landlord.

TB: As a result, all your neighbors tend to keep up their property?

sw: Yes, and my neighbors continue to have pride in themselves as well as in their property. Plus it's an old block, and the majority don't have lots of children. Right now on our block I think we have two teenagers—my daughter and one other teenager who is in high school, but last year, to give you an example, on our block we had four girls graduate from high school, and all four of them have gone away to college—which I think is a pretty good track record!

TB: What kind of work do most of your neighbors do?

sw: We have lots of teachers, lawyers, and people who own private businesses—but we also have lots of retirees and elderly people, and some of those people are on welfare. The people next door to me—well, they just put them into a nursing home. The state came in and did that because those people weren't able to take care of themselves any longer—but that man and his wife, they were the first blacks to move in on this block when it was still Jewish, and they've been living here on this block for over sixty years!

TB: Has their house gone up for sale?

sw: Yes, but it seems to me that the only way houses around here go up for sale is when the people have died or when they put them in a nursing home.

TB: And when they have no relatives to claim the property.

sw: That's right.

TB: So you have spent, residentially, almost all of your life in this neighborhood, which is more or less within walking distance from where you were born?

sw: Right, and I can still remember when at Christmastime Forty-seventh Street would be so crowded that you couldn't walk or drive down it, and I can also remember how my father used to wait for Christmas Eve before he would buy our Christmas tree. You know, he would wait until the very last minute and then get one for about a dollar when they were trying to get rid of them.

TB: He'd wait until he could get the best bargain.

sw: And Forty-seventh Street would be all lit up. There were no vacant lots. There were all those stores. It was great, and then I remember as a teenager how we used to enjoy going to the Regal for the stage shows.

TB: Who were some of the people you saw?

sw: Oh, Jackie Wilson, B. B. King, Bobby "Blue" Bland, Ray Charles, Smokey Robinson and the Miracles, Gladys Knight, the Drifters, the Impressions. You know, my cousin, she met one of the Impressions backstage, and now he's her husband, and they've been married for thirty years!

TB: Is that right?

[*Laughter.*]

sw: We didn't miss any of those stage shows. We would go for the first stage show on Saturday, and we wouldn't leave until the last show was over!

[*Laughter.*]

So on Saturdays, especially if it was a good show, our parents did not have to worry about us because they knew where we were going to be all day, and you know something? As those shows went on through the day and into the evening, they just got better and better, you know what I mean? Remember Al Benson? He used to be the MC for most of those shows.

TB: Yes, and Al Benson was also the DJ who helped to change—whether for better or worse—what people were listening to on the radio because at that time all the other DJs, like Daddy-o Daylie, were mostly playing jazz, and Al was the first one who started to feature the blues.

SW: Well, I do remember that Al Benson played songs on the radio—this was in the fifties—like "Annie Had a Baby" and "Dance With Me Henry," and, oh, there was such a big stir about that! They banned those records off the radio because of the language. I remember that because my sister, who was older than me, went out and bought all those records, and we were playing them when my mother wasn't at home because they said things like "Annie had a baby, and she can't work no more," you know? We just loved those songs!

[*Laughter.*]

TB: Because they were considered to be off-limits?

SW: Yes, but of course, today that's pretty mild, and I suppose that people would just laugh them off the radio now, but back then in those days it was quite different. That's when people still had values. That's when it was not fashionable to have a baby without being married. If a girl got pregnant, she would try to hide it because she knew that she was going to be put out of school.

TB: And also be frowned on by the neighbors.

SW: Right, and you couldn't associate with her. I remember one girl I knew who had a baby, and nobody on my block was allowed to go over to this girl's house. We couldn't associate with her because she was a "bad" girl. Girls like that, their parents usually sent them back down South to stay with Grandma or Aunt Mary or somebody like that, and they didn't come back up here till much later in life.

TB: Now, going back to your memories of Forty-seventh Street, there was not only the Regal but also a lot of other places where you could go for entertainment back then.

SW: Yes, the Sutherland Hotel. That's where all the stars went. They stayed there on Forty-seventh and Drexel.

TB: And then there was another little hotel on Forty-seventh and what is now King Drive where some of the entertainers also used to stay.

SW: Oh, yes, but I can't remember the name of that place. Is it still there?

TB: No, they've torn it down. The last time I saw Miles Davis, he was staying at that little hotel. He was playing at the Sutherland, but that's where he stayed. It was a cozy little hotel, you know, and there were a lot of other nice little hotels, like the Grand up on Fifty-first and South Park.

SW: And people used to go to Jerry's Palm Tavern.

TB: Oh, yes!

SW: And then they used to go down on Fifty-eighth Street to the Rumpus Room, but the Brown Derby—that lounge that was also up there on Fifty-eighth—that was really the cat's meow!

[*Laughter.*]

TB: All the cool people would go there!

SW: And everybody was very civil and nice to each other.

TB: When did that all begin to change?

SW: Well, I'll say this: I think lots of changes came about after the city started putting up all of the projects. With the projects being sixteen stories high, people couldn't control their children anymore. A kid can say, "I'm going to Mary's house," and the mother would say, "Where does she live?" and the kid would say, "Well, here in the building"—but to say she lives in the building doesn't mean anything, not when there are sixteen floors and ten apartments on each floor! *Where* in the building does she live? And if your child is outside playing in the front, you can't even see your child from the sixteenth floor. You're not always able to go outside *with* your children. Even if you have grandchildren and your grandchildren come to visit and want to go outside to play, you're not always able to stop what you're doing or feel like going outside to watch that child. But if you're living in a house or a two- or three-flat apartment building, then you are always able to go and look out the window, and you can see exactly what that child is doing—and so that child always in the back of his mind knows, "My mother, my grandmother, my grandfather, my aunt, uncle—or *any* adult for that matter—might happen to look out the window or happen to come out on the front porch and see what I'm doing." So you always had to be on your p's and q's. Even someone who lived across the street might be looking out the window! [*Laughter.*]

But when you have people stacked on top of each other, you lose control because nobody knows each other. Even at Ida B. Wells or Altgeld Gardens, people used to think that like those were so big and impersonal, but those projects still are not as bad as the high-rises because at least there you know who lives next to you, who lives in back of you, who lives in front of you. That's because they are row houses, and so parents are still able to look out the window or walk out the door and see what their children are doing.

TB: It's the same sort of thing over at Cabrini-Green. Before they built those high-rises, Jerry Butler and all those guys, they'd stand on the corner and doo-wop while somebody was looking out to see what they were doing. They were singing that way because they didn't have enough money to buy any instruments.

SW: You know, I remember, when I was a child, my mother was sickly, and she would say, "It's OK for you to go outside, but don't you go off this front." Well, I knew my mama was going to go upstairs and go to sleep, but there was still always the chance that she may wake up and look out her window—but if she did, I'd better be on this front! So no, I didn't go off the front. But, if she'd told me, "Don't go off the front," and if I lived on the sixteenth floor, there was no way on God's green earth she would have been able to see me—so I could have been here, there, or anywhere else that I wanted to go. That's why I feel that those high-rise projects have *destroyed* our communities, our neighborhoods, and our children. This is why the drugs have been able to start to come in so rampantly. It's because we have lost control over our children. Some have survived, however, but there are more who haven't survived than those that have.

TB: Let's go back to when you first came to DuSable as a student in 1958. What was that like back then?

SW: Wonderful. Just wonderful. I loved *every* minute at DuSable. Just loved it. It was big, and there were so many things to do. I could go to Social Center legally because my older sister was already here.

TB: What was her name?

SW: Nicolette Jones.

TB: I remember her.

SW: And so I always used to come to Social Center with her on Friday nights because my mother was working those evenings. You see, she didn't want to leave me at home by myself, and so if my sister wanted to come to Social Center, I *had* to come as well. That way I got to know lots of the older boys because they would dance with me at Social Center.

TB: Or roller-skate.

SW: Roller-skate—right! We'd roller-skate a lot on the first floor. It was just wonderful, and I can say that in those four years at DuSable I saw, maybe, two fights inside of this building. You know, back then we didn't fight. We had fun. I still remember walking through the halls singing "Mickey Mouse, Donald Duck." You know, somebody at one end would start out with "Mickey Mouse" and then somebody at the other end would holler "Donald Duck."

TB: What about the teachers?

SW: The teachers cared about us, and we respected them. You weren't ever late for a class. You didn't disrespect anybody. I remember going to the football games and the basketball games. Every game that there was—I was there. I felt that they couldn't have a football or a basketball game without me! So we had a lot of good times, you know, and I graduated in June of 1962, but then in September of 1962 is when the kids started to come in from the projects.

TB: They had moved over there during that summer?

TB: Yes, and when you think that the average parent over there in the projects is only fifteen years older than her child, let's face it, all these young mothers are still children themselves!

TB: Yes, and they've already seen too much.

SW: They've seen much too much. You have parents there who are doing drugs, and people like that, they feel, "This is where I live, and I'll do what I want," but their children are seeing all of this!

TB: And all of that becomes part of their own lives.

SW: Right, and if you would take even one of those high-rise projects and put it up in Forrestville, even Forrestville would change! There are no ifs, ands, or buts about it. The people in that high-rise would not try to keep up with the lifestyle that is already there. They would try to bring *down* that lifestyle.

TB: And so people would begin to move out of what had been a stable neighborhood?

SW: People would move. Panic and run!

TB: So, since that time, most of the kids here at DuSable do not come from neighborhoods like Forrestville?

SW: No, 90 percent of our kids come from the projects. We have a very low percentage rate of kids who are not from the projects. At least 95 percent of their families are on public aid.

TB: When you graduated and left DuSable, you went where?

SW: When I left DuSable, I got married, and then I went out to California and went to school for a while out there. Then I came back and started working for the Board of Education in 1965, '66. I went down to the Department of Teacher Personnel when they first started having the teacher aides. They had decided that the teacher aides should at least have a high school diploma, and so we sent out all of these thousands of letters for the teacher aides to bring in their transcripts, and I had to combine all the records together and check off the ones that hadn't sent in their transcripts—and those who didn't, we sent them another letter, and those who didn't have a high school diploma or a GED were laid off their jobs. After that was over with, I was the first black to sit at the front reception desk in Teacher Personnel. Then in 1969 I went out to have a baby, but in 1970 I came back to the board, and that's when I went to Dunbar and became a library assistant. I stayed at Dunbar nine years, and then I had another baby!

[*Laughter.*]

When I went back to work, I went over to Spalding.

TB: Spalding was a special school, wasn't it?

SW: Yes, Jesse Spalding High School at 1628 West Washington was for children with physical disabilities. It was the only high school of its kind in the whole city.

TB: There was only one high school to service the whole city?

SW: Yes, and Spalding was just for those with *physical* disabilities but not mental disabilities. They had to have a physical handicap, and it was while I was working at Spalding that I really started to grow as a person. I learned to have respect for the disabled, which is something that I didn't have before. Like so many people, I felt pity for them, but I shied away from them. I didn't want them to touch me or be near me. I was prejudiced.

TB: Yes, you were!

SW: And I'm not ashamed to say it.

TB: You didn't know better.

SW: That's right. I didn't know, and so I was like so many other people who are prejudiced toward those with disabilities. But when I went through Spalding and saw those kids trying to do everything that other children would do, it brought tears to my eyes. The first time I saw a kid who had no legs get out of a wheelchair, sit on the ground, and hit a baseball, I had chills go through my whole body. To see those kids play basketball from wheelchairs. To see them at a dance—well, you might say, "What do they do at a dance?"—so I'll tell you: they dance! They move their wheelchairs to the beat of the music. They do not let anything stop them.

TB: That's something that everyone needs to see.

SW: But when they first told me that I was going to Spalding, I said, "Spalding! That's the handicapped high school!"—and the director of the library said, "Sylvia, I think you will enjoy working with these children. Go there. Stay at least thirty days. We're not counting holidays, and we're not counting Saturdays and Sundays. You have to give me at least thirty days—and then after those thirty days, if you can look me in the face and say, 'I can't deal with it. It's too depressing,' I will move you. I give you my word on that, but I think you can handle it." And that was one of the best things that ever could have happened to me in this life. Going there, I grew as a person because I was able to see all the ways those kids would help each other. The ones who could walk would push the ones who couldn't walk. Maybe somebody would be on crutches, and her friend was in a wheelchair. So the one in the wheelchair would hold the crutches while the other one pushed him to where they were going. When we had a fire drill, they all helped each other get out of that building. They respected each other. Now, they still had their fights, of course, and some of them were nasty, ugly fights because they would fling crutches. They would even pull the arms up off the wheelchairs and swing them around! You see, at Spalding we had all of the different gangs from all over the city. We had boys who were there because they had been shot. It was a bullet in the back that had put them in their wheelchairs! We had a lot of that sort of thing, but the students all had to learn to get along. Sometimes we had to jump in there and intercede when stuff was getting too rough, but that didn't bother me because I've always been able to relate to those kids and talk to them. So when things started to get rough, they would always come and get me because I knew how to handle all those "bad" boys, and they didn't mess with me because I would threaten them. I'd tell them I was going to lock them out!

[*Laughter.*]

But they respected me for this, OK?

TB: And you weren't afraid of them.

SW: No, I wasn't afraid of them.

TB: And you demanded that they respect you.

SW: And that's what they did. Let me tell you one of the things that I learned at Spalding. I had one boy who was a gang leader. He was so bad. Nobody could do anything with him, and, instead of calling me Mrs. Walton, he was determined to call me Sylvia. So one day the principal said, "Why is he calling you Sylvia?"—this was Arthur Shapiro—and I answered, "Mr. Shapiro, is he going to give me more respect if he calls me Mrs. Walton, or if he calls me Sylvia? If I can reach out to this child, I don't care what he calls me. If I can stop him and his boys from having a big fight up in here, would you rather he call me Mrs. Walton and I can't stop the fight, or would you rather for him to call me Sylvia and I can stop the fight?" And he said, "Well, if he wants to call you Sylvia, I guess he can call you Sylvia!"

TB: He said that because he wanted to stop that fight!

SW: Right, and when they felt like calling me Mrs. Walton, they called me that, but I always called them by their last names. I would tell them that I did that all the time, "because you all are older than me, and I have to respect my elders."

[*Laughter.*]

Let me tell you about another one of the experiences that I had at Spalding. There was a girl who was my friend—a student, you know?—who was a troubled child, and I used to talk with her and help her and everything, but one day she stole my money, and they made an announcement over the intercom about my money being stolen. Well, all those children were at lunch, and when they came out of the lunchroom, they wanted to know, Did I have two twenties and a ten? Was that the money that I had lost? Then they told me how it was folded and told me who had taken my money. They did that because I was their friend. There wasn't a child there who couldn't come to me if he needed something, and if I had it, I'd always give it to him. Those kids were so upset with her for stealing from me that the administration finally had to transfer her out of the school. Of course they had been having lots of trouble with her stealing from other people too, you know? After all, she was a troubled child. But I enjoyed Spalding, and when I left Spalding, I went to Richards Vocational, which was an all-girls school.

TB: Where was it located?

SW: At that time it was on Fifty-fifth and Maplewood, but I hated that school, and I started to think about how soon I could retire. It was the only school that I've ever worked in that I felt that way about.

TB: What was wrong with it?

SW: It was just a horrible school. Eight hundred girls. Ugh! Eight hundred women in one place!

TB: Too many?

SW: Yes, too many women, and every day there were fights and stealing and cursing.

TB: Were these mostly white girls or black girls?

SW: It was everything. It was white, black, Hispanic, Arabs, Indians, Mexicans, Puerto Ricans—it was just too many women!

[*Laughter.*]

Too many, too many, too many! Oh, I just could not stomach it! But then, luckily, the Lord was good, and He let me fall! So I went out on sick leave, and then my transfer came in for DuSable, and since then, I've loved every minute of it.

TB: And you've been here ever since?

SW: Since about 1989—'88, '89. Love it, love it, love it!

TB: Why?

SW: Why? Well, I like the kids, and I feel that Mr. Mingo is doing a lot for these children. Those who don't get a good education here, it's because they don't want it. It's here for them, and I feel that he has put in everything that he possibly can put into this school for these children, and if they don't try to learn every drop of it, they're the ones who are to blame because Mr. Mingo is really in these children's corner. He may be the principal. He may have moved on up, but he does not forget where he came from. He came from right off of West Fifty-first Street. So many times when our people pull themselves up by the bootstraps, they seem to forget where they came from.

TB: Let me say, not many DuSable-ites do that—for whatever reason!

[*Laughter.*]

SW: Right, he grew up in this neighborhood, and I feel that he has done everything he can to help these children. I've seen him take money out of his pocket to give them. He makes certain that every senior registers for somebody's college, and I don't know of another principal in the city of Chicago that does that.

TB: He's unusual.

SW: He's unusual in that he cares, and he wants these children to have the very, very best.

TB: Another thing, as you have indicated, is that they know that he's not afraid of them.

SW: No, he's not afraid of them—and I'm not either. Yes, these children are a challenge, but most of these children, all they want is love. They want somebody to care for them, and, you know, there are two ways that you can fuss at a child. There's the motherly "I care" kind of fuss, and there's that other kind of "I don't give a damn about you" sort of fuss. Well, most of the time when I fuss at them it's the "I care" kind because I really care. There's nothing I won't do for these children. If I had all of the dollars that I've given out in the last twenty-six years, I could go home and sit down. I wouldn't have to be at work, but I love what I'm doing. I love, I care. Most people cannot say that they really like their job, but I don't just *like* my job—I *love* my job. I love working with these children, and I feel these children come first because these children have been beaten down.

TB: So, the generation that you're nurturing now is different from the one that you came from.

SW: Right, and I think that lots of that difference has to do with the fact that my generation grew up in homes with our grandparents. You had your grandmother living right there in the house with you, and your grandmother was old, but, well, now these kids are growing up with a grandmother in the house who may be only thirty-five or forty! They're growing up with a grandmother who is still going out doing the night clubs and sitting on the bar stool, whereas when we grew up, our grandmothers were talking about going to church on Sundays and saying, "Praise the Lord," and Grandma was always there to wash the clothes, iron the clothes, grocery shop, and she always had that dinner ready when you got home from school. In those days you went home for lunch, and Grandma was there with the food on the table ready for you to eat because you only had an hour for lunch, and that included coming home, eating lunch, and then getting back to school.

TB: And getting back there on time!

SW: But now there is nobody at home for these kids, or even if they are home, they don't have time to cook because they're still so young that they just want to go out and party. The average mother of a student here in DuSable is thirty-five, forty years old at most—and if she's forty, she's probably got some children who are older than the ones that are here! So you basically have children raising children, and the parents are still trying to find *their own* youth.

TB: Because they missed it. They missed those teenage years.

SW: Because they missed it. But you can't go back and get that.

TB: You can't recapture that lost time.

SW: You can't ever go back. I used to hear my mother say, "Youth is wasted on the young." I never used to really understand what she meant, but now at fifty-two, I understand a little better.

TB: Yes, yes.

SW: Because these children just don't know what to do with their youth. If I had the energy that these children have, oh, Jesus, what I could do!

TB: But in your younger days there was always someplace to focus that energy.

SW: Right, and now these children have nowhere to go. You can't even go across the street around here because then you're in a different gang territory. Even if I drive over there, they may beat me up and steal my car.

TB: When I was going to DuSable, we had a good relationship with the kids that went to Phillips. We played ball together. But I doubt seriously today whether there's even the possibility of a good relationship between those two schools, and yet they're just a few blocks away from each other.

SW: Well, even when I was here in 1962, when we played Dunbar our motto was "We may lose the game, but we're going to win the fight." You see, we knew there was going to be a fight after the game, regardless of who won. Oh, there had to be a fight, but it was just a fight. You might come out of it with a bloody nose or a black eye or something like that, but there were no knives. There were no guns. There was none of that.

TB: Now the kids don't even go out of their own immediate neighborhood.

SW: No, they don't. It's too dangerous.

TB: Now, given all of those external and internal handicaps and problems, in addition to the creativity and the energy that you and other dedicated people give to these young people, what do you believe might be needed to make this situation better?

SW: I think more adults should be available and willing to talk to these young people. Not to lecture them, but just to talk with them and listen to what they have to say. Let them talk to you. Learn to laugh with them, to cry with them, and to *be there* for them. As their teachers, we need to be more like their extended family because so many of them don't really have any kind of a family life of their own. Our young ladies, our young men, so many of these young people have never left Forty-third, Forty-seventh, Forty-ninth, or Fifty-first Streets. Most of them have never been north of Thirty-fifth Street. Someone should take them over to River Oaks, Ford City, Evergreen, and just let them shop! The way it is these young ladies, they go out in the neighborhood and spend good money for their clothes, but it's the wrong kind of stuff, and they don't have anybody to teach them. Nobody is there to help them know what to wear.

TB: Another example of what you're talking about that I've noticed is the insecurity that these young people experience when their food is served in a restaurant.

SW: Right, not knowing what to do or how to do it, they resort back to, "Oh, I don't like this. Oh, I don't want that thing!" But it's not because they don't like it. It's because they don't know what to do. A lot of our kids are really poor. They don't have any money, and so I feel that we adults should be here not only to educate them but also to nurture these young people. What I'm saying is that I feel that there should be someone to see to it that every child that is *really* poor has some graduation pictures. Even if it's only one eight-by-ten and one five-by-seven. I'm not saying that they should have two hundred dollars worth of pictures, but that child who has made it that far in life should have something, and that child should also be able to attend his or her prom.

TB: One way that they could do that would be if a fund were set up for that purpose.

SW: Right, and that kind of fund should be set up not on the basis of personality or popularity. No, it should be for the needy, not the greedy. There are lots of kids here who won't be able to go to their prom because they don't have enough money for a dress or a tuxedo, and they're too embarrassed to say anything about it, but something should be said! Why isn't something set up for these children? There are enough people here that could help that we don't even need to go outside of the school to get those funds. I mean if every teacher here—every adult employee—donated anywhere from two to five dollars a month, starting in September, to start that kind of fund, do you know how much money there would be?

TB: There would be enough to take care of that problem that you're talking about.

SW: It would be enough, and then no child who graduates from here would not have a picture taken because he or she couldn't afford it, and no child would graduate who didn't go to the prom because he or she couldn't afford to go. But, like I say, the fund would have to be for the needy, not the greedy, and let me tell you, I'm sick and tired of things going to the greedy instead of the needy!

March 18, 1996

CHARLES MINGO

INNOVATIVE PRINCIPAL

In recent years, Charles Mingo has been the driving force that has helped turn DuSable High School from a drug-infested, gang-ridden, leaderless, lackadaisical, attitudinally dispirited place into one which is increasingly vibrant, creative, purposeful, and safe. To accomplish this, he has moved ineffective teachers out (whether black or white) and moved effective teachers in (whether black or white or any other color). He has introduced innovative programs, such as utilizing the small schools approach to restructure and personalize the educational environment for the benefit of his students. He has encouraged volunteerism from former students and residents of the community. He also has opened new college opportunities for those who stay in school and graduate. Most important, however, he has created a safe haven from violence for the students, and as a result, many get to school early and leave as late as possible in order to avoid the violence that exists outside the building's doors. He is truly a strong and inspirational leader who has in spite of all the obstacles turned DuSable once again into a place from which tomorrow's leaders may well emerge.

TB: Where were you born?

CM: I was born in Mississippi.

TB: But it is my understanding that you came to Chicago quite young and that your father was a union leader here.

CM: That's right.

TB: And your mother was a housewife?

CM: Yes, she was a housewife, but she had been a teacher down in Mississippi.

TB: Did you and your brothers attend DuSable High School?

CM: Generally speaking, this neighborhood is where we all grew up, but only one of my brothers went to DuSable. My older brother and I graduated from Englewood.

TB: You have been a school administrator for quite a long time.

CM: Well, I taught for five years, but I have been in school administration for twenty-six. First at Austin High School from '70 to '74, at Whitney Young High School from '74 to '85, at Central High School District from '85 to '88, and then at DuSable from 1988 on until the present.

TB: In that time you must have seen a lot of changes.

CM: Well, when I first came to DuSable High School you already had all the ingredients that were necessary for a good school, but everybody was going around and just doing whatever they wanted to do. What I had to do for the school was to help the staff members establish a coordinated central vision and to take all of the talent we had and try to channel it into one direction rather than in a number of different directions. In some cases that meant that I had to get rid of some folks who were not doing their jobs as well as they should be done.

TB: Were you able to select your staff in the same manner as you were able to do at Whitney Young?

CM: No, not with as much freedom as I had at Whitney Young. This was a different type of situation, but even so, I was very selective anyway.

TB: At Whitney Young you had more freedom?

CM: As a matter of fact, I didn't have the freedom—I had to take it there too. What you do is to learn that power is not given—it is taken. Where I could move folks, I moved them, but luckily there were already very good people here at DuSable High School. At a school like this you cannot have a mediocre teacher. If you do not have an *excellent* teacher, the students won't understand what is expected of them.

TB: Where do your students come from?

CM: All over. The vast majority of our kids come from right here in the neighborhood, of course, but through our options program we take in kids from all over. As a result, we have students coming here from as far south as 133rd Street all the way up north to Howard Street. We encourage this, and since we have gotten the Internet Lab set up, now we are getting an even more diverse group.

TB: And the student body is how large now?

CM: The student body fluctuates between fifteen hundred and thirteen hundred. This year I am doing something that I have been threatening to do. I have stopped trying to be a missionary about kids coming to school. This year I say you either come to school on a regular basis or get out!

TB: You're adopting a kind of tough-love policy?

CM: That's right: tough love! If you want to come to school, come on, and we will be happy to give an education to you. But if you are not going to come to school, I am not going to allow you to have your name on the rolls and attend sporadically whenever you want to. Now it's either you must establish a regular pattern of attendance or get out of here.

TB: Do your students feel comfortable and safe in this building?

CM: Yes, they do. That's one of the things that we try hardest to achieve. See, kids can't learn when there is always a lot of turmoil around them. Kids have got to know that they are safe, and so we spend a lot of time and money to kind of keep things under complete control. At present I am spending over three thousand dollars a month for security, but what price can you put on students' lives?

TB: Yes, but in this blighted neighborhood, in this neighborhood of poverty and sometimes violence, what happens when the children leave this building to go home?

CM: Many of them try to stay inside here as long as they can stay. As a matter of fact, we would have kids staying here until eight o'clock in the evening if I would allow them to do so.

TB: So for many of them this is better than their homes.

CM: Right, for them it's a better place to be than their homes. This is their sacred place. Given the gang configuration, and so forth, this school is one of the few places that young people like them can socialize safely with people from different areas.

TB: Even when I was back here teaching, which is a long time ago, students still were able to walk home in groups over into the Washington Park area or over into the Willard School area.

CM: Well, they still do, but back then kids used to come from a much wider area. Now 80 percent of our kids only have to cross the street. So our school has become the only place where they can do what they want to and get to know people from different areas. Unfortunately, these kids can't get out and go anywhere else that they want to in the neighborhood.

TB: They can't go to the party at Fifty-fifth Street if they are living on Forty-ninth Street.

CM: Because that's different turf. But here at the school we say, "That stuff stops at the door!" That means hats, colors, everything, and if you try to come in here and pull in all that mess with you, I will set you right back out on the street where you can be with it just as much as you want. But you can't have any of that in here. That's not something I am going to argue with kids about. It is just what we do.

TB: Another thing I've noticed here is that the relationships between most of the members of the faculty and the students tend to be a mutual respect kind of thing.

CM: Yes, but that's taken a long time for us to develop. We are trying as best we can to personalize this high school. I do not believe that a large high school needs to be a place where a kid can go for four years and later on nobody will even remember that he was ever there. We want our students to come into this school and know that there is someone in the school who cares for them. We are trying to get away from the idea that kids can just be absent, and nobody will say anything or even bother to notice. That's the way that some kids get lost between the cracks. If someone is not here, someone is going to say, "Why weren't you here yesterday? What happened?"

TB: In other words, by personalizing the education of these young people you are attempting to eliminate the depersonalization that many people associate as being intrinsic to the environment of a large urban high school like this.

CM: That's right. Back when the big-factory model of schooling was first developed, we thought that giving our students a variety and a diversity in everything would be the answer to their educational needs, but we were wrong. That was not the answer. Kids need personalization. They need to know that people really care about them. They need to know that people are concerned about their education, and so we've kind of had to move away from that big-factory model and into the creation of a more personal learning environment.

TB: But physically, because this is such a huge building, how do you avoid having students feel lost within its vastness?

CM: Most of the classes that they have are in rooms that are right around the corner from each other. All day they are generally in those same three classrooms whether they learn math or whether they learn history or anything else.

TB: But in each one of those groups, someone is always in charge?

CM: Yes, each of these small schools within the larger school has a facilitator that was selected by the small school itself.

TB: They run the small schools?

CM: Yes, but they are not administrators. The facilitators are always teachers. She or he also always teaches classes.

TB: How many of these smaller schools are there?

CM: Ten.

TB: How long has this reorganization been in place?

CM: It's been coming for five years, but this is the first year that we have restructured totally.

TB: What happens when the students in these smaller groups decide to participate in what might be called elective courses such as music or physical education?

CM: There are some classes that are called global classes in which kids from everywhere participate, but for most of the core courses they are always with people who know them and understand them and in places in which they are comfortable and familiar.

TB: How does this system differ from tracking?

CM: Well, tracking actually organizes groups by different levels of ability and achievement. What we are trying to do is to let students pursue their own interests. We feel that we can get a higher level of academic achievement by letting them pursue things that they themselves are interested in. This means that we let them go to different activities. Different little groups can go different places. Today some of our students are going to hear *The Barber of Seville*.

TB: So you believe that a great deal of latitude and freedom leaves room for more creativity.

CM: Yes, and all of their learning does not have to take place on this campus. Keep in mind, I was the only African-American on the Carnegie Foundation NASSP (National Association of Secondary School Principals) Commission on the restructuring of the American high school. We studied the American high school for two years, and we came up with the recommendations for what the high schools for the twenty-first century should look like.

TB: And what kind of recommendations did you make?

CM: First of all, we decided to do away with the Carnegie Unit!

TB: The Carnegie Unit is what?

CM: It's when you have seat time, so that a student has to have so many hours seated in a classroom in order to get academic credit. We also almost said that we should disband traditional departments entirely. We did say that technology should no longer be considered just a frill. It has to be an integral part of the pattern of instruction. We said teachers shouldn't have to deal with more than ninety students a term. We said that no student should ever be able to go through school anonymously, that every student should have his or her own personal learning profile, and that every teacher should have his or her own inservice profile. We said that principals should model the behavior that they expect other people to follow. Altogether we made eighty powerful recommendations along those lines!

TB: Who was that young man that you were talking with when I came in?

CM: He is here as an intern.

TB: Well, he certainly seems to be full of vigor and enthusiasm about what he is getting ready to do, and he is not African-American. I was impressed by his positive attitude.

CM: He is an example of the kind of teacher that folks need to have in our schools. He is open-minded, and he is learning to become an excellent teacher.

TB: How many interns do you have?

CM: We have four from the Teach for Chicago Program.

TB: Is there any possibility that under certain circumstances they could return to this school on a permanent basis?

CM: They are going to! I am going to hire them.

TB: What is the composition of your faculty?

CM: About 72 percent African-American, 28 percent non-African-American. My only requirement is that they be good teachers.

TB: And what about the age of your teachers?

CM: Well, we have a lot of people that are near retirement and a lot of young teachers just starting out, but not too many people in the middle.

TB: Gender?

CM: About 60 percent are women.

TB: Sixty percent women? That's a much different ratio from when I went to high school.

CM: Yes, now the majority of our teachers are women.

TB: You have how many schools that feed into here?

CM: Thirteen or fourteen.

TB: And what is the geographic area?

CM: Well, we have feeding into us Terrell, Farren, Beethoven, McCorkle, Burke, Hartigan, Coleman, Dyett, and Carter, and then we always get some from Hoffman, and now we have some from Overton over there and from Mollison over here, and through our options program, people can come from even wider areas of the city.

TB: Now, besides your own genius at organizing, what kind of communication and articulation, if any, goes on between those schools you mentioned and your school?

CM: Well, we have a very proactive program of going out into those feeder schools and talking with the people that are there. We also invite people from the feeder schools to come here and see our assemblies, pep rallies, and everything else. So we are very inclusive. We try to have exceptional programs, and as a result, we are in the newspaper all the time, and that way people know what we are doing.

TB: Do you have activities after school?

CM: Yes, swimming, roller-skating, basketball, computers—whatever it is that the students want. We also have established the Scientific Literacy Program, which meets after school, as well as the Social Center Program, where kids from other places can come here after regular school hours.

TB: So these programs are not just for your students?

CM: No, we are a multigenerational school. We have many of the parents going to school here as well.

TB: Yes, as a matter of fact, I just met one of the parents, who seemed to be quite enthusiastic about being here with her son.

CM: That's because they all know that they are welcome to come here and partake of anything that we have. That's why we have to have an open school. It has to be a place where the parents who come here feel that the teachers are doing something in those classes that they themselves might really need to complete or update their own educations.

TB: How many incoming freshmen do you usually have?

CM: About five hundred.

TB: And how many of those stay the full four years?

CM: Although I have five hundred coming in, maybe three hundred might not stay here, but the main reason for this is that in Chicago we have a promotion policy that promotes the students from the elementary schools into the high schools just as soon as they get to be fifteen. In other words, the thing that moves kids on to high schools like ours is not academic achievement. It is age. Any student who will be fifteen the next school year has a right to come to our school whether or not they have graduated from the eighth grade!

TB: Well, now that he's on your roster, what do you do with a kid like that, who comes here but didn't even go to eighth grade?

CM: Yes, he's on my roster all right, but hell, I don't know even what his elementary school background is like because I don't get those records until two or three months *after* he enters the school! For example, suppose a kid comes in here who has a previous record of not coming to school on a regular basis. Well, the only way we will know about this is when that student is already established in our own tardy system. So what I have been doing is actually going physically to the elementary schools myself and copying down by hand all those absent days from their eighth-grade records and putting all of that information into our computer so that I can check the backgrounds of those kids who have had attendance problems in the past.

TB: How big is your staff?

CM: I have two assistant principals that I get for enrollment, and I have hired two other assistant principals with Chapter 1 money. One is in the area of discipline and the other in the area of curriculum.

TB: I know that at one time you had a kind of advisory committee that included a group of the parents.

CM: We still have it. We have a group of parents who meet here every Wednesday morning, and they know that this school is supportive of whatever it is that they need. We also have volunteer parents in this building every single day.

TB: So, if they want, the parents can come here to see what is happening.

CM: Most of them start as what I call involuntary volunteers. I talk to the parents, and what I am saying is, "I don't have the staff to run after your child every day to make him behave — so you ought to come over here and volunteer some of your time, and then when your child is behaving and doing what he is supposed to do, *then* you can go home if you want to. But until that time, if you want this kid of yours to be successful, like I said, you've got to come here and help out because I don't have enough staff people to run behind him and follow him and make sure that he always does the right thing." And so what happens is that these parents usually start as involuntary volunteers in that way, but once they come in and find out what the culture of the school is like and find out what is really going on, they discover that being here makes them more in control of their kid, and after a while, although they could stop if they wanted to, they still continue to come here.

TB: Because they begin to like what they are doing here?

CM: Yes, but you also have to realize that most of these parents — whether they be either poor or rich — want the best possible education for their children. The only problem is that poor parents don't really understand the system and —

TB: Too often they have been rejected.

CM: That's right. They feel that they have been rejected by the system. So we are one of the few schools that say to them, "Come right in here. You are always welcome, but you cannot get in the way of instruction. You cannot talk to the teacher when it's teaching time." I am not a principal that will allow a whole lot of mess and confusion to be coming in our door. "If you are coming to be disruptive, you have got to get out of here!"

TB: Here at DuSable you've had a Hall of Fame for some time. Tell me something about this new Wall of Fame that you have recently established.

CM: Well, the Hall of Fame was here before I came. It is governed by a board, and they have had only one new induction since I have been here. By the time I came here, parents and people who were graduates were saying, "Mr. Mingo, we really want to do something for DuSable, but we don't feel that we have access to what's happening at DuSable." So that's when I started a yearly open house, and so now every year, in the second week of June, anybody who has ever gone here can come back and visit the school, and when they do, we invite everybody to join the DuSable Foundation. If you join the foundation, one of the benefits is we put your picture up in the building. Eventually I would like to see pictures of all the people who went to DuSable up on that wall because I think that it is important for our students to know that this is Mr. Black when they see him walking through the building and to recognize that person is Judge Cousins. I think it's important that these kinds of connections are being made.

TB: I was talking with Bill Daniels about a month ago. He is a graduate of DuSable, and now he's a dean at the Rochester Institute of Technology. He went there after graduating from the University of Iowa. Would he be of any help to you in terms of enabling these youngsters to go on to the university level?

CM: As a matter of fact, we already have many of our former students at the University of Iowa. Iowa is more user-friendly for us than the University of Illinois.

TB: Is that right? How do you account for that?

CM: Well, one of our graduates—Duke Slater, the famous All-American football player of the twenties—went to Iowa. So they have quite a long history of accepting students from DuSable.

TB: Yes, and as I'm sure you know, Ozzie Simmons also went to the University of Iowa. When I was going to DuSable, he was one of our heroes.

CM: They have a long and honorable history of working with minority kids. My daughter also graduated from the University of Iowa, and she had one of the highest averages in her class. It was like 3.60 or 3.70, but when she needed support, there was the right kind of support right there for her, and this was a long time before affirmative action was initiated. What they have at the University of Iowa is a true commitment to diversity. There is that same sort of approach at Brown. That's where my son is. If you need help, they will always give you the help you need at a place like that.

TB: But your son and your daughter would be exceptions because they are what I would loosely call among the privileged. How do the less-privileged students from DuSable fare at places like these?

CM: At the present time we have juniors and seniors down at the University of Iowa who are graduates from DuSable, and they are doing just fine. You see, the University of Iowa has established a program where the African-American and Hispanic kids can get the right kind of tutoring if they need it. They have established a program that truly helps the kids. But at present I don't have any of our graduates at the University of Illinois because at Illinois you're completely on your own, and you either pass or get out!

TB: And arbitrarily they used to flunk the bottom third of the class, which usually was composed of minority students.

CM: I still remember that when I went to the University of Illinois at Navy Pier, when we came in the first day, the man in charge said, "Look to your right and look to your left. By midterm both of those people will be gone!"

TB: That meant two out of every three members of the freshman class would flunk out.

CM: Yes, they had a flunk-out rate of two-thirds, and they made no bones about it. They didn't have enough space on their campus to keep any more students than that!

TB: What about college scholarships? In what ways are your former graduates involved in that process?

CM: As you know, each year various classes that have graduated in the past will give scholarships and money to the kids who are graduating, and it's just really a warm, warm situation when you see these kids going across the stage and getting their awards from our past graduates. That way the kids really feel connected with the earlier generation. Last year, when DuSable was sixty years old, we invited the classes from '35 to '39 to come here, and we let those former students proceed down the aisle just like it was their own graduation, and we allowed the class of '95 to be their escorts as they were coming down the aisle. Some of the older people were on crutches and walkers and so on, but they were so glad to be here, and the students in the class of '95 were so proud to be walking with them! Even some of the boys that are usually just little thugs in here most of the time were running to take one of those past graduates down the aisle and to hold their arms and give them support. We didn't have to tell them how to do anything. They just went over to them and said thank you. I really think that what happened did more for the class of '95 than it did for the older people. Then afterwards we gave a reception, and although the members of the class of '95 were supposed to go back to their classes after the reception, they continued to stay and were still trying to take their people around. So it was a very good experience for everyone!

TB: What was the reaction of the people who were in the audience?

CM: Well, the audience was made up of any other former graduates who wanted to come and also the students who were not in the graduating class, and all of them were just in a state of shock. I mean they all were very quiet, probably because most of them were sitting down calculating things like, "Let's see: in 1935 my mother wasn't even born yet!"

TB: And in some cases, I would imagine, their grandmothers weren't even born!

CM: Right, and one of the older ladies got up and talked about what had actually happened when Phillips burned that day in her youth. In fact, she even had the name of the person that someone said had set the fire! When she told them about that, the kids were just spellbound.

TB: So it was a good day.

CM: It was a very good day. The students here really got a chance to look and see where they fit into the overall picture. That's why we want to have those pictures of everybody who ever graduated from DuSable placed up there on the wall. You don't have to be a great doctor or anything else. You could just be somebody who drove cabs or worked at International Harvester. But if you graduated from DuSable and if you are in the foundation, you are entitled to have your picture up there.

TB: At the present time everybody that's involved in education is competing for the same limited resources, and regardless of the quality of your desires and the integrity of your own position, what kind of help is needed politically to carry forth and expand this vision and these activities that you are initiating so successfully?

CM: Well, as principal of this high school, it is necessary for me to participate in a wide range of activities. That means that I am very, very active in educational circles, in college circles as well as high school. You see, I want the teachers of DuSable to be recognized for what they are doing. I try to bring the best possible staff to the school, and those things that we do that we think are great, we try to shout them to everybody. Those things that we think are not so great, we just bury them in the backyard and don't mention them anymore. They're part of the past and not the future. What we've got to do is to celebrate our current successes, and we try to learn from our former failures.

TB: As an administrator, what do you consider your greatest challenges to be?

CM: Well, at the present time I would have to say that the two biggest problems that we have here at DuSable High School are attendance and academic achievement. One of the things that really bothers me is when kids don't come to school. Another thing that upsets me is when kids come to me and say, "Mr. Mingo, why is it that we get a high school diploma and still can't get a job?" How can I answer a question like that?

TB: Particularly when right across the street or somewhere down the street there is someone about their own age who is making five hundred dollars a day by selling drugs.

CM: Yes, but everybody here also realizes that those people with their five hundred dollars from the drug trade, they don't ever live very long. We as a nation and a city and a community within that city, all of us had better start getting serious about this entire drug situation. The major problem for us at this school is that drugs are considered to be acceptable in this neighborhood. Everybody around here can tell you who the local dope dealers are, but they never seem to be the ones who get arrested.

TB: It's only the young people at the very bottom end who are going to jail. The producers—I mean those people who are bringing it here from Colombia and all those other places—none of them are getting caught. Why is that?

CM: Well, let's deal with specifics. For example, let's look at this whole issue with crack cocaine versus natural cocaine. Natural cocaine carries a much lighter penalty than crack cocaine. Why is that? It's because the consumers of natural cocaine, or powder as they call it, happen to be upper middle class, usually white kids—or white adults for that matter—and if they get caught, all they get might be a slap on the wrist.

TB: If even that!

CM: Things like that make our students feel that they do not get a fair shake in the criminal justice system—and now the students are telling me that these inequities are getting even worse. They feel that they don't even have to do anything illegal to go to jail. These kids and other people are saying to me that all of this is developing into something like a new form of slavery. I hear young people saying this sort of thing consistently, and sometimes it makes me wonder if what they are saying might not be true.

TB: Most of these young people have seen or been close to people who have died by violence or have been seriously hurt.

CM: Unfortunately that is absolutely true!

TB: And almost all of them also know or are related to someone who has been incarcerated.

CM: Right, but most of them do not want to be part of either of those kind of statistics. That's why so many young people are trying to do what they are supposed to and go to school and do everything in the proper manner, but like I said, a number of them remain convinced that—even if they did do everything right—the system is not going to be fair to them.

TB: That level of despair runs pretty deep, but there must be a spark of hope there somewhere.

CM: What we keep saying is that those statistics do not necessarily have to apply to you as an individual. If you are prepared for a career, if you can do something that is useful and legal, there's always going to be somebody out there who will be willing to buy those services that you are providing, and as a result, you will live longer and have a better quality of life and everything else that you desire. These kids have got to see that real opportunities exist ahead of them, but they

have got to put away the immediate pleasures of every day. They have got to delay certain things, parenthood being one of the most important. They have got
to adopt the philosophy that in spite of everything negative, they are going to
make it and become successful. They have got to realize that in this life you
might not get everything that you pay for, but you will pay for everything that
you get!

TB: No one who has something ever gives it away for free, especially when that
something is power and privilege.

CM: Yes, and those concepts that someone is going to give you something for nothing and that it is always somebody else's fault rather than your own if they
don't—well, it is concepts like those are that are getting in the way of our young
people reaching their true potential. They have got to wake up and realize that
what they do is what determines what happens to them.

TB: Life is always a struggle.

CM: Right. Life is a struggle, and nobody told you it is always going to be fair.

TB: Beyond what you are accomplishing here at DuSable, if you had the necessary
power and the glory to do with this school exactly what you wanted, what else
would you do?

CM: Well, I would make certain that all the parents of our students have a job that
pays a decent wage, and I would do my best to change their living environment.
What I would do is I would go over on State Street and take every other building
and blow it up, and then take the other two that are left and rehab them thoroughly. I would change those projects from low-income to mixed-income buildings. Then I'd build some parking garages where people could put their cars in-
doors, and that way those Robert Taylor Homes would soon become another
Lake Meadows, where people could live in safety and begin to reestablish some
standards for their children's behavior.

TB: Did you happen to know Mr. Taylor?

CM: I know who he was, but I never met him.

TB: Well, before that housing project named after him was built, he was the manager of the old Rosenwald complex, and I have said to his daughters, "How
could you let your father's name be placed on those buildings? You ought to sue
to have his name removed, because I knew him, and he had a genuine sense of
responsibility toward the people of this community. He was one of the first board
members of the first Chicago Housing Authority, and that Robert Taylor project
is an abomination to his memory!"

CM: There are two major sociological decisions that caused that abomination to
occur. Number one, it was supposed to be temporary housing, and then they
decided to make it permanent housing. Number two, the Cook County

Department of Public Aid made a ruling that a woman can't be living with a man in the house and still draw public aid. So that restriction gave all the men a kind of illegal status over there, and what happened was that the basic family structure became destroyed. Now you had boys growing up with no adult males around to monitor them and become their role models, and so those kids took their models from their neighborhood peer group, and this is where your gangs came from. Fathers should raise sons, but when the father can't be there until after midnight, then half-raised sons are raising the rest of them.

TB: And, of course, the girls are in need of male role models as well.

CM: Another mistake they made is that at Robert Taylor they never got any black maintenance people. All the people who service those places have been white.

TB: Is that right?

CM: Yes, and they got those jobs because they were politically connected, and there is no accountability to the community whatsoever.

TB: At the present time, as you were saying, there is almost nothing outside of this building that is available to youngsters. After you have restructured Taylor, and reorganized the neighborhood, what would you bring into the neighborhood of a recreational or entertainment nature?

CM: I would reopen the Met Theater. I would even go and take the auditorium of DuSable High School and open it up as a theater on the weekends. I would stimulate small businesses in the area. People who have money can purchase services, and if we had full employment for the parents, then there would be cleaners and other services that people could use. Someone could own a grocery store. Someone could own some other kinds of stores and provide other kinds of services. But, you see, when you have a poverty community, all of the strength of the neighborhood moves out, and then you have nonresident people who have no interest in the community coming in and providing all the service. Just try and find a first-rate supermarket between Twenty-second and Fifty-fifth Streets!

TB: And there are no movie houses at all!

CM: That's right. The closest movie house you can go to would be at Evergreen Plaza or downtown or maybe the Hyde Park Theater, but they don't want people from our community over there in places like that, and they make that perfectly clear!

TB: So our youngsters have to go out of their neighborhood just to have a good time, and when they do, it often becomes a form of social embarrassment for them and their friends.

CM: It's more than just an embarrassment. It's much worse than that, and all because places such as the Evergreen Plaza have a theater, and we don't have one of our own down here anymore.

TB: When you were still a young man, I would imagine that the ma-and-pa kinds of businesses and various recreational facilities also afforded some opportunities for young people to get jobs.

CM: That's right. You could always find work at places like that. As a matter of fact, my brothers and I, we grew up around the Court Theater at Fifty-third and Wentworth, affectionately known as the dump, and you could always get a summer job there working as an usher or something.

TB: And when there were small ma-and-pa grocery stores, you could also always get a job as a delivery boy. That's the way that communities are built and maintained.

CM: Right, and at one point I worked in the Wentworth Supermarket on Calumet, but now those stores that you do have here are hiring people who do not look like the people who come into those stores to shop. That's not the way things should be. So what I am basically advocating is that we tear down a third of each one of those project buildings and then build some parking lots and some recreational areas, even some tennis courts and things like that. But the most important thing is to give these folks some jobs so they can earn some money and be able to rebuild their neighborhood and turn things around.

TB: That's a good note to end on. Thank you very much.

April 1, 1996

HERMENE D. HARTMAN

PUBLISHER, ACTIVIST, SOCIAL HISTORIAN

Hermene Hartman, the founder and publisher of the weekly magazine N'Digo, was born and raised in Chicago. Her father, Herman Hartman, along with several of his siblings, was a successful businessman who obtained a franchise to distribute Pepsi-Cola and several other popular soft drinks. He was the first African-American to own a distributorship and one of the first Pepsi-Cola distributors in the country in 1935. One of her other uncles was the late great ballad and jazz singer Johnny Hartman. My conversation with Hermene and her mother, Mildred Bowden, focusing on her mother's experiences, is a chapter in the first volume of Bridges of Memory.

I first met Hermene in the late sixties when she was very active in supporting the Reverend Jesse Jackson's work with Operation Breadbasket, which was the forerunner of what is now known all over the world as Operation PUSH (People United to Save Humanity). In addition to this, for many years Hermene was a professor at City Colleges of Chicago and became the first woman to be Vice Chancellor of External Affairs. Hermene Hartman is a vivacious, aggressive (in the best sense of the word), creative, and extremely well-informed person who, in my opinion, has always endeavored to focus her energy in such a manner that her efforts will be of service to her community and all of its residents, whether they are black, brown, or white. With the continuing success of N'Digo, her efforts and influence have increased in their significance and importance, and her annual gala that raises scholarship funds for college-bound youth has become a great contribution to the future of our community. I am so honored to have been given the opportunity to have this informative conversation with such a talented and dedicated person.

HH: I was born here in Chicago, but just don't ask me when.

TB: Why?

HH: Well, it's like something Etta Moten told me years ago. She said, "If you're going to lie about your age, don't start lying at fifty. Start right now—so they can't catch you!"

[*Laughter.*]

TB: Were your mother and dad born here as well?

HH: My mother was born in Apex, North Carolina, but she remembers nothing at all about it because she's been living here in Chicago since she was eighteen months old. My father was born in a little town in Louisiana called Houma, which is outside of New Orleans. He came to Chicago when he was twelve years old.

TB: And so they met here in Chicago?

HH: That's correct.

TB: Do you remember anything about your grandparents?

HH: I know that my father's mother was deceased before I was born, and his father died when I was maybe about seven. That's my paternal grandparents, and my mother, as I think she must have told you, was orphaned. Her mother died in childbirth and her father died when she was less than two years old. The family that raised her were Gina and Leo McHenry—my Big Mama and Bo—she was from Louisiana and he was from Texas. These are the only real grandparents I know.

TB: When you were a child, do you remember where your parents were living?

HH: When I was born, they lived at 4714 South Park Way, now King Drive, right across from the Regal Theater. My childhood until I was twelve was at 5943 South Indiana. That's where I grew up. Then we moved to Lake Meadows. My father had his business at Fifty-fifth and Wabash. He was one of the pioneer distributors of Pepsi-Cola.

TB: That was back in the early 1930s when Pepsi-Cola was trying to invade the market that Coca-Cola had already established.

HH: Yes, and my father helped to build that company.

TB: That's right. Pepsi-Cola was built right here on the South Side of Chicago (the headquarters were at Twenty-fourth and Wabash), and I might even have helped him just a little bit to accomplish that because back then I was working after school in a ma-and-pa grocery store!

[*Laughter.*]

Anyway, that's where I got to meet your father and his brother Edward.

HH: He was the first black to be granted that type of franchise, and my understanding is that after he did so well with Pepsi, all the other soft drink companies
wanted to work with him, and so Edward became a distributor for a brand of pop
that was called Old Dutch, and a friend of theirs became the distributor for another brand named Green Mill.

TB: So when your father couldn't handle those other accounts directly for himself,
he created businesses for his brother and one of his friends?

HH: That's right, because he was too busy with Pepsi-Cola and by contract could
not take on another soft drink. It was something new—sort of like the new kid on
the block—and it needed his full-time attention. He told me some wonderful
stories about how they would get people to drink Pepsi. One of the things he said
was that they didn't try to deal with anybody that was older than thirty. That was
part of his marketing strategy because his thinking was that when people get past
thirty, it's harder for them to change their ways, and Coca-Cola already had a
lock on that market. So he decided to go after the youth market, and that's when
he began to become successful.

TB: Another factor in his success back then was that Coca-Cola had no black
people out on the streets making deliveries, and Pepsi was the first to have blacks
making deliveries for them.

HH: Well, that's because my father hired them.

TB: Now, your dad and your uncle were always continuing to expand their business
during this period, weren't they?

HH: Yes, and my dad set the record, which still stands even to this day, of maintaining his distributorship for the longest period of time in the history of the
company.

TB: Now, what about the uncle that you haven't mentioned so far: Johnny Hartman, the famous singer?

HH: Well, my uncle Johnny was the youngest of six children. He was born here in
Chicago and attended Willard Elementary School and DuSable High School.

TB: When did he first start to demonstrate his talent as a singer?

HH: When I asked my aunt Helen, who was my only living aunt on the Hartman
side at that point, "How and when did Uncle John start singing?" she said, "In
church, of course!" It seems that one day he just got up in church and said, "I
know that song," and started to sing in that beautiful, rich, deep baritone voice of
his. She also told me that one of the other people that he was singing with in that
church was a young lady named Ruth Jones, who later became known as Dinah
Washington. But even before that, she remembered that when she was about six

years old and Johnny was a little younger, sometimes she and Johnny would go outside to play, and he would say, "Helen, I want some candy," and so they would go up to somebody passing by, and he would start to sing—and that's how he would get the money that he needed to buy his candy!

[*Laughter.*]

There was so much young talent in the neighborhood back then. Redd Foxx, Dorothy Donegan, Nat Cole, Dinah Washington, Eddie Harris, Gene Ammons—I've heard so many wonderful stories about them that I feel like I was there myself.

TB: Tell me what you remember about Johnny when you were a child.

HH: Well, he was my special uncle. When I was a young girl, he was the love of my life, but he did not live in Chicago. Most of the time he was in New York or out on the road. That was where he had to go in order to do his art—and it's interesting because all of those people we just talked about—Nat Cole, Dorothy Donegan, and all the rest—had to leave the city in order to pursue their talent. Everybody would always come back home from time to time, but New York was where the money was.

TB: We had the Club DeLisa, the Rhumboogie, and the Beige Room, but they were showcases, and the big money and the challenge to make it was in New York.

HH: Right, so that's where they all went.

TB: And for the ones who were singers and musicians the ultimate challenge was the opportunity to play with Duke Ellington.

HH: Duke or Count Basie.

TB: Duke or the Count—if you could make it in one of those bands, then you knew you had reached the top of the ladder.

HH: Johnny went to New York right after he got out of the army at the end of World War II. He sang be-bop with Dizzy Gillespie's band.

TB: What do you remember about him during those times when he came back home?

HH: He was such a nice man. Always very courteous, but he held to the highest standards. Whatever you'd do, it had to be worth doing, and you didn't do it just to do it. It had to be excellent—and that's the way he was about his craft. That's something that he taught me, that he transferred to me. I can remember once, when I was about twelve years old, I went to New York to spend the summer with him, his wife, and my cousins. One day I saw in the newspaper that Jackie Wilson was playing at the Apollo, and so I told Uncle John that I wanted to go see Jackie, and, Tim, you would have thought I'd said, "Let's go to the moon!" "You're not going there. That guy can't sing. He's a dancer." "What do you mean

Jackie Wilson can't sing? He can sing *and* dance." "Dancers dance. Singers don't do that." "Yes, they do. That's the way they make a song come alive." "Real singers let the lyrics tell the story" — and, well, we got in this argument, and it went on and on. I mentioned James Brown, and my uncle said, "Well, he can't sing either," and we went through this one and that one, and he said, "You haven't named a real singer for me yet. I could not possibly take you to the Apollo to hear Jackie Wilson or anyone else like that." So I called home, and I told my father what he had said, and I said, "I've got to come home because he won't even let me go to the show." My father said, "Right now you are in New York. You are not in Chicago, and you'll just have to wait to see shows like that when you get back home." Well, I told my Uncle Johnny what my father had said, and he got even madder and said, "I told you that you weren't going to see that type of show in New York, and you're not going to see it in Chicago either!" So this became an all-day argument, and it was just awful. Then he quieted down and said, "Come on, let's go out to a record store." So we get on the elevator, and I'm still crying, and who do you suppose was on that same elevator? Dinah Washington! You see, she lived in that same building, and she said, "What's the matter? What's wrong with you?" So I told her that I wanted to go see Jackie Wilson, but that my Uncle John wouldn't let me go and that he wouldn't let anybody else take me either, and she said, "John, what's the problem?" "It's because that guy can't sing. She should be exposed to good music but not bad like that." So Dinah just started laughing, and she said, "Well, maybe it ain't the singing. After all, that guy's pretty cute!"

[*Laughter.*]

You see, she was relating to the fact that this little girl was crying, and so then she says, "When you come back from the store, why don't you all stop on by, and let's have some lunch together." So, Tim, when we came back, we had some lunch and then sat on the floor and listened to records. We played Dinah. We played Johnny and also people like Frank Sinatra, Arthur Prysock, Joe Williams, and Tony Bennett. She played an album for me that she'd made with Brook Benton. You see, both of them were determined that I was going to know the right kind of music, and so I listened while they played those records for me, and I had a great time, and they played all those records for me until it was night. Then the very next day Uncle John took me uptown to hear a jam session with Miles Davis and Cannonball Adderley and people like that, and he told me, "This is what the real music sounds like." That's what made me a lover of jazz. At first I made the mistake of thinking that he was jealous because he didn't have a record high up on the charts or because he just sang songs and didn't dance, but I was wrong, and that taught me an important lesson. Something that is popular is usually popular for only a very short time. Real music is what lasts and continues to be listened to. He would always say, "Now listen to this lyric. What does it mean?" And then he would play "Fly Me to the Moon" or "Lush Life" and say, "Let's talk about what this means." So these were valuable lessons for me, and I've never forgotten them.

TB: He always maintained the highest standards in all the music that he chose to perform.

HH: Yes, he was always true to his craft. He did not abort his craft. He did not prostitute his craft, and it cost him. He would not compromise, and that cost him dearly because he could have made a lot of money doing commercials and things like that, which he never did.

TB: When he'd come to town, all of his old friends and acquaintances would come out to hear him, and he'd look around at the audience and say, "Well, it looks like we've got all of DuSable in here tonight." Then the room would get quiet because no one wanted to miss anything. They wanted to hear all the nuances and subtleties that he expressed in his songs.

HH: He spent a lot of his time in Europe, where they really appreciated his art, and he was a big star in Australia. He even had his own television show there for a while, and then in later years—the late seventies, the early eighties—he spent a great deal of time in Japan, where they also really loved his music.

TB: But back here he continued to be underrated.

HH: Yes, and it was only after his death that the critics began to call him the greatest jazz singer, the man with the most beautiful voice, and things like that.

TB: Which is another indicator of the quality of talent that has existed in our community but has been ignored unless it had great commercial success and that is not familiar to most of the current generation.

HH: Now it seems that the bottom line means everything.

TB: And when the bottom line becomes everything, then the craft is minimized and appears to lose its relevance.

HH: That is certainly true.

TB: And so you got your musical education from your uncle and his friends. What about your academic experiences? Where did you start to go to school?

HH: I went to nursery school at Cosmopolitan, which was on Wabash, right down the street from where my father had his business, and then I went to Betsy Ross. That was my grammar school for all eight years, and then we moved to Lake Meadows, and I went to Phillips for a year and a half, but the rest of my high school education was at Jones Commercial. That's the school from which I graduated. You see, my father was always pushing me to prepare myself for a career in business. He said that was the only thing that made any sense.

TB: We did not have anything in the black community that was the equivalent to Jones Commercial.

HH: That's right. Jones was a specialist business school, and my father's goal was always that I should go to college and be prepared to get a degree in business administration. My mother's thinking also was that if you can get the basic business skills as well as the academics, then you will always be able to make a living. She knew that it was important for people to be able to take care of themselves at an early age because she had lost both her mother and her father by the time she was eleven. So she was determined that I was going to be a self-sufficient person. After that, she said, "The sky's the limit, and you can do whatever you want."

TB: While you were at Jones, had the racial barrier just been broken?

HH: Not really. For all practical purposes it was still a white school. There were 625 students, but there were only three blacks in my class and a total of eleven in the entire school. I can still remember those exact numbers until this very day.

TB: And all the students were girls?

HH: No, I think there were about ten boys.

TB: What about the faculty? Were any of your teachers black?

HH: They didn't have any blacks on the faculty. Zero. None.

TB: And yet that school was located on land that a black man had once owned.

HH: That's right. A man named Mr. John Jones.

TB: What irony!

HH: Tim, I hated that school, and I tried to do something that I'd never tried before, and it was about the dumbest thing I ever did. I tried to flunk out.

TB: Really? Is that because you were so uncomfortable?

HH: Oh, it was terrible! It was my first time encountering the race thing.

TB: And yet in terms of economic background, you came from a class that was superior to most of them.

HH: But they didn't know that, and so even though I was smart, I tried to play dumb because I thought if my grades started to slip badly enough, my parents would send me back to Phillips. But my mother wasn't having any of that! Instead she said, "Well, since you've got all these problems at school, then all your time when you're not at school has to be study time." But she knew I was unhappy, and so one day she said to me, "Hermene, if you're so miserable in that situation, here's what you should do. Don't decelerate. Accelerate and you can get out of there much sooner!" Well, I'd never thought of doing anything like that, and so she went on, "You can go to summer school. You can do extra-credit work. That's a better way to meet your goal than trying to be stupid, because you are not stupid and I am not going to tolerate that kind of attitude and behavior." So that's what I did. I began to accelerate. I became a real whiz in business machines. I became president or some officer in all my classes, and I graduated early. In just three and a half years!

TB: So, after you left there, what did you do then?

HH: I was only sixteen when I graduated, and I got accepted at Howard, Northern Illinois, and the University of New Mexico, but I couldn't decide which of those places I wanted to go to, and then my mother happened to read in the newspaper that they were having a special fall session at Loop Junior College. So she said, "Hermene, you are not going to be out of school for an entire semester. That's just ridiculous"—and she took me by the hand and enrolled me at Loop, and I liked it! I was doing fine as a student. A lot of the other students were Jews, and as you may remember, the Jewish schooling pattern for higher education in those days was that you went to a junior college like Loop for two years, saved yourself some money, and then transferred to the University of Chicago or Roosevelt or someplace like that. So I said to my parents, "Do you know how all these Jewish people manage to go to school? They stay here for two years and then transfer, and the money that they save helps put them through graduate school." My father said, "But you don't have a money problem. That's not your concern. Your concern is school. Money, that's my problem. You let me be the one to worry about that." But my mother understood exactly what I was saying, and she took my side. So I stayed there at Loop, completed my courses, and then transferred just like I had planned.

TB: Where did you go?

HH: Well, my father wanted me to go to the University of Chicago, but St. Clair Drake and Charles Hamilton were teaching at Roosevelt, and so I wanted to go there.

TB: You certainly couldn't go wrong with teachers like that! Charles Hamilton had been a student of Drake's, and I had been one of his students as well.

HH: You were a Drake student? Well, let me tell you, when I was there, you had to register for Drake's classes about one year in advance because he was so popular. There wasn't a room at Roosevelt that was big enough for all the students that wanted to hear what he had to say. When he lectured, people were sitting all around on the floor and even out in the hall. I was so mad that I couldn't get into his class that I waited for Drake one day, and I said to him, "I came here because of you, and now I can't get in any of your classes." I was crying and just raising all kinds of hell, and so he said, "Well, I'll tell you what we're going to do. I'm going to be your counselor. That way you've got access to me whenever you want." From that point on, Drake laid out my academic program, and I used to go and talk with him once a week. We would spend an hour together just walking and talking, and I could ask him anything I wanted to. I would even go to conferences with him, but even so, I still couldn't get into one of Drake's classes! [*Laughter.*]

While I was there at Roosevelt, he would alternate semesters because he also taught in Ghana.

TB: Yes, he was the head of the Sociology Department at the University of Accra. He got set up there because he and Nkrumah were friends, but he was in demand all over. He was fabulous. I can still almost see him now, walking around the classroom, writing on the board—

HH: Writing on the board and smoking that cigarette: a piece of chalk in one hand and a cigarette in the other! [*Laughter.*]

He taught me so many things that are still with me. I can still remember him saying things like, "You should learn at least as much from your students as you teach them because if you don't, then you're not doing it right." He's always been my model.

TB: And also for many others. While I was at Roosevelt, my classmates were people such as Harold Washington, Warren Bacon, and so many other outstanding young men.

HH: Was Charles Hamilton there then?

TB: Chuck was a younger guy.

HH: His classes were also very popular, until some of the most militant black students told Hamilton that he had no business teaching black politics to white students, and so they broke up his classes, and he had one section that was black and one section that was white. But even that wasn't enough for them. Those students continued to put on so much pressure. Some of them even went over to Drake and said to him, "You've got a serious conflict of interest. You've got to divorce your wife!" They said that to him because his wife was white, and, of course, Drake told them that they must be out of their minds, but they continued to increase the pressure so much that both Drake and Hamilton left Roosevelt. I cried like a baby when Drake and Hamilton left there.

TB: Drake, of course, left and went to Stanford. Hamilton was also very much in demand because by this time he and Stokely had already written *Black Power*, and so he went to Columbia.

HH: You know, now I'm on the alumni board at Roosevelt, and we have a St. Clair Drake Award for Academia, but I was absolutely amazed to discover that some of the people who were sitting on that damn board did not even know who St. Clair Drake was!

TB: While you were still a student at Roosevelt, isn't that also when you first met Jesse Jackson? Wasn't he just arriving on the scene?

HH: Yes, I first met Jesse while I was at Roosevelt. I was about seventeen, and he was just out of the seminary at the University of Chicago.

TB: This was at the early stage of Operation Breadbasket.

HH: Yes, originally Operation Breadbasket was meant to be the economic arm that Dr. King had designated for the Southern Christian Leadership Conference, and since the parent organization was based in Atlanta, when Dr. King gave Jesse his initial assignment, Jesse expected that he would be going to Atlanta, but SCLC was growing and branching out, and Dr. King wanted Jesse to be his point person here in Chicago.

TB: So it was Dr. King's decision to have Jesse stay here in Chicago.

HH: Yes, because right from the beginning we were very successful in what we were doing, but then, after Dr. King's death, a conflict arose between Breadbasket and the parent office of SCLC. At that time we had a huge Black Expo that I helped initiate. By then we were raising enough money to pay for salaries as well as for our operating expenses, but Ralph Abernathy would say to us, "You all can't keep that money. Send that money down here to Atlanta, and we'll tell you what your budget is and how those funds should be allocated." Well, we thought that was crazy. I mean, we had worked hard to earn that money, and we thought that it should be ours. Who did that guy think he was? So the staff got very angry, and Jesse decided we wouldn't turn the books over to them or give them the receipts or any of the money. After all, we didn't need them anymore!

TB: And so this led to the founding of Operation PUSH?

HH: Yes. By this time we had grown so large that we had to move from the Parkway Ballroom over to the Capitol Theater on Seventy-ninth Street, but before very long that place wasn't big enough either. Thousands of people came there every Saturday, and you just couldn't get in the place—and so we needed bigger quarters for our permanent home, and then we learned that this old synagogue, K.A.M. Temple, on Drexel was available . . .

TB: And you've been there until this very day.

HH: That's right. I date back to the Parkway Ballroom, after Dr. King's death.

TB: As I remember it, by this time you and David had already gotten married.

HH: That's right. David and I got married in August of '73, and I started my grad work in September. At that time David was the PR and media person on Jesse's staff, but since I was still in school, I was there only on a kind of part-time basis working on special events and things like that.

TB: You were involved in the first Black Expo, weren't you?

HH: Yes, the first two were very successful, but then on the third Expo Mr.

Winbush came in and did all the graphics for us. He's a fabulous man and an absolutely wonderful artist. He really put the finishing touches on what we were doing. He did for us exactly what was needed, and he did it masterfully, just masterfully. So our third Expo was such an overwhelming success that, all of a sudden, I was starting to have people come up to me and say, "Could you do this for me?" or "Could you do that for me?" You see, what I liked best about the Expo was the emphasis on art. I always felt that the civil rights movement missed an important opportunity by not doing more with the visual arts, and so I got very involved with certain artists whom I knew. I was trying to understand their problems with museums, like the Art Institute, which did not display black art, and I wanted to challenge all of that. So I began to represent these black artists and to work with museums in trying to get their work displayed.

TB: What degree of success did you achieve?

HH: Well, by representing these artists, what happened is that I got very involved in the cultural community. I really learned how to do PR because, believe me, if you can promote black art, you can promote practically anything! One of the artists that I represented was named Paul Collins, and one day he came to me and said, "I think you might have a real opportunity to do something for George Johnson because it's the twenty-fifth anniversary of his cosmetics company, and he wants to do something really special! Do you have any ideas?" So we went over to see Mr. Johnson and asked him what type of thing he wanted to do. "Well, after twenty-five years in business, I want to say thank you to my customers in a way that will make a contribution to the community." So we came back to see him the next week and presented him with a proposal that Paul would do a series of twelve paintings which would be a salute to the great, beautiful black women of history. Each of these twelve would be not just a pretty face but also a beautiful woman who had made important civic contributions, and these twelve women would be selected by a blue-ribbon committee made up of historians and community leaders. Well, needless to say, Mr. Johnson just loved the idea and said, "Let's put a budget together and do it!" So we got a committee together with Lerone Bennett, Etta Moten Barnett, Robert Stepto, and people like that! This was my first real corporate type of promotional project, and we toured that exhibit in cultural institutions all around the country.

TB: So now you were promoting the arts not just in Chicago but all over the entire country.

HH: Yes, and what happened is that we pulled people into some of these museums that had never been to a museum before. So we were very successful, and I was beginning to become recognized as someone who was bringing some new ideas and new artists to the table. Then I started getting calls asking me to be a consultant or a member of some arts-related board, and so I started learning how to do that kind of thing effectively. I was really lucky because both Margaret Burroughs and Etta Moten were willing to become my mentors.

TB: You couldn't have better teachers than that!

HH: And so eventually I became a member of the board at the John F. Kennedy Center in Washington, D.C., and from that level we were able to do some really impactful things.

TB: Was this during the Carter administration?

HH: Yes, and we were able to get Carter to do a special salute to black artists such as Romare Bearden and Margaret Burroughs as well as others that formerly had been ignored by the cultural establishment. What I was trying to do was to break into the mainstream and get for these artists the kind of recognition that they deserved.

TB: How long did you stay in Washington doing this type of work?

HH: I commuted for our meetings for about ten years, and one of the things that I am really proud of is that at that time they were just developing the concept of the Kennedy awards for excellence in the performing arts—

TB: Which is where they recognize five or six artists every year for their lifetime achievements.

HH: Yes, and one of my very good friends at the Kennedy Center was a woman named Grant—who was the granddaughter of Ulysses S. Grant—and she was in a very powerful position there. She told me she wanted to do a tribute to Duke Ellington during Black History Month in February, so I said to her, "Why limit Duke Ellington to just Black History Month? He is one of the greatest composers, if not the greatest, that this country has ever had." You see, I had done a lot of research on Duke and found out that he has written more songs than any other American composer. He wrote on average three songs a day!

TB: And half of them have never been recorded.

HH: Or even heard by anyone! I mean, there's all this new music that we've never even heard, and, Tim, when I told this woman that you could play different examples of Duke Ellington's music every day for ten years and *still* not hear all of his songs, that's when she got really excited about the idea of including at least one black person each year among those that would be honored for their achievements.

TB: But then you left Washington and came back to Chicago.

HH: I didn't live in Washington. I commuted to meetings. I felt that maybe I had accomplished the maximum of what I could contribute. So when I came back to Chicago, as you can imagine, I was asked to be on every single board in town in the art community, and I served on several of them. You might remember the tribute to Etta Moten Barnett at the Art Institute—that was one of the projects that I did. Then, when Harold became mayor, Ed Berry asked me to serve on the transition team for cultural affairs, and I ended up being a one-person team! So I called Mr. Berry, and I said, "I don't care how much you believe in me. No one can be a one-person team because you don't have enough varied opinions"—and he said, "Well, Hermene, just go on and act like you're four different people!" So what I did, Tim, is I went around to all the museum people here in the city and got their input on what they thought that the city needed, and my recommendation, reporting directly to the mayor, was that the City of Chicago should establish a cultural affairs department that would coordinate the needs of all these separate institutions. We'd never had anything like that previously, and everybody loved the idea.

TB: From what you've been telling me, you've certainly been very fortunate in your family background, and those advantages plus your own natural talents and creativity have continued to make you successful in all of your various endeavors.

HH: Well, the way I was raised I always got consistent messages from my parents. They always provided what I needed. You know, seven years ago I was a guest on John Callaway's television show, and he asked me, "When you were growing up, how did you feel about segregation?" And when he asked me that, it hit me like a ton of bricks because when I was growing up I never thought about segregation. I never thought of myself as being segregated or deprived in any way. What was he talking about? I never thought of my life like that. Of course I could see how he thought of it like that, but when I was young, we lived in Lake Meadows, and everybody's father was a doctor, a lawyer, or a judge. I was Herman Hartman's daughter, and I had everything I needed. I had a famous uncle who was singing, and he sent me presents from Germany and Japan and England.

TB: What about your early encounters with white people?

HH: When I was around white folks, it seemed to me that *they* were the ones who were deprived!

[*Laughter.*]

TB: If you don't mind, I wonder if you'd care to reflect a bit now on your opinion of what is happening with other people of your generation who happen to be less fortunate and less successful.

HH: Well, for one thing I think that what has happened to many people of my generation is that they never got those same, consistent kinds of messages from their parents that I was fortunate enough to receive. I learned that there was always a group responsibility as well as an individual responsibility.

TB: And that recognition of group responsibility is something that has been lost.

HH: Yes, and so now there is a kind of decadence that has leaked in, and I attribute that in a large part to the media. Tim, I was not a television child. I didn't like TV. I mean it was OK, but I wasn't a child who just sat around looking at TV for five straight hours. There was a cousin of mine who lived with us, and he'd watch that stuff all day long and never moved away from in front of the television set, but I was never a child like that! I had to read. I had to go skate. I had to go ride my bike. I had to do something active, and I believe that if you look at TV for four or five hours a day—and I don't care what kind of programs you're looking at—your body is not perked, and your mind is not properly stimulated.

TB: You certainly can't talk to it and ask it questions.

HH: And so you become robotic. You learn things, but you learn things in a different way. You learn sound bites as opposed to learning in depth. You know, I was always taught to do research. "If you want to go to New York, you have to go read about it before you go there." But now most people don't see any need to do research. They just get on a plane and go to New York or wherever, and whatever they see, that's it.

TB: What about the current generation?

HH: In my last year of teaching high school, I taught the top 5 percent of the students in a College Acceleration Program, and book reports and research papers were always mandatory in my class. When I first started, my students had no trouble writing term papers, but then it started to become increasingly difficult for them to write. I'd have students say, "Ms. Hartman, I've never read a full book before. Why do I have to do this? Just let me look at a television show, and I'll write you a report on that."

TB: And, of course, watching a television show is not at all the same thing as reading a book.

HH: No, it isn't, and then a little later, when I went over to Truman College, I discovered that many of the black students were not able to compete with the other students.

TB: Why was that?

HH: Well, for one thing Truman is very much an international school. I've taught classes in which out of twenty-five students no two people had come from the same place in the world! I mean, you've got the Korean, you've got the Arab, you've got the African, you've got the Haitian, you've got the Polish, you've got the Russian, you've got the Vietnamese, and you've got everything else in that one class!

[*Laughter.*]

Jewish, Muslim, Buddhist—everything! We have a global community in that one little classroom, and we've got maybe one or two American black students in there as well, but just guess who can't compete! The American black students.

TB: And at the same time in that same situation the black African students can and do compete. Why is that?

HH: Our young people seem to be lost in a world of their own. You know, sometimes I would see one of them standing up and doing rap for some of his friends, and I'd say to myself, "What's this got to do with anything that's happening here?" There's a real richness in the classroom that they're just not participating in.

TB: Is that because they can't relate to all the stimuli that are no doubt foreign to them in terms of their experience?

HH: I guess that's what I'm saying. For example, I had some Polish people in one of my classes, and in their home country they venerated a black Madonna. For them that was the ultimate in their religious experience. So when they first saw a person like me, they thought that I must be sort of holy, but when the black kids in the class heard this, they thought the Polish student was saying that I was some kind of rock star like Madonna!

TB: What happens when you mention people to them such as Robeson or DuBois?

HH: The Russian students related better to Robeson than those from our own South Side. At least they knew who he was! Most of my Russian students on the average were over sixty years old and could not speak proper English. So here they were in my classroom with all these other students who are much, much younger. I suppose that this is an example of diversity at its finest, but as their teacher, I found it very frustrating because I could not understand them, and I couldn't tell if they could understand me! So I went to the school's administration and said, "We are setting these students up for failure. There's no way in the world that these Russian students can succeed under these conditions." But then when I go back to my classroom, one of the Russian women comes up to me and says, "Why do you want us to leave this class? That is what they do to us in Russia, but we are in America now. You can't put us out." Then she grabbed my hand, and she says, "Why you want us to go?"—and I say, "Because you're failing, and I can't communicate with you." So she says, "That's because you think you are teaching sociology. That's what you think, but here we are learning America, and we don't care whether we learn your sociology or not! You are teaching us America, and it is helping us because we've got to survive here." She told me I was like a daughter to her, and I said, "No, I'm not your daughter," and she says, "Oh, yes, you're my daughter because I have a daughter just like you back at home, and I'll never see her again." Well, when she said that, I stood there and cried like a baby.

TB: Of course you did. What else could you do?

HH: What was so frustrating about my experience with the Russians, Tim, was that when I gave them their first test, not only did they all flunk, Tim, but they all had exactly the same flunking score! So I said, "Hey, come on, you can't do this. All of you cheated on this test," and they said, "We didn't cheat. We helped each other. What you call 'cheat' we call 'help.'" So there's this cultural factor that enters in. In their country it seems that they don't have a concept of cheating, and there in that same classroom, sitting right next to them, you've got this seventeen-year-old hip-hopper! That's one hell of a contrast.

TB: But that's their world. These young blacks have to learn to cope with situations like that all the time.

HH: That's right. Now here they are in a global environment, and they haven't even left the neighborhood. The grocery store man is an Arab. The guy at the cleaners is a Korean. Let me tell you about another experience. I had a lot of Filipino students, and one of them was a young lady—Tim, she had been a perfect student—and she came to school one morning so differently attired that at first I thought I had a new person in my class. This is midsemester, and so I'm saying to myself, "Who is this? Where did she come from?" So she explains to me in front of the entire class that she had been working late and did not have time to go home and put her school clothes on. Well, Tim, to be frank with you, she looked like a prostitute. She had on this very short skirt and was wearing a lot of makeup and everything, and so I asked her what kind of work she did, and she says, "I prostitute." I was shocked, and she says, "What's wrong with that? Men like me. They pay me. That's how I get money to come here to school." It seems that where she came from at the age of ten or twelve years old your mama and your daddy make you a prostitute, and for you this becomes just another kind of job. It's like someone saying, "Hey, man, I had to wait tables late last night." No big deal, but you can probably imagine the reaction she got from the class! So after class was over, I say to her, "Look, here in America, you can't just go and announce to everyone in the class that you're a prostitute," and she says, "Why not? I'm in school not to be a prostitute. I'm in school to be a nurse, but I got to be a prostitute till I can be a nurse." So that's how I learned that for most of these students of mine school was a socializing process—language, customs, culture—as much as anything else.

TB: But your parents and my own as well did the same sort of thing. Migration from the brutal, rural South to a more free opportunity in the urban, industrialized North was also a difficult process of socialization.

HH: Yes, but it seems to me that these young people of today have developed a totally different kind of culture. I really don't know what hip-hop is. I do not understand anybody calling me bitch and then thinking that I'm supposed to be responsive to them in some kind of polite way. What kind of talk is that? What good does it do?

TB: Where does it lead? What are the consequences?

HH: Yes, because then what they say is "Fuck the political process." Frankly, that's just what they say. I mean that seems to be the general attitude, and I don't understand that attitude at all. You know, one of my students—a young black man just as bright as he could be—came up to me one day, and he said, "Ms. Hartman, I've got to go. I've got to drop your class." You see, I had a rule in my class that you couldn't drop out unless you gave me a good reason. So he said, "Listen, I got something I got to do." "What have you got to do that is more important than your education?" His answer was that he had an opportunity to make a lot of money. "Doing what?" "Well, I really don't want to tell you this, but I got me a job to be a doorman." I was shocked. "You're dropping out of school to be a doorman?" "Well, it ain't quite a doorman." It seems he'd found a job in an Arab and Chinese hotel up on the North Side, and he was being hired to be a doorman all right, but his real job was to go out and bring back dope for the people living there. That way he said he'd be making as much as three thousand dollars in a single day! So here I am trying to tell him the value of education, and he says to me, "Ms. Hartman, with that kind of money I could take care of my mama, I could take care of my sister, I could take care of my baby." So I ask him, "Yes, but what about the police?" and he says, "The police ain't going to try to kill me or lock me up for any of this shit. Remember, I ain't on the South Side with no niggers. I'm up here with some Chinamen, and don't nobody bother no Chinese!"

TB: How did you respond to that?

HH: What could I say? He was already gone. There was really nothing more I could do. He had already made his decision, but what a terrible waste!

TB: You did all you could do. You continued to be active in both politics and education. At what point did you start to publish N'Digo?

HH: Well, I started publishing it in 1989, but let me give you some background as to why I made that decision. I had been a college professor at the city colleges since 1973. I started there as an intern from Roosevelt, and I taught psychology, sociology, and history. During my last five years with them, I was in administration as director of communications and eventually became vice chancellor for external affairs. Because of the civil rights movement, I also started working in the media, and I was a television producer at CBS, but very quickly I became frustrated because of the fact that for the most part the major media overlooked or totally ignored the existence of a black middle class. Black people were always either super poor, super tragic, or super rich. I didn't see anything relating directly to people like you and me. I didn't see that normal person who goes to work every day, who sends the kids to school, who makes plans for the future, who wants to make some sort of significant contribution to society. That is your norm and that is my norm as well, but all of that was missing. I didn't see anything like that on television, and so I got very frustrated.

TB: Television doesn't so much reflect our culture as it creates a culture of its own, which can be very misleading.

HH: That's right, but the final straw for me was during the Gene Sawyer–Tim Evans mayoral race.

TB: How were you involved with that?

HH: Well, as you know, I had pretty extensive experience with the media by then. When I was working for Jesse Jackson, I discovered how the media can take someone's spoken words and twist their meaning by taking them out of the proper context. Then, after that, I worked with Harold Washington as a kind of troubleshooter and was able to help him with some special media things that were going on. Then comes the Sawyer-Evans race, and some businesspeople that I knew, namely Paul King and Prince Asiel, came to me and asked me to write an analysis of the economic issues that were involved. So with their help and some research of my own, I wrote an op-ed analytical piece for one of the major newspapers. What I was saying, basically, in that piece was, "Let's take a hard look at what we are doing and where we are going and what the consequences might be." So I quoted all of the relevant statistics on the jobs which would probably be lost if Sawyer did not win that election. Now, I had already written several op-ed pieces that had been printed by this newspaper, but this one is one they wouldn't publish!

TB: Did that come as a surprise to you?

HH: Well, I thought that they might be somewhat surprised, but I certainly wasn't expecting a total negative reaction—and when I asked them why they wouldn't print it, they said that my article didn't fit their current format, which indicated to me that there was a damn near conspiracy to prevent Sawyer from winning that race. So I took what I'd written to a black newspaper, and can you guess what they told me? They told me they wouldn't print it either. They even went so far as to say, "We have to stay in business no matter who the next mayor is."

TB: And so they didn't want to be accused of helping to determine which way the race was going to go.

HH: They decided it would be better for them if they just lay dormant on reporting the issues that were involved in that election, and that made me really mad—so I went back to the businesspeople I'd been talking to and said, "I can't get it printed!" Well, they responded by saying, "Tell you what. We'll pay for it and run it as an ad. Go back there and tell them we're going to have it printed as an ad." But guess what, Tim? They still would not print that article! I went to one of the editors and asked what the problem was. Isn't it well written or what? And that person said, "Oh, it's written very well, but that's why we're *not* going to print it. It's just too powerful!" Whatever happened to freedom of the press? So I went back to those businesspeople, and I said, "The problem is that we don't have a paper of our own. We do not have a voice that allows intellectual discussion and analysis from our own perspective. That is a tragic and unnecessary situation. What we need is a newspaper of our own!" That was the genesis of *N'Digo*. That's when I really started exploring the possibility of publishing a newspaper, and so I pulled some friends of mine together—photographers, PR people, media people, graphic artists, and writers, and so forth—and everybody started saying that yes, this is something we can do! That's when I took this challenge on—and now here we are!

TB: Yes, and so you went on and created a biweekly newspaper that is aimed specifically at the part of the black community which had previously been underrepresented from the editorial standpoint of the established press.

HH: But then I started looking at the numbers of this demographic from a business standpoint, and I recognized the fact that there was a severe underrepresentation of this market on the advertising side as well. At that time—this is in 1996—the African-American market share here in Chicago was $22.6 billion. This is disposable income after taxes! So I thought that a Marshall Field's and a Carson's and a Nordstrom and all those others should be taught to look at this market differently from the way they had viewed it in the past.

TB: That market is bigger than the economy of most countries!

HH: That's right. This is a serious and important market, concentrated right here in Chicago. What's more, it's still growing. So people have to take you seriously when you make them aware of things like that. So that's why we've been able to develop a contemporary, progressive, intelligent publication that speaks to issues of direct concern to the people of Chicago—but even so, it was a struggle to get started. Let me give you a concrete example of what I'm talking about. Before he died, my father was always telling me, "You've got to go to Pepsi-Cola and get some advertising from them for your paper." Then, when he died, Pepsi-Cola wrote an article in their internal publication about how important his contribution had been to the company, and so I decided to follow his advice and went through all the proper channels that he had told me about, and I spoke with the president of Pepsi-Cola and asked if they would be interested in advertising in *N'Digo*—and do you know what he said? He told me I was hustling! So I said to him, "Thank you for your time, but I don't have to hustle. In fact, I've never hustled anything in my entire life!"

TB: He knew that, of course, but he was intentionally insulting you because he wanted to get rid of you. He was cutting you out of the marketplace which your own father had helped to establish. It's the same old story all over again!

HH: Even in my generation.

TB: Even in your generation.

HH: Tim, one thing that I've learned about business is that our people have been on both sides of the equation: the creative side and the consumer side. But we have *not* been on the distribution side, which is the controlling side. I don't care what kind of publication you come up with, I can tell you who the distributor is because there ain't but two of them! I went to one of them—Charles Levy—to get them to distribute my paper, and do you know what? They wanted to take me out of the South Side! They said, "We will tell you where it will be distributed," and they had me in Naperville. They had me in Highland Park and places like that. So I said, "Wait! Hold it! You can't take me out of here. This is my market! You all will put me out of business. So, thank you, but I'm gone."

TB: In other words, you were not willing to give up control of your own distribution. What is your circulation at present?

HH: A readership of half a million.

TB: And the majority of these regular readers are middle-class and upper-middle-class?

HH: Yes, but the specific components of that readership are constantly changing, and that's a challenge. Now there's a new generation of blacks that just as soon as they get out of school start making forty or fifty thousand a year. For them that's a beginning salary! Some of the opportunities that have opened up for them are global. So I see these successful young people as being mobile in terms of their careers but also as being transient in terms of their lives because what they lack is any true sense of community.

TB: Yes, and that same sort of opportunity to break away from the community in order to be become successful is what happened to so many jazz musicians in the forties and fifties. They felt that they had to go to France or England or even Japan to get the recognition they deserved but were denied back here.

HH: Well, now that same sort of thing is happening in the business world as well. A whole lot of black businessmen are going not just to Europe and Asia but places like South Africa as well. You know, when Mandela was here, he saw a copy of *N'Digo*, and his first question was, "Why can't you come to South Africa and do this same sort of thing?"

TB: I can understand his saying that because your publication delivers positive information about a different class of people—which is the growing middle class of black Africans—on a more regular basis than anything they currently have.

HH: Let me tell you something else. I recently participated in a seminar up at

Northwestern. The black students there had gotten together and invited an executive from a company called Frito-Lay—which, by the way, is owned by Pepsi—to talk to them about how to manage racism in the corporate world. So this executive started out by saying, "I'm going to talk to you today about how to manage racism because if you do not know how to do that you will not be able to succeed in the corporate world. It isn't going away. It's here to stay. What is going away is how you manage it. That's what will change it." He told the story of how when he was being considered to be the vice president of Frito's and went for his interview with the president and the people on the board, he went through the gate of the corporate parking lot, and a guard stopped him and said, "You ain't going nowhere. We don't have no niggers in this parking lot!" Now, this guard was acting like he might be going to pull his gun out, and so he said, "OK, sir, but I have an appointment to meet with the president. Would you please call his office and verify this? I would really be most appreciative if you would allow me to park my car on the lot wherever you say." So, after he was hired and they told him what his responsibilities would be, he asked them, "Who manages the parking lot?" They told him, and he asked if he could add that to his other responsibilities. Well, they probably thought that was a little odd, but they said, "All right, fine, if you want the parking lot, we'll let you handle it." Then, after he'd been there for three months or so and got that parking lot to be just the way he wanted it, he called that guard into his office, and he said to him, "Do you remember that day when I first came in here for an interview and you called me a nigger? Well, I want you to know that today is your last day here. You're fired because we don't have any place here for anyone with that kind of attitude." After that, he went back to the management and said, "Now that I have accomplished what I wanted in terms of restructuring the parking lot, I would like to give it back to you for someone else to manage because I think it is no longer appropriate for me in relation to my other responsibilities." He shared that with those students as an example of how to manage racism. Then he went on to say, "I wasn't going to stand there and cuss that man out because that man had a gun—so that would have been a stupid thing for me to do. I could have gotten myself killed, and besides I wasn't going to let anything like a parking-lot attendant spoil the success of my interview."

TB: Without the advantage of hearing examples like that, too many of our young people are led to believe that the only way for them to manage the racism they encounter is with a gun of their own.

HH: And that only serves to get them killed. It doesn't begin to solve the problem.

TB: As a matter of fact, it just makes the problem worse.

September 10, 1995

CONCLUSION

It is my fondest hope that the reader and all of his or her relatives and friends have enjoyed this second volume of *Bridges of Memory*. It is also my hope that all of these readers will be reminded that there is just as much (if not slightly more) diversity of personalities and individual talents in the African-American community as there is in any other community identified in terms of socially defined ethnicity. The only essential difference is that for the African-American community de facto segregation and institutionalized discrimination have continued to deny and withhold equal opportunity despite proven merit. Why else was a University of Illinois and Michigan Law School graduate such as Earl Neal denied the opportunity to become a comissioned officer in the United States Army while his white fellow graduates readily became officers? What caused Chicago-born Betty Stell, a graduate of Hyde Park High School and the University of Chicago, to be relegated to predominantly black high schools when there were better-paying vacancies in her field of counseling all over the city in racially mixed institutions? These and other stories in this second volume continue to illustrate the role that racial prejudice has played in determining the specific arcs of the lives of African-Americans in a city such as Chicago. No doubt similar stories could be found in every other large American city as well, but stories such as these are not just chronicles of frustration and despair. Much more important, these narratives reveal the dreams, the deep spirituality, and the continued determination of all of these individuals to break the color line and thus to make the stated promise of America become a shared reality for all of its citizens, no matter what the color of their skin might happen to be. People like those whose narratives have filled these first two volumes of *Bridges of Memory* have proven that this is indeed the home of the brave—and they will continue to struggle until it is, in fact, the home of the free as well.

INDEX

Abernathy, Ralph, 369
Abner, Ewart, 180
Abner, Willoughby, 54, 66, 103, 180
ACLU (American Civil Liberties Union), 14
Adamowski, Benjamin J., 67
Adams, Dr. Jo Jo, 91, 228–29
Adderley, Julian "Cannonball," 364
Ademola, Lady Kofo, 6
Adkins, Nelson, 80
Adkins, William "Bill," 78–87
AIDS (acquired immune deficiency syndrome), 219, 308
Al (union organizer), 59–60
Alfred E. Smith Fellowship, 272
Alhambra Theater (Milwaukee), 123
Allen, Bill, 116
Allen, Henry "Red," 86
AME (African Methodist Episcopal) Church, 33, 104, 152, 160–61, 175
American Federation of Musicians, 125
American Federation of Teachers (AFT), 259
Ammons, Albert, 125–26
Ammons, Gene, 83, 131, 171, 363
Anderson, Bobby, 145, 146
Anderson, Marian, 103
Anderson, Mrs. (fifth-grade teacher), 265
Annex, The (nightclub), 125
Apollo Theater (New York), 86, 182, 363–64
Aristide, Jean-Bertrand, 19
Armstrong, Juanita, 191, 192
Armstrong, Louis, 119, 124, 154, 156, 170
Armstrong, Mrs. Louis (Lil), 119
Art Institute of Chicago, 370, 372
Arverette, Arvis, 199
Asiel, Prince, 377

Aspen International Design Conference, 147–48
Attica prison riot trial, 70

Bacon, Warren, 162, 368
Bailey, Pearl, 89
Baker, James, 97
Baker, Josephine, 103
Baker, Oscar, Jr., 97
Baker, Oscar, Sr., 97
Balaban and Katz circuit, 122
Baldwin, Kit, and Baldwin Ice Cream, 44
Bamboo Lounge (nightclub), 171
Banda, Hastings, 19
Banks, Ernie, 251
Barnett, Etta Moten (Mrs. Claude), 26, 361, 370, 371, 372
Barrymore, John, 126
Basie, Count, 86, 171, 182, 363
Battles, Rose, 277
Battles, Wilks, 277–82
Bearden, Romare, 371
Beasley, Dr. Anthony, 110
Beiderbecke, Bix, 84
Beige Room (nightclub), 363
Bennett, John, 174, 188–89
Bennett, Mrs. John (Pearl Butler), 188
Bennett, Lerone, 284, 370
Bennett, Tony, 364
Benson, Al "Reverend Leaner," 91–92, 278, 335
Benton, Brook, 364
Berry, Ed, 372
Bethune, Mary McLeod, 103
"Big Six," 111–12
Bilandic, Michael (Mayor), 73

Billings Hospital, 10

Black, Timuel D., Jr., vii, ix, x, 74, 206, 238, 241

Black, Walter K., 167

Blackburn, Jack "Chappie," 110

Blackburn, Leo, 251, 252–54, 255

Black Expo, 369–70

Black History Month, 371

Black Metropolis (Drake), 189

Black Panthers, 316, 318

Black Power (Carmichael and Hamilton), 368

Blackstone Rangers (street gang), 107, 136, 218, 302–3

Black Student Alliance (University of Chicago), 317

Black Student Association, 316, 317

Bland, Bobby "Blue," 334

Block, Douglas, 110

Boatman, Adelaide, 131

Bodrick, David, 369

Bogan, Kate, 212

Bonner, Bob, and Bonner brothers, 214

Bosnia, 241

Bousfield, Julia, 131

Bousfield, Maudelle B. (Mrs. Midian), 131, 227, 296

Boutte, Al, 75

Bowden, Mildred, 360

Braddan, William S. (Reverend), 79, 80–81

Bradshaw, Tiny, 84

Bradshaw (brother-in-law of Winbush), 147

Brazier, Arthur (Bishop), 102

Bridgeport Park confrontation, 60–61

Bright, Delbert, 126

Bronson, James, 214

Bronzeville, paintings of, x

Brooks, Arthur and Richard, 179

Brooks (runner), 145

Brown, James "Jim" (coach), 280

Brown, James (singer), 364

Brown, Jesse, 203–8

Brown, Oscar, Jr., 34

Brown, Oscar, Sr., 227

Brown Derby (nightclub), 336

Brown v. Kansas City Board of Education, 297

Buckner, O. C., 146

Burger, Warren (Chief Justice), 274, 275

Burks, Willie, 229

Burroughs, Margaret, 35, 144, 371

Burrus, Clark, 158–66

Bush, George H. W., 18, 19

Bush, Margaret, 235

Butler, Dorothy, 188

Butler, Jerry "Iceman," xi, 173–86, 188, 191, 194, 201, 337

Butler, Joey, 188

Butler, Mattie, xii, 187–202

Butler, Pearl (Mrs. John Bennett), 188

Byrne, Jane (Mayor), 73–74, 137, 138, 200

Cabrini-Green, 175, 185, 189, 196, 337

Caesar, Shirley, 103

Caldwell, Mrs. (sixth-grade teacher), 263

Callaway, John, 372

Campbell, Floyd, 151–57

Campbell, Mrs. (music teacher), 112

Capitol Theater, 369

Capone, Al, 85

Carey, Archibald (Bishop), 47, 160

Carmichael, Stokely, 368

Carnegie Hall, 86

Carter, Burnett "Bo," 167–72

Carter, Clotele, 167, 169

Carter, Jimmy, 274, 371

Carter, Lucille, 167

Carter, Vivian, 179

Casey, Eddie, 22–30

Casey, Stanford, 22, 24, 25

Catholic Church, 50–51, 102, 103, 175

Cats and the Fiddle (jazz group), 144

Cavern Inn, 169

CBS (Columbia Broadcasting System), 376

Chandler, Muriel, 31–41

Chaney, James, 215

Channel 2 News, 198

Charles, Prince of Wales, 207

Charles, Ray, 334

Charlie and Ella Mae's Chicken Shack, 28

Cherokee Indians, 117

Chicago: first and second migrations to, xi, 39, 141; Great Fire (1871), 117

Chicago Bee (African-American newspaper), 104

Chicago Board of Education, 46, 78, 81, 158, 216, 338

Chicago Board of Election Commissioners, 94

Chicago Civil Liberties group, 14

Chicago Defender (African-American newspaper), 104

Chicago Herald-American, 246

Chicago Historical Society, ix

Chicago Housing Authority (CHA), 20, 282, 357

Chicago Police Department: blacks in, 134–35; blacks as heads of, 68, 114, 115, 128, 137–42; Red Squad, 324; Youth Division, 107

Chicago Sun-Times, 246

Chicago Transit Authority (CTA), 165–66, 277, 280

Chicago Tribune, 96, 239

Chicago Whip (African-American newspaper), 104

Chicago World's Fair (Century of Progress Exposition, 1933–34), 168

Chili Mac's (eatery), 85

Circe Ceroines (student club), 35

Civil War, U.S., 129

Clark, Charley, 270

Clark, Irma (librarian), 212

Clark, Miss (math teacher), 212

Clay, Robert, 316

Clinton, Bill, 152, 203, 283, 328

Clubs (nightclubs), 120, 125–26, 171, 336. *See also* DeLisa; Rhumboogie "the 'Boogie"

Cobb, Clarence H. (Reverend), 244

Coca-Cola, 26, 361–62

Cochran, Johnnie, 70

Coffee, Mrs. (second-grade teacher), 265

Cole (ballplayer at Phillips School), 228

Cole, Billy, 227

Cole, Nat King, 25, 28, 90–91, 164, 170–71, 363

Coleman, Mr., of Coleman Real Estate Company, 49–50

Collins, Paul, 370

Communist Party, 14–15, 54, 66

Congress of Racial Equality (CORE), 285–86, 292

Constitution, U.S., 319

Cook County Jail, 105

Cooke, Sam, 102

Cooper, Jack L., radio show of, 104

Coordinating Council of Community Organizations (CCCO), 42, 65, 286

Cosby, Bill, 30

Court Theater, 359

Cousins, William "Bill" (Justice), 95, 97, 131

Crawford, Alice, 226, 294

Cress, Ida Mae, 118

Crest, Paul, Company, 147

Croix de Guerre, 232

Crosby, Israel, 126

Crump, Freddy, 122

Cupids (singing group), 249

Dackens (worked with Winbush), 147

Daley, Richard J. (Mayor), 20, 54, 71–76, 133, 164, 286

Daley, Richard M. (Mayor), 76

Daniels, Alice and Roland, 262, 263

Daniels, Professor William "Bill," xii, 259–76, 353

Daniels, Mrs. William (Fannie Pearl Hudson), 259, 268, 271, 273

Dash, Leon, 219

Davis, Allison, 13

Davis, Angela, 216

Davis, Hazel Thompson, 120

Davis, Miles, 163, 172, 182, 336, 364

Davis, Milton, 283–92

Davis, Sammy, Jr., 164

Dawson, William Levi "Bill," 6, 66, 72, 73, 97, 113

Daylie, Daddy-o, 335

Deas, Harry, 114

Deas, Milton (Captain), 134

DeGaulle, Charles, 271

DeLisa (nightclub), 36, 85, 88, 89, 171, 363; musicians at, 83, 116, 125–26

Democratic National Convention, 140

Denison, Colonel Franklin A. and Mrs. Edna and family, 118–19

Depression. *See* Great Depression

DePriest, Lydia, 26

DePriest, Oscar, 26, 103, 105

Detroit, migration to, 32–33

Dewey, Thomas E., 13

Dickens, Sarah, 221

Dickerson, Earl B., 11

Dirksen, Everett, 14

Disabled American Veterans, 203

Disciples (street gang). *See* Gangster Disciples (GD)

Donegan, Dorothy, 7, 363

"Dope Street, U.S.A.," 135

Douglas, Paul, 73

Drake, St. Clair, 189, 367–68

Dreamland (nightclub), 120

Drifters, the (jazz group), 334

DuBois, W. E. B., 374

Duffy, Mrs. (French teacher), 266–67

Duncan, Melvin, 261

Dunlap, Alexander (Reverend), 140

DuSable Foundation, 353

DuSable Museum of African American History, 144

Duster, Benjamin and Alfreda ("Ben" and "Freda"), 103

Dyett, Walter Henri (Captain), 211, 280; as bandleader, 116, 131; students of, 79, 82–83, 169

Eagleburger, Lawrence, 19

Eames, Charles, 148

Ebony magazine, 148, 251

Eckstine, Billy, 157, 163

Eighth Regiment Army Headquarters, 168

Eisenhower, Dwight D., 7, 13, 34

Elizabeth II, queen of England, 207

Ellington, Edward Kennedy "Duke," 98, 116, 124, 150, 182, 363, 371

Ellis, Mr. (assistant principal at Phillips), 298

English, Henry, 317

Espenchez, Ms. (music teacher), 36

ETA Theater, 299

Evans, Tim, 76, 377

Evergreen Plaza Theater, 358

Farmer, James "Jim," 285

Farrakhan, Louis, 104

Farrell, James T., 79

FBI (Federal Bureau of Investigation) 14, 69

Fine, Mr. (gym teacher), 60

Finney, Dr. Leon, 102

First Amendment rights, 324, 326

Fitzgerald, Ella, 164

Fletcher, James, 288

Folks (street gang), 302

Ford Motor Company, 29, 33

Fort, Jeff, 107, 136, 302–3

Fosche, Ruth, 34

Fourth Amendment rights, 324, 325–26

Frank, Mr. (teacher), 221

Franklin, Aretha, 103

Franklin, John Hope, 5

Frazier, E. Franklin, 110

French, Avery, 211, 263, 298

Frito-Lay Company, 380

Fuller, Buckminster, 148

Fuller, Samuel B., 16, 105

Future Teachers of America, 220

Gaines, Dan, 29

Gallagher, Miss (teacher), 248

Gangster Disciples (GD), 136, 302

Garfield Boulevard hospital, 100

Garvey, Marcus, 103

Gaten, Junius, 22

GI Bill. *See* World War II

Gibson, Hoot, 25

Gibson, Truman K. and T. K., Jr., 11

Gillespie, Dizzy, 163, 172, 363

Gold Coast, 118, 175, 185, 189

Golden Lily (nightclub), 126

Golliday, Jim, 226, 229, 230–31

Gooden, Sam, 179

Goodman, Andrew, 215

Goodman, Benny, 84

Graham, Elwood, 14

Graham, Julie, 211

Graham, Ward, 214

Grand Hotel, 336

Grant, Roy, 82

Grant, Ulysses S., 371

Great Depression, 41, 47–48, 56, 101, 121, 157, 205

Great Fire (1871), 117

Green, Benny, 83

Green, Ernest, 215

Griffin, Ernest, 118

Griffin, Johnny, 82, 95, 131

Griffith, Gerald, 253, 254

Grimes, Captain (white racist), 62–64

Griswold, Edwin, 274

Grzywinski, Ron, 288

Haberman, Mr. (clothing store owner), 145

Hall, Mattie, and Hall family, 159

Hamberlin, Dr. Emil, 209–25

Hamer, Fannie Lou, 69, 100

Hamilton, Charles "Chuck," 162, 367, 368

Hampton, Fred, 73, 316

Hanrahan, Edward, and shoot-out, 73

Hansberry, Carl, 11

Harlem Globetrotters, 84–85

Harlem Harmony Hounds, 144

Harlem Renaissance, 94

Harlem Scandals, 122

Harris, Dillard, 226–41

Harris, Eddie, 363

Hartman, Edward, 362

Hartman, Helen, 362–63

Hartman, Herman, 360, 361–62, 364, 365, 372, 378–79

Hartman, Hermene, 360–80

Hartman, Johnny, 131, 360, 362–65, 372

Hawkins, Coleman "Hawk," 171–72

Hayes Center, 220

Head Start program, 218

Henderson, Horace, 126

Henderson, Jonas, 88, 89

Henderson, Mrs. Jonas (Alvena), 88–92

Henrotin Hospital, 175

Henry, William, 66

Herb's (nightclub), 126

Herrick, Mary, 131, 248, 259, 260–61, 280

Higginbotham, J. C., 86

"Hi-Jinks" shows, 211

Hill, Bertha "Chippie," 125

Hi-Lo Food Stores, 249

Hines, Arthur, 131

Hodges, Johnny, 116

Hoffman, Walter E. (Judge), 274

Holiday, Billie "Lady Day," 7, 86, 167, 169

Holly, Bishop (Apostolic Church), 102

Holman, Claude, 70–71, 72, 73

Holt, Leo, 70

Houghton, Mary, 288

Howard Theater (Washington), 86, 182

Hudson, Fannie Pearl. *See* Daniels, Mrs. William

Hudson, George, 86

Hudson, Mrs. (math teacher), 263

Hunt, Raymond, 13

Hyde Park Bank, 288–89

Hyde Park Theater, 358

Ida B. Wells housing. *See* Wells-Barnett, Ida B.

Immigration and Naturalization Service, 19

Impressions, the (jazz group), 179–80, 334

Indiana Theater, 119, 120, 122, 249

International Design Conference, 147–48

International Musicians Union, 125

Irving, Ryan, 318

Italian Mafia, 58

Jack and Jill's ice cream shop, 333

Jackson, Abraham Patterson (Reverend), 42–53

Jackson, Aileen, 42

Jackson, Ed, 272

Jackson, Jesse, 104, 238, 360, 369, 377

Jackson, Mahalia, 102, 103

Jackson, Michael, 205

Jackson, Mrs. (French teacher), 131

Jamaica Gin Gin (drink), 153

Jenner, Edward, 190

Jerry's Palm Tavern (nightclub), 336

Jet magazine, 14

Jewel Companies, 16–17

Job Now program, 194–95
Johnson, Buddy, 182
Johnson, Donald, 270
Johnson, Eddie, 78, 143
Johnson, Elijah and Lolita, 118
Johnson, George, and Johnson Products, vii, 370
Johnson, Glenn, 214
Johnson, Lyndon B., 107, 218
Johnson, Priscilla, vii
Jones, Jimmy (pianist), 143
Jones, John (landowner), 46, 366
Jones, J. T. (corporate official), 238
Jones, Lovana "Lou," 173
Jones, Nicolette, 337
Jones, Ruth. *See* Washington, Dinah
Jones, Ted, 66
Jones, Vonteil, 221
Jordan, Louis, 143, 155
Jordan, Michael, 30, 236, 281, 292
Juanita (student at Englewood), 96

Kalven, Jamie, 31
K.A.M. Temple, 369
Kelly, Edward J. (Mayor), 113, 114
Kennon, Lawrence, 54–77
King, B. B., 334
King, Dr. Martin Luther, Jr., 42–43, 100, 103,
    203, 215, 284, 286, 369; assassinated, 43, 140,
    216, 317
King, Martin Luther, Sr. (Reverend), 103
King, Paul, 377
Knight, Gladys, 334
Kofo, Lady (Lady Kofo Ademola), 6
Korean War, 61–62, 93, 97, 132–33, 231, 268,
    285

Lafontant, Jewel Stradford, xi, 3–21, 47, 110
Langford, Anna, 70
Latimer, Ira, 14
Laverty, Mr. (grocery store owner), 184
Lawrence, David "Baby," 171
"Leaner, Reverend." *See* Benson, Al
Lee, Bruce, 273
Lee, Noble, 5
Lee, Rosa, 219

Leighton, George, 98
Lemon, Mrs. (fourth-grade teacher), 265
Levy, Charles, 379
Levy, John, 7
Lewis, Anthony "Tony," 274
Lewis, Ramsey, 175, 189, 306
Lewis, Virginia, 227
Lipscomb, Frank, 269
"Little Italy" or "Little Sicily," 175
Lonigan, Studs, 79
Louis, Joe, 42, 47, 110, 144, 244, 278
Louis, Mrs. Joe (Marva Spaulding), 42, 47, 144,
    244
Lucas, Bob, 286
Lydel's Barber Shop, 248
Lyric Opera club, 131
Lytton, Henry C., clothing store of, 333

MacArthur, Douglas (General), 132
MacArthur (insurance company owner), 28
Madden Park, 228
"Mad Dog Killer" (gangster), 58
Madonna (rock star), 374
Major, John, 207
Malcolm X, 75, 104
Malone, Mrs. (sixth-grade teacher), 265
Mandela, Nelson, 379
Marable, Fate, 156
March on Washington (1963), 69, 271
Marlow, Ora, 33, 34
Marquette Park confrontation, 286
Marshall, Thurgood, xii, 274–75
Marshall Field's, 214, 378
Mayfield, Curtis, 178, 179, 180, 183, 189
Mays, Benjamin, 284
McCarthy, Joseph, 14
McCoy, William and Ethel, 262–63
McGee family, 13
McHenry, Gina and Leo, 361
McShann, Jay, 170
McSween, Cirilo, 27, 252
Meagan, Joseph, 280
Metcalfe, Ralph, 51, 73, 244
Met Theater, 358
Mexican Campaign (1916), 118

Miller, Ernest "Punch," 170
Million Dollar Round Table, 27, 252, 253, 255–56
Mingo, Charles, 221, 310, 341–42, 345–59
Minor, Byron, 212, 221
Miracles, the (jazz group), 334
Mirsky brothers (drugstore owners), 113
Mix, Tom, 25
Montgomery, Connie, 221
Montgomery, James "Jim," 15
Morelli, Fred, and Morelli family, 58
Morris, Jeffrey, 275
Mosby, Ben, 131
Mosby, Curtis, 122, 123
Mosely, Mr. (teacher), 211
Moten, Etta. *See* Barnett, Etta Moten (Mrs. Claude)
Motley, Archibald J., Jr., x
Motley, Archibald III (Archie), ix
"Mr. Six," 112
Muhammad, the Honorable Elijah, 103, 104, 105
Muhammad Ali, 16, 256
Murchison, Ira, 226, 229
Murray, Charles "C.D.," and Murray's Superior Products Company, 34
Mussolini, Benito, 26

NAACP (National Association for the Advancement of Colored People), 14, 64, 65, 272, 286; Chicago units, 54, 65–67; convention (1963), 73; Youth Council, 66
Nance, Raymond "Ray," 26, 150
National Baptist Convention, 46
National Guard, 231
National Negro Congress, 14
Nazi Party, 140
N'Digo (newspaper), 360, 376–79
Neal, Earl, 93–99, 160, 381
Neal, Langdon, 93–94
Neeley, Jim, 269
Negro American Labor Council, 66
Negro History Club, 316
Nelson, George, 148
Net Studio, 120
Nigeria, 6

Nightclubs. *See* Clubs
Nimocks, Rudy, 138
Nixon, Richard, 18
Nkrumah, Kwame, 368
Nolan, Sam, 107–15
Nolan, William, Jr., Walter, and Clifford, 109
Noone, Jimmie, 122, 125
Northwestern University, 48, 212, 215, 230–31, 380

O'Brien, Ms. (homeroom teacher), 36
O'Connor, Timothy J., 114
Odom, Annie, 268
Old Timers' Club, 145–46
Olympic Games (1952, 1956), 231
Operation Breadbasket, 104, 360, 369
Operation PUSH (People United to Save Humanity), 104, 360, 369
Owens, Frank, 126
Owl Theatre, 25, 249

Parham, Alonzo, 26
Park City skating rink, 279
Parker, Charlie "Bird," 163, 169–70, 172
Parker, Jr. (worked with Winbush), 145, 147
Parkway Ballroom, 279, 369
Patterson, Floyd, 144
Patterson, Kathleen, 214
Patterson, Vern, 144
Paul Crest Company, 147
Peabody Hotel, 154
Peace Corps, 210–11
Pearl's Kitchen, 174, 183–84, 188–89
Penson, Joe, 272
Pepsi-Cola, 361–62, 378, 380
Perkins, Carl, program named for, 294
Perkins, Ike, 126
Pershing Hotel, 161
Phillips, Wendell, 44
Plantation Café (nightclub), 120
Plique, Eddie, 146
Polk Street crowd, 58
Posey, Mrs. (eighth-grade teacher), 331
Positive Evolution of Bongo Baker, The (play), 299
Powell, Adam Clayton, 64, 103

Powell, Austin, 144
Presley, Elvis, 91, 154, 228–29
Pritchett, Al, 229
Prohibition era, 58; ends, 123–24
Promised Land, The (Lemann), 264
Provident Hospital, 8, 94
Prysock, Arthur, 364
Pugh, Frances, 243
Pullman Foundation, 260, 261
Pullman porters, 57
Purple and White Club, 35
PUSH. *See* Operation PUSH

Rainbow Beach confrontation, 67–69
Ramsey, Mrs. (third-grade teacher), 331
Randolph, A. Philip, 66, 100, 103, 232
Randolph, George, 154, 156
Ravens (singing group), 86
Rawls, Lou, 102–3
Rawls, Reverend Dr. Louis, 100–6
Regal Theater, 145, 210, 211, 264, 279, 335,
    361; built, opens, 47, 120; performers at, 85,
    86, 124, 182, 334
Republican National Convention, 100
Rexall Drugstore, 145
Rhumboogie "the 'Boogie" (nightclub), 84, 88,
    89, 126, 171, 363
Rice, Booker, 230
Rice, Fred, 128–42
Ricks, Bob, 268
Ridgway, Matthew (General), 132
Ripley, Robert L. "Believe It or Not," 279
Robeson, Paul, 94, 100, 103–4, 105, 374
Robinson, Jackie, 27
Robinson, Smokey, 334
Rockefeller, Nelson (Governor), 272
Rockets basketball team, 29
Rodriguez, Matt, 138
Rogers, John "Jack," 3, 11–13
Rogers, John W., Jr. "Johnny," 3, 13, 14
Roosevelt, Franklin D., 123
Rosenhaupt, Hans, 270
Rosenwald, Julius, 47
Ross, Mrs. (third-grade teacher), 265

ROTC (Reserve Officers Training Corps), 64,
    231, 236, 279
Royal Theater (Baltimore), 86
Ruby Henderson's Chicken Shack, 28
Rumpus Room (nightclub), 336
Russia, 49, 374

St. Louis Cardinals, 125
St. Luke's Hospital, 159
Salter, George, 243–44
Salter, Mrs. George (Frances Pugh), 243, 244
Salter, George, Jr., 246
Salter, Lonnie and Edna, 247
Salter, Philip, 247
Salter, Roger, 242–58
Salter, Ronald, 246
Saunders, Edmond, 125, 126
Saunders, J. H., 119
Saunders, Lucille, 119
Saunders, Sonny, 125
Saunders, Ted "Red," 83, 116–17, 118–20,
    122–27, 182
Saunders, Mrs. Ted (Ella), 116–27; brother Earl,
    118; sister Sue, 119, 121, 124
Savage, Gus, 74
Savoy Ballroom, 120, 144, 145, 156, 279
Sawyer, Eugene (Mayor), 76, 377
Schmidhauser, John, 269–70
Schwerner, Michael, 215
Sears, Roebuck and Company, 136, 261–62,
    263, 269, 297
Service Link (ice-cream parlor), 44
Sexton, A. O. and James A., 176
Shanks, Earl, 122
Shapiro, Arthur, 340
Signs of the Times (magazine), 146
Silent Six, 71, 134
Simmons, Ozzie, 353
Simms, Arthur, 80
Simpson, O. J., 70
Sims, George, 137
Sinatra, Frank, 164, 364
Skyles-Hammonds, Patricia Henderson, 88, 90
Slater, Duke, 353

Smith, Doris, 293–305
Smith, Eddie, 83
Smith, Fred, 22
Smith, Gaylord, 251
South, Wesley, 74
Southern Christian Leadership Conference
    (SCLC), 369
South Shore Bank (later ShoreBank), 283,
    288–91
South Side Community Arts Center, 59
Sportsman, Mrs. (seventh-grade teacher), 265
Spraggins, Langford, 27, 252
Springs, Henry, 226, 229, 233, 234–35
Stack, Eileen, 263
Stalin, Joseph, 49
States Theater, 168
Steinhagen, Judith, 221
Stell, Betty, 306–11, 381
Stell, Roy, 306
Stepto, Robert, 370
Stevens, Willie, 230
Stevenson, Adlai E. III, 288
Stewart, Potter, 274
Stradford, Cornelius Francis, 3, 4, 9, 12
Stradford family name, 7
Strayhorn, Earl (Judge), 13, 180
Student Nonviolent Coordinating Committee
    (SNCC), 69, 286, 292
Summers, Mrs. (Ingleside home owner), 204
Sunset Café (nightclub), 120
Supreme Court, U.S., 11, 271, 272, 274–75;
    Brown decision, 297
Sutherland Hotel, 335–36
Swift & Company, 26–27

Tate, Erskine, 157
Tatum, Art, 126
Taylor, Charles, 169, 170
Taylor, Hobart, Jr., 97
Taylor, Robert, 51, 357; Robert Taylor Homes,
    185, 211, 220, 223, 267, 292, 357–58
Taylor Street crowd, 57–58
Teach for Chicago program, 350
Tennessee Valley Authority, 129

Terkel, Studs, ix
Thirteenth Amendment, 216
Thomas, Norman, 122, 123
Thomas, Ms. (property owner), 10
Thomas (or Thompson), Ms. (elementary
    school teacher), 33
Thornton, Homer, 146
Till, Emmett, 215
Tom C. Clark Fellowship, 274
Toole, Connie, 71
Travis, Dempsey, 7, 162, 254, 255
Trent, Alphonso, 156
Trojans Club (basketball team), 29
Trotter family, 47
Truman, Harry S, 13, 132
Tucker, Juanita, 234, 293
Tulsa, Oklahoma, terrorism and riots in (1921),
    xi, 3, 4–5, 19
Turner, Mrs. (eighth-grade teacher), 265
Tuskegee, 152; Tuskegee Airmen, 12
Tutu, Desmond (Bishop), 43
"Two-Gun Pete." *See* Washington, Sylvester

Under Fire (Braddan), 79
Underground Railroad, 285
Underwood, Jim, 273
United Nations, 18, 61
U.S. Department of State, 19

University of Accra, 368
University of Chicago, 7, 12, 19, 34, 94, 114,
    187; black runner not sponsored by, 146;
    blacks at, 286, 317; blacks barred from cam-
    pus, 111; blacks dispossessed by, 129, 201–2;
    first black woman graduate from, 103; Police
    Department, 138
University of Chicago Law School, 94; first black
    woman graduate from, 3, 10

Van Dyke, Vernon, 269–70
Vaughan, Sarah, 89, 163–64
Vaughn (slaveowner), 6
Vice Lords (street gang), 136
Vietnam War, 203, 272, 277

Voting Rights Act, 74
Vrdolyak, Ed, 139

Walker, Madam C. J., theater named for, 124
Walton, Sylvia, 330–44
War on Poverty, 194, 218
Ward, A. Wesley, 228
Warwick Hall (nightclub), 171
Washington, Bernadine, 302
Washington, Dinah (Ruth Jones), 89, 158, 362, 363, 364
Washington, Harold, 93, 158, 162, 368, 377; as candidate, 74–76, 138, 200, 247, 318; and Chicago Police Department, 128, 137–40
Washington, Sylvester "Two-Gun Pete" (policeman), 81, 90, 114, 135
Washington Post, 219
WECAN (community organization), 199–200
Wells-Barnett, Ida B., 103; housing named for, 175, 226, 227, 299, 303, 315, 336
When Children Want Children (Dash), 219
White, Charles, 143
White Sox Park, 60
Wiesel, Elie, 205
Wilkins, J. Ernest, 7, 34
Wilkins, Mrs. J. Ernest, 34
Wilkins, J. Ernest, Jr., 34
Willard Theater, 279
Williams, Curtis, 145
Williams, Jean (Judge), 70–71
Williams, Joe, 7, 78, 228, 278, 364
Williams, L. K. (Reverend), 46
Williams, Mrs. (seventh-grade teacher), 331

Williams, Dr. Richie, 94
Willie Gray's Chicken Shack, 28
Willingham, Alex, 272
Willis, Standish, 312–44
Wilson, Jackie, 334, 363–64
Wilson, Nancy, 7, 302
Wilson, O. W. (Police Superintendent), 68, 114, 140
Winbush, LeRoy "Roy," 143–50, 370
Winfrey, Oprah, 30, 236
Winkfield, Clyde, 25–26
Wonder, Stevie, 74
Woodlawn Organization, 187, 198–201
Woodley, Nelson, 131, 212
Woodrow Wilson Fellowship, 260, 269–70
Woolworth, F. W., store, 249
World War I, 23, 79, 118, 153, 314
World War II, 143; black civilians in, 27, 41, 48, 278, 313–14; black servicemen in, 37–38, 102, 271; postwar, 39, 133, 141, 143, 227, 232, 363, (GI Bill) 39, 163, 177, 216
Wright, Richard, 59

Yates, Troy, 228
YMCA (Young Men's Christian Association), 29, 56–57, 58, 59, 228, 245; as employer, 177, 194, 195
Young, Andy, 286
Young, Claude "Buddy," 112, 145, 160, 296
Young, Dave, 83
Young, Lester "Prez," 84, 167, 169, 171, 172
Young, Marl, 82
Younger, Charlie, 115

ABOUT THE AUTHOR

Timuel D. Black Jr. is a prominent civil rights activist and a professor emeritus of social sciences at the City Colleges of Chicago.

PHOTOGRAPHS